JEALOUSY

JEALOUSY

A Forbidden Passion

GIULIA SISSA

polity

First published in French as *La jalousie: une passion inavouable*, © Odile Jacob, 2015

This English edition © Polity Press, 2018

Polity Press
65 Bridge Street
Cambridge CB2 1UR, UK

Polity Press
101 Station Landing
Suite 300,
Medford, MA 02155
USA

All rights reserved. Except for the quotation of short passages for the purpose of criticism and review, no part of this publication may be reproduced, stored in a retrieval system or transmitted, in any form or by any means, electronic, mechanical, photocopying, recording or otherwise, without the prior permission of the publisher.

ISBN-13: 978-1-5095-1184-6
ISBN-13: 978-1-5095-1185-3 (pb)

A catalogue record for this book is available from the British Library.

Library of Congress Cataloging-in-Publication Data

Names: Sissa, Giulia, 1954- author.
Title: Jealousy : a forbidden passion / Giulia Sissa.
Description: Malden, MA : Polity, 2017. | Includes bibliographical references and index.
Identifiers: LCCN 2017025320 (print) | LCCN 2017038667 (ebook) | ISBN 9781509511877 (Mobi) | ISBN 9781509511884 (Epub) | ISBN 9781509511846 (hardback) | ISBN 9781509511853 (paperback)
Subjects: LCSH: Jealousy. | Love. | Semiotics. | BISAC: LITERARY CRITICISM / Semiotics & & Theory.
Classification: LCC BF575.J4 (ebook) | LCC BF575.J4 S57 2017 (print) | DDC 152.4/8–dc23
LC record available at https://lccn.loc.gov/2017025320

Typeset in 10.5 on 12 pt Sabon by Toppan Best-set Premedia Limited
Printed and bound in the UK by CPI Group (UK) Ltd, Croydon

The publisher has used its best endeavours to ensure that the URLs for external websites referred to in this book are correct and active at the time of going to press. However, the publisher has no responsibility for the websites and can make no guarantee that a site will remain live or that the content is or will remain appropriate.

Every effort has been made to trace all copyright holders, but if any have been inadvertently overlooked the publisher will be pleased to include any necessary credits in any subsequent reprint or edition.

For further information on Polity, visit our website:
politybooks.com

CONTENTS

Introduction: I am Beside Myself with Anger…   1

Chapter 1   Being Medea   9

Chapter 2   A Forbidden Passion   58

Chapter 3   Sexual Objects and Open Couples   100

Chapter 4   The Despair of Not Being Loved   154

Chapter 5   Art of Love, Art of Jealousy   193

Conclusion: Confessing the Unconfessable   229

Notes   237
Index   293

INTRODUCTION

I am Beside Myself with Anger...

Love gives us pleasure. Love makes us suffer. What turns exaltation into distress, trust into anguish, serenity into despair, is very often jealousy.

A sullen and sorrowful fantasy; a cruel and petty passion; the confession of a secret indignity; a forced feeling of how little one is worth; the agony of an indigent and miserly creature who is afraid to lack; a symptom which betrays a distrust in one's own merit and reveals the superiority of a rival; an anxiety which usually hastens the very evil it dreads; an emotion so base that it has to be hidden; a foolish pride, a feeble love, a wicked heart and a ludicrous bourgeois absurdity; a prejudice created by education and enhanced through habit; a pathology of the imagination; the projection of an unconscious penchant for infidelity; repressed homosexual urges converted into paranoia; a failing phallus, problematic narcissism, deep self-hatred, poor self-esteem, insecurity, envy.

Blame is unleashed. Contempt roams free. Laughter resounds. No one would boast of being jealous. 'Pride, like other passions', claims François de La Rochefoucauld in one of his famous *Maxims*, 'has peculiarities of its own; while we are jealous, we feel ashamed to confess our jealousy, but when it is past we are proud of it and our capacity to feel it.'[1]

That says it all.

How many of us, during the course of our lives, could swear to never having experienced such shame? I, for one, must plead guilty. It is terrifying to call myself jealous. To the extreme numbness which comes upon you when a love eludes you and a life together disintegrates, jealousy adds the burden of humiliation. All the connections, familiar and unnoticed, which have bound together the habits and the hours suddenly dissolve. All the mundane small gestures of everyday intimacy remain, suddenly, in suspense. And even if this love was more of an ephemeral liaison than a common life, that does not prevent us from being thrown into disarray. Lies destroy confidence. The more we are surprised, the more we suffer. Our material, social or professional conditions may not change dramatically – that much we know – yet nothing will ever be the same as it once was. There will be nothing more. And, in addition to nothingness – the shame.

I have known this shame. In the midst of the anguish, however, I also felt a strong sentiment of injustice. Why should the victim (for such one is) of an infidelity also have to bow down before this additional suffering? Whether he or she turns, in search of consolation, to philosophy or appeals to the various therapies of the soul, anyone who admits to being jealous will be very ill-received. The repertoire of available ideas is monotonous. The great pontiffs of the social sciences, of moral philosophy, of political theory and of psychology compete in speaking ill of amorous jealousy. It comes as no surprise that one hides, blushes, denies and proclaims with one voice: Jealous? What, me? Never!

I wanted to rebel against this nonsense. I wanted not only not to be silent, to attenuate or to embellish my jealousy but to recognize it for what it is – without euphemisms, without denials, without any kind of kitsch Stoicism. And I wanted to think jealousy historically. What, I asked myself, has happened to our experience of love that we have come to be ashamed to admit to what is, above all, a form of suffering? Has it always been improper to assert one's erotic dignity?

Duelling is no more, and crimes of honour have been outlawed. Adultery is no longer the end of the world, seduction is practised openly and desire circulates widely. We enter freely into erotic contracts. All of this is marvellous. But, in this casual and plural euphoria, the jealous – and, above all, jealous women – are alone. The disapproval once attached to sex has now been transferred to love. Love is a desire for reciprocity, in the singular. Love is the desire for desire. Love is therefore jealousy – but you must not say so.

Jealousy is a forbidden passion.

It has not always been so. It has become so. I have, therefore, dared to attempt what the great eighteenth-century philosopher Charles de Secondat, baron de Montesquieu, had intended to do – had begun but never finished – namely to write a history of jealousy.[2] In doing so I discovered a curious fact. The ignominy which moralists of all stripes have attributed to the emotion itself is, on reflection, the predictable response to a massive cultural repression. We are ashamed only because we are made to feel so. We are afraid to look bad because we have been intimidated. We are afraid of ridicule because we have been ridiculed. We conceal our feelings because we lack the strength to suffer cruel comments, condescending advice or knowing smiles. Shame is a social passion.

Like all emotions, whose cultural subtleties we understand better and better, jealousy calls for careful thought. I'm not the first to become interested in it. Far from it. The philosophical and literary representations of jealousy are both immensely rich and very ancient. If we look at jealousy from the perspective of the seventeenth century we will discover that this emotion, for which La Rochefoucauld offers a brilliantly condensed description, is characterized by an altogether peculiar feature. On the one hand, unlike other states of mind such as courage or emulation, about which one is eager to brag, jealousy is a source of embarrassment, which demands discretion. 'We are ashamed to confess [*avouer*] that we are jealous', he wrote. The difficulty with this confession depends upon social perception. Of this La Rochefoucauld was well aware. 'The reason why the pangs of shame and jealousy are so bitter', he noted, 'is that vanity cannot help us to bear them.'[3] Later, Stendhal echoes this maxim and adds: 'to let oneself be seen to harbour a great unsatisfied desire is to allow oneself to be seen as inferior, an impossible thing in France, except for those who are beneath contempt, and it is to expose yourself to all manner of mockery.'[4] Vanity, for Stendhal, was a French national passion. Self-love precedes love. The shame of jealousy silences us.

And yet, on the other hand, unlike emotions such as envy which are always indecent, jealousy makes you talkative – when we remember a bygone experience or envision hypothetical situations. Inadmissible in the present, jealousy becomes praiseworthy, even honourable, in the past and in the conditional. Ignominious and respectable, abject and heroic, a shameful defeat and a surge of dignity. The experience of those who feel jealous changes over time and, above all, in the very expression of their feelings. It is unspeakable when it occurs, yet commendable from a distance. That is its paradox. And this paradox invites historical reflection.

Jealousy can be a triumph. There was a time when a self-respecting person, especially a woman, was expected to take pride in responding to amorous infidelity. The situation was the same – the loss, real or feared, of the singular desire of a beloved to another person – but the framing of the affect, the form it took in both thought and language, was entirely different. Jealousy was erotic anger.

What occurs is an injury: there is a breakdown, one feels disappointed, betrayed, humiliated, dishonoured, abandoned and derelict, but one takes the liberty to admit it and has the courage to speak it loud and clear. Multiple emotions concur in this complex state of mind: the pain of suffering a slight; the pleasure of planning a vengeance; the eagerness to discuss the injustice; the sympathy of all onlookers. This is how it was in ancient Greece. And this amounts to what the ancient Greeks understood as anger (*orgê*). Eros made that anger all the more excruciating. We will not start, therefore, from the premise that jealousy, being akin to envy and emulation, is invariably felt as a disadvantage in an unwanted competition and that sexual or romantic jealousy are merely specific forms of that pre-defined emotion, which is familiar to us.[5] We will look at a situation, and at the affective experience of that situation, in its cultural context. This will demonstrate that anger is what we happen to call 'jealousy'.

A history of amorous jealousy is a history of anger.

Anger was the unbound, dramatic, resounding passion of jealous women *à l'antique*. Grandiose and fully acknowledged, this passion was also noble, worthy of goddesses, warriors and queens. To be able to see this, we have to reread the classics, in Jacques Lacan's words, without 'blinders'. In ancient Greece, he wrote, women 'had a role that is veiled for us, but that is nevertheless eminently theirs in love: quite simply the active role. The difference between the woman of Antiquity and the modern woman is that the Ancient woman demanded her due – she attacked men.'[6] The woman he probably had in mind, the woman who casts aside every social mask, and destroys everything for a man who was everything for her, is Medea.[7]

Medea will take us to ancient Greece.

There we shall see the richness of a thought which values the expression and the recognition of pain. Anaesthesia, Aristotle tells us, is stupid, cowardly and fit only for slaves. Those who refuse to be covered in mud know how to become angry when it is right and necessary. Before Medea turns her anger on her own children, everyone sides with her as the aggrieved wife. We will have to wait until the Stoics before this passion is transformed into something horrifying, monstrous and inexcusable. In the hands of the Roman Stoic philosopher and playwright Seneca, Medea's story becomes one of simple cruelty. Medea herself is reduced to nothing more than a furious and reptilian, jubilant and cloying creature. The tragedy sets

INTRODUCTION

before our eyes only the caricature of failed wisdom. Centuries later, Pierre Corneille's seventeenth-century version offers up a Medea who, although similarly 'all wicked', is yet capable of attracting the sympathy of a Christian audience. She has been so oppressed, and her just wrath is so eloquent, that it is easy to grasp her reasons. Nonchalant and insensitive, Jason couldn't care less. Although he doesn't have the last word, he does give voice to a new sensibility, one which will no longer understand erotic anger.

The jealousy of the moderns becomes something else. Competition with a rival acquires more importance. The nature of anger changes radically. Exclusive attachment relies, in the words of Denis Diderot, on the assumption 'that a being which feels, thinks and is free, may be the property of another being like himself.'[8] Jealousy now becomes an agonistic confrontation which provokes an automatic reaction of anger, whose effectiveness remains doubtful and whose claims are abusive. 'Delicate lovers', as Diderot says, 'are afraid to admit it.'[9] In the euphoria of the Enlightenment, French philosophers multiply their condemnations, of which we are the heirs. Immanuel Kant came up with the argument, now familiar, yet absurd, that all erotic relationships are the mutual use of sexual organs and faculties, and consequently that they transform people into things. An object of desire is therefore only an object/thing, ready for use, destined for exchange, available on the market, liable to be acquired, owned and put to work. The idea of 'sexual object' is one of the most compelling premises for our intolerance of jealousy.

Marxism is responsible for the subsequent consecration of the analogy between the possession of a woman and private property. It is a thesis which, although Jean-Paul Sartre rejected it, became for Simone de Beauvoir a guiding principle of feminist thought.[10] The 'objectification' of women has since become canonical, to the degree that it crops up regularly in the daily press. The 'hatred of the bourgeois' inspires the denigration of jealousy. The bourgeoisie are accused of having turned love into a property transaction. This social connotation is particularly damning. Not many people have ever been proud of being called 'bourgeois'. Greed, narrow-mindedness, conventionality and boredom: the bourgeoisie conjures up images of all these unsavoury attitudes. It is unsophisticated, distasteful, and – capital sin – laughable. So is jealousy.

The modern critic of amorous jealousy re-enacts, ironically, a very old aristocratic scorn. As the marquise de Rétel, in Charles Duclos' *Considerations on the Manners of the Present Age* of 1752, jokingly observes, 'We are not as jealous at Court as we are in the City. Jealousy is no more than a ludicrous bourgeois absurdity [*un ridicule bourgeois*].'[11] The imaginary noblemen of Diderot's *The Indiscreet Jewels* share the same uncharitable views. The desire for reciprocity in the singular seems to be worthy of a money-seeking parvenu underclass. And yet erotic anger is actually very much part of aristocratic sensibilities. At the very beginning of Pierre Choderlos de Laclos' epistolary novel *Dangerous Liaisons*, Mme de Merteuil announces to M de Valmont that her tenured lover is about to marry a young woman. 'I am in a rage...,' she writes. 'But I calm myself and the hope of vengeance soothes my mind.'[12] It is this furious ire (*fureur*) that sets in motion the intrigue of disingenuous adultery, corrupted innocence and self-serving strategies that fill this unabashedly unromantic romance. The marquise de Merteuil and the vicomte de Valmont are the paradigm of cerebral libertinage – yet they act because Isabelle cannot endure a highly predictable slight, her beloved's defection to a younger woman. Has she fallen prey to *ridicule bourgeois*? Not so simple. Laclos readily recognizes amorous susceptibility when he claims that 'jealousy is born out of the love of beauty'.[13] In the same vein, Montesquieu reflects that 'Love wants to receive as much as it gives; it is the most personal of all interests. It is there that one compares, that one counts, that vanity mistrusts and is never adequately reassured.'[14] Intelligence and anxiety go together. The nobility know how masterfully to manoeuvre between infidelity and jealousy, passion and calculus, pride and revenge, but they smother those frightfully common bourgeois with an imaginary disease. And we democratic moderns have followed in their footsteps. It has come to be assumed that the man who makes money and accumulates goods has also to be someone who buys women. We confuse singularity with property.[15]

What a misapprehension! What in fact we desire when we desire is not to possess another person but to arouse that person's *desire* for us. We try to become the *object of* their sexual interest and/or their profound amorous attention. It is reciprocity that makes recognition, gratitude and erotic dignity possible. From Euripides to Stendhal, from Sappho to Proust, from Ovid to Isabelle de Merteuil or Catherine Millet, it is literature and psychoanalysis – more than philosophy – which has taught us these simple truths, which we experience in every way in our ordinary love lives. We expect to be preferred by whomsoever our desire fastens itself upon, even if only partially or briefly. We do not like being treated like an interchangeable, meaningless, replaceable presence. The unfaithful may be jealous. The wives of polygamous husbands, whatever they may say, comply with a prohibition against reciprocity. And even contemporary individuals who form free, contingent, polyamorous relationships are not necessarily immune from the revelation of unforeseen vulnerability. Pleasure for all is great, as long as it is really for all.

There are a few domains in which love appears to be legitimately jealous. Freudian psychoanalysis has opened up a heuristic perspective on normal jealousy. French phenomenology, namely Jean-Luc Marion, invites us to think that jealousy is nothing but daringly enduring love, faithful to itself.[16] Jealousy also finds favour in the eyes of evolutionary biologists, who are now reconsidering the previously shared hypothesis that women are allegedly jealous of their partner's affection while men are troubled more by sexual infidelity.[17] The results of recent experimental research allow for a welcome revision of stereotypical assumptions. In fiction and in life, women are keenly responsive to the loss of physical, sensual, erotic love – unless they are prohibited from expressing their jealousy. Love is jealous. But what for the ancients was a wrong to be righted, and for modern lovers an inadmissible failure, has become for us a folkloric legacy, a moral flaw, a political error. To the injunction against the admission of jealousy has now been added one against *being* jealous, often coupled with the demand that we listen patiently to all our lovers' confessions. Jealousy is now the most obscene emotion of all.

Today, in books and on blogs and websites, we are told that jealousy is a symptom of insecurity, a plea for approval or a mental disorder. All the mirages of a certain idea of the independent individual, confident in him- or herself, swollen with self-esteem – arrogant, in a word – come together in a set of psychological clichés, forever tinged with a tone of reproach. The insinuation is always that you are exaggerating. In the psychological register, if only you would learn to trust; if you loved yourself more (or, alternatively, less); if you had not been jealous of your little sister; if you had not gone through a bad Oedipal phase; if your parents had made you more secure; if, even better, you had had no parents at all – then you would definitely be immune from pain. In a more upbeat version, if only you could bring yourself to believe that you are incomparable, unrivalled, unbeatable, then you would be blissfully happy. Or, in the ethical mode, if only you got the point that desire is a rational choice, you would shed your stupidly high expectations. They don't love you? Why would you care? When we talk about amorous jealousy, all of a sudden the world comes to a standstill. Attraction, arousal, infatuation, seduction, passion, adultery: nothing ever happens. For, as everyone knows, there are no young and beautiful and charming people in the world. Of course, nobody would dream of flirting with your husband (or wife, or lover, or occasional mate), who, in any case, is, as we all know, sex blind, indifferent to sensuality, insensitive to admiration and unable to feel desire. It is all in your head. It is all in your past. It is always *your* problem. Enough!

Jealousy is normal. The more realistic one is, the more jealous one will be.

Jealousy is something that comes about. It comes as a surprise. And in most cases there is indeed a cause: an event sweeps you off your feet. Unlike the censorious, who are always ready to cry paranoia, those who have experience of love know full well its actual freedom of movement. Lovers are always fearful, as Andreas Capellanus, author of a famous twelfth-century treatise, *On Love*,[18] put it, because they – and especially women – are fully aware of how mobile the desire of another person can be. At different times and in different situations, infidelity (and male infidelity, in particular) is, quite simply, commonplace. In ancient Greece, in Ovid's Rome, in Stendhal's Europe, always in Paris and, finally, throughout the Western world, desire leads the game. This, of course, suits me perfectly, as long as it is I who decide how, and with whom, to play. My own infidelity is entirely innocent; my lover's is intolerable. The erotic excursions which I allow myself are wholly insignificant; the adventures of my beloved are always ominous.

In the wisdom of love, we know that we never know. It is now time to recount the history of that wisdom.

1

BEING MEDEA

The ancients fully understood the experience of sorrow, humiliation and the violence caused by the sexual inconstancy of one's beloved, a desertion which places us, against our will, in a position of loss, grief, disillusion, disadvantage and unwanted rivalry. This complex situation, and the passionate reactions that it triggers, formed a powerful narrative.[1] We encounter it in stories, in poems, in the theatre and in philosophical theories of love. To appreciate how significant it was, we doubtless have to recognize its agonistic pugnacity, but first and foremost we have to grasp its affective and narcissistic coherence. If we do so, then we will discover that, in ancient Greece, serious jealousy was anger. It is a distinctive kind of anger – *orgê* – in which *eros*, sensual love, plays an essential role. Jealousy is erotic anger.

Aristotle, as is often the case, is the best cultural interpreter. It is he who offers the most illuminating definition. *Orgê* is the perception of an unjustified offence, which one suffers but intends to avenge. It is a deep pain, because we are forced to swallow our pride at being treated as someone negligible, worth little or nothing (*oligôria*); but it is also a pleasure because it arouses in us the hope of retaliation.[2] Passive and active, painful and pleasant, this seemingly impulsive and thoughtless fury requires, in fact, a chain of thoughts about what actually took place, in what position we now find ourselves, and how we feel about this whole predicament. We are also eager to take action. Anger involves events, affects and agency. Something has befallen me, and I have to respond. It is a paradoxically reasonable and, above all, noble passion. Whereas, in Aristotle's eyes, irascible individuals exaggerate, people who never get angry whatever befalls them deserve only a stinging rebuke: their behaviour reveals not a placid nature but the temperament of a slave.[3]

An aristocratic passion

To find ethical qualities in anger may seem to be inconceivable, dangerous and pre-modern. We have passed the era of vengeance; we live in societies governed by law and respect for the freedom to love whom we want, when we want. Before we get too agitated about this, however, let us look a bit more closely at how Aristotle speaks about anger.

Whatever the degree of violence involved in the act of vengeance, what really matters is the social and emotional dialectic: I expect to be respected. I expect this for reasons that have to do not only with my status but also with my actions. Because of what I have done for the sake of a person, I am entitled to demand recognition and gratitude. Instead of receiving what I am due, however, I receive only contempt. I am ignored; what I hold most dear is belittled, or I am mocked. I cannot just sit still and mope. An insult is a challenge. An obligation has been breached. I have to overcome it: my honour is at stake. For Aristotle, this is why we praise those who, neither being excessively irascible nor allowing themselves to be carried away by passion, know how to be angry as one ought to be (*dei*), following reason (*logos*). Their character is serene (*praos, atarachos*). Since they tend to forgive, you would think they lean towards indifference. But they are not indifferent. On the contrary, their virtue consists in experiencing *orgē* for good reason, against those with whom anger is reasonable, at the right time and for as long as it should.[4] Those who never get angry prove themselves unable to meet all these requirements. They are, literally, insensitive, stupid and slavish.

> Those who do not get angry for reasons for which one needs to be angry seem to be fools [*elithioi*] as well as those who do not get angry against those against whom one ought to be angry, or when necessary. Indeed, it seems that they do not feel anything [*ouk aisthanesthai*] and do not feel pain [*ou lupeisthai*]. And it seems that a man who never gets angry cannot defend himself, because it seems that to be dragged through the mud, or not to worry about (the way others treat) his family is worthy of a slave [*andrapododes*].[5]

The person who gets angry probably knows why, against whom, when, for how long s/he ought to feel the emotion. But taking all these micro decisions – why, against whom, when, for how long – in order to become angry, as 'one ought', is very difficult. Some incline towards too little, others towards excess. We appreciate the latter, calling them 'manly and capable of command'.[6] Between irascibility and apathy, we must identify the middle position, which is virtue. But default is worse than excess. It is even ignoble. A small surplus of anger, by contrast, is associated with valiant and compelling manliness. The purest kind of courage is the willingness to overcome fear and to take risks in the pursuit of what is 'beautiful', *to kalon*. The intent to be courageous, however, must be accompanied by passionate energy, *thumos*. 'Brave men act because of the beautiful, but *thumos* helps them [*sunergei*].'[7] Those who act solely in the heat of anger, *orgizomenoi*, are bellicose rather than truly brave. And yet, Aristotle concludes, 'they have something similar' (*paraplesion de echousi ti*) – to true courage.[8] Heroic action requires 'synergy': it needs *thumos*.

To behave not like a slave, who is insensitive to pain and dignity; not to allow oneself to be 'dragged through the mud', without flinching; to live like a manly man; to feel a passion – courage – which contributes to the political virtue *par excellence*, and to feel that passion exactly 'as it should be', so that the affect, well-tempered, becomes a virtue in itself: this is anger, in all its moral and psychological complexity. Aristotle offers a true phenomenology and a theory of the emotions as experiences to be felt, although they hurt. Aristotle is clearly not Hegel, but we can see here the outline of a dialectical movement, of a struggle for recognition. People have to fight, sometimes, in order to be acknowledged. The will to recover one's honour requires that one is conscious of its loss. For Aristotle, anger leads me to action, but to reach the remedial act I must become fully aware of the offence itself. The whole process starts because it appears to me that someone has failed to acknowledge that I deserve mutual love and the fulfilment of an agreement. I have been slighted, and this perception causes me pain. The slight is presented to me (*phainomenē*). I recognize it as such. I wish for revenge, and that thought gives me pleasure. I will get over it.

The very experience of the passion itself is twofold: pain and pleasure. Consequently, it is absolutely crucial not to pretend that I feel nothing. That would be a stupid form of numbness. It would be the worst of servilities. Indifference, above all, would prevent me from acting. It is therefore up to me to register the infringement of respect and reciprocity. I must acknowledge the fact and, above all, its painful quality. It did happen, and it is a blow. Pain triggers the dynamic of anger.

Now pain and pleasure are essential in Aristotelian ethics: happiness requires pleasure – the pleasure of what one ought to enjoy. Aristotle is not Freud. But we can see here the centrality of a 'pleasure principle' and the precariousness of our hedonic equilibrium: we are 'unprotected' (*ungeschützt*) from narcissistic wounds. Our image of ourselves is fragile and vulnerable, not on account of individual 'insecurity' but simply because we live in a social world, exposed to the feelings of other human beings. And we are never so defenceless, Freud woefully argues, as when we are in love. Aristotle accepts the fundamental dependence of our sense of ourselves upon the way other people – friends or foes – deal with us. The phenomenology of *orgê* proves this sensitivity. It also calls for an offended person to have the courage to suffer, because only the lucid recognition of our own suffering – felt, expressed, articulated – will enable us to prepare a response. In order to understand that this response is required, one must first take stock of the horror. Instead of activating protective mechanisms such as repression, denial, displacement, hypocrisy or self-deception – It's nothing, I'm imagining it, I'm exaggerating, It will pass, It is ridiculous, It is useless, It is bourgeois, I am not jealous, but…etc. – one must admit to the sense of annihilation, until the bitter end. And finally, at the right time and the right place, one strikes. I will get over it, to be sure, but first I must go through it.

That is why anger is a high-level and high-risk passion. It is an aristocratic passion.

Epic erotic anger

Aristotle's definition accounts for the great tumults that we find in Greek poetry.

Think of *The Iliad!* The cause of the Trojan War is adultery. Helen, wife of the king of Sparta, Menelaus, elopes with Paris, a handsome prince from Troy. The wronged husband convinces his own brother, Agamemnon, the king of Argos, and all the other lords of the Greek cities to mount an expedition against Troy and its royal family. The goal is to recover Helen and to punish her lover. Strife, death and misery for innumerable men will ensue from that one act. In the poem itself, the action begins when King Agamemnon is forced to give back a young captive, Chryseis, to her father, who is a powerful priest of Apollo. In order to recover his honour (*geras*), Agamemnon deprives the best warrior in the army, Achilles, of his own enslaved mate, Briseis. Now Achilles is angry. It has become a commonplace that *mēnis* (another term for anger) is the very first word of the poem. It is even the subject of the entire story, since it is Achilles' vindictive retreat from the battlefield that sets in motion the ensuing events. Achilles refuses to fight; his dear friend Patroclus does so in his place and is killed; Achilles returns to the war, so that he can slaughter Hector in response. Once again, all this tragic butchery takes place because of one unforgivable, initial offence: the demand that Achilles give up a woman.

True, we do not have here a romantic triangle. But this does not make the erotic source of Menelaus', Agamemnon's and Achilles' anger insignificant. It is a point of honour, of course. It is a slight. But the warlike, aristocratic and competitive context that makes this kind of insult intolerable does not obliterate the subjective tone of the pain. On the contrary, a king's dignity is at stake in his wife's fidelity. Erotic ownership of a female prisoner is essential to a warrior's standing. Together with precious material objects, women signify prestige. Their aesthetic quality adds value to that prestige. Helen is the most beautiful woman in the world. Captured concubines tend to be young and good-looking. These women provoke sexual desire. Now desire is mimetic. An object of desire causes more desire. Rivalry surges.[9] In a highly competitive group, sensual appeal creates attraction. And attractive women are sexual trophies. Certainly, Chryseis and Briseis are not pampered mistresses, described in a language of sentimentality and idealism. But they are not bronze tripods either. Agamemnon is furious, and this, he explains, is because he prefers Chryseis to Clytemnestra, his own wedded wife, 'since she is not inferior to her, either in form [*demas*] or in stature [*phuē*], or in mind [*phrenes*], or in what she does [*erga*]'.[10] Achilles is incensed because he is erotically interested in Briseis. She was a 'dear wife' in his heart, he said. Although she was conquered with the spear, he loved her (*philein*) passionately, with its *thumos*. He even cared for her, exactly as a husband cares for his wife. And was not the war itself, asks Achilles, 'for fair-haired Helen's sake? Do they then alone of mortal men love their wives, these sons of Atreus?'[11]

Thumos is the affective component of a warrior's personality. It is also the source of courage and ire. By handing over part of their booty, these men had lost face. The total value of their war prize matters a great deal. But the human *and female* quality of their prisoners matters specifically. The Greek princes want to hold on to women who are desirable and comparable to wedded wives. They have regular sex with them. This is not the infatuation of starry-eyed paramours, but it is not brutal rape either. As Ruth Scodel has persuasively argued,

> epic seems to assume that concubinage, even though it begins as rape, becomes something else.... Agamemnon says that he prefers Chryseis to his legitimate wife (1.111–115). Achilles claims to love Briseis, and explicitly compares the feeling he has for her to the feeling that is proper for a man to have for his wife.... Agamemnon and Achilles both received these women as prizes, and the narrative never indicates that the victors selected women they particularly desired; Achilles implies that his feelings arise within the relationship itself. From Briseis herself we hear far less, but the narrator does say that when she leaves Achilles she is *'aekous'* (1.348). She does not want to leave him; at any rate, she is not completely indifferent to who has her.[12]

The erotic and affective connection makes it particularly difficult to give them up.

This mix can only sound disturbing in sentimental, democratic, egalitarian erotic cultures. In the pathetic apparatus of an honour culture, however, such feelings are unsurprising. According to Julian Pitt-Rivers's classical definition, 'honour is the value of a person in his own eyes, but also in the eyes of his society. It is his estimation of his own worth, his claim to pride, but it is also the acknowledgement of that claim, his excellence recognized by society, his right to pride.'[13] On account of such a claim, social status is not just a matter of one's stable station in society. An individual, especially a man, is constantly worried about his status, and this uncertainty generates powerful narcissistic passions, such as pride – more precisely, the sense of self-worth and the anxious expectation of proper deference. In these societies, female sexuality is crucial for men's honour, hence the significance of women's premarital virginity and conjugal faithfulness. A monopoly on women's bodies and women's devotion enhances men's self-importance. Sexual appetite and a claim to sexual exclusivity are felt with great satisfaction, therefore, as personal emotions *as well as* signifiers of status. Sex becomes a particularly sensitive issue. Men prove to be extremely prickly in this domain. They are prone to erotic anger.

Unruly wives

The Iliad offers us the very first example of the passion that is unleashed by amorous disappointment. Fifth-century BCE Athenian tragedy deployed a wide range of scenarios and nuances on the same theme. These are not merely literary genres. They are staples of popular culture. The Homeric poems were the cornerstone of education in the classical polis and were recited in front of the people during the official celebration of Athenian power, the Panathenaia. The theatre was not a private space, home to a marginal or elite form of entertainment. It was a public forum, hosting widely attended festivals. The performance of epics and drama infused ancient mentalities with their language and their content. But this infusion was no complacent conformity with common sense. In tragedy, the constant re-elaboration of the same plots and characters allowed playwrights to create possible worlds and conduct thought-experiments in all possible domains, from politics to love. One major feature of such creativity was the focus on the feminine. In the theatre, women are frequently the protagonists. And they are angry.

The shift from one gender to another is no accident. Anger in the feminine creates a radically new perspective. The archaic conjunction of licence and dominance, promiscuity and jealousy, as a twofold prerogative of men only, finds a renewed legitimacy in the classical polis. Both the aristocratic past and the democratic present sanction the belief that women should accept the obligation of premarital chastity, the duty of conjugal fidelity and the prohibition of jealousy. They have to submit to a non-egalitarian erotic culture. Women must be faithful, whereas men are not bound by the same rule. Their submission is unilateral. It is, moreover, the condition of possibility of men's own behaviours. Women must enable their men's ordinary unfaithfulness by renouncing any pretence to jealousy. If women were jealous, they would challenge men's rights and disturb the tranquil enjoyment thereof. If women were to voice their jealousy, they would be asking to be treated equally, at least in bed. Jealousy is a claim to reciprocity.

In the theatre, however, this matrimonial compliance is endlessly questioned, challenged and upset. Women, especially wedded wives, take the lead and revolt. Tragic wives denounce the unfairness of their own condition. They were constrained to virginity, destined for marriage and, once married, had to observe absolute fidelity *and* tolerate their men's systematic promiscuity. Their jealousy is a resounding 'no!' to this arrangement. It is still, more than ever, erotic anger, but it is now a struggle for recognition within the heterosexual couple. From the standpoint of their own loyalty and their own eros, these slighted spouses fight for mutual love. They, too, refuse to be 'dragged through the mud'.

On the tragic stage, Deianira, Clytemnestra, Hermione and especially Medea 'were honoured', to paraphrase La Rochefoucauld, to proclaim their erotic dignity. A variety of words – *thumos*, *cholos*, *orgē* – express the fury of violated pride. Achilles was angry; now Clytemnestra and Medea are angry. Once again, the erotic situation does not change the structure and the dynamic of the passion. Anger in love is still what the (Homeric and Aristotelian) Greeks understood as 'anger' in its generic definition: the sense of having received an affront (*oligōria*), which is unfair and unjustified because it denies respect and destroys reciprocity. Love, however, makes anger specific. The same emotion becomes *erotic*. This means that eros is the remote cause of what occurs and the trigger of what is felt. As eros is a strong emotion, it brings about a particularly intense response. More to the point, tragedy shows that love makes us intrinsically vulnerable to wrath. Since love is the desire to be desired in return and, therefore, to be admired, preferred, praised, lovers are exceptionally sensitive to respect and extremely keen on reciprocity. What matters is that our beloved should love us. And this is what seems to be lost. This is, therefore, what really hurts. Like any other slight, infidelity causes offence and pain, and one that we are eager to repair. The repair will be targeted. We suffer; we will make suffer – in love as in war – that is to say, valiantly and intelligently.

In tragedy, a woman who has been replaced in the marital bed by a mistress, or another wife, receives an injury that she will not tolerate and which she intends to redress – hence dejection, prostration and collapse but also lucidity, wisdom and a determination to act. In Greek, in short, all this is anger. Confronted by men who do not hesitate to behave as they wish, tragic women take up the challenge. First, they shout loud and clear that this is not right. Because, they say, what touches them so painfully in the domain of erotic love is truly an injustice. This claim is often represented as a physical place: the marital bed, where marriage is consummated in intimacy and lovemaking. To speak of the expectation of gratitude at the heart of their eros, these offended wives say that there is a 'justice of the bed'. These women can be dangerous. I am not attempting here to make murderesses into models to emulate. Tragic choruses are categorical on this point: murder (voluntary or involuntary, of an unfaithful husband or innocent children) is not a good thing in itself. But these women are not bound by a prohibition against what they feel; even less are they bound to remain silent. Of their distress, they have no shame. They are not afraid to confess. They suffer and they are proud of it.

Tragic erotic anger

In this world, it is not ignoble to admit to suffering. Quite the contrary. The greatest of these vocal women, Medea, lays claim to it and exalts in it: 'I am in my torments, and I do not fear that they may be insufficient.'[14] For to express her *ponoi* is, for her, to denounce the outrage, the mortification and the injustice. It is to demand recognition from the beloved. On stage, the whole extent of the damage is brought into full view. Firstly we hear about a ravaged body, an emaciated face, a sickly pale skin. Then the raw affect explodes into inarticulate cries. Finally poignant sentences explain in detail what happens, what has been done, how it feels. Lament gives the measure of a lived experience in real time. Medea screams: 'Woe! Distraught, destroyed by pain, Woe is me, me! How to die?'[15] Everyone hears her voice, *phone*, and her cry, *boa*, and her chant, *melpein*. The theatre of Dionysus must have resounded with all of those *Io! Aiai! Pheu! Pheu!*

Medea is not ashamed. Many passions shake her: anger in all its forms (*thumos, orgē, cholos*), but also fear (*phobos*), love (*eros*), maternal affection. Among all these passions, however, there is not the slightest trace of a 'shame to confess'. La Rochefoucauld's maxim would make no sense to her. In the pathetic language of ancient Greece, shame, *aischunē*, is a torment caused by 'evils' – that is to say, actions and vices, such as cowardice, flattery, weakness, greed – which bring dishonour.[16] Medea has done nothing of the kind. Instead, she plays the role of the innocent victim, proud of her pain. It is her outspokenness that drives the drama because what she says gives weight to Jason's acts – while Jason himself seems to be unaware of the effects of what he is doing. *Her* words convey the severity of *his* act: unforgivable gratuitousness/ungratefulness of such an act, its devastating impact and, ultimately, Medea's own reasons for reacting. Here's what it is for me, she keeps on saying; these are the consequences! She has nothing with which to reproach herself except to have loved her husband too much. Jason is the only one to blame. She has no hesitation in letting him know.[17] Everything Medea feels goes into speech.

No awkward silence, therefore, but rather an explosion. Medea complains of suffering badly from many things: the breakage of the 'contract' with Jason, who fails to honour his promises and oaths; the breach of trust, symbolized in the ritual gesture of the handshake; the ingratitude of a man who, after all she has done to help him, is now rewarding her by breaking all his oaths and promises, by renouncing gratitude and reciprocity. Jason has disavowed himself. All this is a matter of amorous disillusion as well as of social disintegration: Jason is guilty of a violation which, while affecting the most intimate place of sensuality, the bed, dishonours Medea before the world.[18] The justice of the bed has been shattered.[19] Medea's complaint has a moral and social content, therefore, but it responds to an event that is sexual *and* endured with great emotional intensity. Her humiliation is a loss of face *and* its cause is erotic, otherwise the 'injustice' would not concern the *bed*. The bed signifies the specificity of her social shame. Medea's pain is about justice, honour *and* carnal love, all at the same time.

Seen through an Aristotelian lens, this scenario corresponds perfectly to the dialectic of anger. Medea's nurse explains to the public the cultural implications and the pathetic symptoms of her mistress. She fears that all this pain, although understandable and warranted, will lead to a frightening plan of action: something one cannot predict in detail, but something new and unheard of, worthy of a great and terrifying woman. 'For she is terrible...because I have seen her throwing onto the children the eye of a mad bull, as if she were to go and commit a crime. She will not give up her anger [*cholos*], before coming down on someone.'[20]

The reading of the symptoms is clinical. Anger, as we said, with Aristotle's help, is an emotion defined by a perceived insult, a narcissistic wound, and the desire for revenge. Before anything else, anger involves assessing what hurts. This is an insult! And this insult is undeserved for reasons of social status and recognition. In the past, the injured party has acted in favour of those who now wrong them. They are benefactors, but they are badly treated. Medea finds herself in exactly this situation. She is the target of contempt and the victim of ingratitude, the subjective consequences of which come together into a passion, which the Greeks call *thumos*, *orgē*, *cholos* – namely, 'anger'. Euripides' language is full of such words.[21] But there is even more: the deployment of anger commands the very structure of the tragedy. Medea discovers the insult done to her, a scorn she feels she does not deserve. She admits what she is feeling, with foresight and objectivity. She sinks into a pain that crushes her. But she rebounds with a double project of vengeance. First, she wants to kill Jason and destroy his 'new home'. Then she changes her mind. When Jason claims that he is leaving her not for the love of another woman but for the sake of their children – more precisely, for the sake of his *own* beloved sons, who would have a better life in a new family – Medea decides to kill them instead. She now prefers to let the father survive, so that he will be able to feel the loss. He has revealed his soft spot. That is where she will strike. Medea's words, the symptoms of her body, the comments of the other characters and, above all, the plot of the play converge towards one coherent diagnostic: Medea is angry. Which means that she's jealous.

Medea is angry in a complex and yet unambiguous fashion. Her rage is not to be confused with that of other tragic heroes such as Ajax, Achilles or Hecuba. Hers is a specifically *erotic* anger, caused by the 'great eros' that Jason, she says, now feels for his new wife.[22] Her own eros for this man, who is all for her, brought her to leave everything for him, to harm her dear ones, and to venture into an unknown world.[23] Jason repays her eros by another eros – for another woman. This is the slight. If Medea did not love that man erotically, she would not feel what she feels and how she feels. If her passion were not overpowering, disproportionate, totalizing, then she would not ache so much.

Amorous sensibilities

When we read Euripides' moving text, we cannot possibly fail to understand that Medea's misery and her wish to take revenge have everything to do with love – and therefore with the sexual quality of her passion. Injustice, dishonour and betrayal affect Medea because she is in love. The justice in question is that of the bed, not of the city. The honour is that of a wife, not of a warrior. Treason is spousal desertion. Medea is suffering as a woman who is married – and in love with her husband. Her sexual attachment to this man is the cause of her unquenchable tears.[24] Her own eros, as she insists, collides with the 'great eros' Jason must now feel for his young wife. And the erotic nature of her agony is the only thing Jason seems to be capable of grasping. He does not empathize with her, of course, but even he can see where the emotion comes from. Medea, in turn, never refutes this interpretation of her subjective experience – either explicitly or 'implicitly'.[25] There is, on the contrary, a focal point of her experience – a place where her tragedy crystallizes. This is, as I mentioned, the marital bed. A piece of furniture, a concrete, mundane and yet highly symbolic object, the bed is ubiquitous in the play.[26] It is the metonymy of sex.

The erotic specificity of Medea's emotional suffering has been denied by many modern scholars. Medea raises the tone of her reproaches against Jason, David Konstan writes, on account of a love affair that threatens her status in the household. King Aegeus agrees to help her because he sympathizes deeply with her predicament, but 'Aegeus, like Medea herself, focuses, from beginning to end, on what threatens her well-being, not her amorous sensibilities.'[27] With all due respect for a scholar I admire, I would ask my readers a simple question: can we really reduce the discourse of the nurse and the chorus on eros and 'the bed', Medea's emotional and physical symptoms, and especially her anger to a matter of mere survival? If that were her only problem, she could pack up and clear off to some other place where she could exercise all her powers. Medea is a divine creature, after all, and a magician. Expert in the rejuvenation of old people, she could immerse herself in a cauldron of youth and move on. In Athens, where King Aegeus, touched by her distress, vows that he will welcome her, she would have had a bright future. Instead, she suffers a thousand ills. Why all this fuss? Much ado about nothing? Let's listen to her!

When she opens up to Aegeus and tells him that Jason ignominiously dishonours her, although she was his friend (*philoi*), the Athenian king does not doubt for a moment that sex is at stake. He asks if it is love (*eros*) that carried Jason away, or if he was seized by 'hatred for her bed'.[28] When Jason himself, standing horrified before the dead bodies of his sons, cries out: 'You chose to kill the children, because of a *bed*?', Medea replies without hesitation: 'You think *that* is a small misfortune for a woman?'[29] The bed is indeed a cause of great concern, for a woman. It is because it matters so much that it is made to bear such significance.

This is Medea herself, expressing her amorous sensibility, in her own (Euripidean) voice. Her strong feelings – for an undeserved offence that is socially humiliating as well as erotically hurtful – are crystal clear. The text speaks for itself. The context corroborates this evidence. We can certainly call this embodied, emotional, cognitive and social experience 'jealousy'. But, in order to find the right words, and to understand what happens, we must not look for terms that we could *translate* as 'jealousy'. The problem is not to translate but, rather, to make sense. Erotic anger: this is how we should define – now, more than ever – what we now happen to call 'jealousy'.

Rain and tears: Andromache's art of love

In ancient societies marriage was a social transaction. A father gave his daughter to a young man who would become a husband and a son-in-law. This was the standard procedure. The begetting of legitimate children was its function. This does not preclude, however, an erotic dimension to conjugal life. Quite the contrary. Reproduction requires heterosexual intercourse. To fill its purpose, a marriage must be fruitful, which implies sex. Now sex means arousal and coition. In ancient Greek medicine, pleasure was considered necessary for the emission of seminal fluid by the man as well as by the woman. Both partners were supposed to enjoy the act, and to be attracted to it, lest they fail to procreate. What we might see as the most unromantic and unsentimental, impersonal and instrumental end of the family required a mechanical, corporeal activity but also a subjective experience of reciprocal desire and shared pleasure. The societal imperative needed lust. Eros was present in the ritual of the wedding, as vase paintings abundantly show. The wedding itself was a celebration of the alliance between two families, made possible by the conjunction of two bodies.

In the fifth century BCE the spectators who watched Euripides' *Medea* knew that her union with Jason was not a regular marriage. They knew that the two lovers had eloped, against the will of her father. This could only reinforce the erotic core of the couple's togetherness. *A fortiori*, Medea's domestic arrangements were infused with passion. Eros was everything for her.

We should place the play against this cultural background but also remember Euripides' own variations on monogamy. In *Andromache*, Euripides creates a vivid contrast between Andromache, a Trojan woman and the widow of Hector, and Hermione, the Spartan daughter of Helen and Menelaus. The war is over. Neoptolemus, the son of Achilles, has taken Andromache as a war prize. When they returned to his homeland, Phthia, Andromache was still a young mother. Now, however, she has become a miserable, deracinated, enslaved alien. Meanwhile Neoptolemus has married Hermione, a Greek princess. Hermione and Andromache lie in 'twin beds' with Neoptolemus. The starting point of the plot parallels the situation of Jason between Medea and his new bride, the princess of Corinth, so much so that the two plays ought to be read together as experiments in the construction of characters and the permutation of narrative options. From a very similar situation, the storylines take two very different directions. Andromache, as Tristan Alonge felicitously put it, is a 'potential Medea', a 'successful Medea', who overcomes her man's desertion and ultimately survives without resorting to revenge and murder. Hermione, on the other hand, comes across as a 'Greek Medea'. 'The barbarians now dwell in Sparta.'[30]

Now Hermione and Andromache face each other in a memorable antagonistic dialogue. The former expresses her sorrow. She feels 'hated by husband' (*stugoumai d'andri*), and she cannot conceive any children. Andromache, she claims, must be responsible for this double calamity. In response, Andromache lectures Hermione on marital submission. A woman must love (*stergein*) whichever man she might have been given to, no matter how bad (*kakos*) he might be. She must also avoid any competition of high-mindedness.[31] Neoptolemus has good reasons for hating her, she explains, because she does not understand how a wife must make herself loveable. Beauty is not enough: one must show many forms of excellence (*aretai*). This highly meritorious conjugal behaviour consists of doing what Andromache herself used to do in the past with her beloved spouse, Hector, when she gave her breast to his illegitimate children.[32] Young Hermione, she points out sarcastically, would not even let the rain fall on her own man![33] Her erotic attachment to Neoptolemus is far too obsessive. And she does not keep silent about what she suffers because of Aphrodite.[34] She is indeed the daughter of Helen, the seductive, adulterous, sensual creature who caused the Trojan War. Hermione's jealousy betrays the legacy of that infamous mother. 'Do not try to emulate your mother in lusting after men [*philandria*], Oh woman!'[35]

Jealousy grows out of undue eros. Andromache mocks Hermione's amatory fascination for her husband on account of excessive sexual interest. She, for her part, has got over that kind of feeling very fast. Her breast was so completely de-sexualized that it has become a source of food for her rivals' babies. Her body did not have to be beautiful, and every good wife should learn this indifference. The aesthetic dimension of desire is irrelevant. Marriage is but an 'emotional shelter' in which hyper-maternity and total, unconditional devotion to a man must exclude any form of 'bitterness'.[36] Ultimately eros does not matter at all. It was not a big deal with Hector; it is even less of a concern in her current domestic arrangement. 'She [Hermione] says that with secret drugs I make her childless and hated by her husband', Andromache laments, 'and that I wish to take her place in the house, forcibly casting her out as a wife. I took this bed unwillingly to begin with, and now I have relinquished it.'[37] Andromache insists on her dispassionate detachment from a household (*oikos*) and a bed (*lektra, lechos*), which she entered against her will. At the beginning, there was aversion. Now the relationship is over. In the meantime, she has begotten a child, Molossus, who is dear to her. Andromache's maternal fibre is unbreakable. Her affection is concentrated on her children rather than on any of her men.

From Andromache's point of view, Hermione's expectation that Neoptolemus should love her exclusively is only a consequence of innate sensuality, youth and inexperience. Her lesson in wifely behaviour seems to be persuasive: in a sudden reversal, Hermione changes her mind. This happens when she tries, but fails, to kill Andromache and her innocent child. Her own father, Menelaus, has now disappeared. She is all alone. She has to face the results of her aborted act. Her husband will certainly punish her for such a daring attempt. She is terrified. It is in this instant of dread and dejection that Hermione regrets having cared so much for her husband. She should not have 'watched' (*phulassein*) him. She could have enjoyed her wealth, her highly regarded position as a mistress of the house, and her superior status as the mother of legitimate children. In Neoptolemus' house, Andromache, a Trojan captive, would always have been a second-rate mate, mother of half-slave bastards.[38] Hermione reminisces: what a pity that she did not give more weight to those aspects of her life at the time, instead of fretting about a man! All that eros was not worth it. To forget about love, and to content herself with the privileges of being a free, respected queen, not a contemptible slave – that is what she should have wished for.

Hermione's recantation could be seen as the triumph of conventional Greek wisdom about gender roles. Resignation to a male's plural interests in sex is a crucial part of the normative expectations for women. As Plutarch recommends later, a bride should very soon learn to put up with her husband's erotic amusements *and* to be absolutely devoted to him.[39] In classical Athens, the double standard was brutally explicit. Let us remember the proud, unsentimental account of this asymmetry in both the law and public oratory. On the one hand, the orator Demosthenes proclaims that all Athenian men must have one wife to bear legitimate children and be the faithful guardian (*phulaka pistēn*) of the household. They themselves, however, may have as many mistresses for the sake of pleasure, and concubines for the daily care of their bodies, as they wish.[40] On the other hand, female adultery is such an egregious transgression under Athenian law that husbands may kill the man caught in flagrante. After such an event, a husband is not permitted to continue living with his wife lest he be struck with *atimia* (loss of his civic rights). A woman taken in adultery may not attend public sacrifices; and, if she does, 'she may be made to suffer any punishment whatsoever, short of death, and that with impunity.'[41] These are acts of social and physical abuse. Should an adulterous woman dress up and attend a religious event, she may be expelled, humiliated and even assaulted. 'Any man who meets her shall tear off her garments, strip her of her ornaments, and beat her although he may not kill or maim her; for the lawgiver seeks to disgrace [*atimao*] such a woman and make her life not worth the living.' In the vehement words of a colourful orator, Aeschines, adulteresses deserve to live an 'unliveable life'.[42]

The same wives who are expected to accept their husbands' promiscuity as a matter of course are exposed to extremes of ignominy should they commit one single act of infidelity. These are two aspects of a single form of domination: men hold the right not only to enjoy sexually but also to *monopolize* as many women as they wish (except, of course, for prostitutes). This right requires women's compliance with the prohibition to express, and even to feel, jealousy. They must rein it in. They must do what Andromache tells Hermione to do: turn the other breast. Women's erotic anger would disturb men's licence to adjust the institution of monogamy to their own sexual pleasures. Any wife who is angered by her husband's systemic adultery would, in effect, be taking what is a perfectly functional division of tasks in the interest of men as an offence and an injustice against *her*. By feeling hurt, remonstrating and seeking revenge, she would be reclaiming her own honour. By lamenting the loss of her beloved's eros, she would be appealing to reciprocity. She loves, and wishes to be loved in turn. This is the meaning of erotic anger. But, once again, this struggle for recognition would be a challenge to the gender asymmetry of erotic power. Whereas male jealousy is built into the legal and societal sanctions against female adultery, a woman's jealousy is as inadmissible as her unfaithfulness. Both promiscuity and jealousy are men's privileges.

Unfaithful and jealous, men are entitled to their women's exclusive attachment. Women must tolerate this double supremacy in silence. This is the cultural background. This is the norm. Euripides, however, does something much more complicated than simply to reflect it. Initially, Hermione stands proud and experiences an awful disappointment: her husband dislikes her bed, and she suffers. She is not loved erotically, she complains, and this is unjust. But then, suddenly, she seems to discover the virtues of conjugal anaesthesia and to renounce mutual eros. Her change of heart is very striking, but it is nothing more than a spell of retrospective, submissive, domestic realism. As we have seen, Hermione regrets her infatuation after she has failed to kill Andromache and little Molossus and because, as a consequence, she now trembles at the prospect of confronting her husband. It is in this perilous predicament that she hastily embraces Andromache's views. The alleged repudiation of her past jealousy amounts to a reassessment of her social standing within the house. She was safe then. She was, after all, the wedded wife of the master and a victor. She should have appreciated the kind of advantage she had over a rival who was nothing but a war captive. She has now lost everything: her wealth, her station, her security. This is her only regret. There is no argument against jealousy as such, only vain wishful thinking. Even her new feelings, furthermore, are ephemeral: as long as she is frightened of incurring Neoptolemus' revenge, she seems to conform to a dismal vision of marriage. As soon as a male saviour, her cousin from Argos, Orestes, enters the picture, Hermione seizes the opportunity to flee with him. She votes with her feet. Life with her husband in an accommodating, docile, passive fashion no longer seems to be attractive to her. She is done with Neoptolemus and his uncomfortable twin beds.

There is, however, a further paradox. While reconsidering her place in the triangle – a place she should have enjoyed only because a humiliated queen was still better off than a Trojan slave – Hermione acquiesces to a line of thought that comes precisely from that slave. Andromache was not born in slavery, of course, but she has adapted well to her unfortunate condition. In Greece, she has grown comfortable with obedience and servitude. Euripides draws attention to this particular aspect of her mindset. Andromache is a barbarian.[43] More to the point, her role models are not Hellenic. She takes the example of alien mores very seriously. At the beginning of the play,

Hermione sports her luxury and her looks. She is self-confident and demanding. She insists on her conjugal due. What would she do, Andromache asks sarcastically, if she were one of the many wives of a Thracian king? Would she kill them all?[44] Let us imagine the scene: an enslaved Trojan queen challenges a Spartan princess. She prompts her to envision herself in a polygamous royal family. Would she not bow down? For Andromache, polygyny is obviously to be embraced. To reject it would be a matter of lust, the 'insatiability of the bed' (*aplêstia lechous*).[45] This is the provenance of her views on marriage, therefore: 'snowy Thrace, where one husband divides his bed in turn among many women'.[46] And in this freezing land women would not dream of protesting. Thrace is one of the regions from where the Athenians typically used to import their slaves.[47] Andromache's thinking is impeccable.

Whereas Athenian culture, as we have said, accepted a heavily lopsided double standard, marriage was compatible only with men's extramarital sex, not with other simultaneous marriages. For a Greek wife, to renounce any pretension whatsoever to her husband's erotic interest would mean to emulate not only a Trojan captive but also the members of a Thracian seraglio. It would be one step further into slavishness, a disposition that, as Aristotle brutally explains, precludes the capacity for anger and makes one consent to being 'dragged through the mud'. This is precisely what Medea, a fierce princess from Colchis (on the Black Sea), and Hermione, a fearless Spartan girl, are not prepared to do.[48] The most important point, however, is that Euripides casts Medea not as a slave but as a king's daughter who, from beginning to end, acts daringly in defiance of authority. Andromache, by contrast, was a queen who has become a meek servant and bedfellow; she has dutifully submitted to her husband in the past, and now she lectures Hermione on the 'excellence' of never interfering with a man's will, including his sexual wanderings. A woman must love (*stergein*) her husband, no matter what. He might be bad (*kakos*), but she must oblige.[49] Andromache fits the image of Eastern propensity to bend uncomplainingly under a 'yoke', as opposed to the Hellenic tendency to rebel.[50] Medea, for all her alleged 'barbarism', does not fit this Asian stereotype. Jason is 'the worst of all' (*pankakistos*), and she throws this insult in his face.[51]

None of this is remotely funny. We are, of course, in the possible world of tragedy. People hurt and agonize there. They struggle in vain for recognition. There is blood on the floor. What is felt is anger, and it is erotic: a passion whose definition and symptoms are comparable (but not identical) to what we may very well call 'jealousy'. Provided that we agree on Medea's and Hermione's wounded eros, the fetish of the magic word, that philological delight, does not really matter.

What is more natural?

Medea is jealous. But the way in which she suffers is entirely normal.

There is indeed such a thing as 'normal jealousy'. Sigmund Freud described it as grief for the loss of the object of love, wounded narcissism, self-devaluation and hostility towards a rival.[52] This strong language might sound melodramatic to modern Anglo-American ears, but it is appropriate here because erotic infidelity does, indeed, elicit a sentiment of all-encompassing, devastating failure. Love is paradoxical. It elates, excites, exalts us, but all these wondrous things occur only because someone we love loves us in return. We are hopeful yet apprehensive, flattered yet self-conscious, enthusiastic yet exposed. Love makes us feel great, but it also puts us at risk.

Sigmund Freud develops this disturbing, uncomfortable, unbearable truth. Caught between pleasure and displeasure, pursuing the former and fleeing the latter, human beings have found a very effective way to fulfil their 'passionate striving for a positive fulfilment of happiness'. Perhaps, the kind of life that 'really comes nearer to this goal than any other method' is a life centred on love. In this mode of existence, Freud argues,

> One anticipates that any joy comes from loving and being loved. This attitude is quite close to all of us; one of the forms in which love manifests itself, sexual love, gives us our most intense experience of an overwhelming pleasure, and thereby provides us with the prototype of our aspiration to happiness. What is more natural than that we should persist in seeking happiness along the path by which we first encountered it? The weak point of this technique of life is as clear as day, otherwise it would not have occurred to anyone to abandon this path for another. We are never so defenceless against suffering as when we love, never so forlornly unhappy as when we have lost our love-object or its love.[53]

The strongest pleasure of all is also the most precarious, because we are at the mercy of its very cause – another person who might disappear, or whose love might disappear. The other is a mortal being, of course, but s/he is above all a desiring being, a free-floating affective agent whose preferences can change. In this situation we are, literally, 'defenceless' and 'unprotected' (*ungeschützt*). This is blindingly obvious; it is true to our personal experience and is natural. *Was ist natürlicher?* Now, if this is love, then jealousy is simply normal (*normale*), as Freud also claims.[54] Jealousy is nothing but the unhappy consciousness of the paradox of love – empowerment at the expense of alienation. Jealousy is the intelligence of the potential displeasure that awaits any lover, simply because love entrusts them to someone else's pleasure. It is not jealousy but its absence which demands explanation and which should drive us to the psychoanalyst's couch.[55] And there, the pretension to be independent, secure, full of self-esteem, safe and immune would be revealed for what it is: the symptom of a crippling fear to face what we really feel.

Jealousy humbles us. It utterly annihilates us. Jerome Neu, one of the finest phenomenologists of the emotions, argues that a genuine sense of disintegration explains the quality and the strength of this particular form of suffering.[56] Those who admit to such a forbidden emotion can testify to this. It will pass, of course, and we will get over it. But the shock is there.

Medea is right when she speaks of her shattered soul. Only one aspect of Freud's account of jealousy is missing in her erotic anger: self-criticism. Freud argues that jealous persons tend to devalue themselves deeply, up to the point of feeling responsible for their own misfortune. They blame themselves for the loss they suffer.[57] Medea does not. Certainly she claims that she is undone: 'I am dead!'[58] The unforeseen event that befell her destroyed her soul entirely, she says.[59] But she feels no guilt. Following the script of Greek erotic anger, she plunges into nothingness, but what happens to her, she claims, is absolutely not her fault. Medea is proud of all she has done for the dismal hero, the 'total bastard' (*pankakistos*) that is Jason. More Lacanian than Freudian, therefore, this 'antique woman' [*femme antique*] attacks the man and demands her due.

Greek erotic anger is not only comparable with one of the most astute and realistic accounts of jealousy ever offered in modern times – that of Freudian psychoanalysis – it also captures the subjective intricacies of a situation that occurs across cultures, and it does so with exemplary intelligence. Far from processing sexual and amorous infidelity in an exotic, distant and generically 'different' fashion, tragic thought gets the point of what we happen to call 'jealousy'. If by this word we mean a purely contentious, bourgeois and ridiculous passion, and if in uttering it we obliterate the narcissistic nature of love – in which trust and pride, dependence and self-assurance, lust and honour are always intermixed – then we are simply wrong. Euripides' insight is culturally pertinent for the Greeks, who were expected to follow Medea's logic. It will also enlighten us, if only we receive our sentimental education through great literature and good psychoanalysis and shed the defensive embarrassment at acknowledging what we feel. To see that jealousy is indeed erotic anger is as good for us as it was for the ancient Greeks.

The total bastard

Medea's speech is a cry of pain but also an analysis. Others, on stage, share her perceptions. 'The chorus, the nurse, the messenger, and also Medea then proceed to reason, to issue general and definitive judgements on happiness, virtue, the condition of women, the errors of learned authorities, or the disadvantages of having children, and all this in contrast to the violence of what is taking place.'[60] She suffers (*paschein*) an offence, she says, which affects her honour.[61] She is the target of an undeserved injustice: 'Jason is unfair with me, who has done him no harm.'[62] This injustice is a betrayal. And everyone agrees. 'It seems to me that by betraying your wife you are not doing the right thing,' the chorus comments.[63] Aegeus, the king of Athens, is on her side.[64] As long as she does not target her children, everyone supports her.[65] But since she is already thinking about how to reverse her situation, through action, Medea is in no danger of losing her honour. Certainly, she has endured a *hubris*, a stinging humiliation. But, in admitting to it, she shows the dignity that she attributes to herself; she expresses her self-respect.

Only in the text of Euripides can we see plainly the distance that separates jealousy-as-anger, which is far-sighted and courageous – in short, heroic – from the *zelotupia*, the trivial, gauche and unsavoury pretentiousness at which, as we shall see in a moment, Aristophanes and Plato used to make people laugh. Jealousy is subjective, silly and ridiculous, comedy tells us. Jealousy must be taken seriously, and no one wants to joke about it, says tragedy.

Master of playfulness between the two genres, Euripides goes so far as to suggest a comic response to the distress of his protagonist. Medea herself speculates that someone might make fun of her! The thought of becoming the laughing stock of her enemies, especially of her hateful rival, torments Medea, but, instead of paralysing her, this very thought makes her act. 'But what has come over to me?' she asks, overwhelmed with anguish. 'Do I deserve their mockery, while leaving my enemies to go unpunished?'[66] Once again, she has no qualms in disclosing her anguish, for it is precisely to avoid laughter that she dares to kill. And, to come to the point where she can act, she must recognize what she suffers. Not to take revenge: that would be ridiculous. In acting, on the contrary, she achieves her *kleos*, her heroic glory. Laughter remains a threat. But tragedy bypasses it.

The 'total bastard', the unmanly and shameless coward, he who reaches the height of infamy (in the words of the king of Athens, Aegeus) is Jason.[67] Lucid, straightforward and dignified, Medea interprets to perfection this double emotion – passive and active, painful and pleasant, positive and negative – that anger is in Greek: desire for revenge in the consciousness of having been insulted. Her jealousy has no other name but anger – the passion of warriors and kings, the noble response to misfortune.

In Athens and Corinth, in the fifth century BCE, we are in a world quite unlike our own. Granddaughter of the Sun, a barbarian princess, a magician and a witch, Medea is not the woman next door. She is not a bourgeois, of course, but not because she refused to be 'a simple jealous wife', as if the very word 'jealousy' summoned up the most conventional image of conjugality, as it does in the nineteenth century, and as if jealousy were a trivial emotion.[68] On the contrary, Medea is heroic because she is indeed a jealous wife – which, in Greece, was said and thought otherwise. When reading a classical text, we ought not to misidentify the emotions. It should be understood that the jealousy of the ancients was a protest against ingratitude, a call for a reaffirmation of reciprocity and dignity. In all her *kleos*, her reputation and the hope of victory, Medea is furious. This is not only legitimate but also admirable.

Comic jealousy: an excess of zeal

We entered the cultural landscape of ancient Greece by outlining a situation. Usually, philologists venture into the same world by looking, instead, for possible translations. Let us follow them for a moment, and let us see where this kind of concern may lead us. Let us take a linguistic path.

At first, we will feel disoriented. The English word 'jealousy' derives from the Greek word *zelos*, which means 'competitive emulation'. This meaning has come down to us, in English, in French and in other modern languages, as the word 'zeal'. The jealous person sins, or is distinguished, by an excess of zeal. We can play the etymological game, but verbal correspondence will not be of much use to us. A language is not a dictionary. In order to recognize relevant distinctions of meaning, we need definitions. So let us make a detour via metalanguage. Once again, let us open the great encyclopaedia of Greek culture, which is to say: the works of Aristotle.

In his *Rhetoric*, Aristotle offers the first systematic classification of the passions. As a specific emotion, *zelos* figures among the unpleasant *pathemata*. *Zelos* is the displeasure of seeing someone other than us, but who is like us, enjoy goods that we covet and believe we could obtain. We will therefore strive to emulate that lucky person. Aristotle distinguishes 'zeal' from two contiguous passions: firstly, *nemesan*, which means 'to feel indignation', or the suffering caused by the good fortune of another when it seems to be undeserved; and, secondly, *phthonos*, which means envy, or the suffering we experience when confronted with the good fortune of another simply because the other person is like us, *homoios*. The indignant person protests: 'Them? What a scandal!' The envious person complains: 'Them? And why not me?' And the zealous person shouts: 'Them? OK, well, me too!' All these forms of displeasure, when challenged by the pleasure of others, relate to material, but above all symbolic, goods such as power, fame, honours, friendship. Aristotle makes not the least allusion, however, to erotic situations.

It is the compound *zelotupia* that carries the meaning of intense, exclusive and combative attachment between lovers.[69] One is struck (*tuptein*) by *zelos*. *Zelotupia* occurs, first of all, in a comic context. Aristophanes was apparently the first to use the word. In *Wealth*, a play that makes a mockery of romance, an older woman, who is blind to the real interest which her young and impoverished lover has in her, is astonished when he leaves her as soon as he ceases to have any need for her money. But he loved me, she exclaims! The proof is that, when she went to the Mysteries, the young man threatened to strike anyone who dared to ogle her. 'He was violently jealous!'[70] Plato uses the verb *zelotupein* in the *Symposium*, a collection of speeches in praise of love delivered during a party by Socrates and his friends. Aristophanes himself is part of that charming company. By late evening, a handsome young man, Alcibiades son of Cleinias, drunk and staggering, knocks on the door. Socrates knows him well, and is even in love with him, or so he says. And yet he mocks him mercilessly. Since he began to love him, Socrates says, Alcibiades has become impossibly possessive: every time he (old, ugly Socrates) looks at a handsome boy, or tries to chat him up, Alcibiades exhibits both *zelotupia* and *phthonos*. Alcibiades makes a scene, complains at Socrates, and they almost come to blows. In short, he is mad![71]

From Aristophanes' wit to Plato's irony, in a dialogue where Aristophanes' presence looms large, the term *zelotupia* stages jealousy as comic illusion. It is a ridiculous passion. A young man simulates his improbable possessiveness of an older woman; another young man fails to understand Socratic eros. In both cases, *zelotupein* is nothing but folly and vanity. We witness, in short, the birth of the cuckold, so dear to vaudeville. His feelings are stupid; his torments, useless; his assaults, derisory. From his first inception, the *zelotupos* will stay in character.

In Latin, the same Greek words are simply transliterated to become *zelotypia, zelotypus*. They survive in literary genres such as comedy, satire and romance. 'Do not get caught in the trap of an adulteress who pretends to be jealous, *zelotypa moecha*!', warns Juvenal, in an invective against love and women. Beware! This type of woman complains and wails about your alleged boyfriends and mistresses, but this is only to hide her own infidelities.[72] In the *Satyricon*, a story that takes us through the labyrinth of debauched Rome by night, Petronius can only laugh ceaselessly at devoted love and the suffering that ensues.[73]

This uncharitable language is clearly not the one in which to express the pain of disappointed and deceived love, a pain that is no laughing matter. When taken seriously – for oneself, as well as for others – jealousy becomes something quite different. On the tragic scene, Medea is devastated by the betrayal of a husband she loves – to the point of killing their children to make him pay for his desertion. The feeling of being spurned for the sake of another woman genuinely crushes Hermione. These characters certainly cannot be represented in the register of *zelotupia*. Neither Euripides nor Seneca (as we shall see in a moment) attributes to Medea that kind of emotion. For the elegiac poets of Rome, and in Ovid's *Art of Love*, jealousy is, of course, an object of constant discussion, but never in terms of *zelotypia*. This also applies to Roman tragedy. In elevated genres, and especially when we stop making fun of other people's love, we choose other words and we see something else.

This short repertory of texts and contexts might persuade us that, in ancient Greek, there never was a technical term which corresponded exactly and exclusively to the meaning of what we call 'jealousy', a wide semantic field that includes, among other specifications, 'jealousy in love'. It has been argued that, for the ancients, jealousy belongs to a network of concepts centred on honour and power, not sex.[74] Some have even spoken of 'before jealousy'.[75]

I disagree. Certainly the vocabularies do not coincide. The ancient Greeks did not have a single word whose value overlaps perfectly with that of the English term 'jealousy'. There is no doubt that this is both significant and remarkable. But it is no reason to freeze in awe at cultural otherness. To stop at the dissonance between lexica would prevent us from understanding an even more remote and distinctive aspect of ancient erotic culture.[76] We would miss the difference between taking seriously a painful situation and describing it in terms of 'erotic anger', on the one hand, and cruelly making fun of the same situation by labelling it as *zelotupia*, on the other. Furthermore, we would fail to understand many things about language. We speak in utterances, sentences, paraphrases, allusions and metaphors; the mind apprehends complex situations by a dynamic, reflexive and *metalinguistic parole* because, while we speak, we never stop defining and redefining what we mean; the history of the passions must proceed by comparing phenomenological tableaux. Of course, since we can only think historically and across a plurality of idioms, we have to be aware of the difficulty of translation in the first place. And yet it would be a mistake to stop there. We should question the 'untranslatable', to be sure, but only as a first step towards discovering how better to decode and re-encode.[77] Situations can be defined. Definitions can be converted into new sentences, in different systems of signs, which belong in different contexts. Those sentences, codifications and contexts can be compared. If we confine ourselves to verbatim similarities, however, we rush full speed into the dead end of cheap exoticism. No word? Then no thing! The richness of Medea's subjectivity disappears. We lose sight of eros.

The Stoic turn

Aristotle offers a rationalization of anger which fits perfectly what, almost a century earlier, was taking place on the Athenian tragic stage. It is as if Aristotle had extracted his theory of the passions from dramatic performance. Euripides' Medea does not hide the humiliation she suffered. The 'phenomenal' aspect of her pain appears in full light. She cries out loud and clear. In a very different cultural environment – Rome in the first century of our era – a philosopher and playwright, Lucius Annaeus Seneca, wrote a *Medea* in which he profoundly changed the character of the protagonist. As a follower of Stoicism, Seneca injected into the composition of his *Medea* a normative theory of the passions, especially the principles he formulates in his treatise *On Anger (De ira)*.[78]

Medea's jealousy, more precisely her erotic anger, is thereby rethought in a new context: the condemnation of everything that might affect us, namely the *affectus* that the Stoics prefer to call 'perturbation' (*perturbatio*) – that is to say, 'disturbance'. Whereas the Aristotelian perspective invites us to enjoy the passions (*pathemata*) when they are balanced, intelligent and virtuous, the Stoic approach requires us to remove all troubles from our soul. We must evacuate, eliminate and root out what we feel, with zero tolerance.

This is a sudden and significant change that gives a new, and decisive, orientation to ethics. By undermining a moderate vision of emotions and virtues, Stoicism played a key role in our intellectual history. The Stoic turn has radically transformed the way we think of all the passions, but mostly anger and, therefore, amorous jealousy. If we frame the Roman Medea in this anti-Aristotelian and much more rigorist moral theory, our fictional character becomes a symptom of this transformation. The thought at work in Euripides' theatre was compatible with Aristotle's ethics: this is why we read them together. A similar line of thought runs through Seneca's works, from his philosophical reflections to his fictional creations. This is why we will read *Medea* and *De ira* side by side.

Revenge is the confession of pain

Anger is the desire for revenge. Like all strong and disturbing emotions, this desire is, for the Stoics, unforgivable. It is an error of evaluation. When angry, we give a hasty consent to a perception instead of taking time to reflect and to place what affects us in the proper light. 'Do you know how the passions are born, grow and develop?', asks Seneca. The reply is that there are different motions, from a first impulse to a wish, to a strong feeling that overrides reason.[79] A full-blown passion is nothing but a stubborn will. More specifically, will and passion are triggered by consent:

> There is no doubt that anger is roused by the appearance of an injury being done: but the question before us is, whether anger straightway follows the appearance, and springs up without assistance from the mind, or whether it is roused *with the assent of the mind* [*animo adsentiente*]. Our [the Stoics'] opinion is, that anger can venture upon nothing by itself, *without the approval of mind* [*animo adprobante*]: for to conceive the idea of a wrong having been done, to long to avenge it, and to join the two propositions, that we ought not to have been injured and that it is our duty to avenge our injuries, cannot belong to a mere impulse [*impetus*] which is excited without our *will* [*voluntas*]. That impulse is a simple act; this is a complex one, and composed of several parts. The man understands something to have happened: he becomes indignant thereat: he condemns the deed; and he avenges it. All these things cannot be done without his mind *agreeing* [*adsensus*] to those matters which touched him.[80]

Emotions are not instinctual gut feelings. Tears are 'intellectual things', as Jerome Neu put it. Passions are, as was the case for Aristotle, consequential thoughts. More important, they cannot possibly be felt unless the mind gives its consent. Only if we admit that something really serious, positive or negative, is touching us can we experience a troubled state of mind. This is why affective perturbations are liable to intelligent, strategic, wilful handling. Pleasure, desire, pain and fear – i.e., the basic affects that underscore all the passions – can be either minimized as measured and stable sentiments (*constantiae*) or allowed to escalate into over-the-top, exaggerated, hyperbolic agitation.

We must especially beware of pain. The Stoic sage (the paradigm of wisdom is a man) does not allow himself to be brought down. He does not yield to suffering. Pain is a sign of weakness. Furthermore, pain elicits violence. When something happens that might cause offence and sorrow, the truly independent man, immune from the events of a changing world and impervious to its threats, must reason and talk himself out of whatever seems to affect him. He must reach the conclusion that what appears to be a devastating blow is, actually, nothing. He must come to the point of not feeling a thing. He must remain indifferent, unscathed and insusceptible – as if nothing ever happened *to him*.

BEING MEDEA

Add to this that, although rage arises from an excessive self-respect and appears to show high spirit, it really is *small and mean* [*angusta ac pusilla*]: for a man must be inferior to one by whom he thinks himself despised, whereas *the truly great mind, which takes a true estimate of its own value, does not revenge an insult because it does not feel it* [*at ille ingens animus et verus aestimator sui non vindicat iniuriam, quia non sentit*]. As weapons rebound from a hard surface, and solid substances hurt those who strike them, so also no insult can make a really great mind sensible of its presence, being weaker than that against which it is aimed. How far more beautiful is it to throw back all wrongs and insults from oneself, *like one who is impenetrable to any arrow* [*velut nulli penetrabilem telo*], for *revenge is an admission that we have been hurt* [*ultio doloris confessio est*]. That cannot be a great mind [*magnus animus*], which is bent by injury [*quem incurvat iniuria*]. He who has hurt you must be either stronger or weaker than yourself. If he be weaker, spare him: if he be stronger, spare yourself.[81]

Inflexible, the Stoic never bends. Invulnerable, he feels nothing at all. He stands upright, caparisoned, detached, rock-solid. The wickedness of other people cannot touch him because he pays no heed to insults and attacks. Should someone try to cause him offence, he does not even feel it. This true anaesthesia makes him superior to others both objectively, because the 'shots' never get to him, and subjectively, as he values himself highly, and fairly. He knows his worth, and he intends to remain *à la hauteur*. The Stoic does not enter into the dialectic interplay that places human beings in relation to each other and commits them, therefore, to a struggle for reciprocal recognition. What matters to this rigid and safeguarded self is the esteem he himself feels for himself. His own respect is enough. Looking out over the world from the summit of his impassivity – the famous *apatheia* of the sage – he will not fight to restore his humiliated dignity, for the simple reason that there can be no humiliation. I insist: a great spirit 'does not avenge an insult because he does not feel it [*non vindicat iniuriam, quia non sensit*]'.[82] According to Aristotle, this would be the portrait of slavish idiocy. It is an ideal ego entirely dedicated to what Sigmund Freud defines as 'repression'.[83]

The Freudian self operates a repression (*Verdrängung*) of its drives whenever we fear that they might be unbearable. These uncomfortable wishes disappear from our conscience and become unconscious. This manoeuvre seems to protect us, Freud argues, but it actually exposes us to the return of the repressed via the formation of symptoms, and ultimately to a paradoxical loss of control over our own desires, which, although unseen, forgotten, inaccessible, are, nevertheless, still there. A repression cannot be entirely successful, says Freud, because we can never escape ourselves. Hence the therapeutic usefulness of a talking cure in the hope of recovering that mass of concealed emotions. Now, Stoicism elevates this kind of self-defence to a moral feat. The Stoic must feel compelled to bury (*obruere*) and hide (*abscondere*) the very first manifestations of his emotions. He has to shield himself against whatever might reach him and pre-empt any emotional response. He must resist all affectivity. Like psychoanalysis, Stoic ethics postulates that, in all circumstances and events, the human subject has the chance to modulate pleasure and limit displeasure. We play the strategic game of desire and aversion. The Ego chooses to accept what it can bear and to entomb what causes discomfort. But while the neurotic is doomed to fail, since repression is useless, the Stoic prides himself on cultivating successfully deliberate self-defence and self-sufficiency. What for a Freudian would be unhappy pathology is the Stoic's highest achievement.

The ability to build such armour for oneself is not, however, within the reach of everyone. The theatre shows precisely this sad fact. In the eyes of the spectators and/or the readers of Seneca's play, Medea will have to embody the hypersensitivity and, therefore, the raw vulnerability of a lover who is overexposed to another person's desire and bears the full impact of its vagaries. Jason's infidelity did happen. She is now unable to protect herself. She was not sufficiently *hard* (*durus*). She has been 'curved' – literally, she has crashed down on the floor, incapable of lifting her head – by the shock of the outrage (*incurvat iniuria*). Medea impersonates, in a monstrous caricature, the failure of Stoic wisdom.[84] Her mission is twofold: to carry the burden of the illusions of an indulgent ethics, that of Aristotle, and to correct an overly nuanced theatre, that by Euripides. Medea will exhibit the truth of passion: how it takes shape in our consciousness; how, as soon as we give assent to an impression, its power becomes irresistible; and how pain is responsible for the worst aberrations, for oneself and for others.

Now I am Medea!

The fury (*furor*) that ravages Medea is the exact opposite of what a philosopher should make of his emotional experience. She has felt too much on all levels: too much love, too much desire and, above all, too much pain. She is in love. She is in pain. All her turbulence arises out of *dolor*. 'Let a heavier pain rise up!...Gird yourself with anger and prepare yourself for the ultimate act, with a total fury!'[85] Light is the pain that can be softened by advice: hers, on the contrary, is immense.[86] The crimes that, because of her grief, she was able to accomplish in the past were only a prelude. It was nothing more than the anger of a little girl! 'Now I am Medea!' she proclaims. Her intelligence has grown in misfortune.[87] To give heart to her endeavour, she addresses both Pain (*Dolor*) and Anger (*Ira*): 'Look for reasons to suffer, Oh Pain! You do not bring to the crime an inexpert hand. What do you reach out to, Oh Anger, or what weapons do you plan to point against the perfidious enemy?'[88] Driven from one passion to another, in a stormy tumult, she will feel love, anger, pity, grief. 'Pity chases anger; anger, pity. Yield to pity, Oh Pain!'[89] But the pain does not yield, and finally: 'Oh Anger wherever you take me, I will follow!'[90] She stabs the first child. And, immediately afterwards, while the anger subsides (*iam cecidit ira*), pleasure takes over.[91] She savours what she has done. But, to complete the second murder, she needs one last surge of pain: two deaths are not even sufficient to assuage her *dolor*. 'Enjoy the crime slowly, Oh Pain, do not be so hasty! This day is mine! We will make use of the time allotted.'[92] Murder of the second child. Extinction of pain, finally: 'It's good! That's it! I had nothing else to offer you, Oh Pain!'[93]

Medea is tossed by the violent waves and winds of her particularly severe 'perturbation'. But first and foremost, let me insist, she suffers. *Dolor* is truly the source of her many unruly feelings. It is Pain that calls for murder and leads her hand – not once, but twice. It is this exacting power that she must 'satisfy', by 'enjoying' her vengeance unhurriedly. She concedes to *Dolor* everything he asks. Anger only precipitates the acting out. Anger is the intentional turn that suffering will take: when pain leads to a thoughtful, unstoppable plan of action – that is anger.

Medea *dolorosa* enacts perfectly the Stoic script of passionate chaos. Unlike an invulnerable sage, Medea wears no armour: she does feel the sting, and she agonizes. Unlike a self-assured, thick-skinned, inflexible, impenetrable, beautiful and great mind, she acknowledges what she feels: revenge will be, indeed, a confession of how much she has been hurt. She gives her assent, she admits and she yields to that *dolor*. More precisely, she confesses. It is here that confession, the all-important speech-act that is inherent in the normative definitions of jealousy, emerges for the first time.

A praise of repression

In *De ira*, Seneca argues that, for a Stoic, the crux of any emotional experience is a preliminary moment, when we sense that we are beginning to feel something. Either we accept this initial premonition or we reject it.[94] This instant is decisive. It is the time when we can still say: 'no!' Hence the uncompromising command of Stoic morality: 'Concede *nothing* to anger!' Why? Because anger wants to take *everything*. Passions consist of movements of the soul, which acquire momentum. Without our permission, however, these drives cannot move forward. If we feel love, desire, hate or fear, it is because we have already given our approval to an initial perception – which was a mistake. We had, therefore, a choice. Seneca's ethics demands that we make that choice. It demands, more precisely, that we bury the anticipatory signals of the emotion as deep as possible inside our soul, and that we keep them concealed and secret. This effort will prove particularly arduous with anger, because anger wants to explode, until it spreads over the whole face. Once we let it overflow, however, it dominates us completely. It is now too late. Anger is time sensitive.

> Fight with yourself! If you want to conquer anger, it cannot conquer you. You start to win if it does not show itself [*si absconditur*], if it is not given a way out [*exitus*]. Let us bury its symptoms, and as far as possible let us keep it hidden and secret [*signa eius obruamus et illam quantum fieri potest occultam secretamque teneamus*]. It will give us great trouble to do this, for it is eager to burst forth, to kindle our eyes and to transform our face; but if we allow it to show itself in our outward appearance, it is our master. Let it rather be locked in the innermost recesses of our breast, and be borne by us, not bear us [*In imo pectoris secessu recondatur feraturque, non ferat*]. Let us replace all its symptoms by their opposites.[95]

This authoritarian prose explains first why everything is decided at the beginning, when anger is brewing. There are signs of disturbances that we must learn to detect immediately. Seneca tells us, on the other hand, the reasons for the urgency: very soon, it will be too late. Anger is an extrovert, exhibitionist, ostentatious drive which seeks to show off through the colours, the gesticulations, the sounds of the body. Anger tends to spread out for all to see and to hear loud and clear. It overflows, outside one's self and in front of others. It projects itself into appearance. It is this corporeal reality that, taking an autonomous force, carries us away. We must, consequently, keep everything under cover, in silence and within ourselves. As we have just seen, we must bury (*obruere*), hide (*abscondere*), keep occult and secret (*occultam secretamque tenere*), and conceal this emotion in the depths of our breast (*in imo secessu recondere pectoris*).[96] All that psychoanalysis has exposed as the portal to neurosis constitutes the supreme virtue of Stoic ethics.

Seneca describes an affective state that is intrinsically discursive, demonstrative, spectacular. He then explains that it must be silenced and suppressed. Precisely because it struggles to get out, it has to be kept inside. Precisely because it is shameless, it must be considered shameful. This imperative accompanies, of course, our reading of the tragedy. It is its most eloquent comment. But what matters is not simply a literary resonance. Seneca's moral philosophy claims that anger belongs in the theatre, because it is theatrical per se. Furthermore, this philosophical project needs the theatre. *De ira* teaches us that, in order to heal an irascible character, it is essential 'to place before our eyes' (*ponere ante oculos*) the monstrosity and ferocity of those who are prey to anger.[97] Many furious figures from the mythological tradition, such as Atreus, Hercules or Medea, bring the overflowing effects of the passion into full view. All the violence we fail to lay to rest deep down, within ourselves, bursts onto the scene. Anger – as loquacious as it is doomed to silence – is the tragic passion par excellence. It is in tragedy that it is finally brought to light, before our very eyes.

Medea, barbaric tigress

One of the remedies recommended against the passions, Seneca points out, is the contemplation of their effects in a mirror. We should take a good look at our altered face and our upset body. Seneca, however, disapproves of this empirical approach: first, if one is able to go and look in a mirror, this, he argues, presupposes that one is already in control. Worse: frantic people find nothing more beautiful than to contemplate themselves as they appear at that time, with their deformed, atrocious, horrible face.[98] Once we have been carried away, that is, is not the time to worry about ourselves. Either it is no longer necessary, as anger has already subsided, or it is impossible, because we are enjoying our rage. To see oneself in a mirror is useless. It is useful, however, to stare at anger when one can still *prevent* it from exploding (which is the key to Stoic morality) – that is to say, when one still has a clear head and is in a position to learn and reflect. The visualization of the physical consequences of passion can be highly instructive, therefore, but only when it brings before our eyes the bad example of other people's troubles. This kind of training of the self can only occur in experimental, artificial settings, in fiction. Fictional representations provide the perfect playground for emotional education. We can observe the perturbations of souls and bodies in real time and in peace – without being distraught, but retaining our full ability to meditate upon what we are seeing, at leisure.

> Let us paint [*figurare*] anger looking like those who are dripping with the blood of foemen or savage beasts, or those who are just about to slaughter them – like those monsters of the nether world fabled by the poet to be girt with serpents and breathing flame, when they sally forth from hell, most frightful to behold, in order that they may kindle wars, stir up strife between nations, and overthrow peace; let us paint [*figurare*] her eyes glowing with fire, her voice hissing, roaring, grating, and making worse sounds if worse there be, while she brandishes weapons in both hands, for she cares not to protect herself, gloomy, stained with blood, covered with scars and livid with her own blows, reeling like a maniac, wrapped in a thick cloud, dashing hither and thither, spreading desolation and panic, loathed by everyone and by herself above all, willing, if otherwise she cannot hurt her foe, to overthrow alike earth, sea, and heaven, harmful and hateful at the same time.[99]

The fictions of the poets are the most effective moral spectacle. To read a poem or a play or to attend a theatrical performance allows you to observe anger in action, but at a distance, in a state of mind that is conducive to thought. Imagine (*figurare*) Anger, Ira, 'as our poets have described her – / Bellona when she shakes her blood-stained scourge / and Discord when she rushes, enjoying her torn cloak.'[100] Rather than catch a glimpse of ourselves in a mirror, let us envision Ajax, 'driven to suicide by madness, and to madness by anger'. And let us watch carefully those who go astray, to the point of wanting to destroy everything including themselves: 'Let my children perish! Let poverty overwhelm me! Let my house collapse!' These are the wishes of these madmen. Ira makes you an enemy of your best friends; it makes you dangerous to sentient beings that you love the most; it makes you forget all law.[101] In order to know what this passion really is, we have to highlight its grim feats and listen to its clamour. And if the poets are not sufficient, we have to invent (*excogitare*) even more awful ways, if possible, to paint this dreadful perturbation.[102] Seneca's colourful, gruesome and extremely detailed language tries to capture the performance, visible and audible, of an extreme passion. It is from the literary repertoire, he insists, that one can draw a truthful tableau of anger.

To this traditional repertoire, Seneca adds his own tragedies. His Medea is a barbaric tigress. Unleashed as a bacchante, haughty like a queen, fierce like a tiger of the Ganges, she rushes about here and there. She jumps and she bellows. Sometimes scarlet in the face, sometimes sickly pallid, she 'does not know how to slow down her rages, Medea, nor her love; now that love and anger have made common cause: what is going to happen?'[103] Hot, cold, loving, furious, she's entirely lost in her disparate impulses. Should a hint of hesitancy stop her, she resolutely plunges into her pain. Unable to refuse her assent to grief, love, terror or rage, she has never known the slightest trace of wisdom. A nocturnal witch, familiar with every creature that crawls and coils, she kneads with bare hands knots of snakes, drenched with venom – she summons them all in macabre, revolting, special effects. Swarming vermin, frantic turmoil, sinister bellowing – she has everything to repel any reader or spectator and no redeeming features whatsoever. Seneca's monster is wrong, only and exclusively wrong. This *figura* of anger is perfectly abominable. Doubtless she can act as a successful deterrent. Medea's feral jealousy is illegible.

Seneca the tragedian 'places before our eyes' just what kind of monster a furious person is, and with what impetuosity she springs forth to strike and destroy, precisely as he advised in *De ira*, only now in real time and in the optical device that is a theatre.[104] A theatrical performance is a powerful magnifier, which allows us to treat this emotion exactly as Seneca the philosopher recommends. Once *ira* is brought to our attention, we must focus our full attention on it. We can fight anger only if we 'place it before our eyes' (*nobis subinde proposuerimus*). We must compare (*comparare*), scrutinize (*perscrutare*), assess (*aestimare*) and thoroughly clarify (*in medio protrahere*) all its evils. These are cognitive efforts. We must understand analytically and intelligently this counterproductive passion, which destroys the very people who allow themselves to feel it. We must then accuse and condemn it pitilessly (*accusare, damnare*).[105] To know the reality of anger, therefore, is to ban it from our life altogether. As soon as one understands (*intellegere*) this absurdly ruinous passion, one wants only one thing: to remove oneself from it (*se removere*) altogether.[106] This is the aesthetic, intellectual and moral mission of the theatre.

Let monsters abound!

Among modern playwrights, it is Antonin Artaud, the creator of the 'theatre of cruelty', who has best captured the inhumanity of the mythical giants that fill Seneca's theatre. Artaud emphasizes the 'supernatural horrific atmosphere that transpires in Seneca's truly magical text', and especially the primitive and divine nature of the characters, which are irreducible to what he calls 'a miserable anthropomorphism'. In this theatre, we are in an uncanny, unrealistic universe, 'among monsters'. We have to let these monsters 'leap and bound'. Accordingly, in the dramaturgy of *Medea*, a director should not diminish the myth by presenting plausible, familiar figures. There is no place for a human being 'small in size, stupid, ultimately naked'. Modern drama should take up the challenge of tragic cruelty. Diction should be modulated in such a way that 'our bowels would twitch and our soul jolt inside the body'.[107] On the stage, lights and voices must express the disarray of the characters in all its cataclysmic intensity, while deeply unsettling us.

Artaud understood perfectly that a theatre of cruelty implements a philosophical project. In Seneca's *Medea*, we have to see and hear what happens when we give free rein to a passion that, for Seneca, we should keep to ourselves. The theatre utters what should be silent; it makes visible what should be concealed. The theatre is the instrument of transgression. Against the odds of convention, truth springs forth. To find an image worthy of this scandalous performance, Artaud writes, we must use allegory.

One such iconic, stylized, eloquent representation can be seen in the Cappella degli Scrovegni in Padua. It is an allegory of Wrath, Ira. Giotto painted this Stoic *monstrum* as perfectly feminine. It shows an ugly woman, head thrown back, mouth wide open, loose hair. With both hands, she tears her dress, exposing her indecent cleavage. This is a pale, chalky, minimalist picture which fits the vivid description we have mentioned above, in the *De ira*. The personification of anger is fully focused on exhibitionism. The emotion is seized in its vocal trespassing. Ira does not strike. Ira bares herself both by her gesture and by her voice, the eruption of which we can imagine out of her big mouth. Ira undresses and confesses.

The fresco looks like a picture of Medea.

She does not dare even to admit

Seneca's philosophical theatre shows Medea's wheezing, yelling and, finally, thunderous anger. Women, says Seneca, need time to warm up to their rage.[108] Accordingly we follow the gradual rise of fury. We behold, in slow motion, the crippling dilemma of all passions – to consent or not to consent.

Seneca the philosopher theorizes the categorical imperative to say: 'no!' Fight against yourself! Stop the progress of the affect as soon as you can, from its initial signs. Keep it all in! Repress! Do not let it overflow! Clean up your act! Seneca the tragedian puts on stage the conspicuous, flamboyant, hyperbolic spectacle of the same imperative. The theatre shows how easy it would have been to resist, *earlier*; how definitely impossible it is to do so *now*. Now it is too late.

Seneca the philosopher intimates that 'revenge is the confession of pain' (*ultio doloris confessio est*).[109] It is a confession we must forestall, because we ought rather to fight (*pugnare*) the actual feeling of pain, as well as the admission of it.[110] To admit is to consent, which means to approve and, ultimately, to reinforce the feeling itself. To confess is a performative speech-act: when I confess, I do something. Seneca the tragedian sets all of this on the stage. Just before Medea says 'yes!' to her desire to pursue her revenge and kill the children, there is a momentous interval when she senses that a decision is being made in her. 'My ferocious soul has decided *I-don't-know-what*, inside' (*nescio quid ferox decrevit animus intus*), she says. 'And my soul *does not yet dare to confess it to itself*' (*nondum sibi audet fateri*).[111] There is an uncertain, suspended, open-ended instant when she still could stop – when a wise Stoic man would recoil.[112] But, instead, Medea opts for murder. This is how she espouses the motion of anger. Passion and will, in one stubborn thrust, take over. This is how the desire to retaliate fits the pain that is its cause: by a quasi-unconscious thought – a thought that she hesitates to confess (*fateri*), and which a solid, resilient, reasonable person, as we read in *De ira*, would never permit. Revenge itself, let me insist, is the confession of pain. As the emotional trigger of revenge, anger is the consent given to that pain, by its very admission and its immediate expression. Instead of being entombed in silence, the affect comes out in symptoms and screams. And then: murder!

For the very first time, what will become the most crucial idea in the history of amorous jealousy emerges. This emotion is better left unspoken. There is, in erotic anger, something truly inadmissible: something we should not say.

Aristotelian Medea, Stoic Medea

Seneca against Aristotle: let us stop for a moment on this contrast, which sets up two models of passion. It will help us to understand how the Stoic turn changes erotic anger forever.

Aristotle had defined anger, as we have seen, as the pain for having been unjustly offended, accompanied by a desire to avenge oneself. He had also insisted on the moral legitimacy of this response, to be executed as 'it should be', by correctly determining why, against whom, when and for how long one should be angry. Well-tempered anger was a virtue. It was also an exercise in intellectual acumen, for it was first and foremost a matter of assessing the perceived affront. Passion begins, indeed, from an insult that 'appears' to us (*phainomenê*). It all begins with a phenomenon. We need to analyse this phenomenon. We must decide how to react, knowing that exaggeration would be vicious but that indifference is simply not an option: not to feel, not to suffer, would be stupid and worthy only of a slavish coward, incapable of defending himself and of protecting his own people. We praise those who know how to get angry. We crush the indifferent with blame. There is therefore no question, for Aristotle, of rejecting, purely and simply, the phenomenon of offence. The offence is there. There is no question of ascribing any moral value to impassivity. The pain is there. Rather, we must learn to deliberate while we are already experiencing the pain.

Thus, the favourite example of heroic anger, Achilles, shows how one can restrain one's physical violence and, nevertheless, suffer. Insulted by Agamemnon, Achilles succeeded in preventing his arm from drawing the sword and slaying him, but he could not obliterate the outrage. Containing anger, not acting with immediate vindictiveness, does not, however, put an end to what he feels. The pain persists in its phenomenal reality. Achilles will go and cry on the beach, calling out to his mother for help. This melancholic Achilles, tearfully savouring the resentment that drips in his soul, has nothing to do with the Stoic sage. Achilles knew how to rein in his body against Agamemnon, but he never made any attempt to render himself impenetrable to the slight he had suffered. He persists in his grief, no matter what might be the cost for the Greek army, which he now wants to see defeated. He will take up arms only to avenge the death of his friend Patroclus. Aristotle makes of Achilles the paradigm of anger, as he understands it.

Seneca openly criticizes Aristotle. The disagreement concerns the value of the emotions themselves. Natural, amenable to moderation and to conversion into virtue, the *pathemata* are, for Aristotle, an essential component of human life and happiness. For the Roman Stoics, the 'perturbations' of the soul, as they called the passions, are to be proscribed, banished completely (*ex toto removere*), uprooted (*extirpare radicitus*) and evacuated from the soul (*purgare mentem*), because it is impossible to weaken them and to temper (*temperare*) them in any way.[113] To this intransigence of principle, directed against the Aristotelian conception of the virtues, one must add two considerations: the Stoics hold a very different view both of the 'phenomenological' experience of passion and of the benefits of the theatre.

Seneca, as we have said, follows the Stoic imperative, which obliges us to refuse our assent to pain and pleasure. We must say 'no', for the simple reason that the phenomenon which appears to me depends on my consent. As soon as I refuse to admit to a perception, I repress it for good: I forestall the affects that such a perception might trigger. I cease to feel. This is why I have the power to make myself truly invulnerable to insults. Anaesthesia. Analgesia. But I must act right away. I have to bury the first signs, before the disturbance begins to toss, to throw, to carry me away. Once these signs become visible outside – once, by consenting, my reason turns into passion – it is too late. The feeling has overflowed. It now goes down like a stone in free fall. It swirls. It drags me like a torrent. The physical and meteorological metaphors, of which the Stoics are fond, say that the movement of passion is irreversible.[114] All or nothing. This rigour is the consequence of a unitary conception of the human soul: there is no separate faculty that counters the affects, that would see them grow, and thus would be able to judge and appease them. There is one soul that is capable of reasoning, but that may also dissolve into a state of turbulence whenever it fails to say 'no' to pleasure and pain, fear and desire.

The theatre cannot help eliminate unwelcome passions by the homeopathic action of beneficial passions, namely pity and terror. No passion could possibly be a remedy. There is no *emotional* catharsis. Seneca speaks of *purgare*, as we have seen above, but what he means by this is a treatment of the soul, which is drastic and definitive. 'Let us preserve ourselves from such a disease, let us purge [*purgare*] our soul, let us extirpate passion to its roots!'[115] We must eradicate, we must 'drain completely' our affectivity, instead of seeking in vain to moderate it. We achieve this by an unconditional refusal to give our assent to the passions – *all of them*, including compassion and dread. The theatrical spectacle of anger helps us understand (*intelligere*) why we have to free ourselves from its clutches: the enraged are the first victims of their fury; it is a form of violence that causes them the greatest harm. Watching their derangement in full swing, we have said, sharpens our intelligence and judgement: it makes us examine and compare.[116] Seneca does not say that the spectators of his tragedies shudder with terror and that this commotion would cause a visceral repugnance for the plight of their characters. The sight of the perturbation in all its unbound, chaotic, ruinous thrust does not produce, in other words, a *pathetic* relief but, instead, an intellectual conversion. In order to rely on a cathartic deliverance, in the manner of Aristotle, we must admit that the passions themselves, or at least two of them (pity and fear), can do good. But this, for a Stoic, is inconceivable. This is the reason for Stoic inflexibility.

Euripides' Medea evaluates the validity of her anger. She has suffered injustice, dishonour and *hubris*. She is a victim of ingratitude, whereas she has done so much for her man. She is treated as a miserable stranger, while her grandfather is a god. They want to get rid of her, when she deserves her place as a mother. She is not given credit for acting on her own free will, for, according to Jason, Aphrodite has accomplished for her all that she seemed to do. Jason treats her as if she had done nothing, while he owes her everything – and as if she were nothing, when he is everything for her. In light of Aristotelian thought, Medea has a thousandfold right to ride her *orgê*. The slight is real. And a slight (*oligôria*) goes far beyond blame: it means, precisely, to consider people as nothing. This is the cause of anger. There is a reason for Medea to suffer and, therefore, a reason for her to seek revenge. The nurse, the chorus and Aegeus: all try to understand this overwhelmed, afflicted, derelict woman who is crumbling under the weight of disregard and thanklessness. But Medea puts herself in the wrong when she chooses her children as victims. At this point all sympathy ceases. On every possible account infanticide is inadmissible. As Aristotle says, killing relatives, when you know who they are, does not even make for good tragedy.[117] This murder is an anti-tragic flaw.

The Stoic Medea – the *monstrum* Seneca sets before us – displays the stubborn, unstoppable will that is passion. Being responsible, she is also unpardonable. If she lingers for a moment on the threshold of her decision, it is to lay bare before us, in the middle of the stage, the path to wisdom she fails to take. Nobody could ever see anything but a crescendo of ferocity and turmoil. No one could ever have pity for her – not the characters, nor the spectators, nor the readers. Her murder will be the ultimate triumph of who she truly is: 'Now I am Medea!'[118] That will be her masterpiece.

'We must make a masterpiece'

It is precisely this project – to create a masterpiece – that inspires the *Medea* of Pierre Corneille.[119] After the Stoic turn, Medea becomes modern, French and, paradoxically, Christian.

Close to Seneca, to the point of interpolating translations and paraphrases into his text, Corneille composes a new version of the play that offers, also, a new theory of jealousy. The word 'jealousy' emerges gradually. Medea is angry, a prey to anger, to rage, to wrath, as in classical texts, but here we begin to hear about her 'jealous mind'. She is now a 'jealous woman'.[120] She has forgotten her role as the monster she was for the Roman Stoics. In 1635 in Paris, Medea is not the hyper-realistic caricature of a failed philosopher. Corneille explains as much in the *Epistle* that accompanies the play.

> So it [the play, *Medea*] describes equally good and bad actions, without offering the latter as an example, and if it intends to horrify us somehow, it is not because of their punishment – which the play does not care to make us see – but because of their ugliness – which the play strives to represent as it is, naturally. There is no need here to warn the public that the actions of this tragedy are not to be imitated. They appear in a sufficiently open light, as to inspire envy in no one.[121]

Half ironic, half impatient, these words are part of the controversy that raged over the aesthetic and moral effects of dramatic poems. A poet had to please. A fiction had to be useful by contriving the purgation of vicious passions, and by exposing in full light (*à découvert*) actions and manners which no one would ever dream of taking as examples. Ugliness and horror do not make you want to do the same, says Corneille. Needless to say, the play is not meant to suggest that you should emulate an infanticide. Yet Medea here becomes a hero of justice with whom the public can only commiserate. In another text, *The Examination*, which commented on the same play, Corneille explains how Creusa, Jason's young bride-to-be, and her father, Creon, all perish on stage, consumed by an invisible flame, the effect of Medea's lethal spells. These two unfortunate characters 'annoy more by their cries than they inspire pity for their misfortune.' Pity indeed is all for Medea, as she is the victim of 'injustice' in the first place. This injustice 'draws to her side all the sympathy of the audience, which excuses her revenge after the undeserved treatment she received from Creon and her own husband.' For Corneille, there can be no doubt: Medea was reduced to 'despair'; she has 'suffered' to such an extent that the spectators will have more compassion for her than for those who are actually dying in agony. Creusa and Creon are responsible for her immense misery. They deserve their punishment.[122] Jason too, for that matter – and this is why, in this version, he commits suicide.

The author's programme could not be clearer. It fits his characters. Medea never ceases to declare her 'righteous anger' and 'righteous rigour'.[123] She has endured an 'unjust affront'.[124] Nerine, the nurse, recognizes her 'fair ardour'.[125] Creon is aware of the abuse. Creusa even admits that she deserved her punishment.[126] He who understands nothing, as always, and still more stupidly, is Jason. He begins with banter: 'For I am not one of those vulgar lovers; / I adjust my flame to what's good for my business.'[127] He burns for the daughter of the king of Corinth, he proclaims, but it's always the same story. He loved Medea (as he loved Hypsypile, queen of Lemnos, before her) because, in both cases, it was advantageous. Now he has everything to gain from a marriage with the local princess, who happens to be the young Creusa. A reason of state. His friend Pollux tries to make Jason think twice: treating Medea this way is 'so rude'; he should show at least 'a bit of gratitude'. All she did for him is 'poorly rewarded'. Beware! Jason should fear the woman's 'offended courage'. But Jason couldn't care less. Medea will only moan, scream, cry, wish him a thousand ills, as Hypsypile had done. Then she will calm down and be patient. What could the voice of these women ever convey for Jason? 'Bursts of useless anger', nothing more.[128] Medea will leave soon, he predicts. All will be well.[129]

Frivolous, selfish and lazy, Jason is blind to the logic of anger. Rather, he makes his own self-serving little deals, and in the words saturated with pain from the women he keeps deserting he hears nothing significant, only verbiage, whining, complaint – in short: 'useless anger'. But he is wrong. The wrath of Medea is anything but useless. This is a justified, courageous and, above all, tremendously effective anger. In this dissonance, a new redefinition of jealousy emerges. On the one hand, there is Medea's noble jealousy, which is excruciating and active; on the other, there is the same jealousy, but as it appears in Jason's eyes, as clownish desperation. What is tragedy for her is comedy for him. We can see in Jason's Don Juan-like thought the 'powerless rage' Stendhal will speak about. It is ridiculous to be seen with a large unmet desire, especially in France. Jason's mistake ruthlessly flouts the immense love that Medea is not ashamed to confess. But we're not in a *theâtre de boulevard*. Corneille's scene remains tragic: with her 'aristocratic Ego' (*Moi aristocratique*), Medea loves, aches and speaks.[130] She thus draws to herself 'the favour of the audience'. Jason discovers that his 'jealous one', as he mockingly calls her, was unexpectedly right. Creusa burns to ashes. Medea escapes in triumph. He kills himself. Curtain.

Jason was perfidious

Jason's suicide is not a minor variant. Corneille returns to Medea in his *Discours de l'utilité et des parties du poème dramatique* (Discourse on the utility and parts of dramatic poems) (1660). He compares tragedy ancient and modern. The ancients prized plays that ended with the survival of the villain and did not mind when they went unpunished. The French, however, despise this kind of intrigue. They much prefer another way of ending dramatic poems: 'the punishment of evil deeds and the reward of good ones'. In 'our theatre', Corneille writes, we want to leave the playhouse satisfied that our characters have all received their just rewards. We want crime to be punished. 'The awful issue of crime or injustice is capable of increasing our natural horror for it, by the apprehension of a similar misfortune.'[131] The baddies must end badly. We shiver, and we love it.

Medea, however, is an exception.

> The second usefulness of a dramatic poem is found in the naive painting of vices and virtues, which never fails to have an effect.... The ancients were very often content with this painting, without taking the trouble to reward good deeds and punish bad ones.... Jason was

a traitor in abandoning Medea, to whom he owed everything; but the slaughter of his children was something more in his eyes.... Our theatre has no patience for such subjects: the *Thyestes* of Seneca was not a great success. His *Medea* has found more favour; but, to be sure, the perfidy of Jason and the violence of the king of Corinth make her seem so unjustly oppressed that the listener easily comes to understand her point of view, and to look upon her vengeance as a form of justice which she herself exacts against those who have oppressed her.[132]

Despite its dramatic horror and moral monstrosity, Seneca's *Medea* produces on Corneille (and, according to him, on the French public at the time) a pathetic or, more precisely, a sympathetic effect. One can empathize with her and can even forgive her. She has exaggerated slightly, to be sure, but, unlike other furious characters who pushed their vengeance really too far, she is, first and foremost, a victim. The contrast with the vicissitudes of Atreus, in Seneca's *Thyestes*, is eloquent. Atreus and Thyestes are brothers, doomed to fight each other. Thyestes commits adultery with Atreus' wife, Aerope. Atreus' revenge takes the form of a macabre culinary trick. He slaughters Thyestes' children, then carves, minces, roasts and boils their bodies. He mixes their blood with wine. Feigning an invitation to a family meal, he serves this repast to their father. Thyestes falls into the trap. He greedily ingests all this food, except for the heads and the hands of the boys, which are offered to him as seconds on a separate plate, after dinner. Only then will Thyestes realize that what he thought was delicious meat was, actually, his own flesh.[133] Atreus' anger is a response to sexual infidelity, but it is also part of a struggle for power between two cursed brothers. Seneca's play does not allow for any extenuating circumstances for this deceitful murderer. Atreus has no excuse. Yet he outlives his deeds. For a Christian audience, Corneille insists, this is unbearable.

On closer examination, Medea's is a case of legitimate defence. A modern listener has qualms in taking her side. In the case of her deadly love, in other words, the outcome *à l'antique* remains acceptable even in Paris, for French Christians.[134] So Corneille does not feel compelled to change the fate of Medea after she stabs her children but lets her fly away with impunity, in a chariot drawn by two winged dragons. 'The fairy cries of a triumphant Medea at the end of the play', Marc Fumaroli writes, 'accompany the victory of the theatrical genius over cowardice, hypocrisy, pharisaism, the mindless lymph and the wicked deep feelings of the holders of legitimacy.'[135] Corneille has Jason commit suicide instead – a novelty in comparison with Euripides and Seneca – in order to satisfy the taste of his public. Whereas Medea was 'unjustly oppressed', Jason is in the wrong. The drama must impose an unequivocal punishment on him. Jason, therefore, kills himself. Narrative retribution ultimately absolves Medea for her jealousy. This infanticidal mother becomes a paradoxically Aristotelian heroine. She is angry, and rightly so. We do not even blame her for choosing her closest possible kin whom she knows so well as her innocent victims. We easily come to share her 'interests'.[136]

To purge, moderate, correct, and even uproot...

This indulgence takes us a long way from ancient Stoicism.[137] Corneille admired Seneca's tragedies. But his dramatic staging performance of the emotions is not at all the same.[138] A philosophical and religious gulf separates the French tragedian from the Roman philosopher. Their moral theories are profoundly dissimilar, as are their aesthetic strategies. There are forgivable passions, for Corneille, such as the erotic anger of a woman devoted to an opportunistic, unreliable and treacherous husband. This woman deserves to get away with her crimes. Mercy and sympathy, on the contrary, are inadmissible for Seneca.

Never did Seneca dare to say that Medea attracts the favour of the public. Fierce, furious, bloody, her hands thrust into a bundle of snakes, his own Medea was not meant to please – except an audience made of monsters. She was meant, rather, to encourage people to rely on their intellect as the sole sound basis for knowledge and agency. The viewers (or readers) of this theatre were supposed to benefit from the staging of the passions. The exhibition of strong feelings was expected to eradicate and purge them. Seneca's *On Anger* prescribes exactly this use of fiction. Poets visualize, display, magnify the emotions, especially anger, so that we can measure the damage they do. The spectacle of rage offers us an anti-narcissistic mirror in which to see the physical effects of this disturbance of the soul. Those rolling eyes, that purple colour, those grinding teeth, those uncontrolled gestures, those shouts: Oh! My! And all this to destroy yourself! It's cruel, disgusting and, above all, absurdly irrational. Just think!

Corneille also explains in detail how the theatre helps us to purge our souls, but he does so in a completely different manner. The theatre has a powerful *pathetic* impact. It triggers therapeutic passions.

So pity embraces the point of view of the person we see suffering; the fear that follows suit turns to our own point of view, and only this transition gives us enough open-mindedness to discover how the purgation of the passions occurs in tragedy. Pity for a misfortune into which we see our fellow fall leads us to fear the same misfortune for ourselves; this fear leads us to wish to avoid it; and this wish leads us to purge, moderate, correct and even uproot in us the passion that plunges the people we pity into this misfortune. And this for the simple (and yet natural and unmistakable) reason that, in order to avoid the effect, one must remove the cause.[139]

We start by *sympathizing* with characters who fall into misfortune. Then we feel *afraid* that we too might experience the same pernicious outburst of emotion. Finally, we sincerely *hope* to escape these intense feelings and *wish* to pre-empt their consequences. In the theatre we are delivered from disastrous emotions, therefore, but thanks to other emotions: pity and fear. The 'purgation of the passions' is a process quite different from the Stoic *purgatio*, which was a metaphor for the radical expulsion of all the affects from the soul, by thought and reflection. Emotion, not reason, is therapeutic. This is why the theatre is a pathetic apparatus capable of creating a moral experience, a theory which Corneille attributes to Aristotle's famous theory of *catharsis*.[140]

In the terms of this logic, Medea's jealousy as anger appears to be a pastiche of disparate ideas. Since her misfortunes are the result of a passion, and the passion is justified, we feel pity, Corneille argues. Pity for the effects leads us to fear their cause. The terror of being carried away by hazardous passions counteracts any inclination we might have to indulge in them. So even if Medea commits an act of extreme ugliness, we can nevertheless feel sorry for her predicament. Compassion inspires, in turn, the cautious desire not to do the same. What would Aristotle have thought of such a theory? That in a theatre we feel a peculiar kind of pity: for misfortunes that depend on unintentional *mistakes*. We are terrified of making the same disastrous blunders.[141] We're not afraid of the passions themselves, however: felt 'properly', emotions are virtues. What would Seneca have said to this? That, like all the disorders of the soul, pity too was to be banished. It was surely not fear (yet another disturbance) that could help us dispel the effects of the passions. Only a deliberate refusal to yield to all of them could do the trick.

Corneille mixes everything together. We want 'to purge, moderate, correct, and even uproot in us the passions', he wrote.[142] But 'to moderate' or 'to correct' is not the same as 'to uproot' or 'to purge'. It is precisely on this point that Seneca attacks Aristotle: it is simply impossible to dose, regulate or mitigate the passion, he argues. We must suppress all disturbances in the depths of our soul; we must prevent them all by denying them our consent. The slightest trouble must be buried or flushed out as soon as it begins to surface in our conscience. It is all or nothing. Once an affect overflows, it's too late. This rigour explains the hopeless gloom of Stoic tragic characters, including Medea, the ultimate *monstrum*. The result of Corneille's pastiche, however, is that, because of her calamitous and uncontrollable passions (which is reminiscent of Seneca), Medea inspires pity and fear (as Aristotle claims). This creates a hybrid ethics that Aristotle would have rejected (because passion here replaces the tragic, involuntary error), on the one hand, and that Seneca would have abhorred, on the other. A raging and voluntary passion (anger) is supposed to awaken other passions (pity and terror), which, for a Stoic, are no less blameworthy. One needs an antidote; there is no cure in evil itself.

This modern Medea invites a Christian audience to embrace her point of view, and to empathize with her just wrath, while shuddering at the thought of imitating her. The Medea of the *Grand Siècle*, in other words, asks for forgiveness.

Ancient anger responds to a failure to offer recognition. A pact is broken. Promises have not been kept. Reciprocity is shattered. An affective experience has gone wrong. What I am for you! What I've done for you! The triangle exists, but it is not that which commands words, deeds and feelings. Anger occurs between *two* lovers (Jason and Medea) or rivals (Achilles and Agamemnon). There was something between *them*: something serious, intense and painful. When jealousy is seen first and foremost through the prism of three-sided rivalry, on the contrary, everything that was lived becomes insignificant. Exit the cry of pain, the performance of pathos and the dignity of pride. End of tragedy: time for vaudeville.

A forbidden passion

The reframing of jealousy as erotic anger shows us the importance of a reflection that covers a very long period. From this, as I have said, I shall single out a few decisive moments where historical gaps widen, debates begin and ideas change. I will try to construct a cultural history, in tableaux.

There is, first of all, the Stoic turn that, in Seneca's work, dislodges anger from its privileged place among the ancient passions and downgrades it to the level of a mean and narrow feeling (*pusilla et angusta*). Stoicism, however, was not accepted entirely by Christian philosophers and theologians. The early Christians objected to the ideal of the imperturbable sage, insensitive to emotions and invulnerable to pain. This is a haughty man, says Augustine in *The City of God*, in the fifth century CE. An indifferent creature cannot suffer for his sins, love his neighbour or fear God. As heirs to the culprits of original sin, a sin of pride, we must bear regret, contrition, sorrows and agony, and we must live in dread of divine justice.[143] The passions are part of the legacy of Adam and Eve.

By inaugurating the scholastic canonization of Aristotle's philosophy, Thomas Aquinas (1225–1274) re-established the ethics of 'the Philosopher' and, consequently, his reasonable vision of the passions. Anger, love and jealousy intertwine in a morality that is as prescriptive as it is nuanced. I will examine these views in detail. Let me say here, however, that, according to Aquinas, attachment to one person, and the wish to obtain the same particular and unique preference in return, is inseparable from love. This fits the imperative of monogamy, an institution attuned to natural law not generically (because man, as an animal, could copulate and procreate with more than one woman) but specifically, insofar as the good of matrimony is the conception and proper rearing of offspring, which can only be guaranteed by the assiduous and continuous cohabitation of one couple. Interestingly, Aquinas draws attention to the asymmetry of men's and women's feelings. To the question whether polygamy goes against natural law, one might reply that jealousy is a natural desire, because all human beings feel it, universally. Love being reluctant to share the beloved, if many wives were to share one husband it would be contrary to natural law. Women's jealousy and the strife it creates in a household, therefore, would seem to provide a strong argument against what Andromache calls 'the customs of Thracian kings'. Aquinas counters this claim, however, by specifying that wives are more prepared to tolerate their husbands' infidelity than vice versa. Consequently, among human and non-human beings, the male is more prone to jealousy than the female. Wives can easily tolerate their husbands' infidelity. Husbands should abstain from polygyny for different reasons. The crucial point is that marriage is the only appropriate frame of sexual activity, and that, in order to perform its purpose – the proper rearing of children – marriage must entail both uniqueness and fidelity. Gender imbalance culminates with the silence of the law, natural and local, on polyandry. Should a woman have multiple spouses, the purpose of marriage would fail completely, because there would be 'uncertainty of the offspring in relation to its father, whose care is necessary for its education'. There would simply be no fatherhood at all, which would contradict the very definition of marriage. Such a hypothesis, Aquinas observes, is unimaginable.[144] The naturalness of male jealousy, as we shall see, also fits the intrinsic dynamic of amorous emotions. Singularity is love's very intent.

For Andreas Capellanus, as we said, a man in love lives in fear. Jealousy makes love grow. When a lover is apprehensive about his beloved, jealousy and passion increase. He who is not jealous cannot possibly love. Desire for reciprocity, in the singular, is the essence. In the same spirit, from Provençal love poetry to Dante, the experience of love is, in most cases, inscribed in an impossible and triangular relationship that enhances the value of the beloved. In the *Divine Comedy*, while envious individuals with sewn eyelids and a livid complexion are found in Purgatory, jealousy is neither a vice nor a capital fault.[145] Paolo Malatesta and Francesca da Rimini, among those who are guilty of lust, undergo eternal punishment for their adulterous passions. Francesca's husband, Gianciotto Malatesta, who caught them in flagrante and stabbed them to death, will end up in the lowest circle of Hell for having committed an act of treason against his own kin. In itself, however, his jealousy was not a sin.

The theories of the passions are renewed in the seventeenth century. Pierre Corneille shows us how the jealousy/anger of an aristocratic Ego can be forgiven by a Christian public which fully understands Medea's feelings. On the one hand, the spectator sympathizes; on the other, Jason couldn't care less. Tragedy is a potential comedy, but gravity trumps cruelty. That shallow, disloyal, ungrateful man will have to kill himself. In the same world, La Rochefoucauld's *Maxims* offer a melancholic counterpoint to this new emphasis which has now been placed on jealousy. Modern meditations tilt towards the discomfort of rivalry. Jealousy is a reasonable passion (because one fears to lose a precious good), and yet it becomes even more arduous to admit to feeling its pangs (for one is ashamed). Erotic jealousy reveals (and defeats) a sense of self that lies at the forefront of aristocratic culture: vanity.[146] While the Stoics enjoin us to repress our pain, although we are burning to display it to the eyes and ears of everybody, baroque moralists unmask us. We cannot help feeling jealous, and yet we are crippled by embarrassment. Why? Because, La Rochefoucauld said, we care deeply for a person but also for our image of ourselves, hence our sadness at the thought of being replaced as objects of desire. We suffer because of an excess of self-love. Vanity causes jealousy. The success of a rival not only challenges but also undermines our vanity: this is why we refrain, spontaneously and carefully, from letting the world know about our demise. Vanity creates the impossibility of admitting to jealousy. We are so vain that we feel jealous, but too vain to say so. We suffer our indignity in silence.

Our ancient ancestors were proud of their noble jealousy, erotic anger – and they had to be taught how to contain themselves. For the moderns, one passion, vanity, makes us jealous and ashamed of being so. Once again, jealousy becomes a forbidden passion.

2

A FORBIDDEN PASSION

For us, jealousy has become nothing more than a mode of competitive exclusiveness. This may take one of two forms: either another person possesses a good (or receives a favour) which I also want; or I am in possession of a good which I have no wish to share with someone else. From this triangular interaction, between two persons and a 'good', we will single out one particular type: jealousy in love. This approach prevails in contemporary analytic philosophy.

Jealousy is generally defined together, or in contrast, with envy. Its moral value is a matter of robust debate.[1] The specificity of amorous jealousy tends to be discussed in especially unfavourable terms. Even Kristján Kristjánsson, who promotes a 'quasi-Aristotelian' ethics in which emotions, properly tuned, ought to be acknowledged as virtues, singles out its irrationality.

> The reason why romantic or sexual jealousy makes for such a morally (as distinct from psychologically) unexciting case – even if it may, historically, constitute the linguistic archetype of jealousy – is that it seems to fall flat on the first hurdle of appropriateness, that of rationality. The sexually jealous person overlooks the fact that love is not a matter of will and no one deserves to be sexually attractive to another. We cannot decide to love someone (romantically/sexually) because we think the person deserves or owes our love.[2]

This blame of jealous love, on account of its absurd pretence to reciprocal preference, surged in the eighteenth century. Jealousy is an acknowledgement of the superiority of another, and therefore of one's own inferiority; it is an admission of senile impotence. 'Delicate lovers are afraid to admit it.' Everyone blushes. Rightful anger now vanishes from sight, and shame takes its place. What is more, jealousy is now no longer seen as reasonable, as La Rochefoucauld had claimed. It is simply a powerful and embarrassing failure which we have suffered and now desperately wish to disguise. The emotion itself is the flagrant recognition of our defeat and of our lack of self-confidence. This passion is 'cruel' because it is excruciating and persecutory, and it is 'mean' because it reveals our deep insecurity. Jealousy overwhelms and unmasks us. As we shall see, the 'furious' side of jealousy may still be part of the picture from time to time, but the structure of the emotion has changed utterly. A noble passion has become contemptible, ignominious and entirely unworthy of any polite society, wherever it may be found, and so unflattering as to make anyone blush. Jealousy as it is conceived in the Enlightenment becomes increasingly inadmissible, no matter how vividly our gestures and expressions might betray us.

Sullen and sorrowful, and small-minded, jealousy is now greeted with ever-increasing contempt. But why then? Why should it be thought a matter of shame to be in pain, because a person whom we have placed at the centre of our life no longer does the same for us? What has happened to our experience of love, and to our self-respect, that we have learned to blush when we assert our dignity?

Medea has brought us thus far. She enlightens us. Anger gave grandiosity to the jealousy of the ancients. The jealousy of the moderns, although still furious, becomes something else altogether. There are two reasons for this. Firstly, competition with a rival acquires a far greater importance than it once had, and, secondly, anger departs radically from its original Aristotelian definition. As a consequence, jealousy is transformed into an agonistic confrontation, which provokes only a rage that is generally ineffective.

A sudden stop

In the middle of the seventeenth century, an English philosopher who was widely read and much admired brought about a radical change in our understanding of the passions. The greatest theorists of love who wrote in French – Jean-Jacques Rousseau, Denis Diderot and Henri Beyle, better known by his sobriquet Stendhal – would follow in his footsteps during the course of the next two centuries. That philosopher, who exercised an immense influence on the subsequent history not only of political philosophy but also of anthropology and psychology, was Thomas Hobbes.

Hobbes lived for long periods in Paris, where he met Galileo and formed friendships with Marin Mersenne and Pierre Gassendi, the materialist who was largely responsible for the modern revival of Epicurus. Hobbes's ideas, widely diffused, appropriated, denounced and frequently poorly understood, were both influential and provocative. In the *Encyclopédie*, for instance, Diderot provides a brief sketch of Hobbes, whom he describes as possessed of a mind 'vast and just, penetrating and profound'. Diderot was particularly impressed by what he called Hobbes's 'daring thought'. 'His sentiments', he went on, 'are entirely his own, although his philosophy is, as yet, little known.... His errors have done more to advance the progress of the human mind than a mass of works shot through with commonplace truths.'[3]

In 1772, Paul-Henri Dietrich, baron d'Holbach, one of the most contentious figures of the eighteenth century, translated into French Hobbes's 'little treatise in English' *On Human Nature*. This provided an account of Hobbes's theory of the passions, which became well known to the French *philosophes*. Hobbes was a theoretician of human nature, concerned above all with the affects that caused men to feel, think, deliberate and act. He claimed that anger was nothing more than a surge of impatience with an obstacle that stands suddenly before us. The heroic passion of Aristotle and Greek tragedy, but also the 'just wrath' which was still a model for action, as dignified as it was efficacious, in the writings of Pierre Corneille, becomes on Hobbes's account nothing other than an instantaneous, punctual, mechanical reaction, which is neither strategic nor legitimate. Hobbes had ushered in a new language. The consequences were immense.

In *Leviathan*, his masterpiece on the foundations of the state, as well as in *Human Nature*, Hobbes examined and redefined the passions. Taking as his model the laws of motion, he described them as intentional representations capable of being transformed into actions. At first we grasp the world through our senses; then we do so with the mind. The residues of the sensations we first experience become the imagination. Finally, these conceptions are relayed to the heart, where they are transformed into active dispositions to movement. In the case of attraction, preference or the wish to come close to another, this disposition is a positive one. In the case of dislike, repulsion or rejection, it is negative. Appetite and aversion take different forms – love and hatred, hope and fear – hence the variety of what we call the 'passions'. In reality, these are causes for action, the imperceptible beginnings of all our voluntary movements.[4] What we call 'will' is nothing other than the last passion which prevails in the train of contradictory emotions we mistakenly call 'deliberation'.[5]

Each passion fulfils one particular aspect of our natural aggressivity once it has been domesticated by society; it is a perennial competition in a life which is nothing other than an endless race against all our fellow beings and which lasts throughout our entire existence:

> To endeavour is appetite.
> To be remiss is sensuality.
> To consider them behind is glory.
> To consider them before is humility.
> To lose ground with looking back vain glory.
> To be holden, hatred.
> To turn back, repentance.
> To be in breath, hope. To be weary despair.
> To endeavour to overtake the next, emulation.
> To supplant or overthrow, envy.
> To resolve to break through a stop foreseen courage.
> To break through a sudden stop anger.
> To break through with ease, magnanimity.
> To lose ground by little hindrances, pusillanimity.
> To fall on the sudden is disposition to weep.
> To see another fall, disposition to laugh.
> To see one out-gone whom we would not is pity.
> To see one out-go we would not, is indignation.
> To hold fast by another is to love.
> To carry him on that so holdeth, is charity.
> To hurt one's-self for haste is shame.
> Continually to be out-gone is misery.
> Continually to out-go the next before is felicity.
> And to forsake the course is to die.[6]

Within this same catalogue of the passions, anger becomes an impetuous bid to overcome an unexpected hindrance to our will. ('To resolve to break through a stop foreseen courage. / To break through a sudden stop anger.') Anger, therefore, is the audacity to surmount an obstacle which blocks our path or else an impediment to acting in the way we wish.

> ANGER (or sudden courage) is nothing but the appetite or desire of overcoming present opposition. It hath been commonly defined to be grief proceeding from an opinion of contempt; which is confuted by the

often experience we have of being moved to anger by things inanimate and without sense, and consequently incapable of contemning us.[7]

Such a definition is by no means self-evident. Anger, Hobbes explains, has generally been defined as a state of displeasure derived from the sense of having been insulted. But that may easily be disproved by experience. For what most often makes us angry are lifeless things or things lacking in understanding, which are consequently incapable of despising or insulting us. What in fact makes us angry is a hurdle of any kind, be it a person, an animal or a thing, which slows us down, thwarts our momentum, blocks our way, or in any other way interferes with our plans.[8]

A new passion

What now becomes of the ancient drama of *orgê*? Hobbes replaces a culture of honour with a conflict of forces, impressions born out of self-love with empirical experience. Only the vainglorious, 'being more prone than others to interpret for contempt the ordinary liberty of conversation', could possibly imagine that every time he was annoyed he was responding to an offence.[9] This criticism of the classical definition of anger belongs to a political reflection, which goes well beyond the question with which we are concerned here. Nevertheless, Hobbes's incursion into the history of the passions has considerable bearing upon amorous anger.

We have seen how, in the *Rhetoric*, Aristotle had examined the epic passion of Achilles, which is also the tragic passion of Medea. Since he had translated the *Rhetoric* into English, Hobbes was very familiar with this text; he could not, therefore, have been unaware that what he presented as an emotion '*commonly defined* to be grief proceeding from an opinion of contempt' was actually an Aristotelian one.[10] His critique was directed less at Aristotle himself than at the neo-Aristotelianism of the Scholastic scholars, which had dominated theological and philosophical thinking for centuries.

If Hobbes could reduce this theory to a 'commonly' accepted definition, it was probably because, in the thirteenth century, the most influential of Aristotle's Christian commentators, St Thomas Aquinas, had given it a seal of approval.[11] Aquinas takes up the idea that the movement of anger is provoked by an offence for which one strongly desires to take revenge.[12] In reviewing the philosophical mistakes associated with this question, he singles out the mechanistic arguments which had already been considered in his day. Some, he claims, believe that we are capable of feeling anger not only towards persons but also towards irrational creatures and inanimate objects. We grow angry, in other words, with those things that are, by their nature, incapable of offending us. We might, for instance, be taken by an overwhelming desire to throw away a pen when it fails to write adequately.

To this Aquinas replies that anger is a complex passion. There is unreflective wrath, which excites our imagination, and there is reasonable resentment, which depends upon an assessment of the offence. The latter leads us to calculate what chance of success our plans of revenge might have. All animals, including humans, experience the first. But only humans are capable of acting on the second. The fury one might unleash on a pen which fails to do what it is meant to do is clearly an irrational mood swing worthy only of a brute. To organize a response against someone who has humiliated us, by keeping in mind both the desired outcome (that the person who is responsible be humiliated in turn) and the odds of success (are we, for instance, faced by too powerful an enemy?), is quite another matter. This passion, which is both strategic and tactical, is the only truly human anger. It is the passion that Aristotle believes to be impossible to hold against inanimate objects, such as corpses. Since they cannot suffer, it is pointless to harass them.[13]

In reply to the claim of a fourth-century theologian, Gregory of Nyssa, that anger is the armed guard, so to speak, of desire, since it attacks every obstacle that would impede its realization, Aquinas insists that anger is directed towards vengeance – the punishment, that is, of the person who has harmed us.[14] It is not an impediment (*impedimentum*) in itself that makes us angry; it is the intentional action carried out by an agent who is capable of causing harm. On this account, anger is relocated in a dialectic in which justice is effectively re-established in response to an unjust and injurious act. Anger for Aquinas, therefore, retains its heroic value because of the difficulty of the task it faces. While lust easily achieves its objectives, the quest for revenge can often be an arduous one. We are not, in general, incensed by trifles, but only when confronted by words or deeds that offend us deeply.[15] In the neo-Aristotelian language of the Scholastics (whom Hobbes called dismissively the 'Schoolmen'), anger remained, therefore, as it had been for Aristotle, the most noble, just and well-grounded of the passions.[16]

Hobbes takes up the critique of this account with renewed enthusiasm. For him, the specific case of the pen hurled out of the window in an outburst of fury – I want to write, but this instrument, which is meant to help, is hampering my efforts – became the precise example of a fit of rage. Anger is sudden courage before an unforeseen obstacle. Every obstacle will do. It is the idea of obstruction – the 'sudden stop' – that matters. This includes persons as well as things, but it excludes, categorically, any *intention* on the part of any human being who might wish to harm us.

Loving in the singular

It is from the perspective of these mechanistic and kinetic presuppositions that Hobbes centres the definition of anger upon the notion of hurdles and hindrances. As we have said, movement, competition, excellence, triumph are, for Hobbes, just so many aspects of human life, understood as a race. Amorous relations are no exception. In his translation of the *Rhetoric*, Hobbes makes Aristotle say that lovers (as well as the sick and the poor) suffer and become irritated whenever they are confronted by anyone who restrains them, opposes them or refuses to help them.[17] There is in love a demanding and determined impulse that, in the pursuit of its objectives, will brook neither antagonism nor indifference. That is also true for Hobbes. Passionate love is love for one person: '*Love* of one singularly, with desire to be singularly beloved.'[18] While sexual attraction is 'indefinite desire' for any member of the opposite sex (the only kind Hobbes included in this description), love for a particular person arouses a true *need* and, with it, the *hope* that it will be reciprocated.

> But there is a great difference between the desire of a man indefinite, and the same desire limited *ad hanc*; and this is that love which is the great theme of poets. But notwithstanding their praises, it must be defined by the word need; for it is a conception of the need a man hath of that one person desired. The cause of this passion is not always, nor for the most part, beauty, or other passion, with the quality, in the beloved, unless there be withal hope in the person that loveth.[19]

The same passion 'with the fear that the love is not mutuall' is how Hobbes describes *Jealousy*.[20] An excessive love combined with jealousy becomes anger – 'the excess thereof is the Madness called RAGE and FURY.'[21]

These few lines are far from obvious. When one loves, which is something distinct from a purely sensual desire, one yearns intensively for one single thing: to be loved in return. And it is not a matter of indifference how. Just as one focuses one's desire upon a single person, so one hopes to be the only one to be loved in return. Love is not the desire to possess. The other remains other, who, we hope anxiously, will do what we do. Love does not seek to make two into one. It is a question not of unity but of unicity, not of appropriation but of reciprocity. It is a uniqueness desired on both sides, at once. Can I become 'the One' for her or for him who, for me, is unlike all others? Love is always potentially jealous because it is declined in the singular, always hoping, feverishly, for an identical response from the loved one. Love becomes actually jealous when the fear of failure replaces the hope of success. For it is indeed a question of success. If the proper response is lacking, amorous desire cannot achieve its end. Its impetus is halted. Hence that 'sudden stop' which leads to anger, even to rage. Hence, following the same logic, in the words of Stendhal, an 'impotent rage'.

A philosopher who was so concerned with rivalry and vainglory might well have cast love in quite another light. The readers of *Leviathan* and *On Human Nature* might have expected Hobbes to make of jealousy a fundamentally and essentially mimetic passion, unleashed by the clash between two rivals in pursuit of the same object. But he does not. Jealousy does not even appear in the list of passions in Book IX of *On Human Nature*. In *Leviathan*, jealousy adds merely an element of *fear* – not emulation or envy – to the account of the objective of amorous love: to propel oneself towards an end, which is the true end of love. One hopes to be loved as 'singularly' as one loves. A third person would be nothing more than a hitch. So long as you do not despair, you progress. But the moment you lose confidence in yourself, or in your ability to attain your objective, then you become jealous.

These measured and precise observations on love and jealousy complete the juridical framework in which Hobbes places sexuality. The state must promote and protect the growth of the population. It must, therefore, restrain sex within the limits imposed by natural law. 'Them that are in sovereign authority', he wrote, are therefore 'bound to make such ordinances...concerning the same, as may tend to the increase of mankind.' The sovereign must, therefore, 'forbid such copulations as are against the use of nature'. These are 'the promiscuous use of women'; the marriage of one woman with many husbands;

and 'marriages within certain degrees of kindred and affinity'. All such things for Hobbes are prejudicial to 'the increase of mankind'. In conformity with natural reason, it follows that the civil law must enforce monogamous marriage and forbid polygyny, polyandry and incest.[22] Adultery also falls within this category.[23]

From the subjective point of view, desire is indefinite, but infidelity wounds nevertheless. Jealousy is the fear of being disappointed, the awareness of the fragility of all our projects, the foreboding, or the discovery, that the person we love so much, to the exclusion of all others, might love someone other than us. All of which has little to do with a love triangle real or potential. It is a couple which fails to be fully realized. It is between the person I love and myself that the miracle does not occur. Anyone who comes between us is merely an extra. They are nothing more than an impediment along my way. I do not envy them. I am angry.

Tranquil enjoyment

Thomas Hobbes had a thorough command of Scholastic philosophy, much though he professed to despise it. As we have seen, his criticism of anger, as it had been 'commonly' defined, was directed primarily at Aristotle and Aquinas. His conception of love, however, is essentially the same as that of Aquinas. This may seem paradoxical, but it is easily explained if we remember that, for Aquinas, love is a movement (*motus*) directed towards an end. Friendship tends towards the good of a friend; sexual love is meant to culminate in the complete and profound enjoyment of another.[24] Erotic passion is not disinterested. Its intensity, its tension and its intention, by their very 'tense' nature, strive towards their ends and consequently will tolerate no obstacle in their path. Logically, therefore, eros is jealous.

Jealousy, *zelos*, is an effect of love. The more intensely a virtue tends towards something, the more it will resist anything that opposes it. Since love is a movement towards the loved one (according to St Augustine), any intense love will seek to overcome all attempts to thwart it. And since in what Aquinas calls 'love of concupiscence' one desires with great passion, lovers will do their utmost to counteract anything that might impede the full and tranquil enjoyment of the beloved. This is why men are jealous of their wives. The singularity (*singularitas*) they seek in them should not be impeded (*ne impediatur*) by any other relationship: this is their goal.[25] Jealousy is a normal reaction, therefore, when we are confronted by anything that comes to disturb the unique intimacy that is the very aim of love. To this Hobbes had to add only anger, rethought within the same mechanistic model.

Hobbes was a fine Hellenist, and we know that he translated Euripides' *Medea* into Latin.[26] Sadly, that translation has not survived; but we may speculate that the princess of Colchis left a marked impression upon Hobbes's thought. For Medea, too, the other woman – that euphoric ingénue – was nothing more than a stumbling block. It was Jason who had betrayed her, humiliated her, abandoned her, thus stopping her dead in her tracks. Jason had been everything for her. It had been for him, and for him alone, that she had left her family, sown death to left and right, and finally accepted a shameful exile in Greece. It was, therefore, Jason she had to attack, and attack him where he was most vulnerable: his children and his project for a new life. All of that, as we have seen, was anger – noble Greek anger, as Aristotle had defined it, emphasizing injustice and ingratitude. It was also anger as Hobbes could have understood it, in his own way, by simply shifting the focus to the 'sudden stop' in an entire life. In the language of motion, one might say that Jason's new marriage, by brutally interrupting the intense intention of her amorous passion, had brought Medea to an abrupt halt.

A primal passion

Three major writers offer us a reflection on amorous jealousy in the wake of Hobbes: Jean-Jacques Rousseau, who made of it a primitivist inversion; Denis Diderot, who recast it in an ironic mode; and Stendhal, who transformed it into novels.

Rousseau had a profound understanding of Hobbes's thought.[27] His contemporaries, however, considered him to be essentially an anti-Hobbesian. 'The philosophy of M. Rousseau of Geneva', wrote Diderot in the article 'Hobbisme' in the *Encyclopédie*,

> is almost the inverse of that of Hobbes. One believes that man is by nature good, the other by nature evil. According to the philosopher of Geneva, the state of nature is a state of peace; according to the philosopher of Malmesbury [Hobbes], it is a state of war. If one is to believe Hobbes, it is society which has made man better; if one believes Rousseau, it has made him worse. The former was born amid tumult

and civil war; the latter lives in society and among philosophers. Other times, other circumstances, and another philosophy.[28]

In this duel between the two *philosophes* who have come to dominate modern political theory, love and jealousy assume an unexpected importance. As both a thinker and a novelist, Rousseau offers a vision of love in which jealousy plays a paradoxical role. While revealing the very origin of amorous preference, jealousy also brings to light its dangers. If there can exist an art of love, it can only be, as it appears in Rousseau's pedagogical novel *Émile*, a refinement of the drive to jealousy. More significantly, Rousseau also tried to locate jealousy in the 'fable' of mankind's emergence from the original state of savagery. For Rousseau, as for Hobbes, love, unlike sex, does not exist in nature. It is, rather, a product of the perfectibility human beings discover, little by little, as they learn to live together.

In the *Discours sur l'origine et les fondements de l'inégalité parmi les hommes* (Discourse on the Origin and the Foundations of Inequality among Men) of 1754, Rousseau set out to invert the Hobbesian vision of the state of nature as a state of war 'of all against all', which, through an act, or acts, of will had been replaced by society. On Hobbes's account, the mutual hostilities between men could be brought to an end only by means of an agreement through which individuals, while naturally aggressive, are overwhelmingly concerned for their own survival and decide to entrust all violence to an artificial entity: the state. Rousseau reverses the terms of this evolution. He tells the story of the rise of civilization not as a progression but, instead, as a decline. Mankind emerges from the hands of Nature, both good and happy, with an innate inclination to self-love – which is a positive disposition to self-preservation, and on this he agreed with Hobbes – but at the same time with a strong sense of compassion towards his fellow men. In this narrative, Rousseau links monogamous marriage with the creation of the family, the invention of agriculture, the establishment of private property and the creation of the sedentary life. Relations with nature, social relations and sexual relations are all transformed at the same time.

In the course of this unhappy transition, which drew men out of the forest and into rudimentary huts, taking them from innocence to injustice, from blessedness to misery, from promiscuity to monogamy, and from sex to love, desire itself changed. 'The primeval forest', Jean Starobinski has written, 'provides for everything. Desire, circumscribed by the present moment, never exceeds need, and need, inspired by nothing other than nature, is so quickly satisfied that feelings of want never arise.... It is a symbol of happiness.'[29] Physical sex contributes to this well-being. Society destroys it. Furthermore, for Rousseau, sexuality is not merely subject to historicity; it also sets it in motion. Social life begins with love, the first of the passions born in the course of this history, and whose final destiny, as dreadful as it is logical, is jealousy. Erotic jealousy comes together with the desire to possess a house or a piece of land. As this is where civilization begins, jealousy – that primal passion – becomes the keystone on which Rousseau's political theory is built.

The invention of love

In order to appreciate the immense but largely underestimated importance of jealousy in Rousseau's thought, we must return to Hobbes. From Rousseau's point of view, Hobbes had committed two fundamental errors. The first was to have given to natural man one single primordial emotion – the desire for self-preservation – whereas in fact he possessed two: the love of self and also pity, which for Rousseau is the 'only natural virtue'. Pity had been given to man so as to soften 'the ferocity of his self-love' and to assuage 'the concern he possesses for his own welfare'.[30] The second error Hobbes had made was to have misunderstood the psychological and moral foundations of man's life in the state of nature. Savages do no evil because they do not know what good is. 'It is neither the development of the understanding [*lumières*] nor the restraint of law that hinders them from doing ill; but the calm of their passions [*le calme des passions*], and their ignorance of vice.'[31] The 'calm of the passions' is, therefore, the defining condition of primitive man.

Among the passions that threaten to destroy this primeval tranquility, there is one that is 'burning', 'impetuous', 'terrible', furious and destructive, 'which braves all dangers and overturns all obstacles'. It is a 'brutal and unrestrained fury', indecent, uncountable and belligerent, all of which renders it bloody and murderous. This passion that troubles the hearts of men so profoundly is nothing other than love.[32] Love does not exist in nature. It does not exist among savages, as we can see from their ways of life, nor does it exist among those whom Rousseau describes as having only just left the state of nature, such as the peoples of the Caribbean, about whom European travellers had written so much (and on whose accounts Rousseau relied so heavily).³³ Pure and simple sex in the ignorance of love contributed greatly to the peacefulness of the passions. More precisely, the complete absence of jealousy was essential for this primal bliss. For love is jealous. Thus the 'Caribs' are 'the most peaceful [of peoples] in their loves, and the least given to jealousy'.³⁴

Love, which Rousseau paints in such sombre and frightening colours, is a passion that harnesses together preference, possessiveness and competition. The very first transmutation of pastoral sex into urban love comes about through the ripening of mankind's cognitive abilities. At some point, humans find themselves with the need to live together. In these new circumstances, they develop the capacity for comparing things and for comparing themselves with other living beings. In discovering comparison, they also discover that different beings may possess different qualities: that there exists more and less, good and less good. Intelligence leads to taste; taste to predilection; predilection to attachment – and attachment to jealousy. This is how Rousseau describes the first step, the discovery of 'merit', namely what distinguishes every loveable thing.

> Let us begin by drawing a distinction between the moral and Physical in the sentiment of love. The Physical is the general desire which moves one sex to unite with the other; the moral is what gives this desire its distinctive character and focuses it exclusively on a single object, or, at least, gives it greater measure of energy for this preferred object. Now it is easy to see that the moral aspect of love is a factitious sentiment, born of social practice.... This sentiment, since it is based on certain notions of merit or of beauty, which a Savage is not in a position to possess, and on comparisons he is not in a position to make must be almost nonexistent for him. For, as his mind could not frame abstract ideas of regularity and of proportion, so his heart cannot feel the sentiments of admiration and of love that arise, without our even noticing it, from applying these ideas; he heeds only the temperament he received from Nature, and not an aversion which he could not have acquired, and any woman suits him.³⁵

The second step is the sense of possessiveness. The key moment in Rousseau's *Discourse* is the creation of private property. The first man who enclosed a piece of land and said 'This is mine' set history upon a new and fatal path for the entire human race. It was the end of happiness. Before then, in those vast spaces where individuals wandered aimlessly, collecting nuts and fruits, sleeping under trees, crying out to one another in sounds that were as moving as they were inarticulate, sex was performed without courtship, without anxieties, without affection and without consequences. No frills. No strings attached. In the beginning, there was only coitus: occasional, pleasant and swift. 'This blind inclination, devoid of any sentiment of the heart, produced only a purely animal act. The need satisfied, the two sexes no longer recognized one another; and even the child no longer meant anything to its mother, as soon as it could do without her.'[36] Later, once all the first communities had put down roots in enclosed and cultivated lands and in rustic cabins, the attachment between a man and the mother of his children served to reinforce the fixity of human life. Men discovered the pleasure to be had in the possession of their lands – as well as in that of their wives.

Love is a moral supplement to physical sex; but above all it is 'factitious' (*factice*), which is to say, invented and artificial. Today one would say, in the jargon of the academy, that it is a 'social construction'. Selective and elective, this desire immediately creates, for Rousseau, an inequality between an object of love and those that are not loved, or at least not loved enough. 'They grow accustomed to attend to different objects and to make comparisons; imperceptibly they acquire ideas of merit and of beauty, which produce sentiments of preference.' They became attached to the object of their love precisely as they became attached to their possessions, and, thus: 'The more they see of each other, the less they can do without seeing each other still more.'[37] For Rousseau, this was not a commendable experience not of devotion but one of sheer self-love, of egoism and, finally, of violence – and jealousy was its caricature.

The third step in the invention of love is the acting out of competitiveness. 'A tender and pleasant feeling insinuated itself into their souls, which, at the slightest opposition, turned into impetuous fury: with love arose jealousy; discord triumphed, and human blood was sacrificed to the gentlest of all passions.'[38] We want to enjoy what we like, quietly without being disturbed, exclusively and forever. Love, wrote Rousseau in *Émile*, derives from the 'desire to possess what is pleasing to us'. Jealousy is just too much of such desire.

> That it is natural impulse to feel an aversion towards everything that threatens or interferes with our pleasures, is undeniable. Up to a certain point the desire for the exclusive possession of that which gives us pleasure belongs to the same category. But when this desire becomes a passion, it is transformed into fury, or into that sullen and sorrowful

fantasy known as jealousy, it becomes something quite different. Such a passion may be natural or it may not; we must distinguish between them.[39]

There is no mention, in this rudimentary normative account, of the event of desire, the serendipity of encounters, the surprise of discovering the desire of the other person, and the anxiety – will I be, in turn, an object of love, for him or her whom I happen to love already? – which haunts every lover. Rousseau does not care about the complexity and, above all, the instability which Stendhal – who was an attentive reader of his – attributes to love. More interestingly, he seems to forget the nuanced sensitivity he brought to the depiction of love in his fictional and educational writings.

Émile, in love and jealous

Beyond the polemical genealogy of love as a social passion in the *Discourse on the Origin and the Foundations of Inequality among Men*, Rousseau knew how to capture marvellously the happenstance of amorous feelings. When he staged fictional characters, as in *Émile*, he could discern and bring to light the subtlest of sentiments. Here, jealousy is not merely disparaged as 'impetuous fury', or as a 'sullen and sorrowful fantasy', and thus the source of bloody sacrifices. Instead a certain style of affection – assiduous, loyal and trembling – creates an art of love, worthy of praise and worthy of being taught to others.

In an idyllic and pedantic pastoral romance, the perfect training of an imaginary young man culminates with his falling in love. Jealousy immediately becomes an issue. To begin with, Rousseau reiterates a number of claims he had made in the *Discourse*. 'Jealousy finds its motives in the passions of society.'[40] Modern love is more often than not merely self-love, which is 'moved by vanity rather than affection'. The lover 'hates his rivals more than he loves his mistress', since what matters to him most is to take priority and to be the favourite. Such love is 'filled with exclusions and preferences'. At its most intense it becomes 'an unbridled ardour which befuddles [the lover] with the chimerical attractions of an object he is no longer capable of seeing for what it is.' The only difference between love and vanity is that the latter does nothing but take (the lover wishes to be admired and preferred over all others), while the former gives as much as it demands (we admire and prefer another by attributing to them superlative and wholly imaginary charms).[41] One wishes to be loved, therefore one makes oneself loveable, certainly better than another, and preferably better than any other – whence derive emulation, rivalry and, finally, jealousy. 'We wish to inspire the preference we feel; love must be reciprocal.'[42] There is, therefore, in love both perfectibility and reciprocity; but the perfectibility is violently competitive, and the reciprocity nothing other than an exchange of flatteries.

On the one hand, the teacher to the young Émile condemns all that is urban love, gallantry, coquetry, flirting, and the many amusements of seduction. All of that is corrupt, artificial, frivolous and fundamentally egotistical. On the other hand, however, he is prepared to make concessions. Sophie – the object of Émile's devotion – is allowed to give herself, with good grace, to the niceties of a well-tempered jealousy. Without going so far as to torment her lover, she nevertheless knows how to arouse in him doubts and apprehension. 'She can alarm and reassure him just as he needs it; and if she sometimes makes him uneasy she never really gives him pain.'[43] Émile, for his part, knows how to play the role of the jealous lover perfectly.

> Émile, full of love and jealousy, will not be angry, sullen, suspicious, but delicate, sensitive, and timid; he will be more alarmed than vexed; he will think more of winning over his mistress than of threatening his rival; he will thrust him aside, if he can, as if he were an obstacle rather than hate him as an enemy; and if he does hate him, it will not be because he presumes to compete with him for the heart he desires, but because of the real risk he runs of losing it. His unjust pride will not be allowed to enter foolishly into competition with his rival. Since he knows that the right to choose is based upon merit alone, and that honour depends upon success, he will redouble his efforts to make himself loveable, and he will probably succeed.[44]

After having chastised the present as rotten with artifice, inequality and violence, Jean-Jacques indulges in a flattering picture of the mawkish bucolic life of his charming characters. Émile and Sophie are two French aristocrats living on a beautiful estate in the country. Let us forget the rough, wild, uncomfortable forests where every woman would do just as well for any man. In this manicured greenery, where the most refined forms of civility bloom and flourish, we follow a highly sophisticated intelligence of love. In the garden *à la française*, sentimentality is all about captivating desire and creating a beautiful couple. How can one negotiate between the generosity of idealization, on the one hand, and the wish to be given the same consideration and the same tokens of adoration, on the other? Love sets in motion a circular exchange of praise, freely bestowed but also expected in return, and of gifts offered, welcomed and reciprocated. True love, Rousseau concedes, must be mutual. And yet reciprocity is highly suspect. It is a strategic mixture of altruism and egoism, with the aim of becoming more loveable than others to someone who is especially loveable for us. In place of the attentive and uncertain longing of which love is made, Rousseau sees only the calculations and the bargaining demanded by self-esteem. We only love each other by preferring each other.

Émile, amorous and jealous, will take to heart the lessons of Hobbes. In his discussion of love and jealousy, Rousseau's language is, in effect, profoundly indebted to 'Hobbism'. Three ideas are crucial for both thinkers: comparison, self-love, and the concept of the 'obstacle' or, in Hobbes's language, 'sudden stop'.

Firstly, Émile's tender emotions derive from comparison. He has chosen Sophie on her merits. Rousseau, the pedagogue, exposes him to the company of many women, so as better to discriminate the remarkable qualities of that particular one.[45] His 'right to choose' must be based solely upon the physical, moral and social attributes of this enchanting creature, who shows herself to be a perfect mediocrity in all things, as she should.[46] 'One does not love before having judged, one does not choose before having compared.' Although it is commonly described as blind, love in fact derives from reason. '[Love] perceives relationships we cannot see.' It is precisely a judgement, often unconscious, which distinguishes love from a simple, indeterminate 'penchant of instinct'. For anyone who has no experience of love, 'all women would be equally good.'[47] In the account of Émile's upbringing, therefore, we can see the same train of thought that runs through the *Discourse*: sex is natural, but love must be learned and mastered. This is as true of the history of the species as it is of every individual. For natural man, the first experience of the yearning for social recognition took place under a tree, when he became aware that he danced better than his neighbours. The same discovery occurs within every man in society when he first experiences love. 'We wish to inspire the preference we feel...Hence we begin to look around among our fellows; we begin to compare ourselves with them, there is emulation, rivalry, and jealousy.' The whole of social life stems from the election of an amorous partner. 'From the need of a mistress there soon springs the need of a friend.'[48] Love, in short, initiates us into the knowledge – distinctive, individualistic, competitive, and therefore jealous – of others.

As Diderot reminded his French readers in his article 'Hobbisme' in the *Encyclopédie*, for Hobbes the fundamental cognitive act is, precisely, the assessment of qualities relatively to each other.[49] It is only by contrasting or likening things and people that we discover relationships of equality and inequality. As a consequence, it is only by putting *ourselves* side by side with others, and judging our merits against theirs, that we begin to sense our innate, primordial and ineradicable tendency to antagonism. Life, however civilized it may be, is a race.

Rousseau then anchors his anthropology in self-love (*amour de soi*) and self-esteem (*amour-propre*), whose manifestations are pride and vanity. Understood as the 'sentiment of loving oneself', self-love (*amour de soi*) is inscribed in human nature, as much for each of us as it was for our remote ancestors. The first months of our life match the early stages of human prehistory. Self-love is beneficial because it compels us to live and to look upon others as sources of protection and nourishment.[50] It constitutes the primordial urge for self-preservation, akin to what Freud defined as primitive narcissism. What Rousseau famously called *amour-propre*, and we, by contrast, might call 'self-esteem', is only acquired over time. It originates from the multiple relations we have in childhood – that is, from our very first intuition that there exist differences in the world and that we develop preferences between them. It is the love 'that compares itself', and which, on Rousseau's account, gives rise to all 'hateful and angry passions'.[51] Unlike self-love (*amour de soi*), self-esteem (*amour-propre*) is demanding and insatiable. 'What makes a man really good', therefore, is 'the fewness of his needs, [and] the narrow limits within which he can compare himself with others.'[52] Now, love, as we have seen, is not a blind instinctual drive but the outcome of a thoughtful comparative evaluation. Erotic preference, therefore, is an extension of our self-esteem (*amour-propre*). Firstly, I examine numerous objects, in order to choose the one I find most delectable. Secondly, I also compare *myself* with the one I have chosen. And I demand that the other should prefer me to him- or herself, something which is, in effect, impossible.[53] 'We wish to inspire', wrote Rousseau, 'the preference we feel.'[54] As the great theoretician of the dialectic of recognition Georg Wilhelm Friedrich Hegel would say later, I desire, at all costs, the desire of the other, and I will fight to acquire it. For

Rousseau, it is from the craving for predilection that 'spring emulation, rivalry, jealousy'.

Thomas Hobbes too argues that *amour-propre* – or what he calls 'Vain-Glory' – is an essential aspect of humanity. It is even the most distinctive characteristic of human beings in comparison with other political animals, namely the bees. It is also one of the most basic sources of 'quarrel' between men. We attack others, defend ourselves, and strive to conquer respect, fame, admiration. But erotic love is, for Hobbes, a need focused upon an individual by whom one passionately wishes to be loved in return, for oneself alone (*singularly*). The desire for the desire of the other is not a vainglorious contest: it is, rather, a cause for hope.[55]

Rousseau shares with Hobbes the literal distinction between love, on the one hand, and what Hobbes calls 'desire indefinite', on the other. Like Hobbes, he believes that love demands confidence in *oneself* – one must rely on one's own power, one must always be up to the task – but he conflates the erotic drive with an insatiable passion: the urge to possess and, therefore, to expropriate. The emotions that sustain love are pride or vanity rather than hope. Jealousy is not simply the need to be loved as *uniquely* as one loves. One wants to be liked *better* than anyone else, as if a qualitative evaluation were at stake. Amorous attachment entails a battle with a rival over ability or desirability. And this battle can become bloody. In love there are never two but always at least three. Émile, when he is enamoured, must tame love. Émile, when he is jealous, must always, in principle, soften jealousy. Paradoxically, he does this in the most Hobbesian manner feasible: by making himself as agreeable as he possibly can and by refraining from any attempt to outdo any other rival. The quest for a positive, intense, intimate singularity suddenly prevails upon the will to beat others.

In the second *Discourse*, as we have seen, Rousseau describes jealousy as a reaction to an obstacle. 'A sweet and tender affection enters the soul, but *at the slightest opposition* it becomes an impetuous *fury*' (emphasis added). This is anger. And what triggers anger is 'opposition'. Hobbes, as we have also seen, had defined anger precisely as a 'sudden stop', as 'the desire of overcoming present opposition'. Rousseau therefore shares this theory of a purely mechanical annoyance. But here he adds competitiveness. What he sees at work in amorous infatuation is not only an impatience with anything that might hinder that desire but also, and above all, the ceaseless conflict which divides all civilized beings. As a consequence, 'discord' – that is, rivalry – becomes a corollary to erotic anger. 'Jealousy awakens with love, discord triumphs.' Jealousy is a crazed bloodletting: 'the softest of passions receives sacrifices of human blood.' It is also a merciless antagonism with those who might aim at the same goal. This is why Émile must choose which of the two aspects of jealousy – mechanical anger or an old-fashioned duel – will be the one worthy of him. He decides that he will dispose of his rival 'as if he were an *obstacle*, rather than hating him as an enemy'. Rousseau's delicate lover sees in his competitor a physical impediment to the realization of his desires rather than the author of an unfair humiliation which cries out for revenge. His unjust pride will not be allowed to become so offensive that he will stoop so low as to enter into competition with the other man. Life is, after all, a race. One needs fair play. By mechanizing, so to speak, his *amour-propre*, Émile will become a modern gentleman. He will be a Hobbesian.

Imperious, jealous, deceitful, vindictive

On every one of these three points – comparison, *amour-propre* and obstacle – Rousseau appropriates Hobbes's thought, but he also historicizes what for Hobbes characterized human nature as such. In the transition from the state of nature to the social condition, the human had learned how to compare and how to fight. The same apprenticeship begins again for each individual from infancy to adulthood. Furthermore, Rousseau takes up the theme of competition and vainglory so dear to Hobbes but pushes it to the limits of caricature. The infant soon begins to make comparisons, and then to acquire fancies and urges that make it 'imperious, jealous, deceitful, and vindictive'.[56] The adolescent discovers love as a privileged emotion that is manifested in particular tokens of esteem and affection, which, in their turn, demand an 'impossible' reciprocity. I love you; I prefer you; I wish to be preferred; I compare myself with others; I wish to prevail over all others; I challenge those others – I am jealous. Jealousy is awakened together with love, as we have seen, and each and every one of us wishes to be fancied above and before anyone else, but 'there could be no preferences if there were not many who failed to find satisfaction.'[57] The simple fact that we all covet the same thing creates competition. Mimetic desire is mimetic violence.

For Hobbes, such generalized conflict was pervasive in the state of nature, where everyone fought for his or her own survival, to crush all others and to preserve their self-image. In civil society, this tendency is restrained. Under the legal, religious and policing rule of the Leviathan, internal peace becomes possible. Sentiments of cooperation are learned. Eros contributes to civility. Love is the need I have for this particular individual, desired in the singular and whose love in return matters so much to me. Hopefully s/he loves me too! For Hobbes, then, erotic jealousy is nothing other than love itself, whenever hope has been replaced by fear. For Rousseau, on the contrary, the ravages of self-esteem are precisely the consequences of life in *society*. Jealous attachment is not merely a part of this; it lies at its core. 'As soon as a man needs a companion he is no longer an isolated creature, his heart is no longer alone. All his relations with his species, all the affections of his heart, begin at that moment. His first passion arouses the others.'[58] Sociability is not, therefore, the remedy for a nasty, brutish and quarrelsome urge, as it is for Hobbes, but the very cause of that evil. In civil society there thus exists an impasse: the more civilized one becomes, the more one is caught up in the cycle of comparison, inequality, love, jealousy. Blood is on the floor.

Can one ever extract oneself from this baleful perfectibility? In one of those intellectual pirouettes that lend a degree of charm to the man whom Diderot once called 'the first victim of his own Sophistries', Rousseau prescribes for Émile a Hobbesian cure. I have mentioned this already, but it is worth emphasizing the point. The only possible remedy for that 'first passion' (*passion première*), which promises to destroy one's life, is an additional dose of mechanization. To know that anger is a 'sudden courage' against anything that blocks our way forward will help us to thrust our rival aside '*as if he were an obstacle*' (*à la* Hobbes) rather than being humiliated by his presence as if s/he were an offensive human being (in the Aristotelian fashion). 'The aversion to everything which may disturb and interfere with our pleasures is a natural impulse.'[59]

On this account, jealousy has nothing to do with the noble passion of Medea and Aristotle, conceived as a surge of dignity, a demand for gratitude and a reply to injustice. In Rousseau's eyes, all these dramas derived, in fact, from nothing more than 'unjust pride'. The theatre in which they may be represented seemed to him stupid or, worse, contrary to nature. 'What can we learn from *Medea*', he asked in the *Letter to D'Alembert*, 'other than that the fury aroused by jealousy can make a mother cruel and unnatural [*dénaturée*]?'[60] Medea is useless, if not dangerous. To this, D'Alembert replied that *Medea* makes us 'shudder with horror'. Just as the sight of public executions upsets the mob, tragedy shakes even 'the most delicate and sensitive of souls'. *Medea* makes an impression on its audience which is as violent as it is salutary, for although in plays which portray hideous crimes the criminals may go unpunished, still the spectators will regret the lack of retribution.[61] The historian Jean-François Marmontel responded, in turn, by claiming that, before her revolting infanticide, the representation of Medea's many and contradictory emotions led the spectator to sympathize with her.[62]

The passion of an indignant and miserly animal

Let us now be really naive! Open for a moment, without preconceptions, a deceptively amusing philosophical dialogue, Diderot's *Supplément au voyage de Bougainville*, and be carried away to the island of Tahiti in the middle of the eighteenth century. In 1768 the French navigator Louis-Antoine de Bougainville had spent just over a month there. On his return to France the following year he published an account of his journey, which became something of a best-seller and helped to establish Tahiti – called tellingly by Bougainville 'The New Cythera', after the island off the Peloponnese on which Aphrodite had been born – as an exotic and erotic paradise. Diderot's imaginary *Supplement* to this work is, like so many of his writings, complex and allusive. It contains a long condemnatory oration aimed at European civilization by an old Tahitian – called 'The Old Man's Farewells' – and an extended conversation between a younger Tahitian, Orou, and Bougainville's pious chaplain. Two anonymous Frenchmen, called simply 'A' and 'B', then exchange comments on what the Tahitians had to say. These engaging characters are all, in different ways, concerned with the same subject: what is the difference between Europe, old, socially stratified, pious and sophisticated, on the one hand, and the world of the Pacific islands, where everyone has always lived the simple life, unconstrained by religion or conventional morality, greed or the pursuit of wealth, on the other? Which of these two worlds should one prefer, above all, when it comes to questions of sexual habits? More precisely, these amiable debates are concerned with the very special way in which the Tahitians had welcomed the French explorer and his crew.

As soon as he steps ashore, the chaplain is greeted by his host, Orou, with what is, for him, a most startling form of hospitality. He is invited to sleep with Orou's wife and daughters, as he pleases, although Orou warmly recommends the youngest. After a great deal of coquetry, and protestations, and cries of 'But my religion! But my holy vows!', the chaplain finally succumbs, night after night, to one woman after another. Everyone is happy. But, for the chaplain, Orou's gesture is deeply puzzling: why is he not jealous? The Tahitian, therefore, is obliged to explain in detail why he finds it perfectly natural to treat the chaplain as he has, to describe how the Tahitians understand sex, the family and society and to reveal why, by contrast, he finds French Christian morality overburdened with worthless, contradictory and baleful principles. Erotic jealousy – absurd in Europe, non-existent in Tahiti – is the leitmotif of all these dialogues.[63] Reflecting on the exchanges between the Tahitian paterfamilias, concerned for the future of his daughters, and the man of the cloth, anxious about his religion and his moral integrity, the two *philosophes*, 'A' and 'B', come to the conclusion that the best solution is always to adapt to local customs. They will become cosmopolitans.

Jealousy does not exist in Tahiti because the Tahitians know how to live according to nature. No constancy, no fidelity. These so-called virtues Orou dismisses as nothing more than the parochial mores of Europe. Furthermore, they are contrary to nature, he insists, because they 'assume that a being which feels, thinks and is free, may be the property of another being like himself'. Orou then goes on to ask the key theoretical question:

> On what could such a right be based? Don't you see that in your country you have confused something which cannot feel or think or desire or will; which one takes or leaves, keeps or sells, without it suffering or complaining, with a very different thing that cannot be exchanged or acquired; which does have freedom, will, desire; which has the ability to give itself up or hold itself back forever; which complains and suffers; and which can never be an article of exchange unless its character is forgotten and violence is done to its nature.[64]

Immanuel Kant – whom I shall discuss in the next chapter – gave a serious form to these Tahitian ideas. Since some of their ramifications have become common currency, we might say that this claim amounts to what is now often referred to as a 'theory of objectification'. To demand sexual exclusivity is to commit a grave error: it is to treat a person as a thing. It is allegedly a category mistake because, as a person is not a thing, it implies the extension of the rights of property to persons, and this constitutes a denial of humanity itself.

Kant and Orou, however, do not entirely agree. While Kant earnestly prescribed reciprocal possession in marriage as the only corrective for sexual reification, Orou's more libertine understanding of the same logic conveys scorn for amorous devotion. In Tahiti, it is the matrimonial contract that is objectifying, whereas free love is supposedly humane and dignified. Monogamy becomes a juridical monstrosity which overturns our very definition of the human. There can therefore, as we shall see, be no more implacable argument against jealousy.

Delicate lovers are afraid to admit to it

The opinions which Diderot attributes to Orou belong in a long line of thought which can be found in the *Encyclopédie*, that massive project conducted towards the middle of the eighteenth century under the general editorship of Diderot himself and the mathematician and philosopher Jean D'Alembert. The first part of the entry on jealousy was written by Louis de Jaucourt, who defined it in general as a 'disquiet of the soul' concerning 'our own good, which we are afraid to lose, or which we fear another might share. We envy someone else's authority; we are jealous of the authority we possess.' On jealousy in love, he wrote that it was a 'burning fever that devours the peoples of regions scorched by the rays of the sun, and which is not unknown in our temperate climates.' At that point, however, he handed over to Diderot, who continued:

> Jealousy, in the latter sense, is the stormy disposition of a person in love, who fears that the object of his love might not share with him her heart, her feelings and everything else he claims as reserved for him alone. The smallest thing she does alarms him, and he sees in her most ordinary actions the sure signs of the misfortune he fears so much. He lives in suspicion and makes the other person live in torment and constraint. This cruel and petty passion is the sign that we mistrust our own merit and is the confession of the superiority of a rival. It commonly hastens the evil it is afraid of. Few men and few women are exempt from *jealousy*; delicate lovers are afraid to admit it, and it causes married people embarrassment. It is above all the madness of old men, who confess their own inadequacy, and of the inhabitants of hot countries, who know the ardent temperament of their women. Jealousy crushes the feet of women in China and sacrifices their freedom in almost all the countries of the East.[65]

For the philosophers of the Enlightenment, jealousy is about rivalry, a rivalry that concerns goods. In its amorous form, jealousy is a manifestation of unease, a sense of alarm, a fear. It betrays the unhappy insecurity of a person who doubts his or her own worth. All of its effects are undesirable – for both parties. In China, in the Orient, in the overheated South, where masculine jealousy has been institutionalized in a series of odious customs, it is devastating.

The origins of this ethnography are to be found in the writings of the great natural philosopher Georges-Louis Leclerc, count of Buffon, whose *Natural History*, which appeared in thirty-six volumes between 1749 and 1788, provided the underpinnings for much of the thought of the *philosophes* concerning the life of the body. Buffon unhesitatingly decried in the most biting manner what he called 'that little passion which is so mean that everyone wishes to hide it'. By contrast with physical sex, he argued, 'moral' love was nothing more than simple vanity: 'vanity in the pleasure of conquest...vanity in the desire for exclusivity...vanity in the means of enjoyment...vanity, even in the manner of losing what one has conquered'.[66] Furthermore, while animals are jealous only in proportion to their physical capabilities, and because they are always seeking ever greater pleasure, 'among men this passion always presupposes diffidence towards ourselves, some mute recognition of our own weakness.'[67] The champions of this brand of idiocy are what he calls the 'barbarians'. This is why it was they who had invented the anatomical myth of female virginity and the practice of infibulation. Louis de Jaucourt repeats this claim in his article on virginity in the *Encyclopédie*. 'Men, says M. de Buffon, jealous of all forms of familiarity, have always set great store by what they believe they can possess initially and exclusively. It is this kind of madness which led them to make the *virginity* of their daughters into something real.' But, he goes on: 'Why cite barbarous nations when we have similar examples so close to us! Is the delicacy with which some of our neighbours concern themselves with their wives' chastity anything other than a brutal and criminal jealousy?'

In the geography of the passions, the obsession with the need to oversee the sexuality of women is distributed in a very interesting way. For when one has no qualms about the cultural backwardness of non-European societies, jealousy is usually classified as specific to those alien barbarians. Thus Diderot, following Buffon, claims, as we have seen, that jealousy 'crushes the feet of women in China and sacrifices their freedom in almost all the countries of the East'. When, on the contrary, the state of nature is being idealized at the expense of civilized society, jealousy is cast as exclusively the product of European (especially French) modernity. In other words, wherever there is something to blame, there you will find jealousy. Thus Rousseau locates it among the depraved customs of contemporary Europe (except for Geneva) but also in Southern climes, where it is accompanied by polygyny. As more women than men are born in hot climates, it is only natural that the men, surrounded by their numerous wives, their insatiable desire now exacerbated, should be jealous. The cause of this hypersensitivity is not, however, the sun as such but, rather, its effect upon demography, and on sexual activity. Too many females are physically overwhelming for those few males. No doubt they feel inadequate. 'The feeling of his own weakness drives the man to seek to elude the laws of nature, through constraint.' The principle behind the passion itself remains the same in all cases. No matter where it is found, therefore – in this case, men's supervision of a group of wives – jealousy is nothing other than a symptom of lowly self-esteem. The more women there are who ask for sex, and need to be kept under control, the more men doubt their potency and thus have to resort to 'tyrannical precautions'.[68]

Within this logic, Rousseau shares with the primitivists we have encountered in the *Supplement* the absolute conviction that jealousy has no place in the good life of savages. Neither on Tahiti nor among the Caribs would it be possible to imagine such a vain and deleterious emotion. Rousseau is very precise on this point: for those to whom he refers as the 'rude and simple peoples', the purely carnal enjoyment of sex, before the invention of love, precludes jealousy.[69] And that despite the climate. In certain regions, for some unknown reason, the blessings of nature may overcome even the obnoxious effects of heat. 'It is the more absurd', he writes, 'to represent savages as continually cutting one another's throats to indulge their brutality', when we know by experience that the Caribs are 'in fact the most peaceable of people in their amours, and the least subject to jealousy, though they live in a hot climate which seems always to inflame the passions.'[70] In Europe, by contrast, very few men or women succeed in escaping its clutches.

A Tahitian in Tahiti

If we now stop reading Diderot with rose-tinted spectacles, let us question who is speaking in this infinitely deceptive text of the

Supplement. First there is the logic of the Tahitians. Orou offers his wife and daughters to his guest as a gift. The women are clearly quite happy with this, but it is nonetheless the head of the household who distributes them at will, and it is he who negotiates on their behalf with the fearful chaplain – as man to man. The women themselves barely speak. And then the final goal of this custom, Orou explains, is purely demographic. The most cherished things on Tahiti are children, and the interbreeding between the Tahitians and the Europeans will help to increase and improve the population. All this promiscuous sex is not meant, therefore, for the pleasure of the women but is, instead, a reproductive strategy. The Tahitian females have to be inseminated so as to give birth to as many children as possible. Those who are unfortunate enough to be sterile, by the way, are penalized and stigmatized by being obliged to wear a black veil.[71]

Orou treats his wife and his daughters as disposable genital utensils, as fungible bodies ready-made to serve the ends of social reproduction. As Orou enlightens the chaplain on the true reason for his generosity, all becomes clear. Cannot he see, this silly young man, that the wives and daughters of the Tahitians have come to 'drain the blood' from the veins and gather up the semen of a race which is superior to their own? Has he not understood that he has been offered the most beautiful of them for reasons that are purely eugenistic? Did he not even suspect that the first women sent into the eager arms of the vigorous young French sailors were precisely those whom the Tahitians had failed to get pregnant? Was he not aware that in Tahiti the number of women exceeds that of the men and, unbeknown to him, he had been 'enlisted' to help those sexually overworked males? He has been exploited from day one: a 'tribute has been raised on his own person' and on his very 'substance'. But he, in his awestruck gratitude, has been thoroughly duped. Such are the pitfalls of condescending primitivism! It prevents you from detecting the calculating and self-interested intelligence of all human beings when they are not encumbered by that 'bluster about virtue' which blinds Europeans. Such an attitude makes you ridiculous in the eyes of these 'Savages', in whom you fail to see universal egoism. 'Go wherever you will', says Orou, 'and you'll always find a man as shrewd as yourself.'[72]

This lecture on transcultural utilitarianism is delivered with searing irony. The 'Savage' takes the chaplain, who, through an excess of charitable zeal, badly underestimates the true talents of these 'rude and simple people', quite literally for a ride. But the irony does not cease there. Orou justifies his use of his wife and daughters as a matter of right. 'I am in no way exceeding my authority', he informs the chaplain, 'and you may be sure that I know and respect the rights of persons.'[73] This claim is not insignificant. Orou is echoing Roman law, which was responsible for the distinction between persons (who are inalienable) and things (which may be acquired, passed on and sold). Sexual fidelity and the institution of monogamous marriage blur this distinction and consequently cast doubt on nothing less than the humanity of both women and men. In contrast, according to Orou, the use of female bodies for procreative ends, together with the exploitation of male bodies and the extraction of their 'substance', is a perfectly legitimate and natural practice. The good chaplain has only to accept his lot with patience and make himself useful until the end, sleeping night after night with each of Orou's daughters, each night crying out, 'But my religion! But my holy orders', and finally, 'out of courtesy', granting 'the fourth night to the wife of his host'.[74]

The two anonymous philosophers 'A' and 'B' comment on the conversation between the chaplain and Orou. 'B' is not taken in by this exotic tableau of a life that is as tyrannical as it is idyllic. On the one hand, he defines jealousy as 'the passion of a poor and wretched creature who fears to lack. It is an unjust sentiment in a man, produced by our false customs, and the extension of the right of property to a being that feels, thinks, wills and is free.'[75] He seems to echo Orou himself, whose wisdom he clearly admires.[76] On the other hand, however, he rejects the suggestion that jealousy has no more place in nature than marriage, gallantry, coquetry, constancy and fidelity. 'Vices and virtues are all the same in nature.' Just as there exists a strategic and self-centred Enlightenment among Savages, so there exists, among Europeans, a hope that 'senseless laws' may one day be reformed. In the meantime, however, laws must be observed. In the end 'B' replies to Orou's primitivism with his cosmopolitanism: 'Let us follow the good chaplain's example and be monks in France and savages in Tahiti.'[77]

A Parisian in Paris

Diderot, the creator of the *Encyclopédie* and the author of countless works of philosophy, art criticism, physiology, psychology, aesthetics, novels and plays, was a ferociously hard worker. He was also, however, very much a man of the world, sensual, passionate and witty.

His letters to Sophie Volland, his sometime mistress and longtime correspondent, give us an insight into his social life, from a Parisian salon to the country house of Mme d'Épinay, or in the company of Mme D'Holbach. All that survives of this correspondence are the letters Diderot wrote to Sophie, but none of her replies. It is clear, however, that she was often jealous. All those suppers, parties, walks, chess games and other leisurely pastimes, among friends and pretty women, added up to a very agreeable way of life, particularly in contrast with the sheltered and sedentary existence lived by Sophie, alone with her mother and sister. As Jeannette Geffriaud Rosso has shown, Diderot made frequently playful, sometimes gently mocking, allusions to Sophie's jealousy. 'I love the place', he wrote to her, 'where the persons I hold dear have been, I love to touch what they have touched, I love to breathe the air which has surrounded them – would you be jealous even of the air?'[78] But to reassure her he sometimes adopted a more serious tone. 'I love only you, and I would be in despair at the thought that I could love any other. This is not a joke. In truth, dear friend, you are jealous, and I would have only to continue in this vein to torment you. Is it really possible that, after having been together for twelve years, you still do not know me?'[79]

Diderot himself admitted to feeling jealous while at the same time claiming, as we might expect, that he was ashamed of it. 'I have become, so extravagant, so unjust, so jealous', he wrote. 'You spoke so well [of Mme Le Gendre, Sophie's sister], you are so impatient with any critical remark made about her...that I dare not go on. I am ashamed of what takes place within me, yet I cannot find a means to prevent it.'[80] The letters, that is, reveal not a monk in Tahiti, to be sure, but rather a Parisian in Paris. Could he be transported to Tahiti? Possibly. But it is doubtful that he would have wished to move there or even to stay for long.

Diderot plays with primitivism. In this world there exist caves, cabins and palaces. Since men have pushed their control over nature to a point of excessive comfort and complexity, cabins may just be preferable to palaces.[81] But there can be no comparison between palaces and *caves*. In the writings where he is most personal, Diderot drops his guard to reveal just who his primitivist interlocutor really is. It is, of course, Jean-Jacques Rousseau. 'Yes, Mr Rousseau,' he wrote in the *Refutation of Helvetius*, 'I prefer refined vice under a suit of silk to stupid ferocity beneath an animal skin. I much prefer voluptuousness between the gilded, panelled walls and on the soft cushions of a palace to pale, dirty and hideous misery stretched out upon the damp ground, disease-ridden and filled with dread in the depths of the savage's cave.'[82]

In the *Supplément au voyage de Bougainville*, Diderot entertained himself by creating imaginary characters who, through the polyphony of the dialogue, were able to contrast the intricacies of a Parisian lifestyle with the ceaseless merriment of the Tahitians, alone on their island. But his objective was to show that one ultimately had to learn how to adapt to different environments. The chaplain, having sampled the pleasures of love without jealousy, does not in the end decide to remain with Orou in Tahiti. Instead, he returns to France. He too votes with his feet.

In the *Refutation of Helvétius*, Diderot explicitly rejects the idea that civilization, infused with luxury and superfluity, should be destroyed, as Rousseau, that eloquent colourist, forever in bad faith, forever dupe of his own Sophistries, would have us do.[83] Instead, it would be more desirable to discover some social intermediary between the 'baneful perfection' of contemporary France and primeval simplicity. But that would be possible only by going back in time, and progress is as natural and necessary as ageing. The only way to create such a world would be by establishing colonies. Unlike the legislators who had founded the societies of the ancient world, 'a modern legislator, more enlightened than they, would create a colony in some unknown region of the world, and, between the savage state and our wonderful civil life [*état policé*], would find perhaps an environment which would retard the progress of the child of Prometheus, would shelter him from the vulture, and would fix the civilized man between the infancy of the savage and our own decrepitude.'[84] This project for an artificial, and colonial, utopia might come as a surprise to the primitivist readers of Diderot, but certainly not to those who, amid all the banter of the *Supplement*, can discern a parody of Rousseau.

Tahitian love, therefore, must remain in Tahiti, with all the arguments which demonize jealousy. Let us now return to Paris.

A dagger-thrust to the heart

It is in Paris that we will find the philosopher of love who, perhaps more than any other, has inspired our sentimental education: Stendhal.

In his essay *Love*, Stendhal offers a meticulous description, which he calls 'ideological', of the emotions of which love is made up. Although his prime concern is with France, he traces, with infinite subtlety, the distinctions between genres, social classes and erotic cultures all the way from America to Italy. The most compelling of his insights is what he calls 'crystallization'. This is the sudden and immediate transfiguration of the person on whom, by chance, we focus our desire into someone who is stupendous and 'brilliant'. 'What I call crystallization', he wrote, 'is that operation of the mind which draws from everything that happens, new proofs of the perfection of the loved one.'[85]

One of the ideas which is dear to all those who have written about love, from Plato and Lucretius to Ovid, Freud and Proust, is that the idealizing power of admiration is a game of mirrors. True to this perception, Stendhal imagines 'crystallization' occurring in two stages. At first, despite the enthusiasm he might feel towards a love interest, one is still somewhat distracted. It is only with the emergence of the first doubts about the desire of the other person that his or her love begins to grow in intensity. 'He is seized by the dread of a frightful calamity', observed Stendhal, 'and now experiences a profound attention [*attention profonde*].'[86] It is then that the second crystallization takes place. This way of loving, more zealous and less contemplative, more apprehensive and less awestruck, involves sensuality and hope of mutual reciprocity and intimacy. 'Love is to enjoy seeing, touching, feeling with all the senses, as closely as possible, an object of love who loves in return.'[87] But, all of a sudden, we are no longer certain that this object of our love does indeed love us in return. The fact that she or he is, in fact, a woman or a man, with her or his own erotic freedom, becomes suddenly and painfully clear to us. Henceforth his or her desire will be in question.

The lover moves ceaselessly back and forth between three basic ideas:

1) She is perfect.
2) She loves me.
3) How can I get from her the greatest possible proof of her love?[88]

The roots of jealousy are to be found at exactly this moment in the experience of love. Although love makes us crystallize endlessly, since all that we do, and all that happens to us in even the most unrelated of activities, drives us to think continually about our beloved, which means to add constantly 'new perfection[s]' to the idea we have of her or him: 'The moment that jealousy is born, the same mental habit persists, but now it produces an opposite effect.'[89] The process of crystallization itself continues; but now, instead of crystallizing joyfully in the confident belief that our lover will love us with ever-greater intensity – but, of course, our lover loves us! – every new charm we attribute to the other, every thought about what we have done or might do together, renews the possibility that someone else might enjoy precisely that feature, or that situation, in our place. Jealousy is created out of the same thoughts – memories, hopes, fantasies – of which love itself is made. But now, 'far from giving you heavenly joy', all the good you have thought of your lover, all those diamonds which, despite everything, you can still see glittering about her person, become 'a dagger-thrust to the heart'.[90]

Jealousy, therefore, simply *is* love. Because our love makes out its object to be so magnificent, so worthy of every possible consideration, it follows that we cannot easily rid ourselves of the idea that others must see her in the same light.[91] Because in our imagination we multiply constantly the opportunities for happiness in the company of the creature we have divinized, it is quite natural for us to imagine that another might play the same role in the same circumstances. And those others do exist.

Everyone jests and frolics

Jealousy is love in the world, once one has become attentive, profoundly attentive, to the reality of others, in their relationships, their habits and their social life. For if everyone crystallizes in his or her own way and with different persons, the 'desire indefinite', as Hobbes would say, or 'physical sex', as Rousseau would call it, is always floating everywhere. Actual or potential rivals are not spectres, nothing but the outpourings of paranoid hallucination. They are that tall, handsome man we have seen in our mistress's salon or that bubbly woman whom our lover looks at with a lingering smile. For Stendhal, life in society, be it in France or Italy, is a continual dance of relationships as they are made and unmade. In France, love and vanity dominate, which is the cause of endless subterfuges. In Italy, a country closer to nature, husbands are friends with their wives' lovers, and everyone gossips about the latest love affairs. But, no matter where you are, in capital cities or in the provinces, love and jealousy thrive together wherever men and women enjoy the leisure to reflect and use their intelligence, instead of having to struggle merely to survive. Crystallization, for Stendhal, 'springs from nature, which ordains that we shall feel pleasure and sends the blood to our heads. It also derives from the feeling that our pleasure increases with the perfections of the loved one, and from the idea: 'she is mine!'.[92] Nature, pleasure, a feeling, an idea – these are the things which generate love, as a social phenomenon of the kind one can see in Milan or Bologna or Rome, in England and, above all, of course, in Paris. If, therefore, our pleasure is at once natural, intellectual and possessive, jealousy must inevitably be its corollary, for, in our idealization of happiness, not to be loved exclusively and to be replaced by a rival can only cause pain. Natural man, by contrast, is immune to such suffering.

> The savage does not have the time to move beyond the first step. He experiences pleasure, but the activity of his brain is entirely taken up with pursuing the deer as it flees through the forest, and with the meat with which he must recover his strength as swiftly as possible to avoid falling prey to his enemy's axe.[93]

Wholly absorbed in hunting, savages have no time for jealousy. They accept that their wives will have sex with other men. Brothers and husbands 'are only too delighted to be able to extend this little courtesy to their friends'.

At any moment, and for any civilized and cultivated individual capable of reflection, the inclination for crystallization can produce delightful images. But because desire 'accentuates', as Jacques Lacan would say, the very object of desire, this object/subject appears particularly desirable both to us and to others. And it is her desire that we desire.

A trip to Salzburg

In the summer of 1818, Stendhal travelled to Salzburg in the company of an Italian friend, Mme Gherardi, whom he called affectionately 'la Ghita', and her official lover, known, somewhat derisively, as 'Annibalino' – 'Little Hannibal'. En route they visited the salt mines at Hallein. There they were shown some bare, dried tree branches, 'studded with an infinite number of shimmering and scintillating diamonds'.[94]

Here was a beautiful image of love! To see a sad little piece of wood as a constellation of glittering gems: this is to single out and to highlight one or the other feature of a person who might appear to someone else as insignificant as a dead twig. The crystals were made of salt, to be sure, but they sparkled like precious stones. The metaphor of the 'crystallization' was born out of this witty and casual conversation. But there is more.

While Stendhal and Mme Gherardi were out walking, they fell in with a young German officer who began to look adoringly at 'la Ghita'. One could see, Stendhal wrote, that he 'was falling in love before our very eyes'. All of this took place in the presence of Annibalino, who became increasingly irritated by their chirpy, suggestive and complicit conversation. He was not imagining things. At once both timid and passionate, the young German paid Mme Gherardi 'the most exaggerated and sincere compliments', praising, above all, her hands, which, as they had been scarred by smallpox in her youth, were the least attractive part of her body. Stendhal, for his part, took advantage of the situation to offer to his friend, who was greatly amused, the most flattering of compliments, for, knowing her as he did, he could imagine nothing more seductive.[95]

The metaphor of 'crystallization', therefore, arises out of a moment of jealousy. There can be no urbane love, no worldly life, no soirées in elegant salons, no leisurely trips, without jealousy, without the endless stories of couples who make up and then break up, of husbands and lovers, of wives and mistresses. Everyone jests and frolics and flutters around.

It is amusing. And yet it is not. For, while la Ghita flirts nonchalantly with her German admirer, Annibalino is in agony. Jealousy, wrote Stendhal, is a dagger thrust to the heart. 'Its impotent rage and self-contempt are as much as the human heart can bear without breaking.'[96] Nothing will help make it manageable, since we can make no appeal to our vanity. In fact, the reverse is true. It is precisely our vanity that has been wounded. Citing La Rochefoucauld, Stendhal goes directly to the paradox of love: because it is so exhilarating to be loved by this exceptionally dazzling creature, it is much more humiliating to be deprived of that love for the benefit of another. 'This delight', cries a voice, 'is for your rival!'[97] Because our happiness has been projected exclusively onto our intimacy with that particular person, 'one may exaggerate the rival's success'.[98]

The prouder one is, the more one suffers. This is why women, whose pride is immense, are more vulnerable than men. Women in the nineteenth century were understandably suspicious. There was more at stake for them than for the men, fewer other things with which to occupy their time, fewer means of establishing what their lovers were doing; and, finally, they had no recourse to duelling as a means of 'killing a rival legally'. Cruel and abominable, female jealousy is the more unconfessable because a woman cannot even boast about her past. Quoting La Rochefoucauld's maxim on the paradox of jealousy, that 'one is ashamed to admit that one is jealous, but one is proud of having once been jealous in the past and of being capable of being so again in the future', Stendhal adds that, indeed, 'the poor women cannot even admit that they have felt this cruel torment, since it only makes them look ridiculous.'[99]

A pierced heart, a broken heart, silence, frigidity, thoughts that turn black, 'an extreme unhappiness poisoned by a shred of hope' – jealousy is a subjective experience.[100] Vanity scorned, self-contempt, shame, ridicule – jealousy is a social experience.[101] Men seized by anger, ready to kill; women debased because they hide their jealousy through pride: jealousy is a gendered experience.[102]

Does she love me?

We are ashamed of being jealous, Stendhal claims, echoing La Rochefoucauld, above all because of our vanity, which is a particularly French quality. But there are also good strategic reasons for not revealing one's grief. It is wise to hide what one feels precisely in order to avoid the calamity that one fears. We must know how to wait. We have to take the time to persuade ourselves that this jealousy we feel is perhaps, after all, only the effect of crystallization. The rival, perhaps, cannot even see all the diamonds sprung out of our own imagination. We must hide our sufferings in such a way as not to arouse desire in a potential competitor. There is, after all, an art to jealousy, whose manoeuvres form an integral part of the art of love.[103] Protect yourself and win. Afterwards you will feel proud of yourself, both for having been jealous and for being capable of being jealous.

Stendhal the theorist places jealousy at the heart of love. Crystallization is central to this claim. At first one believes that one owns the other as one would a beautiful horse. In fact, however, what we think we 'own' is never anything other than the *love* of the other. Not their body but their desire. From this certainty, confident and unreflective, the euphoria that surrounds the 'first crystallization' arises. 'She is mine!', you cry. It is a solipsistic illusion. You do not truly begin to attach yourself to that person until the moment of the 'second crystallization', at which point you recognize fully that the other is, indeed, another. This occurs because she prevaricates, makes you wait, keeps you at a distance, rejects your invitations to meet, forbids you to visit her, or sends back your letters. In short, she dismisses you. In the same logic, this other person may, of course, love someone other than you. The other is a subject of desire. The second crystallization, the one that makes you both enamoured and vulnerable, is bound up with this, always unexpected, discovery. You become aware of the desire of the other. 'Does she love me?' – that is the real question. *Amorosus semper est timorosus*, in Andreas Capellanus' imperishable words.

Stendhal the novelist shows us in real time, namely in narrative time, just how jealousy can make us love. In this mobile mirror, which for him is the novel, his polished characters pass through the different phases of crystallization. Julien Sorel, the protagonist of *The Red and the Black*, sees immediately all the details which make Mathilde, the daughter of the marquis de La Mole, whose secretary he has become, so desirable. Mathilde has very beautiful eyes. But for him, the son of a carpenter, she remains out of reach. When he discovers, to his great surprise, that this Parisian aristocrat, who is so elegant and so haughty, has taken a special interest in him, he becomes attentive to the improbable desire she seems to be offering him. He is little more than a servant, yet, despite that, Mathilde seems to be falling in love with him. In fantastic and palpitating circumstances he makes love to her. But his seduction is nothing more than a triumph for his vanity and sense of honour. This is an opportunity he could not afford to miss! But although he is delighted, he is not yet hooked. This is the first crystallization.

Julien does not begin to feel passionately about Mathilde until she begins to tell him stories about how she was once courted by fine young men 'of quality' who were habitués of her salon, and whom he also knew well. She tells him joyfully of the 'movements of passing enthusiasm' that she, in her turn, felt for them. For Julien this is agony.

> 'No. For M. de Caylus too!', exclaimed Julien and in his expression was made manifest all the bitterness of a cast-off lover. Mathilde took it this way, and she was by no means displeased.
>
> She continued to torture Julien by describing in full detail all her former feelings, using the most vivid and particular language and speaking in

tones of absolute, intimate sincerity. He saw that she was describing something immediately present to her. He was further stricken to see that as she talked she made new discoveries among her feelings.

The misery of jealousy could get no worse.

To suspect that a rival is preferred is a bitter blow, already; but to hear in detail about the love that rival inspires in the women one adores is beyond any doubt the peak of misfortune.[104]

Mathilde finds that these playful, conceited, wholly gratuitous and frighteningly precise disclosures are just amusing. 'She discovered a distinct voluptuousness in this kind of conversation.' For Julien, however, they are the cause of immense pain. 'A human being cannot sustain pain of a higher intensity than this.'[105] Mathilde 'tortures' him, but he is careful to conceal his 'cruel' and 'bitter' jealousy. He trembles 'lest he be found out'.[106] Overcome by the wholly unexpected intensity of his suffering, he is on the point of falling at Mathilde's feet or crying out in pain. Instead, however, he remains silent and listens. Under the sway of his jealousy he falls more and more in love and becomes more and more enthralled by his lover. 'No word would be strong enough to convey the excess of his admiration.' He also rediscovers Mathilde's body, in all its familiar details. As he walks by her side, he looks 'furtively at her hands, her arms, her queenly bearing'.[107] This is the second crystallization.

Does he love me?

Tortured by anxiety, as if his chest had been filled with molten lead, Julien is driven by his suffering to confide in a Russian prince named Korasoff, whom he had met in London. This cosmopolitan dandy, who had already revealed to Julien the basics of 'higher fatuity', provides him with a veritable art of love. Like Stendhal himself, who was true master in the knowledge of love, Korasoff knows that one falls in love, first and foremost, thanks to the imagination. His beloved, Korasoff tells Julien, sees in him not who he really is, but what she dreams about.[108] This is clearly a variation on the theory of crystallization. As a 'medicine', the prince prescribes three remedies: one, pretend to be wholly indifferent to Mathilde's charms; two, pretend, instead, to love another woman; three, do this in two ways: be discrete in public but passionate by letter. Mathilde de La Mole,

Korasoff explains, is a capricious and egotistical young woman who, by upbringing and wealth, has come to be overly self-confident. She must learn to feel anxious.[109] We recognize, of course, the theory set out in *Love* that one truly loves when the loveable object begins to show signs of mobility. The profound attention that unleashes the second crystallization comes about only through anguish.

The intended victim of this therapeutic little comedy is a certain Madame de Fervaques, a parvenue, a foreigner and a prude who had married a local notable, the maréchal de Fervaques, a year before his death. Under Mathilde's astounded gaze Julien carries out the plan of his 'doctor'. The Russian 'cure' works like a dream. In a poignant scene, filled with all the ingredients of Stendhal's erotic thought, Mathilde ends by confessing her jealousy and her love. One day, in the library of the marquis de La Mole, Mathilde comes across the letters Madame de Fervaques has written to Julien. She 'slowly unsealed them', writes Stendhal. Time stands still.

> 'Tell me, this at least', said Mathilde slowly in the most supplicating manner, but without even daring to look at Julien. You know very well that I am proud, it is the misfortune of my position in life, and, I'll admit it, of my character. So Mme de Fervaques has taken your heart from me.... Has she made for you all the sacrifices into which this fatal love has carried me?'
>
> A gloomy silence was Julien's only response. 'By what right', he was thinking, 'does she think she can ask me for confidences unworthy of an honest man?'
>
> Mathilde tried to read the letters but her eyes filled with tears and she could not.
>
> She had been wretched for the past month, but this lofty soul was far from admitting any such feeling. Chance had brought about this outburst. For an instant, love and jealousy had overcome pride.

Thanks to Korasoff's good advice, Julien is thus able to trap the 'tiger' who is the inconstant, haughty and sullen Mathilde. Jealous, but too proud to admit it, Julien has finally succeeded in making her acknowledge her own jealousy, an emotion which he himself has patiently orchestrated by pretending to love the unfortunate Madame de Fervaques. In an explosion of frankness, Mathilde confesses to her pride and what her true feelings are. This double confession is a revelation to Julien. He was 'staggered at the extremity of pain he read in her eyes; he could scarcely recognize them as belonging to her.'[110]

By means of reciprocal jealousy aroused deliberately by both lovers, the second crystallization has been successfully achieved. Pride has been tamed. Both have experienced the fear of not being loved, of seeing others apparently preferred over themselves. But it is Julien, the man, well schooled in the arts of love, who has carried the game; and it is he who is now obliged to make certain that Mathilde remains in her present state of apprehension. He has to frighten her, subjugate her. He has to 'keep her always occupied with this one great doubt: Does he love me?'[111] He has made the 'medical' knowledge of the Russian prince – which is, of course, the same physiology Stendhal theorized in *Love* – his own.

Thus one is jealous not because one thinks that one owns an object but, on the contrary, because one knows full well that one does not. To show that the object of love is in fact a moving and autonomous subject, whose desire appears to be evanescent and unstable, is a remarkable insight.

On the one hand, Stendhal claims that jealousy, particularly female jealousy, amounts to all that one can bear of self-loathing and impotent rage. Suffering is anger, therefore, but it is an anger that must now be judged from the point of view of its efficacy rather than its legitimacy. Anger, which for the ancients had provided a model for noble action, has become an attempt to establish a balance of power. Clumsy and vain, it seems to be wholly incapable of achieving its ends. To secure what he desires, a lover has now to turn to the art of love – to the physiology of *Love* – or 'Russian politics'. The grand dialectical scenario of a just and justice-dealing anger has become outdated. Now it is a question of recovering from a regrettable accident with a clear head, a question of 'triumphing' over a rival whom one overestimates because one despises oneself.[112] It has become, in short, a question of overcoming an obstacle.

A modern affection

Stendhal was an attentive reader of Hobbes. He had read and greatly admired *On Human Nature*.[113] 'The work *On Human Nature* by Hobbes', he noted in his journal, 'is excellent.' 'It is written in the best philosophical style I have ever encountered,' he claimed, before adding that, in his view, Hobbes prevailed over Rousseau. 'This appreciation', wrote Victor Del Litto, a great scholar who has studied the readings of the young Henri Beyle, 'would lead one to suppose that Beyle had not missed a line. In fact, it was only Chapter IX which seems to have attracted his attention. He copied out the last paragraph where Hobbes compares human life to a race and analyses the passions in function of this simile.'[114] This detail is exceedingly significant. Chapter IX, which we have discussed earlier, describes the experience of the passions in terms of a perpetual forward motion, in which different circumstances – success, speed, failure – correspond to different emotions. 'To resolve to break through a stop foreseen courage. / To break through a sudden stop anger.'[115] Stendhal had not only read those lines, he had also assiduously copied them out, and he clearly thought very highly of them. It was the best philosophical style he had ever known.

We, in turn, should not hesitate to read *Love*, and also *The Red and the Black*, in the light of this excellent philosophy. Love is tension. It is the hopeful expectation of another person's desire. That expectation makes you profoundly attentive to the other but also deeply uncertain as to his or her desire. It is this very apprehension that leads you to crystallize, for 'easiness' – that is to say, assurance, certitude, self-confidence – would prevent that from happening.[116] Jealousy is the most formidable, but also the most probable, of the difficulties which unleash our fearful trepidation about the desire of the beloved. Nor is this merely a question of distrust or suspicion or simple fantasy. In the world, be it in the countryside or in the city, as in a novel, gallantry, flirtation, inconstancy and adultery abound. In Stendhal's world, la Ghita seduces as she breathes. Mathilde flirts every evening. German officers travel. Charming men and women turn up in the drawing rooms of the wealthy. Indefinite, indeterminate or unique, desire is everywhere. It is very likely that my love will be brought up short by the sudden realization that reciprocity is never to be taken for granted. I am jealous because sometimes my love will run up against an obstacle which seems to me to be insurmountable. If I have the courage to fight – in a duel or by climbing perilously up a ladder – I will triumph. If, however, when confronted by the volatility of the other, my desire is forced to concede, then I am overtaken by a 'powerless rage'. I am ashamed to admit it.

Stendhal, however, never falls into the error of equating the desire for the desire of the other – this desire of which the jealous lover perceives the vagaries – with a vulgar wish to possess. He does not, in other words, make the mistake of confusing what he calls 'the object of love' with an 'object', understood as a 'thing'. He does not follow Rousseau on this matter. That, however, is not so obvious. Although he was an admirer of Hobbes, Stendhal was also an avid reader of *Émile* and *Julie, or the New Heloise,* and he went so far as to claim that Rousseau was the 'best painter of love'.[117] His characters read and quote Rousseau's novels with the utmost admiration. The young Henri Beyle was himself fully immersed in Rousseauism, but the *Discourse on the Origin and the Foundations of Inequality among Men* and the *Letter to D'Alembert* seriously diminished his enthusiasm. In the end, he seems to have valued Rousseau more as a poet than a philosopher.[118]

The two writers disagree on the essentials: the difference between sex and love and the idealization of the object of love.

When we read in *Émile* that love dangles before the eyes of a lover the 'chimerical attractions of an object he is no longer capable of seeing for what it is', we hear a language that Stendhal will amplify. 'Ah! I understand', says la Ghita in *Love*, 'at the moment you begin to be interested in some woman, you do not see her *as she really is*, but only as it suits you to see her.'[119] The crucial difference, however, is that, while for Stendhal such madness is a 'treasure'[120] which is inseparable from love, and especially from lasting love, for Rousseau these 'chimerical attractions' are only the result of an 'unrestrained ardour' which 'intoxicates' us.[121] As we have seen, Émile in love judges Sophie's qualities for what they truly are. He never 'crystallizes'.

The long passage in the *Discourse on the Origin and the Foundations of Inequality among Men* on the genesis of love, which we quoted earlier, provides a true sub-text for Stendhal's *Love*. In it we find the binary opposites of Stendhal's reflections on crystallization: savage/civilized; nature/society; temperaments received directly from nature/acquired ideas and feelings (merit, admiration and love); indifference/preference; sex/love. But Rousseau's entire argument resonates with tones of nostalgia and disapproval. Original nature is contrasted with the 'artificial' customs of today. The discovery of comparison acquires here a very particular significance: by learning how to compare different desirable objects with one another, men begin to distinguish, to discriminate, to choose and consequently to reflect upon what is best for them. They cease to be content with whatever or whomever they have. Love is inegalitarian. It is, therefore, competitive. Worse still, love is possessive. We become accustomed to what we believe is worthy of our esteem and cleave to it more than to any other thing. From that, blood then begins to flow. For all of this, modern love is to blame.

Stendhal, by contrast, opposes the life of the savage, too busy with the immediate need to survive for anything more than hasty coupling, to the love life of civil man, capable of appreciation and thus of enduring preferences. In the 'forests of Thessaly' or 'in the savage's cabin' love does not exist. Love is 'a modern affection', a beautiful plant which flourishes between the gilded walls of the court. 'It is there that extreme leisure, the study of the human heart, the cruel isolation in the middle of a human desert, self-love, with all its imperceptible shades of happiness and desperation make love appears to us in all its glamour.' Love is the unique, unexpected fruit of the 'perfecting of societies'.[122] Love requires intelligence, self-esteem, sensibility and a great deal of free time. That is the beauty of it. Stendhal had no use for primitivism or the antiquarian fascination with the ancients.

Starting from these premises, he came to the conclusion that modern love deserved to be praised. So, too, did jealousy. Painful though it is, it is also natural and refined. A man treats a woman he does not yet love as one would a beautiful horse. He only comes to love her with the sudden realization that her desire is in motion. The same is true of a woman's desire. Love is fearful, anxious, trepidatious – 'zealous'. That is why jealousy is intrinsically linked to love. And, because seduction and infidelity are part of the charm of social life, occasions for jealousy will always abound. It is imperative, therefore, to understand its paradoxes between confession, dissimulation, strategies and pride. Stendhal belongs among those who, unlike Jean-Jacques, Orou and 'B' – but like Ovid, Andreas Capellanus, Thomas Aquinas, Thomas Hobbes, Choderlos de Laclos and Marcel Proust – have a realistic understanding of love in its profoundly attentive nature.

3

SEXUAL OBJECTS AND OPEN COUPLES

The vilification of jealousy concerns us all. Not because we might be one of Rousseau's, or Orou's, admirers, but because many of us, in the European and Northern American intellectual world, have been influenced by some aspect of Marxism. It is in this tradition of thought that jealousy reached the lowest level of contempt. In the nineteenth century, jealousy became romantic, but it also became bourgeois.

The vision of sexual intercourse as something which reduces a husband to a possessor was to become the basis of the political theory of Friedrich Engels and Karl Marx. In *The Origin of Family and Private Property*, Engels builds on the work of one of the pioneers of social anthropology, Lewis Morgan (whom Marx knew well), to demonstrate the passage from primitive communism, which was the spontaneous structure of the first human groups, to sedentary agrarian societies. In Morgan's classification of kinship systems, the community of women and children was the most rudimentary form of social organization. The economic communism of early mankind entailed sexual promiscuity and, consequently, the absence of distinctions between consanguineous and cognatic kin, direct and collateral descendants. For Engels, the monogamous family was formed as a unit of production on a plot of land capable of sustaining a well-defined group. Marriage was invented as a contract obliging a woman to live, to copulate and to conceive children with one man, in his household. A whole taxonomy of terms differentiated the members of the group on account of their respective distance from the head of the family.

There is here, as in Rousseau's *Discourse on the Origin and the Foundations of Inequality among Men*, a powerful theory of sexual possessiveness. It is a social drive, as necessary (from the point of view of historical materialism) as it is harmful (in terms of political values). Its genesis is economic. Its destiny comes to full completion in bourgeois marriage. With the proletarian revolution, humanity must rid itself of all this – private property as well as jealousy.

The influence of this theory has been incalculable. Marxist thought stands in the background of many variants of feminist critique. The most systematic criticism of male domination, gender roles and stereotypes stems from this anti-capitalistic and anti-liberal view of history. Such a pedigree explains the negative focus on property, wealth, consumption and commodification. All personal sentiments and lifestyles that could be traced back to these economic phenomena were to be condemned. Beyond all the nuances and controversies, therefore, a self-evident commonplace loomed large in the political culture of the European and American left in the 1970s: jealousy was to be despised, shunned and extirpated from love life. The hatred of the bourgeois leads to the ban on jealousy.

In order to sketch out the history of this development, however, we have first to take one step back.

Desire of desire

We desire desire: the desire of others. We hope to become its object. Love longs for reciprocity. Reciprocity makes possible recognition, gratitude and erotic dignity. From Euripides, to Ovid, to Stendhal, the greatest theorists of love tell us these simple things, which we experience anyway, in our own life. This inclusive plural, this 'we', crosses cultures and historical circumstances. Whereas sexual variety is practised always and everywhere, as soon as one can and because one can, the failure of mutual love disappoints us all. The pleasure of our own liberty does not guarantee that we will appreciate being on the receiving side when it is the beloved who takes that same liberty. Libertinage and jealousy often go together. Mme de Merteuil and Catherine Millet remind us that the unfaithful may be extremely jealous. The wives of polygamous husbands, whatever they say, comply with a prohibition against claiming reciprocity. And contemporary individuals who 'hook up' in free and polyamorous affairs are not necessarily always immune from the vagaries of vulnerability. There is no assurance that we will be as indifferent as expected. Wherever our desire clings, even partially or momentarily, we may discover that we expect a fleeting sign of preference, after all.

The jealousy/anger of the ancients is profoundly different from the jealousy/rivalry of the moderns. But, in spite of distance, one powerful idea runs throughout this long history: each time, and even in ephemeral encounters, love is declined in the singular. Whether it is in the moment of going to a date with no future, or even in a singles bar or swingers' club, we play the game of a flattering comparison, even of a superlative. To give pleasure is to create a bubble of illusory uniqueness, sometimes instantaneous. Everyone is special. Me too, please!

Contemporary philosophy, however, resists thinking reciprocity. In *Le Don des philosophes*, the French anthropologist Marcel Hénaff has shown the strange persistence of today's moralists in denying the dialectical exchange – to give, to receive and to give back – which anthropology places at the heart of the social bond. A gift must allegedly be disinterested. If you give, and anticipate that you will receive in return, you do not really give.[1]

There is something naive and overtly demanding in these normative positions. The experience of love helps us understand that, to open up to another, to offer care, tenderness, fun, presents, compliments, means to engage in a relationship that is, first of all, singular. By these gestures and words we create an encounter that individualizes the recipient. There are always minor differences, distinctive features, even through repetition, even in promiscuity. Every object of desire is almost the same as the previous one – but only *almost*. It is the infinitesimal individualization, in contrast and in a series, that makes all the difference. Secondly, once we have identified this singular object of our desire, we want our partner to do the same. We wish to be desired. And if we have been loved first, how ungracious not to pretend, at least, to be flattered.

Contemporary philosophy is also afflicted by the cult of intersubjectivity. Despite the definitive refutation by Jacques Lacan in 1960, it has resurfaced today, especially in the arguments of a certain righteous and moralistic feminism, on both sides of the Atlantic. Lacan had initially excoriated the attempt to reduce the analytic situation to an intersubjective relationship. This pious intent missed, he said, the structural disparity of transference.[2] Lacan then rejected the idea of what he called *oblativité* (purely unconditional love), this 'highly moral' prototype of 'old issues' (*vieilles questions*). 'You must treat the other person as a subject, not as an object!' This was an ethical posture that, for Lacan, belonged to the 'existential-analytic' vocabulary of the time. It was not just an intellectual fashion, in his opinion, but a serious mistake.

Above all, such language created a misunderstanding of the meaning of what we call the 'object of desire'. 'If we do make [a person] into an object', said Lacan in his characteristically sarcastic tone, 'it will be any old object, an object like any other object, an object that can be rejected, exchanged. In short: it [the person made into an object] will be deeply devalued. This is the theme underlying the idea of *oblativité*.' Against this 'silliness' (*cette niaiserie*), Lacan made two arguments. The first was that the word 'object' in his 'primary sense...aims at objects insofar as we distinguish them, and can communicate'. To speak of 'objects' means to talk of the *distinctive* effects of desire. Desire 'enhances', 'accentuates' (*accentue*), an object in relation to another. Desire draws lines of demarcation. The second argument was that, paradoxically, 'for the subject it is much worse', because a subject, for Lacan, was defined by its *subjection* to language. A subject does not occupy, in other words, a position of dominance and control. The subject is unconscious, or, more precisely, 'in the subject there is a part where it speaks all by itself.'[3]

To these unfavourable comments, I would like to add a few further observations which relate to contemporary debates. The polarity of subject/object produces absurd effects, both ethical and erotic. I mean that we are *now* ready to shed the all too familiar notion of 'sexual object'.

Objectification theory

The American philosopher Martha Nussbaum, whose influence is now beginning to be felt in Europe, has compiled a list of ways in which we may 'objectify' a human being. These are to treat a person: as a means to our ends; as if s/he were devoid of autonomy and a sphere of action of his/her own; as if s/he were interchangeable with other objects; as if we did not respect his/her integrity; or as if s/he were a commodity. Indifference to the experiences and feelings of a person – that is to say, the denial of his/her subjectivity – crowns this catalogue of the ways in which we look at others as objects.[4] Another philosopher, Rae Langton, has added to this the reduction of a subject/person to a body, to body parts or to their appearance and the attempt to silence the person herself.[5] The focus of this feminist take on objectification is a variety of sexual interactions and the enjoyment of pornography.

Because the sexual act involves *my pleasure*, it might appear to exploit another body for this end. Eros is the first culprit of objectification/reification. Nussbaum is willing to forgive the literary eroticism of *Lady Chatterley's Lover* (but not that of *Playboy*), and even she admits that, sometimes, she happens to lay her head on the belly of her lover, without treating him exclusively and forever as a cushion. As the involvement of the beloved's abdomen occurs in a context of respect, it is permitted. No objectification, no reification. This daring confession is, however, only a concession within a Kantian vocabulary, which remains unquestioned.[6] This language has crept not only into many scholarly works but also into everyday speech in the twentieth century. How did it happen?

A human being is not a thing

For Kant, sexuality belongs to a fundamental ethical scheme known as the categorical imperative. This takes a number of forms, but its basic premise is that we must always relate to rational beings as ends, not as a means. Means are things; people are ends.[7] This distinction generates all the laws of the will. 'The practical imperative will therefore be the following: so act that you use humanity, whether in your own person or in the person of any other, always at the same time [*jederzeit zugleich*] as an end and never merely [*niemal bloss*] as a means.'[8]

A human being is not a thing (*Der Mensch aber ist keine Sache*).[9] This absolute principle compels us to condemn the reduction of others (and ourselves) to the status of more or less useful, inert, exchangeable, replaceable, disposable *things*: goods to enjoy, piece by piece. As soon as another exists, or interacts with me, according to my wish, in view of desire or in function of my pleasure, this contravenes the categorical imperative and is, therefore, immoral.

Kant clearly understands that it is impossible always to treat everyone as an end in themselves. In our active, affective, social or professional life, instrumental relationships are endless and inevitable. In handing out a letter to an employee of the post office so that s/he will send it; or in doing our job so that, through us, our students might gain knowledge, receive grades, graduate and hopefully find a job, we engage in relationships that are subordinate to other, and other people's, purposes. We make ourselves useful, helpful, serviceable; others help, care for, serve us. If we were to consider all these exchanges as forms of mutual (yet non-simultaneously reciprocal) reification, and if we were to look for an absolute antidote to this deadly sin, no business whatsoever would be ethically acceptable. Cooperation would be crippled. This is why Kant points out that we must never (*niemal*) treat a human being 'only' (*bloss*) as a means (*Mittel*). This means that we must always deal with the other in their humanity too, namely 'as an end in itself' (*als Zweck als sich selbst*).[10] We admit the existence of utilitarian relations, while ensuring that they are the least instrumental and exploitative as possible. We must preserve the dignity of others and ourselves in all human interaction.

In the *Groundwork of the Metaphysics of Morals*, Kant does not explain how to do this, except by reason, will and duty. In the *Metaphysics of Morals*, however, he describes two ways of protecting persons from mutual, dehumanizing manipulation: the law and good manners. Thoughtful legislation and continuous politeness preserve humanity. It is the law that transforms the dictates of reason into written norms. It is civility, not the categorical imperative, which saves us. By saying 'please' and 'thank you', smiling, and modulating the voice in a friendly tone rather than using one that is imperious and dismissive, we respond to the call of the 'face' of the other. By being treated as such, we do not feel humiliated or exploited. What makes the difference is respect.

Reciprocal usage and mutual possession

Sexuality is part of the juridical and civilized experience of being human. In the first section of the *Metaphysics of Morals* – the *Doctrine of Right* – Kant discusses a peculiar case of legal status: the possession (*Besitz*) of certain kinds of objects (*Gegenstand*) as things, combined with their use (*Gebrauch*) as persons.[11] There are persons who, without being the property (*dominium*) of a master, as a slave would be in Roman law, still belong to another person. They are objects in someone else's possession, therefore, *and yet* they are 'used' as persons. This is a motley notion that Kant readily acknowledges as the product of his own juridical thinking, as we shall see in a moment.

To possess (*besitzen*) an object, according to Kant, means to have the right to defend that object against other people's claims.[12] Now, many human beings, according to Kant, can be such objects. A man's wife, his children and his servants fall into this hybrid category. Technically they are not slaves. But a paterfamilias is forever in possession of the members of his 'own' household. Within this account of a 'real' (from Latin *res*) right concerning persons, Kant then goes on to define the right of marriage. And here comes his much quoted definition of sexual intercourse as the 'reciprocal use [*Gebrauch*] one human being makes of the sexual organs and capacities [*Geschlechtsorganen und Vermögen*] of another'.[13] Such reciprocal use, once legalized in monogamous marriage, creates a reciprocal possession (*wechselseitig besitzen*). Such possession involves first of all the body: 'Marriage is the union of two persons of different sexes, for lifelong possession of each other's sexual attributes.'[14] But it also involves the entire person: 'the relation of the partners in a marriage is a relation of equality of possession, equality both in their possession of each other as a person...and also equality in the possession of material things.'[15]

Marriage is a legal stipulation about a human possession and its proper use, namely the duty to treat that particular possession as a person. In the logic of Kantian ethics, this is not obvious. If to treat a human being as a person means to treat her always also as an end, not a merely as a means, how can we make 'use' (*Gebrauch*) of a human being – who happens to be an object in our possession – as a person? Is not the very fact of 'using' someone incompatible with the idea of personhood? To answer this we need to follow Kant's line of thought, step by step.

Sex is either natural (if it is meant for reproductive purposes) or is contrary to nature, and as such it can occur either with a person of the same sex or with an animal of another species. The natural character of heterosexuality depends on its purpose, procreation. The law can ratify only natural sex, and only a matrimonial contract makes heterosexual intercourse legitimate. All transgressions of the law are 'unmentionable vices', contrary to nature. They 'do wrong to humanity in our own person [*Läsion der Menschheit in unserer eigenen Person*]. No restriction or exception could possibly protect them from total disapproval.'[16] Any extramarital, useless usage of the sexual parts, including one's own, affects nothing less than a person's humanity. Masturbation is worse than suicide.

As far as natural sex is concerned, Kant claims that any sexual act, whatever it is, is defined as the handling of organs – i.e., instruments – which means the manipulation of things for the sake of pleasure. Sex is objectifying. 'The natural use that one sex makes of the other's sexual organs is enjoyment [*Genuss*], for which one gives oneself up to the other. *In this act a human being makes himself into a thing* [*Sache*], which conflicts with the right of humanity in his own person.'[17]

The real *reification* (making oneself into a thing) that is a sexual act can be offset only by its repetition, through legal reciprocity. By having sex, the members of a couple practise the mutual use (*der Wechselseitige Gebrauch*) of their genital apparatuses, thus functioning as 'things' for each other. Such interaction is *de facto* reciprocal, but it is nonetheless dehumanizing for both partners. Those two 'things', however, can be made again into two persons. This can only occur through marriage. Marriage reinstates the lovers' legal status as persons and therefore makes the 'reciprocal use' of their sexual parts into a rightful reciprocity. Once I am married, Kant argues, I 'win back' (*gewinnen wiederum*) my personhood (*Persönlichkeit*) because, although my spouse has acquired me as if I were a thing (*gleich als Sache*), I too have acquired my own spouse 'as if s/he were a thing', and now I have the right to 'use' her/him, in turn and in return. What matters is to acquire (*erwerben*) the other person as if s/he were an object. We are equals in possessing each other. We are human again by objectifying each other. This is the *right* that gives me back my human dignity. 'There is only one condition under which this [giving oneself to another in sex] is possible: that while one person is acquired by the other *as if it were a thing*, the one who is acquired acquires the other in turn; for in this way *each reclaims itself* (*gewinnt sie wiederum*) *and restores its personhood* (*stellt ihre Persönlichkeit wieder*).'[18]

This utterly unromantic and counter-intuitive vision of marriage should make us pause. According to Kant, I use any sexual partner as a thing, I acquire a husband as an object, but then I use this special object 'as a person'. The shift from object to person does not happen thanks to a moral, religious or magical sanctification of sex but because of a juridical reassignment. My husband 'owns' me. It is possession, legally acquired, that makes him into a person as a holder of rights upon me. Vice versa, by taking a man as a husband, I become his legitimate 'owner'. I too have rights over him. *As a wife*, therefore, I reconquer my status as a person. Coition remains beastly and reifying. When we have sex, in the act itself, I use his body and he uses mine, but I am not just a bedfellow. I am also a *rightful* (in the literal meaning of the word) wife. In this sense, therefore, he statutorily uses me 'as a person'. Not because he is gentle, attentive and respectful in bed, but because I have won back my personhood in a legal transaction. Whatever we do, I am a person. Furthermore, Kant adds, the use of organs – that is to say, body *parts* – necessarily commits me to regain my integrity. Since the person is 'an absolute unity' (*ist eine absolute Einheit*), whenever I make use of a member (*Gliedmaßes*) of their body I am actually involving their entire person in such an operation. Vice versa, I cannot separate myself from the pieces of my body that someone else puts to work.[19]

To have a person as mine

Kant's argument hinges on the nuances of property rights. Three points are crucial for our reflections on jealousy: matrimonial ownership, reciprocity and sexual fidelity.

As a general legal principle, I may only use something I already possess, or, in Kant's familiar language, 'possession is the condition of possibility of the use of a thing.'[20] I am not permitted to use something that is not already mine. Monogamous marriage is meant to create exactly this condition vis-à-vis a person: it allows a proper reciprocal use by engaging the spouses in a reciprocity *of possession*. Marriage realizes a real (*in re*) transaction. It is not the transfer of the full property (*dominium*) of a person to another person, since that is impossible. But it is the acquisition of a very significant right over that person: the usufruct. The *ius utendi fruendi*, or 'the right to the use and to the fruit' of an object, is part of Roman law. Bride and groom acquire this particular right over each other, Kant argues, namely the right 'to make use of a person *as if* of a thing [*gleich als von einer Sache*], as a means to my ends, but still without infringing upon his personality.'[21] The rapport is indeed instrumental (I use the other as a means to my ends, as if s/he were a thing), but I do not disregard his/her personality.

How can I square the circle? Because this animate instrument has been made into a person once and forever – by marriage. By acquiring me, my husband (my sexual object) has won back his personhood: he is now a person. And I have done the same: by acquiring him, I (his sexual object) have recovered my personhood. Our conjugal status, therefore, is the context in which I authorize myself to handle a sexy body as I please, because 'in *another* respect' – and this is the crucial point – I treat my husband as a person. By taking care of the repersonification of my spouse, so to speak, marriage allows me to objectify her/him as much as I want, with perfect righteousness.

> If I say 'my wife', this signifies a special, namely rightful relation of the possessor to an object as a thing (even though the object is also a person). Possession (*physical* possession) is the condition of being able to *manage* (*manipulatio*) something as a thing, even if this must, *in another respect*, be treated at the same time as a person.[22]

If I were to try to make sense of this legal line of thought of Roman provenance, I would say that, whereas by making love out of wedlock I would relish abusively a chunk of human flesh that does not belong to me, marriage confers on me the *title* to do so. A marriage is a deed. Does it mean that I own my husband as if he were a piece of real estate, a horse or a car? Not exactly. I am only enjoying the 'right of the use and of the fruits' of my husband. According to definitions of usufruct today, I have the right to 'the enjoyment of the underlying asset and the right to the income generated by the underlying asset', but I do not hold the 'bare ownership' of this asset.[23] I could not sell my husband to another woman, for instance. He is not my slave. I do not dehumanize him in this sense. And yet I use him *as if* he were a thing. He is *mine*. I hold a right to *usufruct* on him. Now, to use a person as a thing is also dehumanizing. Thing versus Person is the master dichotomy of Kant's ethics. What is it then that saves marriage from dehumanization? Reciprocity.

Reciprocity

In his capacity of entering into the legal nuptial agreement, my husband is, precisely, a person who has gained rights of usufruct over me. I have gained the same rights over him. By acquiring (*erwerben*) and possessing (*besitzen*) each other, spouses 'win back' (*gewinnen*) their respective personalities. They exchange not merely their sexual attributes but also their 'very person'.

> A man cannot desire a woman in order to *enjoy* her as a thing, that is, in order to take immediate satisfaction in merely animal intercourse with her, nor can a woman give herself to him for this without both renouncing their personalities (in carnal or bestial cohabitation), that is, this can be done only under the condition of *marriage*. Since

marriage is a reciprocal giving of one's very person into the possession of another, it must *first* be concluded, so that neither is dehumanized through the bodily use that one partner makes of the other.[24]

Marriage confers a 'real' (*in re*) right. This becomes particularly clear when the very definition of 'possession' is put to the test. To possess is to be entitled successfully to compete with others for the claim of an object. I prove that something is rightfully 'what is mine' if, in case of loss or 'theft', the law authorizes me to repossess such a thing. If one of the spouses were to elope, or would like to enter into an agreement with someone else, the other has the right to reclaim her/him, 'as if it were a thing [*als eine Sache*]'. Kant insists that nobody and nothing can interfere with this principle.[25]

We modern readers should not fantasize about a dialogical situation in which a jealous wife or husband might voice their pain, try to understand why the infidelity has happened, and ask whether the other person wants to leave forever or might wish to come back: none of these interpersonal negotiations is in order, for Kant! We should rather compare the relation of possession between spouses with the domination which the owners of a household exercise over their domestic servants, who, Kant claims, are not merely employed to work for a salary but actually *belong* to their masters. They enter into an agreement (since they are not purchased as chattel slaves and they are not bondsmen), but they are not allowed to rescind their contract. Should they flee, they can be brought back. The law, in its rationality, dictates that a possessor will recover his/her possession. For Kant, the right against a person is really akin to the right in a thing. And the right in a thing is empowering. The right human beings exert upon the things – and the persons – they have legally acquired and legitimately own (*besitzen*) is 'right', reasonable and undeniable. We should stress that, for Kant, a human being can never be a mere piece of property. But we should also marvel at his admission that there does indeed exist a vast category of persons whom I may rightly consider as 'mine': spouses, servants and children. The sign of this possession is my sacrosanct right to claim them back whenever they are taken away from me, or whenever they themselves desire to desert me. They are not free to go.[26]

This is the legal effect of marriage. The difference between matrimony and domestic servitude is that the matrimonial possession is reciprocal. Reciprocity is the core of marriage. Not any kind of reciprocity is good, however.

Once again, we have to start from the premise that intercourse is the 'reciprocal usage' of the sexual organs and faculties of another person. Sex creates a merely physical reciprocity, therefore, for the sexual act is the utilization of each other's body parts as things. But this reversible handling and touching is not enough. Sex is just sex. This is the metaphysical, moral problem: sex is a double objectification. Now marriage does nothing but make sex legal. Two legitimate *owners* still objectify each other – sex is still sex – but now with the blessing of the law. They have *acquired* the right to do so.

In conclusion, when Kant argues that only the conjugal covenant transforms the use of the genital apparatus as a thing into the use of a wife (and a husband) also *as a person*, he means something brutally illiberal. The crucial point is not formal wedlock versus free love, adultery or perversion, but bilateral, consensual, mutual *possession*. As with all possessions, this one is also inalienable, hence the provision that neither spouse is permitted to leave. This is the true reciprocity of civilized marriage. Monogamy, therefore, is of the essence. Only strict monogamy creates reciprocity between persons as each other's possessors, which goes far beyond the simple exchange of gestures in lovemaking. Only complete, durable and sexual devotion offers a form of redemption to the intrinsic inhumanity of sex. Marriage must be an engagement to sexual exclusivity, a pact of sexual possession – on both sides. Fidelity and the right to jealousy are the very purpose of marriage.

Fidelity

This is the culmination of Kant's line of reasoning. But there is more.

Sexual fidelity consists in a surrender of one's body to another person, and only to that one person. Monogamous marriage creates an obligation of sexual loyalty for a woman to a man (which is banal) but also for a man to a woman. When a man, by entering into a matrimonial contract, accepts to become the exclusive possession of a woman, he still 'uses' her sexually, but not just as a collection of anatomical pieces or as a disposable playmate. She is now his rightful wife. This makes all the difference. And the difference lies in the man's faithfulness. His unique devotion changes everything. By consenting to belong to one woman, a husband confers on his wife 'real' rights against himself. She is now entitled to claim all of him. Should he leave her, she is authorized to bring him back. Thanks to these rights – which in effect amount to a lawful, compelling, enacted jealousy – she exists as a person. Reciprocally, although a wife enjoys the privilege of taking pleasure from her husband's body, this does not make the man into a sex toy. By consenting to be faithful to him, she has surrendered her own rights: he fully possesses her. He holds real rights over her. Thanks to such bilateral and mutual commitment, both the use *and the possession* become reciprocal. Both partners are still being physically 'used' in sexual intercourse, because this (*Gebrauch*) is what sex is by definition, but, since they are also actively using and legally possessing each other, they interact as persons (*als Person*). Each of them wins back her/his personhood. The faithfulness of a husband makes his wife into a person, and vice versa.

Once again, it all hinges on fidelity. 'In polygamy the person who surrenders herself gains only a part of the man who gets her completely, and therefore makes her into a mere thing.'[27] If I, a woman, surrender entirely to a man who possesses all of me (if, in other words, I am faithful), I treat that man as my possessor. As such he is a person. If, in turn, he gives me only part of himself (if he divides himself among many beds, as Andromache put it), then he treats me only as a thing. He uses me sexually, but I do not possess him. Only by owning him can I win back my personality. His fidelity makes me into a human being. My jealousy corroborates my human dignity.

Sex is incompatible with the perfection of a man

Although Kant's theory of reciprocity may sound fascinating, we must not lose sight of the intransigence that runs throughout the entire account. Sex is immoral in the first place, because it undermines the humanity in the person. Desire and pleasure lower us to the level of the animal, and in most erotic situations they lead us still further down. Because sexual desire is not the attraction of a human being to another human being as such, but a penchant for the sex of the other, this desire causes the degradation (*Erniedrigung*) of humanity. The desire that man has for a woman is directed towards her not because she is a human being, but because she is a woman. The fact that she is a human being is of no interest for the man; only sex is the object of his desire (*nur das der Geschlecht Gegenstand seiner Neigung*). Humanity is thus debased and subordinate. This is why all men and women do their best not to improve themselves as persons but to make themselves sexually attractive. Human quality is literally 'sacrificed' (*aufgeopfert*) to sex. So if a man and a woman want to satisfy their own individual desires, they try to excite each other. Their inclinations meet, but their purpose is only sex, and each *dishonours* (*entehrt*) the humanity of the other. They make humanity a mere instrument for the satisfaction of their desires and vilify their human quality by placing it at the same level as the animal nature (*entehrt und der Thierheit gleich geschätzt*). Sexual desire, therefore, exposes humanity to the danger (*Gefahr*) of becoming equal to the animal (*dass sie der Thierheit gleich werde*).[28]

This danger culminates in extramarital sex. Sex 'against nature' is still worse, since this goes against the animal itself. For a human being, masturbation is not only degradation (*Abwürdigung*) but 'a defilement [*Schändung*] of humanity in one's own person'. Therefore, the pleasure of the flesh (*Fleischeslust*), namely voluptuous pleasure (*Wohllust*), when it is sought independently of reproductive purposes, becomes unnatural (*unnatürlich*). More specifically, pleasure is contrary to nature whenever it is pursued for the sake not of a real object (*nicht durch den wirklichen Gegenstand*) but of an imaginary one.[29] Masturbation, homosexuality and bestiality are forms of sexual desire (*Geschlechter Neigung*) which make a human being not only unworthy of his humanity (for, in practising them, a man ceases to be a person) but lower even than the beast, for non-human animals, according to Kant, do not mate outside their species.[30]

We must also understand that this language is located firmly within the Christian discourse on sexuality. Kant replaces the Kingdom of Heaven with the Kingdom of Ends. Reason, he argues, leads us to moral duty. Revealed religion performs the same edification by other means, such as scriptural narratives, which, although hardly sufficient for a philosopher, are good enough for ordinary people. The story that Christ was born of a virgin and thanks to a virginal conception is consistent with an undeniable moral impulse. God, who, in becoming incarnate, cannot be allowed to share the human penchant for evil, could not possibly be brought to life through sexual intercourse. This impossibility depends upon the evil inherent in the sexual act. 'Since natural generation cannot take place without sensual pleasure on both sides and yet seems to relate us to the mating of animals generally far too closely (for human dignity), we look upon it as something to *be ashamed* of.'[31]

The sexual act is 'something immoral, something incompatible with the perfection of a human being'.[32] Not to mention God. The biblical narrative of original sin and the expulsion from paradise expresses this ethical intuition by telling us that Adam and Eve transmitted a corrupted inheritance (*Anlage*) to their descendants. The Church has institutionalized the same intuition in the practice of monastic celibacy.

Veal roast à la Kant

Degradation, humiliation, disgrace, defilement, sacrifice of humanity: sex is a dehumanizing, animalizing, objectifying, reifying activity. Sex transforms us into beasts and even into sub-beasts. Below the sub-animals, there are only things.

Forgive me for insisting, but let me emphasize once again that there is no true redemption for the erotic experience as such, not even for conjugal sex. By definition, as we have seen, my erotic enjoyment of another is but the instrumental handling (*Gebrauch*) of anatomical utensils, made acceptable only if the other does the same, by legally putting to work the corresponding tools in my own body. The 'person' is saved, paradoxically, only if I push to the extreme this symmetrical reification, which is also a total possession. *Als eine Sache*, as a thing: this is how I belong, and I possess, and I use, and I am used. Intercourse may be somehow balanced in monogamous marriage, but in no way can it be valued per se.

Chastity is a categorical virtue. It is the duty of man to himself. Unless the law frames the procreative purpose of a sexual act, pleasure between men and women is nothing but vice. Prostitution, concubinage, fornication and *vaga libido* are nothing but greed for a flesh, which is just meat. Again, the logic that commands the argument and runs through the metaphors is inflexible.

A man is not his own property. He has no right to sell an organ, not even one of his teeth. For a 'person', to be used by another as the object of satisfaction of sexual desire (*als Gegenstand der Befriedigung der Geschlechter Neigung*), therefore to agree to become the object of the other's desire (*Object der Verlangens andern*), means to treat oneself as a thing. One allows oneself to become a thing (*Sache*) on which another satisfies his appetite (*Appetit*) just as he would if he had satisfied his hunger with veal roast (*Kalbsbraten*). The premise of this crude culinary analogy is simple: 'There is something contemptible in the act itself.'[33] In plain English, sex is bad. And it is bad, as a matter of principle, on account of the kind of desire that it satisfies.

Sexual desire is 'hunger'. It targets a sexually appealing body (not a person). Any object of this craving is to be considered, *ipso facto*, analogous to some appetizing food. Any piece of erotically desirable flesh is (like) a cut of juicy meat, nicely seared and ready to be consumed. Sexual object equals sexual thing.

With her concern for the belly/pillow of her lover, Martha Nussbaum is working within this same formatting of the erotic situation. Sex is potentially objectifying, but it may be justified, permitted, condoned at best – provided that I treat the other person as a person, and *vice versa*. But this is wrong. It is merely the effect of the rhetoric of Man and the Thing. For if we think for a moment about our own experience, we know full well that this is not how it works. We can simply refuse to start from the no-nonsense, down-to-earth postulate that sex is beastly, thus predatory and carnivorous.

Kantian jealousy

The definition of sexual intercourse as a reciprocal use of the appropriate organs (a use that, in a monogamous marriage, becomes reciprocal possession) leads to a normative theory of jealousy. Kant explains this in *Anthropology from a Pragmatic Point of View*, a work in which he examines the common features of human life throughout the world. To take into consideration the natural and social ways of the 'citizens of the world' rather than the members of a given civilization, as Michel Foucault explains in his 'Introduction' to his translation of this work, demonstrates Kant's pragmatic perspective on a concrete universal.[34]

The relationship between the sexes is one of the transcultural characteristics of the species. Women are different from men. They have to please and make themselves desirable. As objects of desire they are in a situation of permanent potential seduction, which rouses systematic jealousy on the part of men. Men marry women as human beings; thus they use their wives as persons, but they are also obliged to imprison them in the domestic space. This confinement is necessary because women are always likely to seduce others. Infidelity is always a possibility. At first, this occurs in polygamy. The harem is a rudimentary form of marriage: a polyamorous and jealous man maintains under his authority a group of women, who must accept to be faithful but have also to accept to be jealous. They fight with ruses and seductiveness to conquer the preference of the lord.[35] Jealousy is part of their life. It is, however, not symmetrical. The women compete, but no one can prevail. Monogamy is more civilized than polygamy, for all the reasons we have already discussed. Yet Kant sees an analogous gender dynamic: even monogamous wives are systematically coquettish and flirtatious, but with men other than their husband. The more luxurious and refined a culture is, the more elaborate this art of love becomes. Women display the quintessential feminine character and, by titillating men's desire, experiment with their liberty. 'Woman lays claim to freedom and, at the same time, to the conquest of the entire male sex.'[36] Men ought to understand that this occurs for a reason: women's ambivalent status in a marriage. Because they enter into the conjugal contract as persons, wives are 'free'; therefore they use their freedom in their own womanly way. Furthermore, Kant adds a demographic consideration: since there is a strong probability that they might become widows, they anticipate the need for a second marriage. This is why they entertain potential suitors.[37] Jealousy of coquetry is therefore unjust. 'Gallantry has become the fashion, and jealousy ridiculous.'[38]

Husbands, however, have to be aware of their rights. Women may well laugh at the intolerance of men for what Freud will call the 'little excursions' (*kleinen Schrittchen*) into infidelity that most societies tend to condone.[39] But women also expect their spouses to be offended by the prospect of actual infidelities. For by not asserting his privileges as the unique possessor of his wife, a husband would forfeit his contractual rights. He would also fail his wife as a person. She would hate him for that.

> Accordingly, one will also find that when the married woman openly practises gallantry, and her husband pays no attention to it, but compensates himself for it by drinking and card-parties, or wooing other women, then not merely contempt but also *hatred* overcomes the female partner: because the woman recognizes by this that he now places no worth at all in her, and that he abandons his wife indifferently to others to gnaw on the same bone [*an demselben Knochen zu nagen*].[40]

Jealousy lies at the core of heterosexual relations. It is a strong feeling that, in rough monogamous societies, can result in murder. In Kant's more refined world, jealousy manifests itself, in the *Metaphysics of Morals*, as the right to repossess an adulterous spouse. In the *Anthropology*, however, Kant mostly insists on what he considers to be a stereotypically female form of behaviour. Across different societies, he observes, women are systematically victimized, governed and secluded. They are also demonized as a constant temptation for any man. The two things go hand in hand. A civilized wife plays the game of seduction and aesthetic exhibition because she is a person, after all – remember, she gets married *als Person*, as a person – but this is the only liberty she is capable of taking. These two ways of thinking about the feminine might seem contradictory; but they have a bright future ahead of them. Men oblige their wedded wives to lead a life of dependence and objectification, to be sure, but, by the simple fact of having married them (rather than just enjoying them sexually), they acknowledge their 'freedom'. In other words, they have consented to treat them as persons, endowed with rights. This is the point of reciprocal fidelity. Married women in turn indulge in the position of objects of desire; thus they cultivate self-objectification – but they do so on purpose, in order to arouse men's lust and their husbands' jealousy. This is the point of femininity. Woman's situation is profoundly ambiguous. Marriage itself hinges on the balancing act of reification and freedom, coquetry and jealousy.

Michel Foucault had also noticed this paradox. 'Jealousy', he writes, 'is a recognition of a woman's moral freedom.' A man is jealous not because he definitely owns a 'thing', but because he is constantly alert to the potential infidelity of a *person* – who never ceases playing the 'thing' for others. It is the woman's indomitable desire that creates this alertness. In Foucault's words:

> But jealousy as a violent relationship, as the thingification of woman (to the point of destruction), is a recognition of the woman's value. It is, on the contrary, the absence of jealousy that would reduce the woman to nothing but an interchangeable commodity. The right to be jealous – up to committing murder – is a recognition of a woman's moral freedom.[41]

A man who, instead of being jealous of a disloyal wife, carried on with his own pleasures – drinking, gambling, mistresses – would, in effect, accept that his wife had become a bone (*Knochen*) for all to gnaw upon. *Osso buco*, then! Even less appetizing than roast veal.

Coquetry and cannibalism

The culinary metaphor deserves our attention.

The publication of the *Metaphysics of Morals* caused quite a stir. Kant was challenged on what he considered to be a truly original contribution to legal theory: the concept of a 'Right to a Person akin to a right to a Thing'. He hoped to demonstrate that this 'new phenomenon in the juristic sky' was a *stella mirabilis* rather than a 'shooting star'.[42] In order to elucidate the meaning of this twofold definition of an odd right – a definition that blurred the line between persons and things – Kant offered the following clarification:

> Apart from this condition (marriage) carnal enjoyment is *cannibalistic* in principle (even if not always in its effect). Whether something is *consumed* by mouth and teeth, or whether the woman is consumed by pregnancy and the perhaps fatal delivery resulting from it, or the man by exhaustion of his sexual capacity from the woman's frequent demands upon it, the difference is merely in the manner of enjoyment. In this sort of use by each of the sexual organ of the other, each is actually a *consumable* thing (*res fungibilis*) with respect to the other, so that if one were to make oneself such a thing by *contract*, the contract would be contrary to law (*pactum turpe*).[43]

One of the first critics of Kant's conception of marriage was one of his pupils, Christian Gottfried Schütz, a philosopher and a classical philologist with whom Kant was in correspondance. Schütz had written a letter to Court Chaplain Schultz, a mutual friend, in which he had raised questions about Kant's notion in the *Metaphysics of Morals* of 'Rights to persons [being] akin to rights to things'. In this letter Schütz had expressed his misgivings about the status of wives and servants. In July 1797, although unsolicited by Schütz himself, Kant responds to those questions.[44] Schütz had apparently argued, firstly, that Kant's marriage looked like 'no more than mutual subordination' and, secondly, that his line of thought started from a mistaken definition of '*Genuss*', pleasure. Kant takes issue with both of these arguments. The 'reciprocal use' is a result of the legal contract, he claims. And sexual intercourse, in its corporeal reality, could only be defined as 'use'. About the meaning of pleasure, Kant is even more defensive:

> Second, you say: 'Kant's theory seems to rest simply on a fallacious interpretation of the word "*enjoyment*".' Granted, the *actual* enjoyment of another human being, such as in cannibalism, would reduce a human being to an object; but surely married people do not become interchangeable goods [*res fungibilis*] just by sleeping together.[45]

Kant reduces sex to anthropophagy! This was Schütz's accusation. Now, if we were to expect an indignant, humanistic rebuttal of such an unflattering (for us) insinuation, we would be sorely disappointed.

Challenged as to his intellectual ability, Kant replied with ironic irritation. Yes, indeed, to ground his argument on the word '*Genuss*' might have been feeble, but one had to understand what '*Genuss*' really meant.

> The word may be replaced by the notion of *using someone* directly (that is, sensuously – a word that has a different meaning here than elsewhere); I mean rendering her an *immediately pleasurable* thing. An enjoyment of this sort involves at once the thought of her as merely *consumable* [*res fungibilis*], and that in fact is what the reciprocal use of each other's sexual organs by two people provides.[46]

Not only does Kant hold his ground, therefore, he also puts his foot down. To have sex is nothing other than to use someone's sexual parts and faculties. Coition is a physical *mutuum adiutorium* (the 'reciprocal use' we have discussed at length). Marriage makes it lawful, therefore, but it does not change the nature, or the proper definition, of what it is. 'The appetite of a cannibal', Kant concludes pithily, 'differs only insignificantly from that of a sexual libertine.'[47]

If we were to translate Kant's language into that of contemporary opera, we could say that, whereas the title character of Mozart's *Don Giovanni* is always ravenous for savoury meat – including the fatal 'mortal food' [*cibo mortale*] he offers to share with the Commendatore – and for female flesh, Don Ottavio waits patiently to legalize, in a connubial mode, his desire for one person, Donna Anna. Don Giovanni rapes, deceives, lies and uses whatever means might be expedient to his ends, including fake promises of marriage to Donna Elvira and Zerlina. Don Ottavio behaves like a genuine fiancé, capable of waiting to wed his beloved, whose affection is everything to him. The former plays with marriage just to overindulge his gluttony. The latter aims at a unique reciprocity in which, thanks to his own fidelity, his wife will be a very special delicacy for him, as he will be for her. The former is an indiscriminate cannibal, the latter a discerning gourmet who expects to be savoured in turn.

In response to Schütz's concern that this way of conceiving the members of a household verges on a justification of slavery, Kant specifies that 'One person's holding another as his own (that is, as part of his household) signifies a right to possession that may be exercised against any subsequent possessor [*jus in re contra quemlibet hujus rei possessorem*].'[48] And this competitive, antagonistic right is exactly the one a husband may, and should, exert upon his wife, as it appears in the *Metaphysics of Morals* (§25) and in the *Anthropology from a Pragmatic Point of View* – lest he abandon her to other men's appetite for *osso buco*. This is the only kind of cannibalism that may threaten a marriage: a spouse's failure to be dutifully jealous, therefore to protect the other spouse from someone else's predatory jaws.

An extremely perceptive reader of Kant's letter to Schütz was, once again, Michel Foucault. In his Introduction to the *Anthropology*, Foucault emphasizes the fact that Kant wrote the two texts during the same period.

> In his letter to Schütz of 10 July 1797, at the time when he was probably completing the draft of the *Anthropology*, Kant responded to the objections made to him. The *mutuum adjutorium* of sexual intercourse is the legally necessary consequence of marriage: that is to say, the 'thingification' [*chosification*] in the relationship between man and woman is not a fact which underpins the law but a fact which results from a state of law, and which does not contest it unless it asserts itself outside such a state. Beyond or within the limits of marriage, the libertinism of a *Freidenker* is no different except for the anthropological form. But, conversely, if the moral significance of sexual intercourse is very different according to whether it is fulfilled or not in the legal form of marriage, the content itself does not change. A partner becomes for the other a thing, an *adjutorium* of his pleasure. The law authorizes the fact: but, by founding it, it does not alter its content, nor does it accomplish any metamorphosis.[49]

Foucault sees in Kant's response the radical coherence of the 'pragmatic' point of view on human sexuality. The law permits, to be sure, but does not alter, through some magical conversion or glorification – a 'metamorphosis' – the simple fact that one partner is the 'accessory' of the other's pleasure. Once again, sex is sex.

Kant does not advocate a change in this status quo. He is no feminist. On the contrary, he identifies an anthropological pattern that fits his normative views about the right of marriage. He brings to light a powerful correlation between the characteristically feminine care of the self (which is frivolous, shallow and silly) and the use of women as things. The former is nothing but compliance with the latter. Both must be blamed. According to Kant, it is by nature that the appropriation/domination/thingification of women goes together with women's obsession with their own bodies and their looks. Women want to make themselves objects of desire, therefore objects. Shame on them! This is a deeply anti-aesthetic way of thinking because it fails to acknowledge the intentional embodiment of our erotic presence beyond anatomical equipment. It also rules out the hypothesis that, after all, women might like to show their own creativity in fashioning themselves, not just to please men, but also for themselves and for (not against) other women.

If one were to imagine an emancipatory development of this logic, then the liberation of women from male oppression would require, first of all, the sacrifice of charm and playfulness. And this is indeed what happens in certain righteous feminism of the second wave: condescension, if not contempt, towards everything that is adornment, seduction and sensuality. A woman who wants to rise against the power of man must renounce, first of all, her lipstick.

This will be the price, fixed at Königsberg in 1798, of our freedom. Man, meanwhile, will keep his own liberty to roam.

Shame on Kant!

There are many ways out of the Kantian kingdom. One is Schütz's contestation of Kant's legal theory. Another radical objection, based equally on right but offering a more ambitious ethical perspective, comes from Georg Wilhelm Friedrich Hegel. We learn to talk about recognition, not objectification; about dialectic, not opposition between subject and object; of relationships between people wilfully surrendering to each other, not between people and things.

Hegel discusses sex and family formation in the *Elements of the Philosophy of Right* (1821). From the outset, he attacks Kant, whom he accuses of thinking of marriage in a way that falls within 'shamefulness, it must be said' [*Schändlichkeit, muß man sagen*].[50] Kant's vision of sexuality was haunted by abhorrence for the 'defilement' (*Schändung*) of humanity in the person. For Hegel, Kant's own vision of the conjugal actualization of sexuality 'is not itself but a form of shamefulness [*Schändlichkeit*]'. Kant's thought, Hegel fulminates, is just disgraceful.

This criticism is violent. Why such violence? Because, in Hegel's opinion, Kant commits a category mistake: he subsumes marriage under the concept of contract (*Vertrag*). But a contract, Hegel objects, is defined as a transaction between two wills – that is to say, two free persons – who alienate, acquire, exchange a thing (*Sache*). Marriage has nothing to do with such a definition. The conjugal association of man and woman creates a union. Two individuals form a society which is itself a 'moral person'. The specificity of this union is love and reciprocal devotion (not use). Be it arranged by families or be it the culmination of passion between two individuals, marriage, the conjunction of natural sexes, 'is transformed into a *spiritual* union, into self-conscious love'. There is absolutely no transfer of objects or things. There is no mutual usage of organs.

These remarks are of crucial importance for the criticism of the theories of the social contract. Conflating the handling of private property and the formation of the State, for Hegel, is a category mistake. But the redefinition of marriage – this is not a contract: shame on Kant! – also opens up a whole new perspective on the erotic experience. Hegel rejects the language of machinery and butchering. The body is not an assemblage of tools, the utilization of which (without a contract) would threaten the human essence and the integrity of the person. The body allows people to personalize themselves even more, so to speak, in the creation of the foundational human community – which is a moral person. Nature is not a domain that the law would counteract by a formal stipulation. Nature itself brings us to the moral finality of marriage. Even more significant, Hegel dismantles the confusion between possessing one another as objects and uniting with another person as a person. Thus the critique of Kant culminates in the justification of monogamy. Monogamous marriage does not ratify the reification inherent in the usage of the sexual apparatus. On the contrary, for Hegel,

> Marriage is essentially an ethical relationship. Formerly, especially under most systems of natural law, it was considered only in its physical aspect or natural character. It was accordingly regarded only as a sexual relationship, and its other determinations remained completely inaccessible. *But it is equally crude to interpret marriage merely as a civil contract, a notion [Vorstellung] which is still to be found even in Kant.* On this interpretation, marriage gives contractual form to the arbitrary relations between individuals, and is thus debased to a contract entitling the parties concerned to use one another.[51]

This could not be clearer: marriage is not wild sex, to be sure; but neither is it just a formal agreement about mechanical sex. Marriage is not meant to legalize the reciprocal utilization (*Gebrauch*) of the sexual organs between two partners who treat each other as their thing (*als seine Sache*). Marriage unites two people who regard each other as persons (*als Person*).[52] Hegel, therefore, asserts exactly this: one has to depart completely from a purely juridical vision and to understand that marriage is the opposite of what Kant had claimed it to be. Kant's approach is nothing less than 'crude'.

It was noted above (§ 75) that marriage is not a contractual relationship as far as its essential basis is concerned. For the precise nature of marriage is to begin from the point of view of contract – i.e. that of individual personality as a self-sufficient unit – *in order to supersede it* [*ihn aufzuheben*]. That identification of personalities whereby the family is a *single person* and its members are its accidents...is the ethical spirit.[53]

Once again, marriage must not be confused with a contract, because there is no transfer of ownership; there is no reification, no possession, no usage, no things involved. Kant was wrong. His was, Hegel points out, nothing less than a logical error: the subsumption of a specific phenomenon (marriage) within a larger category (contract), the definition of which is incompatible with that of the phenomenon in question.

So this is the problem. Within a couple made up of two persons, there will be a reciprocal demand for respect, which means that, on account of their devotion to each other, they both expect to be perceived as they want.

Vaga libido

At this point, two brief detours via the ancient world.

Medea, this Hegelian wife, wants to be recognized as the passionate lover who did everything for Jason. This is why Jason's failure to give her credit for her love is so devastating. She claims her due, in the sense that, once she has helped Jason so generously in his heroic feats, she refuses to be replaced by a younger and more useful wife/mother. But she does not protest against the idea of being treated as a dispensable object. This would be a Kantian accusation. Medea misses the erotic desire of the man she still loves. His lost desire for her: that's exactly what she longs for. She would like to be targeted, 'accentuated' as an object of love. She does not care about being manipulated like an inanimate 'thing', but she suffers from no longer being the *object of* the loving interest of her man.

Kant's theory of love can be read against the background of one of the great philosophical poems from the Roman past: Lucretius' *On the Nature of Things* (*De rerum natura*). For Lucretius, sexual contact is a matter of chance and shocks. The image of a body (*simulacrum*) – which, being made of an extremely tenuous material, is also corporeal – strikes and arouses us. The blow causes a wound and triggers a mechanical reaction: an ejection of seed, directed at the individual source of the *simulacrum*. This is desire! *Haec Venus est nobis*! Should this physical response strike the same object again and again, the 'wound' would worsen: we would then fall in love. All the evils of infatuation would follow suit: foolish idealization, disappointment, wasted time and constant jealousy. Lucretius can think of only one remedy: sexual promiscuity. We must channel our seed towards other bodies and keep swinging, with pure venereal pleasure, in a ceaselessly moving world. The name of this restless desire is *venus volgivaga* (or *vulgivaga*).[54]

Now, *this* is reification. To claim that Venus is nothing other than light films, colliding with the material texture of the soul, thus causing the projection of seed; to say that love is but the rotting of a wound, a pathological turn of events that we must forestall as soon as possible by drifting towards other bodies, with no attention whatsoever to the individual and intentional (personal) dimension of those bodies; to insist that whatever a lover may say about a beloved can only be the misled distortion of a physical defect – *this* is reification. Lucretian lovers are, indeed, made into things. Love is a wandering thing, if I may.

Kant liked Lucretius. It is in *On the Nature of Things* that Kant found the unusual expression *'venus volgivaga'* that he uses in his arguments on sexuality. In *The Metaphysics of Morals*, in the same chapter where we find the definition of the sexual act as 'reciprocal use', Kant argues that 'Natural sexual union takes place either in accordance with mere animal *nature* (*vaga libido, venus vulgivaga, fornicatio*) or in accordance with *law*.'[55] This Venus is beastly, dehumanizing sex. When Hegel responds to Kant, he uses the expression *'venus vaga'*. We have examined his criticism of Kant, guilty of downgrading marriage – an ethico-legal love – to a merely civil contract.[56] Precisely in that context, Hegel calls sexual coition *venus vaga*.[57] The mention of Kant, and his 'crude' vision of marriage, makes it clear that Hegel is mimicking his disparaging, Lucretian language.

An object of desire is not a thing

We can see a major fallacy in the line of thought inspired by Kantian morality: the confusion between an *object of* (*Gegenstand, Objekt*), on the one hand, and an 'object', understood as a thing (*Sache*), on the other. There is no reason why we should conflate an inanimate, inert, tangible, interchangeable, available, consumable and ready-made object/thing with an *object of*. In the philosophical tradition, as well as in ordinary language, the word 'object' refers not to an ontological category – this is a thing; this is a person – but to a relative *position*, with respect to a logical and grammatical subject. René Descartes, for example, commonly mentions *objects of* perception but also of other forms of care or attention, such as love or admiration.

The expression '*object of*' designates a syntactic place – one that anyone and anything can occupy. It is not because I situate a person, or even God, at the centre of my visual field, as the recipient of my curiosity, my devotion, my reverence and my affection, that I convert that '*object of*' into a thing. On the contrary, I value their qualities and even worship them. I recognize their precious existence. In love, I may attribute extraordinary charms to the object of my profound attention. Stendhal would have said that I 'crystallize', Jacques Lacan that I set them apart. Desire makes all the difference, meaning that an object/cause *of* desire does something special *to me*. I cannot help placing a distinctive accent onto it. And I will say that above all, if I desire, I will lend to that object a lively desire for me. Hopefully, hopelessly, wistfully, wishfully, I will try to read the signs of their desire for me. I hyper-personify the object of my desire, therefore, which is the exact opposite of objectification.

There is no reason, however, why we should make this confusion unless we wish to. And we might want to do so if we were to believe, in the first place, that erotic desire as such, because it targets a person's body, objectifies its object. Notwithstanding the clever disclaimer of a sophisticated philosopher such as Rae Langton, this is the unfortunate slippage of objectification theory. We all know, Langton argues, that the term 'object' carries an intentional meaning and a metaphysical meaning.[58] The whole thought process set in motion by this word 'objectification', I contend, reveals the conflation of the two, because it is always a certain kind of intentionality, namely erotic attention, that activates the alleged reduction of a person to a thing. If it is a voice that suddenly sounds attractive, if it is the cut of a jacket on a pair of shoulders that draws my attention, if it is a dress that designs a sexy silhouette – and each of us has our own memories – then eros is indeed responsible for a focalization on the aesthetic presence of a person. That embodied person is the *object of* my desire.

Does the sheer enjoyment of that sensory experience mean to treat a human being as an *object/thing*? I say no. I refuse to call my sensual perception of people 'objectification' because, for me, this is an abuse of language. But if I were to separate the 'body' from the 'person', as Kant does, then sexual desire would *ipso facto* be dehumanizing. The object of *that* desire would always be an object/thing. It would not be 'made into a thing' occasionally, on account of some avoidable wicked intention, but systematically, by the sexual act itself. If I have decided that the body is a thing, and since the body is involved in sex, then sex allows a human being to be used as a thing. Sex degrades, defiles, violates my humanness. *That* desire would be objectifying for the simple reason that it responds to a corporeal reality, which I have disconnected *a priori* from my human essence. *That* desire itself would deserve the blame. To speak the parlance of 'objectification', I would need to despise the facticity of the body *in the first place*. But then eros is doomed.

The neo-Kantian argument takes it for granted that, if I love you, just because I speak of 'you' as a 'direct object' of the transitive verb 'love' (which in the Greek, Latin or German languages would be declined in the accusative case), then my love imposes on you not just a grammatical convention but an ontological status. Along these lines, Luce Irigaray suggests that we ought to avoid altogether the formula '*je t'aime*', 'I love you'. We should instead declare our love by saying: '*j'aime à toi*', 'I love *to* you'. Thanks to an 'indirect object' (dative), you will become the recipient of my erotic interest. You will then not be treated as something passive and thingy.

> I love 'to' you means: I keep a rapport of indirection towards you. I do not submit you, and I do not consume you. I respect you (as an irreducible being). I greet you: I greet in you. I praise you: I praise in you.... The 'to' guarantees indirection. The 'to' prevents a relation of transitivity in which the other would not be irreducible and in which reciprocity would not be possible.... The 'to' is the place of non-reduction of the person to the object. I love you, I desire you, I take you, I seduce you, I command you, I instruct you, etc. – these utterances threaten to annihilate the otherness of the other. They threaten to transform her/him into my good, my object; to reduce her/him to be mine, namely to be part of my field of existential or material properties.[59]

But, seriously: does this grammatical difference create an ontological difference? It is obvious that this is not the case. A verb can take direct objects but does not automatically reify them. The phrase 'I meet Mary' does not make Mary into a thing, just because the verb 'to meet' is transitive. The same is true of 'to desire', 'to love', 'to admire' or 'to respect'. A direct object is no more a thing than an indirect object. Its placement in a sentence cannot perform some kind of metaphysical magic.

What matters, ethically and linguistically, is the meaning of the verbs I am uttering. What matters erotically is the quality of what I feel for you. What matters is the awareness that, whenever I address you as the '*object of*' my love, this language implies that there are sensations, perceptions, sentiments, intentions, *of which* you are, actually, the cause. The so-called object becomes just 'that of which' and 'that thanks to which' there is sensation. It becomes 'that which' is capable of creating a sensation in me. And you are indeed a person, even a hyper-person, mysteriously embodied and keenly sentient: the person whose desire means the world to me – more than anyone else's desire.

But it is true that, if I start from the principle that sexual pleasure violates the humanity of a person, then yes, certainly, I will accuse desire itself of transforming its object (and its cause) into an object/thing. I will accuse desire itself, in other words, of objectifying/reifying everything it touches. In the infamous passage on the veal roast, Kant does exactly that. The logic of the argument relies on the premise that there is something intrinsically despicable in the sexual act. It is eros that degrades a person, *ipso facto*, to the level of a *Sache*. A moral posture of disapproval, religiously adopted *a priori*, generates the rhetorical strategy that leads to the conflation of the grammatical and the ontological meanings of the word 'object'. A systematic *blame* of pleasure, at work in every sentence, word and syllable of Kantian anaesthetic humanism, reduces eros to hunger for inhuman meat.

Feminist theory should get out of this unsavoury cuisine.

Eros as hyper-personification

Where is eros? Pleasure is a sensation, not a usage; the flesh is irreducible to anatomy and physiology, even less to the Sunday roast. A body is never a thing. In an erotic situation, a body reaches out to another body. Desire clings to parts and places, bits and pieces, indeed, but above all it responds to movements and postures, attitudes and gestures – which have nothing to do with 'things'. This way of walking speaks to me of the vitality and energy of my beloved. These eyes I look into twinkle with complicity. This lobe I chew is not a morsel of *scaloppina*. When reading Immanuel Kant, I can only long for Stendhal or Maurice Merleau-Ponty! And, above all: we badly need psychoanalysis! We need a scholarly discourse that touches the real of eros. Not the real as waste, the real as material, the real as tool, but the real experience – sensation, feeling – of pleasure, or pain.

When I desire, I do exactly the opposite of what is meant by 'objectification': I accentuate the privilege, the unique point, the anchorage and the centre of gravity of my desire, which sets that person – the object of my love – apart.[60] I single out the special features of the other person, including her/his lively, expressive, intentional body. Once again, I hyper-personify the other person. I project intentionality onto their body: he looks at me, she smiled; he turns around, she beckoned to me. Careful and apprehensive, my desire guesses, assesses and amplifies the desire of the other. Eroticism deals not with 'organs' but with partial objects that emit eloquent signals, not with the wish to regain a lost personality but with attention to the sensual singularity of the other, and of myself. There is no 'use'; there are only sensations. When I try to make myself desirable, I do the opposite of self-objectification. I am not morphing into a 'thing', but I am aware that I can become a *cause* – the cause of someone else's desire and pleasure. I dress up and perform my erotic persona in order to signify my desire, or the absence thereof. I am not an 'absolute unity' but a subject who does not know exactly why it has to be this, rather than that, which makes me feel. I am not a person whose 'humanity' would be violated by the pleasure of my lover; I feel a pleasure which is good, and which makes me feel good. I have nothing to lose. I have nothing to fear.

What preserves us from the meaty exploitation of others' bodies is eroticism. The arts of love deploy ways to take pleasure and to offer one's own body, in so many fashions, to the pleasure of others. Social graces; erotic graces. Thus, it is perhaps by thinking hard about the context of our interpersonal relations that I allow myself to lay my head – sorry, darling! – on the belly of my lover. But making love is something else. Eros is otherwise demanding. He wants a living and renewed desire. We entwine with others in order to experience pleasant and thrilling, intense and beautiful sensations – together. This is the end. For the time being, and we take the time, this is what matters: the miracle of shared pleasure, not procreation or the greater good. It is not sex that instrumentalizes persons; it is Kant and his followers who instrumentalize sex.

If eros is the end, we want to experiment, vary, discover and rediscover. It is by taking the liberty to isolate the caress of this hand, the sound of this voice, the smell of this skin, that I will feel, perhaps, something erotic. And the other, a particular person with fantasies of her/his own, will want me to do silly little things that trigger their own erotic response. Sensuality demands the opposite of a reasonable 'context'. It might be weird, ritualized, perverse, embarrassing. We actually disconnect. And we do not make 'one' either. We cling piecemeal to each other, in surprising micro-shocks. Whatever happens outside is irrelevant here and now: only pleasure matters. Of course, when we talk about pleasure as an end, not as a means, we choose the antithesis of a morality based entirely on contempt for the useful and the pleasant, in the tradition of Stoicism or of a tortured Epicureanism. We are also very far from a feminist theory that needs to 'condone' eroticism on behalf of some higher, more legitimate end – such as 'flourishing', the new categorical imperative.

To see things everywhere

We owe to Immanuel Kant the invention of 'reification'. Not the noun *Verdinglichung*, or *Versachlichung*, perhaps, but certainly the concept of 'reducing man to the status of thing'.[61] The binary ontological opposition between person and thing is the organizing principle of his ethics. The sexual act blurs precisely this fundamental distinction. 'In this act', Kant says, 'a man makes himself into a thing' (*In diesem Akt macht sich ein Mensch zur Sache selbst*). This 'making himself into a thing' is the worst abdication for a human being: it goes against the law of humanity. Sex threatens human rights. It is in this reflection on sexuality that we see the emergence of a familiar language whose fate concerns us all, well beyond professional philosophy. Everything we say, without really thinking, on the representation of women as sexual objects comes from there. This way of thinking and speaking is of capital importance in any critical theory of social relations, in feminist thought and even in our common political language. We may not agree, but everyone understands what the term 'sexual object' means.

Does a feminist theory focused on the objectification of women refer explicitly to Kant's ontology? The resemblance is obvious, but there is more to be said. In order to understand fully the genealogy I have been describing we will have to take a short detour via Paris at the end of the 1940s. We have to track down, very briefly, the vicissitudes of the terms *Versachlichung* and *Verdinglichung*, which are often translated into English as 'reification', and also *Gegenstandlichung* (objectification).

These words belong to the lexicon of Marxist theory and German sociology. Marx mentions two paradoxes at the heart of the capitalist system of production: the personification of commodities, on the one hand, and the objectification of social relations, in the form of money, on the other.[62] After Marx, a very rich tradition of critical theory multiplies the variations of the initial idea. By maximizing profit via surplus value, exploiting workers, rationalizing the production of goods, and promoting calculation and quantification in all domains of life, capitalism implements a reduction of man (or relations between men) to some*thing* purely instrumental. There are only commodities in the world, the only value is monetary, and people are treated as means to material ends. This language conveys contemptuous disapproval. It is a polemical concept, Frédéric Vandenberghe claims:

> The highly critical, polemical, character of reification should not be overlooked, for its meaning and standard usage invariably carries negative connotations. As a subversive concept, reification designates the becoming-thing of that which *by right* is not a thing. This pseudo-thing can be a concept, person, animal, relation, process, social world or commodity – the list goes on. The reification of these pseudo-things involves illegitimately attributing them with, alternately, facticity, fixity, objectivity, externality, impersonality, naturalness, in short, the ontological thingness deemed inappropriate. In every case, the concept of reification presupposes an ontology which initially is only rarely, if ever, made explicit.[63]

We have seen how Kant makes his ontology quite explicit. Persons are reasonable, free, integral and fully human beings. Things are essentially non-persons. The becoming-thing of a person is, consequently, an ontological degradation, an alteration that affects the person's truest being. Vandenberghe denies that Kant has anything to do with reification. He is probably right in terms of word-for-word correspondence. He is, however, wrong on the substance. The texts mentioned above bear witness to this. The Kantian 'Man' must protect himself against the danger, or the temptation, of 'making

[him]self into a thing'. But sexual desire exposes him to this risk. Whether interactive or solitary, between humans or animals, the sexual act accomplishes exactly that: a 'thingification'. The concept of 'reification', in other words, is at the heart of Kantian ethics – an ethics of Man against the Thing.

Now, Karl Marx takes his idea of reification from there. In evidence of this, I can cite a paradoxical witness: Louis Althusser. In his ground-breaking book on the genesis of Karl Marx's thought, *Pour Marx* (1965), Althusser advanced the thesis that there was an epistemological break between two distinct phases in Marx's thinking: his first 'humanist' philosophical sensibility appears to have been at odds with the properly theoretical and *scientific* theory of capitalism, devised after 1845. Althusser argued that Marx's youthful humanism was based, precisely, on Kantian ethics. It was predicated on a highly idealized vision of 'human essence' (*Menschheit*) borrowed from Kant and Fichte, he insisted, rather than Hegel. For the young Marx, 'Man' was to reclaim his human essence, which had been 'objectified'. This was the core of the critique of capitalism.

Althusser demolished this 'rationalist-liberal humanism' as a merely ideological posture. In 1845, Marx accomplished a 'total theoretical revolution', he claimed, which consisted, precisely, of the 'rejection of the Kantian ethical idea'.[64] In one single footnote, Althusser dismissed the language of reification as merely a 'popular theory' which had become fashionable in leftist circles among intellectuals who had failed to understand Marx's political theory – an essentially *post*-humanistic understanding of the economy and of history: 'An ideology of reification that sees "things" everywhere in human relations confuses in this category "thing" (a category more foreign to Marx cannot be imagined) every social relation, conceived according to the model of a money-thing.'[65]

Althusser showcases a humanist Marx, humanist because Kantian. He is a politically committed journalist who has not yet understood (theoretically) the dialectic of history but who is morally (which means ideologically) engaged against the becoming-thing of Man. 'For the young Marx, "Man" was not just a cry denouncing poverty and slavery. It was the theoretical principle of his world outlook and of his practical attitude.'[66] But to construct a project of revolution on this 'theoretical principle' means, for Althusser, to commit a conceptual error: to confuse all social relations of power 'under the category of the "thing"'. One more category mistake! What a massive misunderstanding! And yet this flawed basic assumption had misled an entire generation of intellectuals across Europe.

To understand the scope of this demolition, it must be remembered that, from the 1920s on, a tradition of critical thinking had flourished from the premise of this 'theoretical principle': reification. György Lukács in Hungary, Georg Simmel and the Frankfurt School in Germany, and Jean-Paul Sartre and Maurice Merleau-Ponty in France all offered variants of the same theory. In 1965, with imperturbable insolence, Althusser discarded this critical endeavour as nothing more than an intellectual trend.

This interests us for two reasons: firstly, the Kantian genealogy of Marx's concern for the 'becoming-thing' of Man; and, secondly, the fact that, among the intellectuals who took up this humanist and Kantian Marx, there is the French philosopher who shaped the conceptual apparatus of feminism in the twentieth century: Simone de Beauvoir.[67] In *The Second Sex* (1949), Simone de Beauvoir endorses the language of Man and the Thing in order to think sexual difference. It is in these pages, which have now become canonical, that several generations of feminists have learned to speak of Woman as the 'Other of Man' and of Woman as a sexual object. This is supposed to mean that a woman may be an *object of* desire, but also that, through sex, she becomes an object pure and simple, understood as 'thing'. The semantic fusion occurs when three lines of thought blend into each other: a philosophy of life; Hegel's dialectic of recognition; and the Marxist conception of history. Here is a brief account of how this came about.

Sinking into the paste of immanence

Humanity is gendered. In all societies and in all historical periods, men emerge as subjects capable of projecting themselves into the world by making decisions and leaping into action. They always take the initiative. Thrown into any situation, they do not stay put; they strive, they 'transcend'. Women, by contrast, are mired in inertia, immobility and repetition – in short, they sink 'into the paste of immanence'.[68] It is not their fault. It is that human subjects have a need to feel recognized. Paradoxically, self-awareness requires from others confirmation and approval, validation and acknowledgement. Since all individuals aspire to the same response, such a need creates competition: it is a struggle between the other and me. Power and domination are the result, but it is always an unstable result. In the most extreme and paradigmatic version of this fight, we try to prevail by reducing the other person to slavery. The slave, while being exploited and humiliated, experiences how essential their role is for the master. 'By a dialectical reversal, the master appears the inessential one.'[69] Revolution is possible, therefore – even inevitable.

Beauvoir endorses here the Hegelian dialectic of master and slave, but it is now a *gendered* dialectic. Men, she writes, have always, of course, monopolized 'the concrete power' to enforce their economic interests and therefore, of course, to exploit women. This domination, however, 'also suited their ontological and moral ambitions'. They need an Other in order to exist. The Other limits the freedom of a human subject, but 'it is still necessary'. If you cease to exist for others, you collapse. It is for this reason that men have always and everywhere subjected women by systematically making *them* into the Other.[70] Woman 'is determined and differentiated in relation to man, while he is not in relation to her; she is the inessential in front of the essential. He is the Subject; he is the Absolute. She is the Other'.[71] Other than man; other *for* men. Unequal *and* indispensable. Inferior *and* complementary. A man's validating reflection in a mirror rather than a rival. At the orders of a loving and despotic man, who is unwittingly reliant on her, Woman finds herself in a situation that is constraining but has the potential of being transformed. She may come to experience herself as the essential partner in a relationship, as opposed to a man who might become dependent and dispensable. A dialectical reversal will revolutionize the couple and lead to an authentically mutual recognition, without struggle. Some day, women and men will relate to each other in fluid commonality and immediate reciprocity. 'In the authentically democratic society that Marx heralded,' Beauvoir prophesizes, 'there is no place for the Other'.[72] For the time being, Woman transcends her situation and conquers her human dignity by working.[73] Emancipation is possible and, indeed, inevitable.

By framing the difference between the sexes in terms of this unstable and paradoxical antagonism, Simone de Beauvoir performs an innovative philosophical gesture. While Hegel had sketched the opposition between a master and a slave, Beauvoir places Man, the sexed and gendered male human being, in conflict with Woman. Woman is the Other who, in the struggle for recognition, has always already lost because she will never be valued as an equal. Woman, however, is the Other a man cannot live without, because she gives him a recognition that is unique.

This uniqueness supports the entire argument of *The Second Sex*. By imposing onto women a secondary, instrumental and auxiliary role, men subjugate women. But they deal with them quite differently in comparison with slaves, because they expect not only social servitude but also sexual service. Although subdued, Woman has to some degree to be respected, protected and even idealized in myth or surrounded with magic, for she 'remains necessary to the mechanism of fertility, life and order of society'. Because she is instrumental to biological and social reproduction, she cannot be exploited like a piece of machinery. She is a servant and a companion. Woman's situation in the world is distinctively ambivalent, therefore. Women's history is the history of such ambivalence. 'This very ambivalence of the Other, of the Female, will be reflected in the rest of her history; until our times she will be subordinated to men's will. But this will is ambiguous: by total annexation, woman will be lowered to the rank of a thing...'[74] And this cannot happen.

Because of the ambivalence/ambiguity of a special relation mediated by sex, the full, literal and permanent reduction of women to nothing but things is just impossible for Simone de Beauvoir. But the story she tells in *The Second Sex* is all about how women have adapted to become – to occupy the place of, to play the role of – things. This language runs through the book.

> But under the patriarchal regime, she was the property of a father who married her off as he saw fit; then attached to her husband's household, she was no more than his thing and the thing of the family (*genos*) in which she was placed.
>
> When family and private patrimony incontestably remain the bases of society, woman also remains totally alienated.[75]

For a male subject, a woman is an object: she is mere flesh, she is a thing, his thing.[76] Woman is a fertile body in which life begins as a 'strawberry of blood' or a blob of 'trembling gelatine'. She is a fleshy and sensual body. Breasts and buttocks are a 'fatty proliferation that is not enlivened by any project, that has no other meaning than to be there.'[77] Perceived and desired as natural, the female body is, at the same time, aesthetically modified, improved, enhanced, prettified, decorated, ornamented. It is made into an elaborate artefact. Make-up, coiffure, clothing and jewellery complete the 'petrification of body and face'.[78] Women not only consent to be objectified, but they love to do so by themselves. They embrace this corporeal care of the self as a mode of existence. Frivolity reinforces facticity. What we might now see as creative self-fashioning is, in *The Second Sex*, mindless self-objectification for the sake of the male gaze. The '*bourgeoise*' is the champion of such stupidity.

When we read these sentences, when we listen to these metaphors, we can see the semantic shift from *object of* (of desire, of sensorial admiration) to *object-thing*: thing possessed and exchanged, taken and delivered; thing made up, touched up and remodelled; thing heavy, thick, dense and inert, incapable of subjectivity and transcendence.[79] We witness the second birth of reification.

We also see the dawn of feminist thought. We recognize the melodic lines of this intellectual music: dialectic of master and slave (Hegel), connection between private property, land and woman (Marx and Engels), but all against the background of a Kantian harmony. Human beings are persons. Persons are not things. Sex reduces persons to things. Sexual desire is aimed at Woman as a sexed and sexy being rather than as a human. The sexual act is the mutual use of the sexual 'tools' with which bodies are equipped. In the sexual act, 'man makes of himself a thing, which contradicts the right of humanity in his own person.' The leitmotiv that woman is an object and, consequently, an object-thing, derives from all these considerations, as severe as they are imperious, on the human essence.

The pages of *The Metaphysics of Morals* and *Anthropology from a Pragmatic Point of View*, which we have discussed above, resonate with those of *The Second Sex*. First of all, the theme of immanence, inseparable from all that is aesthetic in a woman's corporeal experience – sensuality, care, ornament – can be read as an amplified commentary on Kant's remarks on women. They aim at being desired and therefore cultivate coquetry. It is inconceivable that, for women and for men, there might be a concern for the corporeal self in a sensual and erotic playfulness, experienced between subjects of desires, causes of mutual desire, and desiring bodies. Aesthetics has to be reduced to facticity. Look at the fatty clumps of the female flesh! Aesthetics is frivolity: women have nothing transcendent to do. Secondly, Beauvoir agrees with Kant on the ambivalence of marriage, as the acknowledgement of the humanity of Woman as a holder of rights, on the one hand, and her subjugation, on the other. She also insists on the inevitable outcome of this ambiguous situation: systematic infidelity.[80] Whereas Kant theorizes woman's matrimonial destination, however, Beauvoir rejects it entirely, on behalf of genuine freedom.

Sex can only reify Man, says Kant. Sex reifies Woman, adds Simone de Beauvoir.[81] This is a turning point. Its audacity should not be underestimated. Kant theorizes the subjugation of women but fulminates against all forms of use of the sexual organs outside the matrimonial contract, and he thunders against men who degrade their own humanity in zoophilia, sodomy, the *venus vulgivaga* and the supreme crime against oneself that is masturbation. Beauvoir brings to the fore the division of the sexes. Kant is concerned with the Human Being, albeit with a male connotation, *der Mensch*, who, by manipulating his sexual instrument illegally, makes of himself a thing, compromises the integrity of his person, abdicates his humanity. The other (woman, man, beast or fantasy) is only an instrument of this self-objectification. Beauvoir cares precisely about this Other. The masculine man is a sexual subject who, by definition, never takes the position of an object. On the contrary, man is an autonomous, free, active, conquering and desiring consciousness who needs another human being relative and specular to him. This Other will be woman. Woman is to be situated as an object of Man's desire. She has to beautify, adorn and exhibit her appearance in order to make herself desirable, and, in so doing, she remains entrapped in pure immanence – to be there, as a thing.

Beauvoir's ability to blend Hegel's dialectic and the Kantian/Marxian language of reification is quite a feat. Hegel insists that the struggle for recognition necessarily involves two human consciences: domination cannot succeed; there will be a rebellion. A person cannot be made into a thing: this is the point of dialectic. Marriage, as a consequence, is a union of two persons, as persons. Kant, on the contrary, describes the success of 'becoming thing'. This is what sex does all the time.

At first sight, Simone de Beauvoir ignores or neglects Kant, a preacher overflowing with contempt towards women and their coquettish ways, disgusted by all erotic variations, pitiless towards all that gives pleasure. Beauvoir needs a dynamic perspective, open to a project of emancipation. To reconstruct a history of the difference of the sexes over time, she relies upon a theory of the unstable and perfectible relationship between subjects: the struggle for recognition, with its 'dialectical reversal'. Hegelian dialectic makes it possible to narrate the systematic and necessary oppression of women but also to theorize another future for them. Kantian ethics (which Beauvoir had criticized in *The Ethics of Ambiguity*, published in 1947) had little to offer from this point of view.[82] But she could draw from Kant the reproachful language of the sexual object. Ironically, Beauvoir was going to find in Marx – the Marx whose Kantian formation Althusser would later expose – everything she needed to reopen the macabre dance of Man and the Thing.[83]

Beauvoir brings together these two ideas: 'By a unique privilege, Woman is a consciousness and yet it seems possible to possess her in her flesh.'[84] It is exactly with this small phrase that Beauvoir prises open her Hegelian master text to the Kantian language of the 'thing' (*la chose*) which runs through *The Second Sex*. This is where Hegel's and Kant's moralities blend. This intersection should actually shock us, because, as we have seen, Hegel attacks Kant with vehemence precisely on his vision of sex and marriage, nature and the law. A slave is engaged in a struggle for recognition: this is why s/he can rise up and kill the master. A woman may be subjected, but she is no thing: this is why she can rebel and prevail. Dialectic was expected to go beyond the language of contract – once and for all.

If we wonder why Simone de Beauvoir should choose to mould her theoretical meditation in Kantian terms, we might consider first of all that Kant's idiom did something which for Marxist French philosophers at the time was quite fascinating. In its brutality it could be used to deromanticize bourgeois love. But there is more. The vocabulary of use and possession allowed Beauvoir to expose the political significance of heterosexual intercourse in its very physicality.

First of all, Beauvoir declares that the principle of marriage is 'obscene', on account of the transformation into rights and duties of what ought to remain free and spontaneous love. Marriage gives to the bodies involved an 'instrumental, and therefore degrading, character'.[85] Secondly, when envisioning sex, Beauvoir follows a line of thought that echoes Kant's definition of intercourse. She maintains that, as a premise, differently gendered lovers are absolutely heterogeneous. Although both experience a fundamental ambiguity in feeling themselves as flesh and mind, and in interacting as a desiring subject and as the partner's other, for a woman this is a *specifically* divisive conflict. Because in her entire existence she lives as an object, woman finds it difficult 'to reconquer her dignity as a transcendent and free subject while assuming her carnal condition'.[86] When having sex with a man, woman would like to allow herself to feel, therefore, but it is delicate for her 'to find a confident autonomy in pleasure'.[87] Woman, in other words, tends to resist voluptuous abandonment precisely because she is always, already, so much there, in her flesh, as a living thing. In bed, the full enjoyment of her corporeal sensibility threatens her dignity, transcendence and freedom.[88] As a defence, she will inhibit her ability to have sensations. Frigidity becomes a 'no' uttered by the body itself. It is a rejection of the entire situation: of being physically possessed but also of possessing in return. Beauvoir is daringly clear: penetration is *her* possession of the male organ. A woman wants to have a hold on her lover. This is what a frigid woman resists.[89]

When Beauvoir pictures a woman divided between sensuality and subjectivity, she echoes a familiar language. From her entanglement in lovemaking, a situation in which she engages as an object in the first place, that woman wants to 'recover' (*récupérer*) what makes her properly human.[90] She tries to improvise all by herself exactly what, for Kant, only the law could ever accomplish: the 'winning back' (*gewinnen wiederum*) of one's personhood through mutual possession. A woman can consent to enjoy intercourse, according to Beauvoir, if she feels desired as well as *respected*. Respect is the recognition of freedom: 'if he covets her in her flesh while recognizing her freedom, she recovers her essentialness at the moment she becomes object, she remains free in the submission to which she consents.'[91] Then she will also be able to feel that a man 'belongs to her', not for having married him but by ecstatically welcoming his sex inside her own body. There is no struggle any longer. The legalization of sex is not an option for Beauvoir, but Kant's sexology provides a solution (reconquering one's personality through reciprocal possession), one that Hegel's dialectic and romantic marriage could not offer. Respect is the remedy to frigidity. Although Beauvoir admits that physical love is neither an end nor a means but should be always free, thus never in need of a 'justification' by anything exterior to itself, she also claims that pleasure is 'justified' only by mutual recognition.[92] The context, therefore, rescues eroticism from a degrading instrumentality.

In Beauvoir's immediate environment, Jean-Paul Sartre, her lifelong companion, had engaged with the Kantian legacy in a different manner. In unusually candid pages for a mid-twentieth-century philosopher, Sartre, too, theorizes the erotic situation (which he called 'the caress'), but he also insists on the shared experience of 'enfleshment' (*incarnation*), which undermines domination and usage. Whereas sadism and masochism involve objectification, this kind of sex is precisely an antidote to 'reciprocal use'. It is all about diffused tenderness. As Allen Wood persuasively argues, Sartre lifted his views on the manoeuvring of erotic bodies almost literally from Kant. And Beauvoir in turn responded to him. 'The discussion of Beauvoir on sex depends on Jean-Paul Sartre, who resumed Kant's vision of sex with modifications mainly terminological and stylistic. Sexual desire, in particular, seeks to objectify the other in order to capture the freedom of the other.'[93]

We will come back to Sartre's art of love.[94] Maurice Merleau-Ponty, one of Beauvoir's closest friends, understood perfectly that a human being, a human body, could never be objectified – especially not through erotic attention and in sexual situations. It is just not possible.[95] To such impossibility, we should add the very definition of desire. Desire cares not for things but for a desiring consciousness. Or, as Lacan would put it, desire clings to partial objects, which are perceived as its powerful cause. Or, even better, desire responds to its *hundred* causes, as Ovid, before everyone else, had the wit to sing. Desire, unfortunately, is not a matter of respect.

To possess her in her flesh

The impact of dialectical thought on Kantian sexual humanism can be seen through a magnifying glass: it is the Other that becomes a thing. Gender emerges: the Other is female. We see the Marxist inflection: woman has a connection with private property. But we also see the insinuating ruse of the metaphysics of the sexes, which produces anti-modern effects: heteronormativity, obliviousness to women's creativity, idealization of a disembodied masculinity. The prose of Simone de Beauvoir lingers with disturbing complacency and condescension on the details of the female body, blaming the facticity, thickness, gravity, inertia and various prostheses of this body/flesh/thing. Feminine materiality confronts a masculine subjectivity, which may deviate from its essential vocation to transcendence only in the camp frivolousness of the 'pederasts'. These are the only males, for Beauvoir, who take the trouble to dress elegantly, which places them *ipso facto* on the side of women. True men do not play the role of objects of desire. They do not take care of their bodies – which, therefore, never exist as things.

Of course, one needs only to read a bit of history and anthropology (not to mention psychoanalysis) to know that this is false. Love between individuals of the same sex is not a gender inversion. Male flesh does exist, anxiously and narcissistically cultivated. The feminine concern for the body is very interesting, on the other hand, even among coquettes, of all time and in all cultures. It is an exemplary experience of performativity. The woman who makes herself beautiful knows her imperfection, accepts it and corrects it to give pleasure both to herself and to those whose desire she appreciates. A woman who dresses up knows that tastes change and takes pleasure in this change. A woman who moisturizes her skin closely follows her ageing, watching and mastering this fatal metamorphosis with humility and irony. In her own way, the shallowest woman demonstrates an intelligence of finitude. She knows that time is passing.[96] She does not risk collapsing at one stroke on the day when her sexual organ no longer works as well as it once did. Above all, as we have said, a woman who places herself in the trajectory of the desire of the other is not a thing. An object of gaze, attention, admiration, respect is not automatically an object-thing. One is free to confuse them: it is a rhetorical choice. We are also free not to anchor feminist thought in this confusion.

After reading Beauvoir with devotion in the 1970s, I return to these pages today with a mixture of surprise, annoyance and discomfort.

First of all, I see the potential of this thought as a path that was taken and yet interrupted. The dialectical shaping of the difference between the sexes is resolutely interactive and interpersonal. In echoing Hegel, Beauvoir writes that man 'is alone when he touches a stone, alone when he digests a piece of fruit'.[97] Inanimate things are incapable of giving to him that recognition of which he has a vital need. Only another human being can be 'present', specular but active, for another human being: 'It is the existence of other men that wrests each man from his immanence and enables him to accomplish the truth of his being, to accomplish himself as transcendence, as flight towards the object, as a project.'[98]

So what happens when this dynamic, anxious and ambitious man meets a woman? He makes her an 'intermediary' between the world of natural things – stones, fruits – and that of his fellow men. Women do not struggle to be recognized, as their male rivals do. 'By a unique privilege [woman] is a consciousness, and yet it seems possible to possess her in her flesh.'[99] We have already discussed this crucial passage. Woman's flesh could be seen as the expressive embodiment of different kinds of gendered projects. It is merely the locus of inertia. It is the incarnation of a failure, that of transcending oneself towards the world. It is the matter on which men exercise power, as sexual possession.

Secondly, the resonance with Kantian thought is troubling. The fact of 'seeing things everywhere', in Althusser's words, creates an impression of evidence and makes us feel good about ourselves. Let us lash out at any form of stylishness and self-fashioning, and we shall have resisted gender domination. Let us chastise those who prefer blondes and, even more, the blondes who like to be preferred. Let us dress as plainly as we possibly can. But why should this be of any political significance? Because sexual desire objectifies and dehumanizes. The language of objectification presupposes this major premise. To make it into a feminist principle, or a watchword, means to ratify, more or less consciously, this presupposition whose pedigree we have already seen: a conception of humanity that pits the person against the body, will against the senses, goodness against pleasure.

This kind of feminism was timely in the 1970s, when women's focalization on their looks could be associated with inferiority and incompetence in all the domains of active life except the family. It was a prejudice, of course, upheld by actual exclusion. As a matter of fact, for middle-class women, social and professional confinement, not below a glass ceiling but within the thick walls of domestic space, did indeed correlate with what Beauvoir calls 'immanence'. Women were obliged to embrace a lifestyle of docile compliance with men's desires. Their bodies spoke to that submission. And yet: are we sure that there was no creativity at all in their existence? Were they simply conforming to a stereotype? And is conformity to a stereotype the only possible reason why women would ever dream of cultivating their aesthetic persona?

Contemporary women, in North America and in Europe, show that this is not the case. Younger women who have grown up enjoying rights and seizing opportunities (to choose a career, to practise contraception, to manage maternity) want precisely, and even more, to 'lend to palpitating life the frozen necessity of artifice'.[100] They feel free to become 'plant, panther, diamond, mother-of-pearl'. Flowers, precious stones, seashells, feathers, silks, pearls, perfumes: these can be bought at *J. Crews*, *Zara* or *Sephora* for a few dollars. Coquetry goes hand in hand with high social and professional ambitions. I can see this every day, in the streets of Paris and on campus at UCLA.[101] The female body, worked out, shaped up, injected, painted, inked, pierced and imaginatively exposed, has become compatible with self-confident and audacious forms of subjectivity. Made up and conquering, well toned and hard-working, sexy and nerdy, my students are especially not 'pasted into immanence'.

Beauvoir could not foresee that 'transcendence', meaning the ability to project oneself into the world, could be accompanied by an unbridled taste for the sheer joy of affording cheap luxuries and making daily fashion statements. She could not predict the liberal future of democracy and its individualistic outcomes. Neo-Kantian feminism cannot appreciate these women either.

Freedom, infidelity, jealousy

The history of this theory, which has influenced left-wing political culture so strongly, is indispensable for understanding how in all good conscience we have come to despise amorous jealousy. It is on the basis of the transformation of the object *of* love into a thing that erotic anger has been reduced to possessiveness – and unforgivingly blamed.

The Second Sex, which Simone de Beauvoir published in 1949, is the founding text of French feminism. This book combines phenomenology and the language of post-Kantian existentialism (freedom, situation, transcendence, immanence, subject, object, thing, etc.) with a critical adherence to Marxism. Drawing selectively from the writings of Marx and Engels, Beauvoir inscribes the vicissitudes of woman in those of private property.[102] The monogamous family exists only as a corollary of the appropriation of land. The landowner is, therefore, jealous. He is even the inventor of jealousy. We have seen this powerful association of ideas in Rousseau's narrative of the origin of inequality. Although Beauvoir sees the drive to possession as a primordial transcendence of the human subject (not the effect of economic causation), she shares the same adamant certainty. 'When woman becomes man's property,' she writes, 'he wants a virgin, and he demands total fidelity at the risk of severe penalty.'[103] Of course, the man's motivation can only be the concern to preserve the transmission of goods within the family, to an heir who must be his own, safe and legitimate. As long as there is private property, the strain on fidelity will be considered, for a woman, as a 'high treason'.[104] And yet infidelity prospers.

Man has snatched woman from nature, enslaved her, made her into his property, and established the rites of marriage in order to defend his ownership. As a result, he deprives her of charm. Marriage kills love. For having desired 'a lovely young girl, the male must spend his whole life feeding a heavy matron, a dried-out old woman; the delicate jewel intended to embellish his existence becomes an odious burden.'[105] If he is polygamous, he will have several wives more or less ravaged, who in turn pass from gorgeousness to horror.[106] Men watch their precious possessions. But, in spite of everything, women take liberties. Once again, marriage creates a situation of ambivalence. By taking her as a wife, a man raises a woman 'to the dignity of a human person'. While sequestering her in the house, therefore, he recognizes a freedom. Remember Kant! A woman is a sexy thing; a wife is a person. Furthermore, man does things in 'half measures'. A wife is neither a slave nor an inanimate thing. But even this makes her dangerous. She will enjoy the consciousness of her freedom in the only way accessible to her: adultery. As long as there is marriage, says Beauvoir, there will be adultery. On the one hand, therefore, woman is reduced to the servitude and immanence of a corporeal existence (Kant/Marx). On the other hand, she is nevertheless a person, able to escape this role (Hegel). Woman is 'fated to infidelity: it is the only concrete form her freedom can assume.' For to be the object of the desire of another man is her only way of proving that she is 'the thing of no one'.[107]

Extramarital sex is an elementary form of transcendence. The only one to which this sensual being sprawled in immanence, this fleshy thing entrenched between nature and artifice that is woman, can possibly aspire. The Kantian lump of thingness comes to Hegelian life only to make use of her sexual apparatus. On the masculine side, according to Beauvoir, polygyny is natural. Almost all societies practise this form of marriage. It is not known why the Greeks did not embrace it: no doubt it was because the maintenance of a harem was so expensive that only an oriental despot could afford such luxury.[108] The male accumulates women as he piles up wealth. And he is extremely jealous of both. Rightly so, Beauvoir argues, because Woman is unfaithful 'over and above her own desires, her thoughts, or her consciousness'. The simple fact of being the ever-potential object of men's desire, of being offered 'to all subjectivity that chooses to take her', makes Beauvoir's woman similar, paradoxically, to those creatures whom Marcel Proust calls 'fugitives' (*êtres de fuite*).[109] A woman is always available and virtually ready to flee. In addition, in order to put to the test her only chance of freedom, she is flirtatious. Man can only live in the torments of insatiable anguish.

The conjugal situation ruins love, provokes adultery and arouses jealousy. Man dominates and possesses, knowing only too well that he will never be assured of holding full control of his property. Woman enjoys cheating under cover, by telling lies and devising all sorts of subterfuges. She is not jealous of her man, however, because she basically doesn't care. The sex of man has always been a 'lay' piece of anatomy, bereft of religious and magical meanings. The wives of polygamous men do not particularly worship the phallus they have to share and adapt easily to their cohabitation. In modern societies, the secularity of masculine sexuality brings about a generalized tolerance towards flings without 'gravity'.[110] Andromache's blues, again: men are polygamous. Why bother? Eros is insignificant anyway.

Simone de Beauvoir considers with materialistic dispassion the asymmetry of the sexes whose transhistorical advent she describes. She wants to demonstrate how radical and absolutely necessary such an asymmetry had to be. But the arrangement of causes and effects leads to a rationalization of sexual intercourse, which makes love non-existent, as a sentiment in its own rights. The erotic per se is equally downplayed. The real thing is economic power. Sex is merely one of its expressions. The rest is ideology. The Kantian idiom of objectification comes in handy as a convenient parlance, ready-made to cast pleasure and desire in these instrumental terms. Polygamous and domineering men appropriate women who respond by being unfaithful and resigned, if not indifferent. The necessary complement of such unsavoury interaction is female anaesthesia: there is no jealousy.

The Hegelian marriage, a spiritual and conscious union of two human beings, is not part of the picture. Neither is romantic love. Kant has prevailed. But, interestingly, Beauvoir's Kant cannot be the normative theorist of marriage. Marriage, for Kant, creates *mutual* and *exclusive* possession, so that both partners enjoy the privilege of using *each other's* bodies and can treat each other as persons. Reciprocal fidelity is crucial. This is the significance of monogamy. Beauvoir despises marriage altogether. Woman is desired only for the sake of her body and in view of sex. Any passion for singularity is completely foreign to this vision. There is no preference, no quest for reciprocity, and no erotic anger. The desire for the other person's desire becomes unilateral and unidirectional: men impose their domination and appropriation onto women. Females consent to being dominated and appropriated. Woman deviates from her condition of thing only by sexual infidelity. On marriage, Beauvoir espouses Marx's economic vision of the origin of the family and property. The bourgeoisie, chanted the *Communist Manifesto*, 'has drowned the most heavenly ecstasies of religious fervour, of chivalrous enthusiasm, of *petit-bourgeois* sentimentalism, in the icy water of egotistical calculation.'[111]

In the world of the *Second Sex*, there are no petty bourgeois.

Transparency

Words of love abound, however, in the *Lettres au Castor et à quelques autres* (Letters to the Beaver and to a few others), part of the correspondence between Simone de Beauvoir, affectionately nicknamed 'the Beaver' (*le Castor*), and Jean-Paul Sartre. These two thick volumes, which Beauvoir herself saw to print, contain a few letters that Sartre addressed to lovers, such as Simone Jolivet (Toulouse) and Bianca Bienenfeld, alias 'Louise Védrine'. Those addressed to Beauvoir herself are affectionate, tender, and full of narratives and allusions to the numerous affairs the philosopher had had in the past or was currently pursuing. And here we can observe how this iconic couple practised their brand of 'free love': their own relationship, based on a strong, irreplaceable, unique attachment (their love was 'necessary'), combined with the liberty to undertake multiple collateral liaisons (which were, on the contrary, merely 'contingent').[112] The whole thing had to be conducted with no lies, no deceitfulness, no duplicities, but in complete honesty. The letters bear witness, in real time, to this transparency.

With Jean-Paul Sartre, Simone de Beauvoir experimented with a couple as stable as compatible with parallel erotic relationships. The pact was clear. Within a necessary love, we can, or, better, we must, say everything and tell everything about our occasional arousals, tempting fantasies, passing infatuations or actual 'contingent' loves. The more honest we are, the more accurate our accounts of our feelings will have to be. The more sincere we are, the more realistic our perception of the other person involved will have to sound. Our goodness, as the worthy members of such a special couple, is all in this dutiful truthfulness. On the receiving side, we must lend an infinitely generous ear to every single confidence, listen to every evocative detail, read what we are asked to read, look at photographs, give advice, offer consolation and, of course, even make friends with our partner's love interest. Where is the problem? To the virtuous, admirable, heroic frankness of one partner – who is magnanimous

SEXUAL OBJECTS AND OPEN COUPLES

enough to tell all – must correspond the unconditional availability, and even the curiosity, of the other.

Sartre proposed and Beauvoir accepted a polygamous contract. The partners stay together on account of an absolutely free choice of each other, not because of a binding commitment. The full acknowledgement of the other person's freedom requires that their sexual drives should never be hindered. Each one just does whatever s/he wants. The other one just puts up with it. Rather than through a pledge to reciprocal fidelity, the pair is united by a licence to copulate elsewhere. Tough love! In such a situation, jealousy is not welcome. The jealousy that gives you nausea, ruins your appetite, prevents you from sleeping, makes you cry in front of strangers, forces you to look in horror at your image in the mirror because you seem visibly to have lost weight – real jealousy, with its real effects, is simply out of the question. More: it is forbidden. If you dare to suffer from this inferior sentiment, so much the worse for you.

If we place this experience in the context of *The Second Sex*, we can see how Beauvoir borrows from Kant the blame of objectification but rejects the Kantian remedy, namely marriage, with the consequent right, and even the obligation, to claim a spouse as a possession. To be a man's property, and to sneak out of this prison only to become another man's gizmo: this is what women have done for millennia! On the contrary, Beauvoir will not become anyone's object, and she will not make her preferred partner into an object of her own proprietary desire. She will endure Sartre's women.

Comedy

We might ask a few questions.

Firstly, is arrogance the cost of feeling unthreatened by rivalry? In the utterly special relation she had with Sartre, Beauvoir was never in competition. She was above the fray. She was safe. The other women appear to be inferior enough to guarantee her pre-eminence. Wanda Kosakiewicz, alias Tania, had the brain of a dragonfly. What a burden![113] 'Martine Bourdin' was a starry-eyed, manipulative actress who tried to seduce Merleau-Ponty and Sartre himself. She could become unbearable, vulgar and jittery. She did not know what to do about her virginity. She had violent mood swings.[114] We could go on. The letters can be read as a feuilleton of unflattering scenes in the streets of Rouen or Paris, in hotels, restaurants, cafés and various bedrooms. These vignettes were obviously meant to amuse their addressee at the expense of the women involved. Sartre kept Beauvoir posted on the vicissitudes of his *galanterie* in an epistolary sitcom.

The two of them were complicit in their mockery. While writing freely about his sexual relations, Sartre sent continual reassurances to the Beaver: these interchangeable women were more or less sensual, more or less boring, more or less tiresome, more or less capricious, more or less socially inept – and never as intelligent as she was. They were just part of absurd, contingent moments that made him feel 'the nothingness of the flesh' (*le néant de la chair*).[115] In contrast, the Beaver, as Sartre wrote to one of these endlessly belittled mistresses, Bianca Bienenfeld, was *always perfect*.[116] Sartre offered to Beauvoir the constant confirmation that, if anyone might feel a twinge of jealousy, it would have to be one of those second-rate women. And she would have every reason to be jealous of her, Simone de Beauvoir. Who else? Was not she the greatest of them all? The jealousy of other women for her was not proof of their vulnerability, therefore: it was fully justified. Sartre himself gave his blessings to that jealousy, 'which derived from a right sentiment, in [his] opinion' (*Ce qui procède d'un sentiment juste, à mon avis*). He gallantly offered the jealousy of 'little Bourdin' (*la petite Bourdin*) to the Beaver as homage: it enhanced her matchless superiority. She should not feel diminished. And, by the way, he was doing his very best to remain 'all together' with her (*tout uni avec vous*).[117] By publishing these particular letters, Beauvoir created a formidable game of mirrors. She advertised to the entire world that, in the eyes of Sartre, she had always been not the One, perhaps, but indisputably the Best.

Secondly, what kind of love can resist the erotic mobility of the beloved? We might speculate that Beauvoir probably applied to herself the kind of demystified, jaded, cynical attitude she projects onto the women who, in her ethnographic reckoning, happily adjust to polygyny. These women, she claims in *The Second Sex*, do not make a fuss about the phallus. They have given up on eros. This is the secret of their sanguineness. In her own couple, the pact became an 'absolute fraternity'.[118] Just like Andromache, once again, these women find jealousy ridiculous – Hi, Hi! Hermione is jealous of the rain! – only because they find eros utterly insignificant and worthy of sarcasm.

Thirdly, is true equality possible when a covenant is stipulated about sexual adventurousness? Between Beauvoir and Sartre, reciprocity seemed perfect. In turn, Simone and Jean-Paul allowed themselves other loves. The pact, however, had started at Sartre's initiative – he was polygamous. And, while the Beaver takes a serious male lover from time to time, Sartre passes from one affair to another. Is this really reciprocity, or is it a nominal liberty to match the restlessness of a very lustful man? Because of Beauvoir's reticence about her loves with women, it is difficult to answer this question.[119]

The best-known relationship is that with Bianca Bienenfeld. When Beauvoir was a teacher of philosophy at the Lycée Molière in Paris, she had a very special friendship with this brilliant teenage girl. In the summer after Bianca took her *Baccalauréat*, what started as a privileged intellectual intimacy became an erotic affair. Then Beauvoir introduced Bianca to Sartre. They created a trio that was supposed to be unique and to last forever. But, suddenly, at the beginning of the war, the two adults terminated the affair. The experience resulted in a devastating disappointment and serious psychological troubles for Bianca. Being Jewish, she went through a horrible period of danger and persecution, during which her former lovers showed no concern at all for her. And yet, after the war, Bianca resumed her friendship with Beauvoir. An amiable bond was saved. But an even crueller disillusion awaited her. In 1990, Sylvie Le Bon de Beauvoir, another of Beauvoir's younger and closest friends, whom she had formally adopted, edited the posthumous publication of Beauvoir's letters to Sartre. In those pages Bianca discovered how she had been treated all along.[120] Her adored mentor, whom she had so loved all her life, used to speak disparagingly about her, by calling her 'pathetic' and deriding her naiveté. Worst of all was the revelation of this venerated creature's character: her resentment, vulgarity, meanness, hypocrisy, and also her jealousy. Once again, the 'absolute fraternity' of the philosophical couple was glued together by mockery. In response to such disloyalty, Bianca wrote her own autobiographical account, *A Disgraceful Affair* (*Mémoires d'une jeune fille dérangée*).[121]

Was Beauvoir immune from jealousy? What follows might come across as a piece of indelicate gossip or as an unusually candid admission to *Schadenfreude*, but it should be taken as a symptom of the taboo of jealousy. Gisèle Halimi has been a public figure in France: a distinguished lawyer, a member of parliament, a feminist activist and a successful writer. She knew Beauvoir very well. In 2009, she disclosed how surprised she felt one day, when she happened to hear a loud argument from behind a closed door. Beauvoir was shouting at Sartre. She was accusing, recriminating, and asking for some reparation. It was 'a classic scene of jealousy' (*une scène de jalousie classique*), nothing less! Halimi marvelled at the normalcy of the situation. It was liberating. The woman who had sealed a 'pact of liberty' and had seemed 'to overcome with the most complete serenity the contradictions that tear apart the common man', that supernatural creature could sound like a hurt woman and 'yield to a scene of jealousy' (*se livrer à une scène de jalousie*). Halimi acknowledged her relief: having always fought, inhibited and 'forbidden' (*interdit*) her own jealousy, she was now pleased that Simone de Beauvoir was human enough, after all, to suffer 'like a wounded woman' (*comme une femme blessée*).[122] This sounds like *Schadenfreude*. Personally, I feel deeply sorry for Simone, Gisèle, Bianca and all the women who waste their time battling, repressing or denying the most normal of their amorous feelings.

And how about Sartre: was he ever jealous? He ridiculed jealousy, of course. 'A cuckold is to die of laughter' (*Un cocu, c'est à mourir de rire*), he famously said. But he also used a claim to singularity in his courtship. To Simone Jolivet he could write that his deepest desire was to be for her, in her love, not the first man, but the only one (*c'est que je voudrais être non le premier mais le seul dans votre amour*). This was the most painful and difficult (*pénible*) confession to make for him. Why? Because of his 'superficial shame' (*honte superficielle*) and, above all, because of 'the odious fear of ridicule' (*l'odieuse crainte du ridicule*).[123] We shall see that, for Sartre, love was indeed the project to be loved, the desire to become the object of the other's desire, therefore to find a place in that person's love. It suffices here to take in the tragicomic coherence of this erotic *mise-en-scène*. In Beauvoir's and Sartre's eyes, or at least in their reciprocal exchanges (the trustworthiness of which is yet another story), contingent women were pathetic, because love was ridiculous.

Finally, what is the difference between 'the pact' and the good old asymmetry between a womanizer and a devoted woman who endures her trouble in patience? In two of her novels, *L'Invitée* and *La Femme rompue*, Beauvoir gives us the poignant account of this patience, of this suffering. These pages sound true, like those of Catherine Millet's *Jealousy*, Annie Ernaux's *L'Occupation*, or the narrative thought of Stendhal and Proust. Instead of making an immense voluntaristic effort of self-anaesthesia, these voices confess, to begin with, how difficult it is to say: 'I am jealous'.

Cruelty

Another French philosopher, Louis Althusser, who at the same time and in the same political milieu practised a plural sexuality while being married, has left us a brutal autobiographical testimony.

He likes to pursue, boldly and cheerfully, beautiful young women. He likes to do so in front of Hélène, his wife. He also likes to tell her all about his encounters, as quickly as possible. He never stops talking to her about his girlfriends. This is because he is trying to get her approval, he explains. Hélène is too important for him: she must give her blessing on his sexual choices. Now Hélène, it goes without saying, is not jealous. How could she dare to be? She is an intransigent communist. She wants him to be 'free'. She respects his desires, his needs and his whims. He remarks, however, that her initial tolerance for this kind of situation always turns into harshness in the end. Since at first she is patient, Althusser is at a loss, and he fails to understand why on earth her mood should change in this way. To him it is a mystery. As a result, he subjects her to the kind of wild psychoanalytical diagnosis Freud would have loathed. If she goes from forbearance to anger, she must be ambivalent. The thing is: Hélène is afraid of being a shrew. She throws scenes of jealousy, and after the scenes she asks for forgiveness and promises to do better next time. She begs him not to tell her, however, about his affairs. Ultimately, discretion is the only condition she asks him to respect. Could he, please, spare her! Before she knows, he is at it again. He cannot help himself. He is too honest.

One day, in their house on the Côte d'Azur, near Saint-Tropez, Althusser seduces before Hélène's eyes a very attractive young woman. He takes her to the beach and then out to sea. They swim offshore and almost make love in the waves. Then a strong current makes the return unexpectedly perilous. The unhappy spectator of these frolics enters into a state of despair, which Althusser interprets in his favour: Hélène must be awfully worried about him drowning! What else? She runs away and disappears from sight. Later Althusser finds Hélène 'on the seaside, but far from the beach, unrecognizable, completely curled up on herself, trembling with an almost hysterical crisis and with the face of a very old woman ravaged with tears'. Medea. And, like Medea, she finally shouts: Ignoble! Coward! Bastard! – the same words as in Euripides' tragedy. The great philosopher has an instant of clairvoyance: 'Decidedly one cannot treat a human being in this way.' He suddenly realizes that she was not afraid for his safety but was terrified of being killed on the spot by 'his horrible provocation'.

The open couple could seduce as a political project, full of good intentions. Superior synthesis of freedom and sincerity; emotional security and erotic entertainment; trust and confidence – all of the above, in an equal and reciprocal relationship. It might have worked well for some. Between Beauvoir and Sartre, however, the balance was not exactly even. And between Althusser and his unfortunate wife, whom he ended up by strangling: what happens to the erotic contract? The man takes his ease without incurring the least danger, for the (necessary) woman cannot risk leaving him or doing the same – she is simply not beautiful enough. He boasts and shows off without any scruple, for the (Marxist) woman is not jealous – out of the question. He inflicts derogatory interpretations on her, for the (hysterical) woman is either to be blamed or to be cured – he knows better. By its ideological arrogance, its moral intimidation and its ostentatious indelicacy, this version of jealousy as a forbidden passion is undoubtedly the cruellest and crudest of them all.

Rights, habits and bodies

In conclusion, the language of objectification supposes a major premise. Sexual desire, by targeting the body as its intentional object, brings about a change of status: it makes the person into an object/thing. This is bad. Kant frames the erotic experience within a legal, and religious, vision of objectification. Beauvoir focuses on male desire for women as intrinsically objectifying. For both, eros is the culprit. Does eros deserve this blanket accusation? No, he does not, because it is desire for the other's desire. Desire hyper-personifies. Unless we take rape as a paradigm of heterosexual intercourse, in order to do justice to the erotic experience we have to acknowledge this dynamic. Furthermore, whenever we adopt the parlance of objectification, we step into a rhetorical morass in which it becomes only too easy to put the blame on women. They must be complicit in allowing themselves to be part of the game, and they are, therefore, blameworthy. Objectification requires self-objectification. Hence the tone of Kant's prose, but also that of Beauvoir, which roams between offensive contempt and condescending irony. Women's care of the self is mere compliance with men's fantasies. Their life is stuck in the silly facticity of the body. Femininity is the nemesis of feminism.

We should ask, however, two questions.

Firstly: are there conditions in which heterosexual desire deserves to be blamed? Yes, of course. If we do not start from a negative view of sex as beastly and immoral, the criterion is adult consent. There are relationships of domination, humiliation, exploitation of which sexual partners are the victims. Eros can be replaced by violence and by indifference to the other's desire. This is sexual assault, which is the very opposite of eroticism. When we want to define and describe such anti-erotic sex, however, the appropriate language is that of power and status.[124] The larger theoretical picture is the failure to recognize the other person, thus to take seriously what s/he does and, above all, what s/he wants. This language captures the forces at work in coercion and disregard. Failure to give proper recognition can be implemented by forcing people to act in certain ways and to suffer unwanted acts. But this does not reduce people to things. Much worse! It makes them the sentient, humiliated, hurting victims of violence. It may even project an obscene, fantasized desire upon them as an excuse for attacking them. Coercion requires the acknowledgement of people's own will and desires, but only to deny respect to them. Power can only be exercised upon an agent whose agency one thwarts, and who feels pain.

Secondly: what can we say about the focus on self-objectification in the discourse of second-wave feminism? Gender relations involve three dimensions: rights, habits and bodies. Rights have changed. After the original feminism, that of universal suffrage, after the second wave of the 1970s, which successfully promoted a whole range of rights – contraception, abortion, the Civil Rights Act, Title IX, equal opportunity and affirmative action – it is time to recognize the effects of those rights on younger generations. Women who grew up in a largely secularized society and in an increasingly egalitarian erotic culture, namely women who find it obvious to work, earn and spend their own money; women who decide how to live, how to dress and how to educate their children; women who take the initiative in their sex lives – these women cannot then be asked to give up their sovereignty over their own embodiment. For the simple reason that they do not feel like it. This means that habits and bodies have also changed, but not in the direction Beauvoir might have imagined. Younger women take a completely different perspective on their freedom of choice from those who had to fight for self-determination. That first struggle for recognition had to break down the powerful association between women's aesthetic and erotic presence, on the one hand, and exclusionary and demeaning opinions on their abilities, on the other. Women's embodiment was correlated with beliefs about their inferiority. A feminist, therefore, had to start from there. The cost was a critique and a renunciation of typically feminine forms of identity, focused on the body maternal and erotic. But if feminist theory is meant to uphold emancipation, and if the emancipation of actual women brings about a variety of compatible identities, then contemporary feminism should yield to this evidence: this is what empowered women want. They can be proud of their womanliness, because *now* it is compatible with activities, competition and achievements. There is no reason to give it up. There are new aesthetic languages, new trends in love, new lifestyles. There are, in short, not only rights but also new bodies and habits.

All this can be brought to bear on jealousy. For Kant, legalized reciprocal possession is the only redemption from the dehumanizing cannibalism of the sexual act. Jealousy is a claim to a right. For Beauvoir, heterosexuality is objectifying, marriage is the appropriation of a woman, and men are indeed jealous as well as polygamous. Woman has to transcend the feminine body, resist the matrimonial trap, abhor the quagmire of possession, and ban jealousy altogether. In exchange, she will have to embrace polygamy to the full.

We are back to the forbidden passion. But if we refuse to step aboard this vintage train of thought, then we can afford the luxury of being honestly jealous.

— 4 —

THE DESPAIR OF NOT BEING LOVED

Jealousy is suffering. The first feeling, before anger, terror, vanity or shame, is, as Stendhal would have it, a dagger-blow to the heart, molten lead in the chest. It is the tears we shed, whatever we do to restrain them. It is the emaciation of a body that feels so heavy it cannot move; it is fatigue together with insomnia. It is restlessness despite the aching slowness of our movements; it is dehydration coupled with thirst. It is trying to stick to the routines of daily life while being unable to make the simplest gestures. It is the memory of everything that has been done for, and with, that other person, the memory of a time shared and given. Or it is the thought of what one might have done – the longing for a time that has become impossible. It is the crushing proof that *their* presence is even more precious than we had imagined. She, or he, bruises us, and yet contact with them steadies us. The things that s/he did or did not do with us (or did for us), s/he will now be doing with another. We know just how that person described his or her past loves; thus will we, surely, in our turn, be subjected to unflattering comparisons and, doubtless, to a cruel caricature of our failings. Swept away by the sense of an incomparable intimacy, we have now become nothing more than one memory among many. Because being jealous means not conceding one's singularity, not giving up on the irreplaceable, and clinging to privilege, it is absolute despair. We cannot rid ourselves of the object of our love. In its own way, jealousy is a form of fidelity.

Paying proper attention to these brute feelings means re-examining in detail an experience that different normative languages have covered with a moralizing clamour, which is always cruel and not infrequently sarcastic. Only the suspension of judgement as to all that might be behind/before/inside/underneath jealousy will take us back to that first experience which is our own – real, present and vivid.

Neither imaginary nor sublime

If there exists a philosophy which has the right to concern itself with what affects us, with some hope that it might help us, it is phenomenology. We find such a reflection in the work of Nicolas Grimaldi. Relying on his reading of Marcel Proust's *Remembrance of Things Past*, Grimaldi goes into detail about love and longing but then reiterates the woefully mistaken idea, so dear to the censorious, that jealousy is a 'psychopathology of the imagination'. 'It is based on nothing. Nothing can justify it. Dependent upon suppositions, doubt, and suspicion, it is a delirium of the imagination, which sometimes seems to be as gratuitous as a parlour game.'[1] To this idea – which, as we shall see, bears no resemblance whatsoever to the vision of Marcel Proust – he adds another with which we are now all too familiar: for Proust, and apparently for Grimaldi, there would seem to be a 'secret belittling of the self' at the root of jealousy.[2] Grimaldi repeats the constant refrain of the philosophers of the past, whether they be Stoic or libertine, whenever they find themselves annoyed in the face of pain. For them jealousy can only ever be what Rousseau called 'that sullen and sorrowful fantasy', and Diderot, the 'indication that we distrust our own merits, and the confession of the superiority of a rival'. Similarly for Grimaldi, jealousy is a 'scenography of the imaginary'[3] which 'has not the slightest relationship with reality'.[4] It is nothing other than an illusion that makes one 'feel secretly unworthy'.[5] Shame, then, on any jealous person who is unashamed!

By contrast, in a manner less blind to the experience and infinitely more respectful of its suffering, Jean-Luc Marion has written a veritable eulogy of jealousy. His are unusual, and remarkable, observations:

> When he who loves and has been loved is betrayed, he who has loved, and who loves still but is no longer loved, must continue to love. Now, it is in fact he who has the best part, since it is the other who has given up. It is the one who ceases to love who has lost. We must therefore praise jealousy, a sublime feeling which has been unjustly denigrated! What is sublime about jealousy – for so it may be – is that I am jealous not because the other has betrayed me, but because he has betrayed his status as a lover. I reproach him, the lover, because he has stopped playing the game.[6]

This audacious thought is also written in the wake of Marcel Proust's *Remembrance of Things Past*. Proust's narrative shows us that jealousy is love. Marion theorizes this equivalence. Furthermore, his thought asks that we distinguish between the learned discourse on jealousy by La Rochefoucauld and the moralists of the seventeenth and eighteenth centuries, on the one hand, and what *we ourselves* might have to say in the first-person singular, on the other. As Christophe Perrin, a philosopher who is closely associated with Marion, has argued, this thought demands that we move away from the 'one' so as to return to the 'I'. 'One' makes superficial, hasty and overbearing judgements on an emotion which, as soon as 'I' question and examine it, becomes something entirely different.[7] As I am jealous, I know that my jealousy is nothing other than my perseverance in love. It is my fidelity that endures. I have all the appearance of having lost, but I have 'won'. For Marion, love must be a gift which precedes gratuitously any response, and which is perfectly disinterested. Love, as Perrin says, 'belongs to the intrepid, not the chemist, to those who dare, not those who measure', hence its 'rationality', which is generous, explosive, sublime.[8] Love must go ahead. Love must pre-empt any consideration of exchange or competition. Jealousy, therefore, accomplishes such duty.

I am jealous

I share this view. The historical and textual work I have done in this book points in precisely this direction. My wish is to uncover the lineages of the systematic condemnation to which jealousy has been subjected. But, from my own experience as one who has both been unfaithful and suffered the pangs of jealousy, I cannot subscribe to an 'I' who is at once wretched and stubborn, ravaged yet willing to turn the other cheek, in short a Catholic 'I' – like Marion – sacrificial and disinterested. What I am suggesting instead is an ethics of reciprocity and, more exactly, of reciprocal pleasure. For in love there is an expectation of joy, of justice, of worth. I fully agree that jealousy should be praised, but for reasons of equality and loyalty, and not through any wish to make a stingy assessment of our losses and gains, but because anyone who breaks the agreement of desires makes the other *suffer*. Infidelity is unforgiveable. We try, of course, to understand, to turn the page, to make all manner of accommodations; but, for all that, a breech has been opened up in the heart of love.

I therefore recognize myself in the 'I' of the ancients. I also recognize myself in an 'I' which is not 'kitsch', and by kitsch I mean, as Milan Kundera uses the term, an 'I' who takes pleasure in offering an edifying, self-righteous testimony on his or her life, and who contemplates such an image with 'emotional admiration'. All is well that ends well. Thanks to the pain I have become who I am – and I am wonderful. In short, I shall have the last word, and I will use it to declare to the world: look at me; I am the triumphant hero of my own misfortunes! My 'I' is more modestly ironic: furious, candid and realistic. Suffering serves no purpose. I would happily have done without the injuries that have been inflicted on me, and all those that I have inflicted on others. I have bounced back, moved on. Doubtless I have also learned something, but that has not compensated one jot for all this useless unhappiness.

In the end, I recognize myself in a gendered 'I'. Women have no monopoly on the pains of jealousy – far from it – but it is they who have been institutionally denied the right to be jealous. Polygamy – which is in fact polygyny – can only be practised at a price. Whether among the Mormons in Utah or those non-European peoples where it is the custom, this asymmetry cannot work unless the wives are prepared to concede this favour to their husbands. As Montaigne says of his cannibals, their wives are are 'more concerned for the honour of their husbands than for anything else'. This is why they 'take care to let them have as many companions as possible, since that is a testimony to their husband's valour.' In our own cultures, we are, for our part, accustomed to the sight of the wives of politicians whose infidelities have been on public display across the screens of the world. Clenched and mute, pallid and overly made-up, they stand stiffly upright beside their men. And while the husbands proffer profuse public apologies, their wives support them stoically. They are the modern icons of the shame to confess. With barely suppressed fury, they comply with the obligation to behave as if nothing had happened. Seneca would have been proud of them. 'It is virtue proper to matrimony', but from 'an earlier age' – as Montaigne would have said.

In reality it is an abdication. For women to accept with good grace the sexual pluralism of men is a renunciation of both reciprocity and singularity. If one of the principles of feminism is the demand that every woman be recognized as an equal, then to claim the right to jealousy is a feminist gesture. And this despite the fact that Simone de Beauvoir chose to accept, in the most militant way possible, a life of conjugal compliance, even if she did not formally marry. We have followed in her footsteps. Modern woman complies with the social pressures to behave in a manner which is 'dignified' – in other words, to accept her suffering in silence. By contrast, the ancient woman demanded her due. And so do I.

More self-love than love

I believe in following the Epicurean rather than the Stoic line: that, before rushing to condemn, it would be best to suspend judgement. The suspension of judgement is, of course, the founding gesture of phenomenology; but it is all the more essential when, as is the case here, so many ready-made opinions encourage us first to judge, then to be silent. Jealousy, the forbidden passion, tends to hide itself, the philosophers say – and there is a good reason to do so. It is, after all, wicked, mean, rebarbative, sinister and bitter. It is our duty to conceal it. Better still, for our own good, we should refrain from expressing it in any way and even, if possible, from feeling it at all. Our moral quality is at stake. 'Delicate lovers fear to admit to it.' Let us then be delicate. Let us project this ignominious passion onto Ignoble Savages, women, the bourgeoisie or the elites, or onto whatever group we despise the most.

To acknowledge one's pain, and to say so in the first-person singular, is to resist this pressure; it is to challenge the prohibition placed on the language of jealousy; it is to refuse to allow oneself to be intimidated, to disregard the shame, and to let go the vanity, once and for all, in a frank and calm speech-act. One does not need to shout in order to say 'I am jealous.' One can whisper it. But, in order to get there, it is necessary first to reconsider what one thinks of the esteem and respect one has for oneself.

Jean-Jacques Rousseau and the marquise de Rétel, in Charles Duclos' *Memoirs Illustrating the Manners of the Present Age*, tell us that jealousy is a matter of self-love. La Rochefoucauld has explained how this works. 'One is ashamed to acknowledge it', he wrote, because our vanity is undermined. To feel jealousy, one has first to be excessively vain and then be wounded in our vanity. For *'amour-propre* is a greater factor in jealousy than love itself.'[9]

I do not recognize myself in this scenario. Vanity plays only a secondary role in jealous love. Although its importance has been constantly emphasized ever since the seventeenth century, to attribute a central role to vanity is to make a double mistake. Firstly, it obscures the pain caused by the loss of a unique presence; and, secondly, it introduces the idea of self-love at precisely the wrong moment. We are not jealous because we are vain. The reverse is true. We become vain in the process of attempting to hide a pain from which we are already suffering. To deny us the right to be jealous is to create confusion and timidity, fear and apprehension. At that moment, overcome with embarrassment, we try desperately to mask our feelings. But to pretend that this is nothing is the height of absurdity. It is also pointless, since the jealousy we are trying to deny with such hue and cry is precisely that which everyone will attribute to us as a matter of course. It is, in effect, a form of boastfulness, since indifference to pain would elevate us above mere mortals to the celestial loftiness of Stoic invulnerability. Paradoxically, therefore, shame at confessing what we feel, how we suffer, becomes the most extreme form of vanity. No one is more arrogant than the Stoic sage, armoured and invulnerable, who represses, rejects and denies their suffering. Medea, by contrast, is humble enough to make it a point of honour to give expression to her anguish, to admit to it and thereby to overcome it. Once again, I am promoting not murder, but honesty.

Above all, jealousy is a feeling of moral and physical grief, of sorrow and affliction, brought on by the eclipse of the other person's desire, the loss of her or his irreplaceable presence. Anxiety over our image of ourselves (which is what moralists call 'vanity') then intervenes to make us feel that this disappearance represents some failing or shortcoming which reflects badly on us, whereas, in reality, it is pure suffering. The jealous are in mourning.

Suffering in love

Why do I suffer? Because I am stubbornly narcissistic? That is the answer which the detractors of jealousy have given. Those of us, however, who know truly what it is know that this is not the case. I suffer because I desire the desire of that one unique person. This desire, if it encounters mine, fills me with joy. But, if that same desire should cease, I am overwhelmed with immense distress. When we are attentive to the desire of the other we are simply in love. Love is not stubbornly possessive; it is profoundly attentive. This profound attention makes us ever alert to the possibility of another desire that might destroy our fragile privilege, that of being a more loveable object than others – preferable and preferred. And that fall from grace happens all too often. This is something that those who are jealous know full well, which is why we are required to keep silent.

I am not jealous because I am *insecure* – that trite formula from a simplifying psychology of self-esteem – but because, hopefully, I value the love of that particular person. And, if I dare trust that I am worthy of such love, it is not because I might have been led by 'foolish pride' into thinking that I am the most beautiful creature on earth, but because I love so much this person's love. I love the way s/he walks, the way s/he smiles. It is not sublime. It is simply *different*. It is – who knows why? – 'incommensurate'. It sparkles – just for me. And I would love that this or that detail of my person, my body, my habits, my words or my ideas would please him/her just as much or, in any case, with enough intensity to light that flame, to bring about that 'miracle'. The uniqueness of this miracle is none other than the extension of that silly singularity. This encounter is our own. It matters to me. The mutual recognition to which I aspire lies here in this space between us.

The failure to frame jealousy as it should be – that is to say, as suffering – has led to the jealous being accused, most unfairly, of being either too proud or not sufficiently sure of themselves. Whereas in fact they are simply in love. This is why jealousy understood as anger, as in Euripides and Aristotle, corresponds to the reality of our lived experience. Suffering depends on what takes place between us two, not in a love triangle. The jealous lovers of antiquity do not give a damn about their rivals. Jason's new wife is not even a character in Euripides' *Medea*. And Medea herself begins to fantasize about 'the stupid virgin' only in the version by Max Rouquette, in the twentieth century.[10] Achilles is desperate for a young woman who was dear to his heart. Othello wishes Cassio dead, but it is Desdemona whom he kills with his own hands. The narrator in Proust's *Remembrance of Things Past* – Proust himself – is obsessed by Albertine. It is the love-object who counts. It is there that our attention is fixed most firmly. This dual interaction explains why couples can break up and then come back together again.

Despite the humiliation, the ridicule, the gossip, the scandal and all the social, familial and professional complications – and these do most certainly exist – the bonds can be remade, as miraculously as the first time. Despite everything, and after all, her way of walking remains unique *for me*. I love it. It is my business.

If I were a Stoic sage, seated on the pinnacle of my *apatheia*, I would pride myself at mastering sorrow. If, by contrast, I am an Epicurean, I know that pleasure and pain guide our entire psychological existence. I am not afraid to acknowledge my subjection to these two principles and, consequently, my own vulnerability. I am not going to say, for example: 'I am not jealous, *but*: you lied to me. You did not tell me about it first. You have disappointed me. It's with my best friend. It has happened in our professional environment. At this moment I have so much on my plate already' – and so on. I am not going to talk as if these lies and these deceptions were not specific, whereas it is this particular lie (sexual) and this particular deception (amorous) that cause this particular pain (erotic anger). As if there existed circumstances in which one might be cheated upon with perfect equanimity.

In saying 'I am jealous', I have the courage to confess my suffering here and now, exactly as it is: unalloyed, unqualified, raw pain. I refuse to be bullied into feeling this pain as a sign of inferiority in a power struggle. I will say simply that this – this other desire – has wounded me. I will say that the end of the reciprocity I expect from this singular person devastates me. I do not need to scream out my grief like Medea. I am not going to stab my children. I can write, very simply: 'Yes, I am jealous.' In France, where allowing oneself be seen to be 'inferior' is always insufferable, a little phrase like that can ignite a fire-storm.[11] It is an acting out, even if the act, in this case, is a speech-act.

Finally, if I am a Freudian, I will accept the evidence that love is the source of the most exhilarating possible happiness and, for that same reason, also of a misery that can hurt me more painfully than anything else. For, in my love for another, I believe confidently but with trepidation that I will be loved. I place myself at their mercy. I entrust myself to them; I surrender; I give myself; I relinquish my defences. This stance changes radically my illusion of being in command of my pleasure and my pain, for it is the other who is now the cause of both. I could exclaim, literally with Don Ottavio in Mozart's *Don Giovanni*: 'Upon her peace of mind / mine also depends; / what pleases her is what gives me life; / what displeases her is what gives me death.' One can carp at the folly of depending on another person, but, whatever one does to protect oneself, love will always be essentially alienation and vulnerability.

Normal jealousy

Sigmund Freud clearly understood the normality of jealousy. 'Jealousy', he wrote in 1922, 'is one of those affective states, like grief, that may be described as normal.'[12] As a consequence, he added, 'from the analytic point of view' there was not much to be said about 'normal jealousy'.[13] 'It is easy to see that essentially it is compounded of grief, the pain caused by the thought of losing the loved object, and the narcissistic wound insofar as this is distinguishable from the other wound.'[14]

These words have a definitive and disarming precision. Yes, to believe that one has lost, or runs the risk of losing, the object of love is profoundly upsetting. Yes, it hurts our image of ourselves and therefore jeopardizes our self-esteem or vanity, but only insofar as we can distinguish the 'narcissistic' component of our suffering, on the one hand, from the element of 'loss', on the other. This clause indicates that we are dealing with a difficult and purely formal distinction which is fully in keeping with the nature of love. For, as Freud explains in *Civilization and its Discontents* (1929), if loving and being loved make us positively happy – which means full of confidence, including in ourselves, since feeling that we are unique for another clearly does us good – the fear that we might see this mirror shatter unsettles us. And, yes, 'it is easy' to see that all of this is normal – so normal that it is rather the opposite, the denial or repression of jealousy, that, in Freud's view, we should find unhealthy. 'If anyone appears to be without [jealousy] the inference is justified that it has undergone severe repression [*starke Verdrängung*], and consequently plays all the greater part in his unconscious mental life.'[15]

Jealousy is a pain which is fully justifiable. To repress it is to strengthen it and to let it loose in the unconscious, therefore to set off the production of symptoms. This repression corresponds precisely to what, first, the Stoics and, later, the baroque and libertine moralists found so refined and so desirable: the blushing and the shame at having to admit to being jealous. As always, Freudian psychoanalysis is a part of the history of thought while at the same time revealing the defensive strategies that underpin its norms. As always, the wisdom of the couch encounters the literary intelligence of love, from the tragic subjectivity of the ancients to Proust, and thence to ourselves – when, that is, we stop lying about what we feel.

To understand better Freud's insight, we have to examine it in detail. Freud speaks of three degrees, or levels, of jealousy. The first is the jealousy of rivalry, which is normal. My husband deceives me; I am suffering. The second is the effect of a projection onto our partner of our own impulses to infidelity. My husband must surely be deceiving me; I am imagining things. The third degree depends on our repressed homosexuality. This leads us to attribute to our partner an erotic attraction which we experience unconsciously for a person of our own sex. I claim that my husband desires this woman, when in fact it is only I who am smitten by her. Only the projective and delirious forms are pathological and therefore susceptible to analysis.

Competitive jealousy is, for Freud, therefore, an adult response to a real situation. There do, in fact, exist 'actual situations' (*aktuellen Beziehungen*), and 'real conditions' (*wirklichen Verhältnissen*). Suffering, he explains, draws its strength from the infantile experience of Oedipal triangulation, which makes it 'by no means completely rational' (*keineswegs durchaus rationell*), which is to say not 'fully' (*restlos*) proportionate to actual circumstances. But the legacy from childhood adds nothing but a surplus of intensity to a present state of mind. This is true of our entire psychological life. This time that never ends, this child who never leaves us – in short: the unconscious – marks our entire condition as neurotics. There is a crucial difference, however, between the projection of deeply repressed desires, a source of obsessive and sometimes delusional behaviour, on the one hand, and a reaction about which 'there is little to say from the point of view of psychoanalysis', on the other.

Normal yet 'by no means completely rational' jealousy is a reaction to the intense mobility of desire, for infidelity does exist, and it offers a constant temptation for us all. Freud willingly acknowledges the erotic potential of social interaction, what Hobbes called 'desire indefinite', which Stendhal depicts in his novels, and with which we live on a daily basis. All cultures would be wise to accept and codify gallantry and 'flirtation' in this way, for, as Freud writes: 'this inevitable tendency to unfaithfulness will thus find a safety valve and be rendered innocuous.' The flirtations and frivolities, and what he calls the 'little excursions in the direction of unfaithfulness' in social life, allow us to play around before we return to our true partners. The persons who know how to tolerate this 'safeguard against actual infidelity' (*Versicherung gegen wirkliche Untreue*) are precisely those who, rather than misapprehending their own drives by projecting them onto someone else, succeed in participating, with greater or lesser equanimity, in the great social game.[16] Annibalino, for instance, is hardly amused by the adulation with which la Ghita allows herself to be surrounded. But it is easy enough to tolerate this kind of gallantry. A proven act of infidelity, by contrast, will come as a shattering and infinitely painful loss. In this case, Freud's protective strategy will not work. Real infidelity is instantly apparent. Remember Mathilde, in *Red and Black*, slowly opening Madame de Fervaques' letters to Julien, which she cannot read from weeping. Remember Medea, in all her grief. Remember, too, how we have all continually to negotiate the fine line between those gallant complicities which we know how to take lightly, if sometimes reluctantly, and the gestures or the words which can make us tip over into anguish.[17]

The end of the tragic

It is sad, however, that, after Freud, contemporary psychologists seem frequently to amalgamate the normal and the pathological. In the process, jealousy of competition vanishes in favour of delirious jealousy. This distortion fails to do justice to Freud's thought, which places great emphasis on both the cause and the expression of affects. This applies to the past (Oedipus) but also to the present (my husband deceives me). When pain derives from a real event and an actual situation, it has to be recognized as such. Paradoxically, by theorizing that jealousy is never normal, the language of medicine joins the chorus of ordinary blame. The expert legitimizes our spontaneous, self-protective tendency to do whatever we can in order to disavow what we are feeling. Refusing to recognize that reality plays a part in triggering a passion can only result in its pathetic and pathological denial.

In 1937 two English psychoanalysts, Melanie Klein and Joan Riviere, published a landmark study entitled *Love, Hate and Reparation*.[18] In their reworking of Freud's approach they emphasized the intensity of infantile emotions, which they presented as morally tainted. There is hatred and, above all, envy, and it is from them that jealousy derives. It is bad and malicious. As a consequence, the authors claim, we seek to project these hostile inclinations out of ourselves. Adult jealousy, which derives from this infantile experience, thereby loses all social and factual plausibility. Everything takes place inside ourselves, and we then try to drive out this foul morass. It is as if all human beings possessed a congenital allergy to this alien body which is the 'evil'.

There can, therefore, be no complicated pleasure to be found in the negative, only an automatic immune system.

As both a psychological and a moral requirement, projection thus becomes *the* mechanism of jealousy. There is no longer any ambivalence, which might *sometimes* lead to a psychotic projection, but which remains, most frequently, within the limits of a tolerable neurosis. There is a dichotomy here between good and evil, between what is within and what without. 'Without going into the delicate, and probably disputed question of what constitutes normal jealousy,' wrote Joan Riviere, 'there are certain general features on which we all agree.'[19] These are summed up in the claim that, even in 'normal' jealousy, one's narcissism is wounded and one will be plunged into a severe and critical attitude towards oneself. This, however, will always depend on the aggressive impulses the subject experiences and which s/he tries to expiate, condemn and expel. For Klein and Riviere, every form of jealousy is systematically more pathological than it appears. We are very far from Freud's reflections on the nature of love, whose consequences are inevitable and logical. 'Normal jealousy' is the pain we experience at the loss of the object of our love, accompanied by humiliation, because it was that love which had made us at once both happy and proud, delighted with the other and happy with ourselves. Yes, we are more or less neurotic, but this is normalcy in psychoanalysis. This means that we are indeed the survivors of infancy *and* adults in touch with what actually happens to us in the world.

Today psychoanalysis often follows prevailing philosophical verdicts. Jealous women are covered in shame and, overwhelmed by their weakness, they swoon. They are unable to stand upright. This is because they are suffering from a defective narcissism, which reveals a deficient phallicity. Wishful thinking: if only they were more phallic, these unhappy creatures would be perfectly capable of standing up straight. Instead of folding up like a pile of old clothes, they would be able to tell themselves that love's failures do not matter at all, because they are worth more than that. It's simple. But, then again, that might be a symptom of repression. Whichever way you turn, clearly amorous dependence is a terrible thing, and we should all mourn for it.[20]

Once more, everything in this kind of interpretation takes place in the patient's inner self, as if the sudden unexpected impact of what Freud does not hesitate to call 'real infidelity' (*wirkliche Untreue*) did not upset a whole life, an entire social existence, an image of oneself.

Sometimes it is a real trauma, which undermines one's confidence in love forever. But it is always the case that, no matter how strong our economic, professional or affective autonomy might be, love supports us, helps us, reassures us. Even if it is a plus, it is a plus that becomes indispensable. Even if it is a luxury, it is a luxury to which we rapidly become accustomed. By seeing us, in Stendhalian terms, as covered in small diamonds, the other plays an essential role in our life – an imaginary role, but one that is also both symbolic and real and of which we are more or less conscious. As soon as this support is taken away we collapse, exhausted, crushed with fatigue. Not enough phallus, not enough serotonin, not enough self-esteem?[21] Not enough sense of omnipotence, perhaps.

If we were not dependent on the other, we could simply turn the page as if nothing had happened. If we had not trusted, we would not be stunned by the discovery of a lie. If we had not woven a thousand and one singular ties between ourselves and the object of our love, we would have no difficulty in replacing one body with another. If this person were insignificant, we would be indifferent. Yes, indeed. If we were not in love, we would not be jealous. For, if we are not walled in with selfishness and solitude, buttressed by distrust, isolation and the claim to be self-sufficient – in short – if we say 'yes' to love – we cannot but be at the mercy of the people we love.

A trembling hand

Jealousy can only be normal between inverted commas. Worse still: 'why are my fingers so terribly reluctant to write down this word "normal" which Freud, after all, uses so uninhibitedly?', asks the German psychotherapist Hildegard Baumgart. Her book *Jealousy: Experiences and Solutions* gives some idea of the sanctimonious, plodding, anti-tragic turn which a certain kind of contemporary psychoanalysis has taken.[22] From the very beginning, jealous behaviour is treated with unremitting sarcasm. The difference between unfounded jealousy and jealousy based upon evidence is minimized, because what really matters is the intra-psychic experience. Roughly speaking, this means that the jealous person has to work on herself (on her relations with her parents, her sisters and brothers), on her dependence – for love is an addiction – and on her self-esteem (which is clearly defective). What is actually happening to her, here and now, vanishes altogether to the benefit of infantilizing reflections on her character and her feelings. Baumgart's tremor says it all. Freud is miles away. The fine Freudian distinctions which Daniel Lagache repeated and refined in his classic study *Jealousy: Descriptive Psychology and Psychoanalysis* (1947) are handled with extreme caution, precisely because Baumgart is unwilling to set up distinctions.[23] Finally, in an exercise of clinical literary analysis, she embarks on an interpretation of Shakespeare's *Othello*, which imputes to the Moor of Venice – that powerful, confident, loving victim of an infamous tick – a jealousy which she characterizes as 'delusional' from beginning to end. We shall come to this wonderful text in a moment.

Medicalization and moralism have killed the 'tragic figure'.[24] One of the things which I hope to achieve in this book is to recover our ability to enjoy the tragic – that is, to understand the suffering intrinsic to love, whether it be in Euripides, Seneca, Corneille, Shakespeare or, indeed, our own lives. When Freud claimed that great poets and playwrights had the intuition of what psychoanalysis was going to theorize, he meant exactly that. Those poets were smart enough to grasp the potential for pain that lurks in pleasure. There are, of course, other psychoanalysts who have made the same move. Jealousy, writes Jean-Paul Hiltenbrand, provides us with 'an opportunity to restore a sense of the tragic in an age that has lost all awareness of it. Jealousy protests against the injury inflicted on the mirage of harmony between two beings whose love (deemed to be the most perfect vehicle) is supposed to be the remedy for any dissension.'[25] Alas, however, the insight that jealousy can open our eyes to the primordial vulnerability of human beings, who can find happiness only where they are most at risk of losing it, ends, once again, with a diagnosis. The chopper falls. Love is a *folie à deux*. Jealousy proves *that*. But why?

Why should those who are jealous be made into caricatures of amorous idiocy? They dream of harmony and perfection, these simpletons, while everyone should know that, in Lacan's famous phrase, 'there is no sexual rapport'. But is not normal jealousy (and, in writing these words, my fingers are definitely steady) most often the consequence of dramatic *events* that shock and hurt us, precisely because we were expecting something quite different – reciprocity in the singular? Are not the most frequent situations made up of confidence betrayed, wrenching lies, broken projects, reneged agreements, and the collapse of what we believed to be an erotic intimacy? The object of love is nothing but the person with whom, and for whom, we live a unique experience – an experience that has suddenly become no longer unique. We have had lovers in the past, and we will have others in the future, but now, at this moment, all we wish to do is to live somehow happily with this particular person. Somehow, therefore. Nothing to do with harmony. He may sing out of tune, he may snore and sigh, he is certainly less rich, less handsome, older and less amusing than many others, but when he bursts out laughing, then, as the poems and songs say: *La vie en rose*.... *Quando sei qui con me, questa stanza non ha più pareti, ma alberi*[26]...*Something in the way she moves*...Something, therefore. Nothing to do with perfection. We know that.

But, of course, in the beginning, at the source of all this, we will find Oedipus. But who has no parents? Who was never a child or an adolescent? Even Marcianne Blévis, a psychoanalyst who does recognize the fact of jealous suffering, suggests, nevertheless, an evolutionary etiology. Jealousy has to do with the identity of the individual and the sense of oneself. 'It goes back to a time of childhood or adolescence when the person was subject to the absence/need of those erotic and affective reactions, which would have enabled him to feel strong, independent and desirable. Jealousy, therefore, may be seen as a delayed response to a situation that has made a person helpless and humiliated.'[27] Is there not, in adolescence, a fundamental uneasiness to which it is always possible to trace the anxieties of adulthood? Fragility is doubtless there for all of us. A love that dissolves inevitably brings to the surface memories of old wounds, but this past would not explode in our faces were it not for the actual loss of the object of our love. It is this loss that does us harm, just as it was the love itself that did us good. There is reactivation, but there is also what is actual. Adult love possesses its own reality – desires, projects, expectations, pleasures, agreements, bonds – which cannot be reduced to the experiences of infancy. Otherwise everything could be similarly reduced. And nothing would ever affect us, because everything would have always already happened.

Let us re-read Freud. 'It is easy to see that essentially it [normal jealousy] is compounded of grief, the pain caused by the thought of losing the loved object, and of the narcissistic wound in so far as this is distinguishable from the other wound.' And let us also be glad that some psychoanalysts are able to write without quaking. One of these is Anne Deburge-Donnars. In a tone which is unusually free, she asks the following open questions: 'Can jealousy enrich the range of one's emotional drives [*pulsionnalité*]? Is this the way to more love?' Surprisingly, she answers in the affirmative. Normal jealousy is structuring, because it 'makes it possible to leave the fusional relationship with the mother by introducing a third party and is, therefore, in this sense dis-alienating.' By encouraging the awareness that the world is indeed full of possibilities, and by sharpening one's curiosity for the other person, jealousy acts as 'a formidable promotion of the phantasm'. The moment when a patient is able to say 'I am jealous!' is a turning point. The confession becomes a way out of repression. Dependence and the inability to tolerate absence are both diminished. Silence was crippling. Avowal is dynamic. Fortunately, the words of this particular patient fell on the sensitive ears of a good reader of Marcel Proust.[28]

Even closer to Freud, and one of his most subtle interpreters, is Jerome Neu, who has contributed greatly to rethinking jealousy. A complex, legitimate and normal emotion, jealousy, for Neu, is a fear of 'annihilation', inseparable from love. We live the loss of the object of our love (which has absolutely nothing to do with the Kantian 'thing') as the failure of a relationship which binds and intertwines us with another person. If we suffer so much, it is because the person we love is also the object of a true identification on our part. Love involves a strong overestimation of the loved one, but the enhanced value of the other feeds on our own image of ourselves. We identify with this dazzling creature: the crystals that shine on her make us shine in their reflected light, and vice versa. 'Idealization in Freud', writes Neu, 'is a transformation of narcissism.' If I magnify the other, it is because I myself feel magnificent. It's a game of mirrors.

For narcissism is, in turn, a form of dependence on others. As a structural dimension of sociability, our reliance on other people's gaze is inseparable from our very humanity. We have encountered different philosophical versions of this wisdom, from Aristotle to Simone de Beauvoir. We have read insightful and stirring fictions. Sensitivity to respect, vulnerability to slights, taste for fame, self-esteem (*amour-propre*), struggle for recognition or alienation from others: these are all aspects of a fundamental demand. Others must acknowledge us. We need mirrors to exist. And mirrors are never to be taken for granted. Uncertainty is the essence of what, after Ovid and Freud, we call 'narcissism'. If the other whom we love as we do ourselves ceases to be there for us, recognizing and enhancing us, our own image of ourselves crumbles. Jealousy is nothing other, and nothing less, than the terror of this void. Furthermore, what adds to its tragic paradoxicality is the fact that the anguish of loss is doubled by the hope that the other might return.[29]

Psychoanalysis may, therefore, help us to understand the ethical destiny of jealousy. It is important, above all, to free the affect from repression – by admitting to it on the one hand and recognizing it on the other. For being jealous does not mean that, fooled by a chimerical infatuation, we believe that we can make ourselves 'one' with the object of our love. On the contrary, one can perfectly well lead an independent life and cultivate a relationship which is respectful of each other's private spaces. But that does not prevent us from experiencing the collapse of the erotic equilibrium, often very peculiar, in which we believed we lived, as if it were an earthquake. To trust each other in a monogamous relationship – accompanied by Freud's 'little excursions in the direction of unfaithfulness', which, depending on the circumstances, and on how they are conducted, may amuse, titillate or embarrass – is not a 'mirage'. Trust means that a three-way situation can be envisaged, but without fear. Loving from a distance, clandestinely or in a libertine manner, may leave a well-defined place to all manner of variations, so long, that is, as its limits have been friendlily agreed upon. Agreement, however, while it means that some playful complications may be a part of the picture, is no guarantee against jealousy. The unfaithful are well aware of this.

In any case, one can be jealous without the slightest illusion as to the supposed fusional harmony of two beings. We are well aware of the excluded, included or virtual third parties, around whom desire, indeterminate or not, flutters. Here and now, however, we desire a reciprocal relationship with one particular person. And we say so. That is all.

A burning hand

The return to Freud of Jacques Lacan is, as always, at once inspiring and disorientating. Lacan analysed jealousy in *Family Complexes in the Formation of the Individual* (1938), beginning with early childhood, as that is the time when the 'social feelings' of the individual are first created. This is something like the state of nature was for Rousseau. The primordial competition between siblings, when they are infants, articulates love and identification. One imitates the other. To overcome competitors, one wishes to be like them. It is this primordial ambiguity between emulation and antagonism which we should recognize in amorous jealousy. The jealous have a 'powerful interest' in their rivals which takes the form of hatred. This hostility is the negative side of the passion they feel; but there is another side, which can become its 'essential and positive interest'. This interest confuses identification with love. 'Even though this emotion is motivated by the supposed love object,' Lacan wrote, 'it seems nevertheless that the subject fosters it in the most gratuitous and costly manner.'[30] Sometimes, the feeling of love itself is overcome. This is obsessive and psychotic jealousy which is fixed on the third person, at once both scorned and fascinating.[31] Less a rivalry than a 'mental identification', this jealousy belongs with that which every child feels towards the parent of the same sex in the Oedipal triangle: there is an 'obstacle' to the love of the parent of the other sex.[32]

On the other hand, however, Lacan was also capable of some of the most iconic – I would almost say 'romantic' – of phrases that have ever been written about love. Desire, he wrote, is to reach out one's hand, 'to pick a fruit which is ripe, to draw close to a rose which has opened, or to stir a fire the logs of which suddenly burst into flames'. Desire is, therefore a tension towards the object that is its cause.

> If in the movement of reaching, drawing or striving, the hand goes far enough towards the object that another hand comes out of the fruit, flower or log, and extends towards your hand – and at that moment your hand freezes in the closed plenitude of the fruit, in the open plenitude of the flower or in the explosion of the log which burst into flames – then what is produced is love.[33]

This love, which is also 'to give what one does not have', comes into being simultaneously and in an instant.[34] It is not of the order of symmetry or of return, or of a system of calculated exchanges ('the psychology of the rich'). It is a miracle. And who would not want to stay there, within a miracle?[35]

It is with this Lacan that we can understand the logic of jealousy. Beyond the fatal, puerile trio, beyond the occasional obsession with an enthralling contender, it is the very magic of love – the dazzling encounter of those hands – that makes us aware of what horror it would be to separate them.

To deny is to repress

The founder of psychoanalysis and his most radical and provocative successor, Jacques Lacan, were able to think broadly. There is a jealous jealousy (mimetic and morbid) but also an *amorous* jealousy – one, that is, which is inseparable from love itself. Subsequent psychoanalytic writing, however, has usually favoured the first.[36] The clinical perspective and the rhetoric of the case study create a small therapeutic world whose social horizon is severely restricted. Everything is determined in childhood and remains always the same. There is no place for chance, no nuances, no cultural habits and no contingency.

If, today, a woman were to discover a romantic correspondence among her husband's e-mails, to which he had long since given her access, her only option would be to ask herself: 'What is wrong with me?' Were she to see a therapist, first of all she would receive a prescription for sleeping pills and some suitable legal advice in case she felt suicidal. The expert would have to cover herself. Then, she would start to second-guess the patient's sentiments, to probe their remote provenance and their recondite meaning, as if everything were potentially significant under the circumstances – except for the circumstances themselves. What happened, what is happening, is meaningless. Facts are welcomed with medicalizing condescension. On the more or less aseptic settees of contemporary psychoanalysts, everything leads directly to the past and to pathology. The event itself ceases to exist, covered as it immediately is by the curative process. The words are insignificant. The relationship itself is of no importance when compared to the required therapy which will allow the analyst to dig into the patient's infancy, go back to her oral phase, resurrect the rivalry with her sister, uncover a hidden desire for the children she never had. Everything is relevant, so long as the patient is not allowed to believe that she has a *right* to suffer because her world has just collapsed around her. Everything goes except the recognition of a legitimate suffering, everything except the 'justice of the bed'.

Had this woman, however, been able to lie down on that old, tatty, orientalist Viennese couch at Freud's home at number 19 Berggasse, her story would have been heard, and respected, for what it is: the story of a shocking calamity which has suddenly interrupted her life. Then the memory of Greek tragedy, of English philosophy or of French novels would have offered a profound intelligibility to her unoriginal predicament. Shallow nosography, blind to its cultural mean-spiritedness, would have been replaced by the ironic wisdom that led Lacan to say that 'the non-dupes are those who err' (*les non-dupes errent*). Jealousy is useless, as psychiatrists of a certain kind pontificate. Really?

THE DESPAIR OF NOT BEING LOVED

Faced with a 'moralized' Freud, anyone who becomes normally jealous because s/he has stumbled upon something truly atrocious and unexpected – something which is a true 'symptom', in the original Greek meaning of the term as 'coincidence' – is tempted to assert, in the strongest possible terms, that never, never would s/he fall so low. Jealous? What a thought! It was already a source of shame, a lack of taste, a false step, a political error. To that we can now add the diagnosis that jealousy, whatever it may be, binds the sufferer indissolubly to paranoia. In a Lacanian version of the same brand of dogmatism, jealousy is 'joylousy' (*jalouissance*: *jalousie* plus *jouissance*), or 'joyful jealousy'. 'The clinic bears witness to the fact that the moment of "joylousy", from which jealousy itself arises, is overpowering, unconfessable, shameful.'[37] You imagine things, you become delirious, you reveal yourself. By pushing to the extreme the idea that any jealous love originates from ancient struggles between siblings, Marie-Magdeleine Chatel develops Lacan's play on words so as to cast jealousy as a form of enjoyment (*jouissance*). Now, we can certainly speak in this idiom, but only if it is clearly understood that we are talking about that *paradoxical* form of enjoyment which is experienced as irresistible suffering. All symptoms are made up of unconscious pleasure, oddly felt as pain – hence their repetition. This is the definition of neurosis. But, here again, it is as if *every* form of jealousy belonged to the same category. There is no room here for normal jealousy, unless it is placed between condescending quotation marks. Loss, mourning, the destruction of trust, suffering and loneliness – all these banalities have nothing to do with *joylousy*.

The pathologization of jealousy is pernicious because, in our culture, while one might be able to ignore La Rochefoucauld, one cannot do the same for the legacy of Freud. If it is Freud who says, as some of his followers would have us believe, that jealousy can only ever be a morbid affection, to be cured and, above all, to be chastised, then it must be so. Henceforth, let us cultivate kitsch Stoicism, in its medicalized reincarnation. Above all, let us make believe that we can immunize ourselves against love itself. Let us forget its potential tragedy, of which jealousy represents a lucid conscience. Freud himself, however, tells us two crucial things. The first is that one must never conflate all forms of jealousy into projection or, worse, persecution. The second is that not to confess to being jealous is not an instance of moral prowess but, rather, a *defence* against a truth which is too painful to mention and, as such, a symptom of neurosis. To deny is to repress.

Jealous speech-acts

It is, therefore, those who preach silence and 'dignity' who are wrong. They are cruel, because they seek to impose a relationship with the self which only makes the pain even more painful for those who experience it. To speak out, on the contrary, would be the surest way to face the other, to find oneself, to position oneself so as to be able to rebound. These preachers are ill at ease, self-conscious, embarrassed. Possibly, those who refuse to hear about jealousy do not want to see the fragility of others, which may perhaps be contagious. It might happen to me. It has, perhaps, already happened. The mournful face of a jealous person defies you to look the mortality of love directly in the eyes. Or, another hypothesis, they might want to ignore the consequences of infidelity for their own comfort. The people (mostly men) I have heard invoke the Stoic cure – silence, please! – condemn the truth of eros to insignificance. They imagine that all it takes to cut off his wings is a little silence.

To speak one's jealousy, one's own and that of others, requires courage and real dignity. The jealous lover is an honest lover. It is monstrously unjust to try to close his or her mouth. We must admit to our jealousy, albeit *sotto voce*, and claim that admission as a worthy act. Worthy, precisely because it is honest. Worthy of recognition, of empathy, of respect. The expression of jealousy itself must be set free. Why is it thought to be more elegant to tell self-deceptive stories and proffer improbable excuses? Not to give voice or to show what one feels, as the philosophers of the eighteenth century recommend, seems to me infinitely more ridiculous than to acknowledge the wound and the insult – which means to own up to love. Not that I laugh, but I cannot help feeling very sorry for those who pretend to be indifferent. This does not mean that we should bore other people with theatrics and indiscretions, but that we refrain from counterfeiting a particularly hurtful emotion. When we speak our sorrow, we take responsibility. *Non nisi laesus amo*, 'I only love if I am wounded', says Ovid, as we shall see later. To speak openly is a form not of exhibitionism but of self-respect – in the antique manner.

To speak openly means first of all to highlight the realism of jealousy. It is a philosophical banality to claim that jealousy is a disease of the imagination. By insisting on its supposedly fantastical nature, one hopes to make it unreal. Yet there is genuine pain for the loss, no less real, of the other's desire. To say how one suffers means revealing what one is suffering from. Setting out the facts, and detailing the feelings, makes it possible to recognize that something has indeed happened – that it was not nothing. Since the past, the present and the future are intertwined, anger is the narrative passion par excellence. And this erotic anger which we call 'jealousy' is ready-made for narration.

We should, therefore, forget the philosophers, at least those who cast erotic suffering into the mould of either the unconfessable or, by contrast, the sublime. We should listen not to the censorious who only sit in judgement on the passions but, rather, to those who have experienced them and know how to write about them. The psychoanalysts, unless they reduce jealousy to paranoia, are well placed to understand the vicissitudes of jealous suffering. But it is above all to the poets that we must listen. Ever since Sappho, they have spoken to us in the first person.

> That man to me seems equal to the gods,
> the man who sits opposite you
> and close by listens
> to your sweet voice.[38]

Poetry is one place where jealousy is fully acknowledged. The poets (the men, but most especially the women) have never known shame. They are the true phenomenologists, capable of bringing pain into consciousness, without pretence.[39]

The door to truth

Let us, then, turn to the most classical of the classics: Shakespeare's *Othello*. Let us read the text without preconceptions, without footnotes, without scholarly commentaries.

Once upon a time there was a brave warrior, admired by all, who was general of the armies of the Most Serene Republic of Venice. He came from North Africa and his mother was Egyptian. Those who hated him mocked him by calling him 'sooty bosom', 'thick-lips', an old goat, a Barbary horse, an 'old black ram', a lecher.[40] But he paid them no heed. Like the great men of antiquity, the Moor of Venice was conscious only of his own worth. Noble birth, fortune and virtue all smiled upon him. He was also a beguiling storyteller, whose tales of the 'battles, sieges, fortunes' he had endured enthralled a young Venetian girl called Desdemona, the daughter of Brabantio, a

Venetian nobleman.[41] She fell in love with him and wanted to marry him, to follow him on his campaigns. Desdemona and Othello make an unlikely and tender couple. Clearly they love each other. But there is no obvious fusion between them. They do not have the same skin colour or share the same interests. They are simply a man and a woman. They want to be together. They will make love. He will tell her other stories. She will listen.

But in Othello's entourage there is a man devoured by envy. His name is Iago. He is one of Othello's subalterns, who had expected to become his lieutenant but instead finds himself passed over by a Florentine called Cassio, an outsider, an 'arithmetician', in Iago's judgement, 'That never set a squadron in the field / Nor the division of a battle knows', whose soldiering 'is mere prattle, without practice'.[42] Iago loathes them both and resolves to destroy them both. Two birds with one stone. He will make Othello believe that Cassio and Desdemona are lovers. He will sow doubt and suspicion. Unlike Othello, who tells Desdemona tales of his military prowess, Iago will make up erotic fantasies as precise in their details and as realistic as they are false. Carried away by this display of *ekphrasis*, Othello will eventually come to believe what he sees, have his alleged rival killed, and strangle his wife in their marriage bed.

Iago is the precise depiction of that base and wholly negative passion which is the resentment towards one who possesses a good that we desire but cannot attain. From Plato (who condemns it in the *Laws*) and Aristotle (who echoes this same condemnation in the *Rhetoric*) this is envy, a passion which is wholly distinct from emulation, but most especially from amorous jealousy.[43] As we have already seen, the envious do their best to deprive others of their property, material or symbolic. It is easier than trying to compete with them by struggling to do the same, or even better, than they. Their sole objective is the degradation and suffering of others. Paradoxically, they are disinterested. Left to his own devices, Iago has no intention of confronting either Cassio or Othello. Instead he will ruin them by arousing in the latter a murderous jealousy. He will betray them by inventing a non-existent adultery. Both Othello's jealousy and Desdemona's infidelity are equally artificial. Taken together, they constitute Iago's masterpiece. The drama depicts a transition from envy to jealousy in which an envious man creates a jealous one.

The intrigue of the play lies wholly in the steady crescendo of Othello's belief in Iago's strategic confabulation. For Iago carries out his plan with painstaking attention to detail.

THE DESPAIR OF NOT BEING LOVED

> To get his place, and to plume up my will
> In double knavery – How, how? Let's see:–
> After some time, to abuse Othello's ear
> That he is too familiar with his wife...[44]

He plots to 'put the Moor / At least into a jealousy so strong / That judgement cannot cure.'[45] To do this, he will make use of a proof which is both tangible and eloquent. A handkerchief, embroidered with little strawberries, a present from Othello to his young bride, will ostentatiously find its way into the hands of her supposed lover. 'I will in Cassio's lodging lose this napkin, / And let him find it.'[46] Iago even boasts of what he has done to his victim. 'I see, sir, you are eaten up with passion: / I do repent me that I put it to you.'[47] His 'medicine', as he calls it, now goes to work. 'Work on, / My medicine, work!'[48] It is a 'pestilence' poured into Othello's ear, a suppurating boil.[49] In the eyes of the world, Othello's jealousy of a woman as faithful as Desdemona can be explained only as the consequence of a deliberate manipulation. Someone had to have planted these thoughts in Othello's head, thereby setting the murder in motion.[50] Iago is the true author of the dramatic action. It is he who manufactures doubts. It is he who makes things happen. It is also he who will shape the character of Othello himself by modifying his perceptions, his ideas, his intentions. Othello will see and do what Iago makes him see and do. Iago is his director.

This is an epistemological tragedy which reveals the dangers that threaten two kinds of trust: trust in the virtues of certain knowledge and trust in the presumed virtues of a friend. At first Othello refuses to be convinced by Iago's insinuations. He wants proof: he wants to see with his own eyes and hear with his own ears. Iago will give him evidence (Desdemona's handkerchief) and a witness (Cassio himself in a conversation about one of his mistresses, whom Othello is led to believe is Desdemona). It is by means of this highly deceptive staging, therefore, that Othello comes to believe he has reached 'the door of truth'.[51] If he has allowed himself to be duped, it is only because he had failed to question a flatterer whom he took for a friend.

The confusion of flattery with friendship is a major theme in ancient reflections on the nature of power. Plutarch, whose works Shakespeare knew well, had written a treatise on the subject.[52] Othello is not, of course, a king or even in the Venetian context a doge; but he is in a position of leadership, and Iago's career depends entirely upon him.[53] Othello has given the post of lieutenant to someone else, and Iago wishes him dead. Nurturing his hatred, Iago will, nonetheless, go into raptures over him. This will be his strategy. Others there are, he reflects,

> Who, trimm'd in forms and visages of duty,
> Keep yet their hearts attending on themselves,
> And, throwing but shows of service on their lords,
> Do well thrive by them, and, when they have lined their coats,
> Do themselves homage: these fellows have some soul;
> And such a one do I profess myself.
> For, sir,
> It is as sure as you are Roderigo,
> Were I the Moor, I would not be Iago:
> In following him, I follow but myself;

Iago will pursue his own ends while pretending only to be doing his duty, while he wears his 'heart upon [his] sleeve'.[54]

One does not improvise flattery. It is, rather, a rhetorical and social strategy. Throughout the play, Iago's obsequious duplicity towards Othello is conveyed in traditional forms of address, in servility, false modesty and unctuous attentiveness.[55] The flatterer administers his calumnies in small doses, making them credible through homage and professions of devotion. By exploiting the victim's self-esteem, he creates confidence in himself. So much so, in this case, that Othello finally comes to rely completely upon Iago, whom he assumes to be brave, honest and just. In Othello's eyes, he is a model of nobility and, above all, of friendship.[56]

The green-eyed monster

High self-esteem, confidence in a twisted panderer, and a wish to drag everything into the open, which, in turn, leads to an excess of epistemic zeal: it is tempting to accuse Othello of having exaggerated on all three fronts. Here we are, as we were in Seneca's *Medea*, 'among monsters'. Their size is unmeasurable. Othello commits horrendous mistakes, but one might argue that, given his position, and in the context of the 'Venetian' culture in which Shakespeare has placed him, they are, if not exactly inevitable, then at least difficult to avoid. A *condottiere* such as he would find it hard to be shy, to distrust those who praise him in his presence, or to resist the temptation to take immediate control of any challenging situation. He is a leader; he has to leap into action. It was, after all, precisely to help men like Othello to avoid falling into such traps that philosophers such as Machiavelli or Erasmus wrote their 'mirrors for princes'.

It is, therefore, in this context that the two most frequently cited passages from the play must be read. The first is that great classic of anti-jealousy kitsch:

> O, beware, my lord, of jealousy;
> It is the green-eyed monster, which doth mock
> The meat it feeds on.[57]

Often taken out of context, this arresting image says it all. It would seem that Shakespeare himself says of jealousy that it is a filthy and repulsive creature, endowed with a life of its own, which seizes upon us only to haunt, humiliate and harass. 'It is a monster / Begot upon itself, born on itself.'[58] Created by spontaneous generation, jealousy cannibalizes us, while conjuring up only its own fanciful fantasies.

Nothing could be more absurd. It is Iago who mocks Othello, warning him – as a consummate flatterer – against the role he himself is making him play. It is Iago who gloats over how skilfully he has given birth to this monster, the child of Hell and of Night, and it is he who will 'bring this monstrous birth to the world's light'.[59] It is he who will inflame the wound and administer the poison. For it is not, after all, so easy to lead Othello by the nose. He is no ass, but an open and confident man, and Iago must work hard to 'abuse' his ear.[60] He has to satisfy Othello's demand for 'ocular proof'.[61] He has to make sure that Othello will be there to see this irrefutable thing – the handkerchief – at the very moment that Cassio is holding it in his hands. Jealousy is a green-eyed monster only on the lips of Iago, who, when he utters the phrase, is pretending to protect his 'friend' while at the same time revealing to the spectators his determination to make Othello as jealous as possible. Moreover, Iago attributes to jealousy such disconcertingly coloured eyes only because he confuses it with envy, that hag with a livid complexion which embodies his only true passion.[62]

'Trifles light as air / Are to the jealous confirmations strong / As proofs of holy writ: this may do something.'[63] Does this other canonical passage imply that, for Shakespeare himself, jealousy was a psychopathology of the imagination? Absolutely not. Once again, it is Iago who is speaking, at the very moment that he baits the trap with Desdemona's handkerchief. He is alone on the stage, and his sole witness is the audience. Silken, diaphanous, 'light as air', the handkerchief is nothing more than a 'trifle', in the most cruelly ironic sense. For Iago knows that, for Othello, this is an exceptional object, as his mother had entrusted it to him on her deathbed, 'And bid me, when my fate would have me wive, / To give it her.' Its origin ('That handkerchief / Did an Egyptian to my mother give; / She was a charmer, and could almost read / The thoughts of people'), the silk of which it was made ('there's magic in the web of it'), the embroidery ('dyed in mummy which the skilful / Conserved of maidens' hearts') – all contrive to make it unique, and so intimate and personal that Othello believes it to be inimitable and irreplaceable.[64] This fine fabric is heavy with meaning which only Othello, and he alone, can know. He will have one, and only one, inference to make. Wherever it is now, it can only be Desdemona, and she alone, who put it there. Iago relies on the singularity of this almost immaterial object, which embodies the singularity of the couple, to give maximum weight to his lies.

At once a maternal gift and an erotic talisman, the handkerchief becomes an exhibit in a quest for factual proof that corresponds, word for word, to what the doge of Venice himself requires in a trial scene at the beginning of the play. 'To vouch this, is no proof,' he tells the Senate. For an accusation to be upheld, something more than 'thin habits and poor likelihoods', something of a 'wider and more overt test', is required.[65] The ethereal handkerchief fits this description perfectly. And Iago, who is a master at subverting these Venetian principles from the inside, will use it to prove a non-existent complicity between Desdemona and Cassio. This has nothing to do with the crazed imagination of a paranoid Othello.

Too sceptical or not sceptical enough?

Too many readers have insisted on the supposedly 'delusional' nature of Othello's jealousy.[66] Even such subtle and skilful interpreters as Stanley Cavell, the American philosopher who has made of Shakespeare a critical theorist of scepticism, and the French poet Yves Bonnefoy, the most brilliant of Shakespeare's French translators, concentrate their reading of the text upon what they both identify as the enigma of a single monumental error. How could Othello kill his wife? How is it possible for this man, who in all other things appears to be so upright, so judicious, so virtuous, to have fallen victim to such blindness? It is, they both claim, precisely his rectitude, his very inability to accept the existential and sexual reality of Desdemona. A faithful Desdemona, claims Cavell, would be even more threatening than an unfaithful one. Othello cannot tolerate the feminine and carnal humanity, which eludes his insistent inquiry. For Cavell, the 'two bodies lying together on their bridal and death sheets form an emblem of the bare fact, the truth of skepticism.'[67] Blinded by his doubts, because obsessed by the mirage of the 'ocular proof', Othello is incapable of setting any limits on his susceptibility to Iago's insinuations. Yves Bonnefoy, for his part, suggests that Othello should have mounted a cross-examination. 'He could have gone straight to Cassio and demanded an explanation. Even before that, he should have questioned Desdemona directly instead of scolding and insulting her in what is, in effect, a highly enigmatic manner. But he does not because he needs to preserve his suspicion.'[68]

It is therefore Othello, either because he is too sceptical or because he is not sceptical enough, who alone is responsible for his own misfortune. He could, and he certainly should, have distrusted not his wife but his hypocritical subaltern. The theatrical exchange between the two, however, reveals a man who has been overwhelmed by Iago's machinations. I was, Othello says at the very end of the play, 'one not easily jealous, but, being wrought / Perplex'd in the extreme.' He had lost all capacity for judgement and then, 'Like the base Indian, threw a pearl away / Richer than all his tribe.'[69] He had no vicious predisposition to jealousy, but something unheard of had happened. Someone had bent, twisted and shaped him, so to speak. Othello had been 'wrought' – a word that means 'forged', 'artificially transformed'. And it is Iago who is of course the master craftsman. Cassio makes exactly the same diagnosis. So, too, does Ludovico: 'This is thy work!' he says to Iago, pointing to the two corpses, 'the tragic loading of this bed'.[70] In the Shakespearean theatre, being 'wrought' is frequently the fate of men of action and power when they allow themselves to be carried away. In *Julius Caesar*, Brutus finds himself in a similar situation. He is noble, but his 'honourable metal' could be 'wrought' by what has befallen him. 'Therefore 'tis meet', Cassius warns him: 'That noble minds keep ever with their likes; / For who so firm that cannot be seduced?'[71]

Othello's vulnerability lies in his self-love, as La Rochefoucauld would say. Othello's vanity, however, is not directed at his wife, since he knows that he cannot ever possess her desire. It is as a military commander that he esteems himself so highly. He has devoted himself to the service of the Republic of Venice, and it is this excellence that has made him worthy. 'Valiant Othello', 'the Valiant Moor', is how the Doges and the Venetian senators address him.[72] His great deathbed soliloquy begins with the words 'Soft you; a word or two before you go. / I have done the state some service, and they know't.'[73] No one, except, of course, for Iago, his friend Roderigo and Desdemona's father, Brabantio, despises him.[74] No one suggests that his pride is excessive or misplaced. Othello is judged on his due merits and, for this reason, believes in the declarations of esteem and the eulogies he receives.[75] It is precisely that which is so dangerous for all figures of authority. He is mistaken only in the trust that he places in Iago the sycophantic courtier: that reptilian, corrupt and venomous traitor, whose envy he cannot see. Only there is he mistaken. Othello is the victim of his virtues. His great heart, his aristocratic self, his faith in the personal integrity of those around him, all prevent him from seeing through Iago's treachery. What the play gives us, therefore, is an Othello who is both innocent and responsible for his actions (and thus is ultimately a criminal) – like all the great tragic heroes.

As, indeed, are many jealous people, I would add. For, more often than not, one becomes jealous unexpectedly. You find yourself thrown into a situation that simply happens, and then, suddenly, you are thrust brutally to the back of the stage. You are wrenched away from all that you believed to be essential to love – the trust in the loyalty of your lover – and, from one moment to the next, your good faith is made to look like simple naiveté. You did not see it coming. You were insensitive to all the good reasons that your loved one might have had to go elsewhere. You were not in love enough to have become jealous earlier. It is as if all your light-hearted, generous and cheerful confidence had been mere stupidity. Jealousy can make us regret love.

On reading Shakespeare's play in context, in all its theatrical polyphony and dramatic discontinuity, it is impossible to share René Girard's[76] interpretation, which makes of Othello a poor victim who lacks self-esteem because he is a foreigner who is also both ethnically and socially inferior.[77] It is this, on Girard's reading, which leads him to appeal to Cassio, the handsome young man whom he promotes as captain, to act as a go-between. Othello is fascinated by his supposed rival, even before being captivated by his wife. His desire is, from the beginning, mimetic and fatally triangular. On this account, the corner has already been turned, and the events that create the tragic suspense are neutralized from the start. The plot becomes predictable. The text has nothing more to add. Tainted by an inveterate weakness (a social insecurity which is, in fact, completely foreign to him), Othello alone allegedly brings about his own ruin. Iago (whose wicked and successful strategy Shakespeare depicts with precision) thus becomes merely a surrogate – Othello's sacrificial substitute. Above all, jealousy is reduced to envy: a matter to be settled between men – or, rather, between a man and his scapegoat.

As with Medea, alas, we are no longer able to enter into the true concerns of these characters. Murder – it goes without saying, but I repeat it anyway – is awful and unforgivable. But to diminish Othello in this way is, once again, to refuse to lend a benevolent and intelligent ear to erotic jealousy. Those who are jealous must suffer from some character defect. They are always in the wrong. Othello, whose jealousy was by no means easy to arouse, finds himself adrift in an ocean of incomprehension. Seized by the anguish of a normal, but entirely hypothetical, jealousy, he acts as any true lover would and initially refuses to believe what he has been told. He suspends his judgement and goes out of his way to test the normality of his jealousy by trying to discover what has really happened between Desdemona and Cassio. He has, of course, spoken to his wife, but she has replied only with protestations and an obvious and panicky lie about the fate of the handkerchief, followed by persistent requests that Cassio 'be received again'. Every time Othello cries out in anguish: 'the handkerchief!', Desdemona answers him with some further mention of Cassio: 'You'll never meet a more sufficient man.' She insists, 'I pray, talk me of Cassio' – 'A man that all his time / Hath founded his good fortunes on your love, / Shared dangers with you' – until finally, in anger and despair, Othello leaves the stage. When he has gone, Emilia, Iago's wife and the unwitting accomplice of his duplicity, turns to Desdemona and asks: 'Is not this man jealous?' We could also ask why Desdemona was so insensitive, so unsympathetic, so blind to her husband's state of mind that she did nothing to reassure him – quite the opposite. Henceforth Othello will believe only what his eyes and his ears tell him. What he does not know, of course, is that Iago, the true 'green-eyed' monster, has poisoned them both.

Othello is fettered by his own generous-hearted but excessively trusting good faith. Once he accepts the evidence – as false as it is brilliant – of Desdemona's betrayal, he leaps into the void. 'It is not words', he cries out, 'that shake me thus: / pish! – Noses, ears, and lips. – Is't possible? – Confess – handkerchief! – O devil!' And then he 'falls into a trance'.[78] It is this which makes of his suicidal inquiries not the fatal outcome of an ancient malaise, but a tragedy.

Anyone who has ever been jealous will know what I am talking about.

Fugitives

I am talking about normal jealousy – without quotation marks. I shall now continue the same meditation in the wake of a novel which, together with the works of Stendhal, is such a large part of modern sentimental education: Marcel Proust's *Remembrance of Things Past*.

For Stendhal, jealousy creates love because it is jealousy which brings about the 'second crystallization', that 'profound attention' which is aroused when the object of love turns out to be a creature whose 'appetites' one never will possess, as Othello might say,[79] or reveals herself to be, in the language of Proust, a 'fugitive' (*être de fuite*).[80] 'More often than not, a body becomes the object of love only when an emotion, fear of losing it, uncertainty of getting it back, is merged into it.'[81]

Suddenly, everything falters. And I freeze. Out of this priority of jealousy over love, Proust's readers have found a further reason for making of it something phantasmic. If we love only because we are jealous to begin with, and for the simple fact that the other, the object of our love, has slipped away from us, we love nothing, or we love badly. From the height of our Cartesian pulpit we might say, for instance, that suspicious jealousy is wholly despicable because it reveals a love that is not 'of the right kind', because one clearly has a 'low opinion' either of oneself or of the other person. One does not love the faithless lover but only, in Descartes' words, 'the good that one imagined to consist in being in sole possession [of him or her]'. Understood as the anguish of losing an entirely imaginary good – which is nothing but the *idea* of possessing the other in exclusivity – jealousy is paradoxically incompatible with real infidelity. 'For to try to avoid some evil when one has reason to fear it is not properly jealousy.'[82] Thus, while La Rochefoucauld recognizes the reasonableness of normal jealousy, Descartes divides it into two: by definition, amorous jealousy is related to suspicion and mistrust (which is unseemly), while the fear of loss is, precisely, only a justified fear (not jealousy proper).[83] In short, once one has been deceived there is nothing more to be jealous about. Jealousy is either silly, or it is something else. Such are the joys of 'clear and distinct ideas'!

The grip of agonizing pain

It is precisely in between these two extremes that Proust locates the experience of jealousy. For him, the suspicious imagination is inseparable from the knowledge acquired suddenly and by chance of the infidelity – past, habitual and therefore probable – of the other. We become distrustful because our trust has been betrayed. We begin to ask questions, form hypotheses, conduct inquiries, not because a secret sense of indignity gnaws at us or some dark menace corrupts our desire, but because – from one moment to the next – we have been blighted by the epiphany of eros – the winged deity. In Proust, all the wings are worn by fugitives. 'To such beings, such fugitive beings, their own nature and our anxiety fastens wings.'[84] Odette, in whom Swann has an intermittent interest, has a life of her own. Swann is, of course, aware of this; but, one evening, he suddenly confronts the reality of such existence, and his attention deepens accordingly. Albertine, who has become for the narrator – Proust himself – a daily, homely presence, has transformed his own house into a gilded cage. She is safely there. He wonders whether they should continue to live together. But every time he catches some new glimpses of her female liaisons, this same young woman suddenly becomes irresistible all over again. Now he can no longer leave her as he had intended to do.

Jealousy is a 'thirst to know'.[85] We investigate, we explore, we make conjectures because we are in the interstices between 'prickly', suspecting, apprehensive jealousy, on the one hand, and what Descartes calls a 'just subject of fear', on the other. We know, but we do not know for certain. Our pursuit of knowledge is driven by two very real circumstances: the falsehoods which we have experienced in the past, thus learned to foresee, without being able to prove them; and the shame of confessing our jealousy, which prevents us from asking direct questions. To find out the truth about Albertine, the narrator relies on his friends Andrée and Bloch and his valet, Aimé, because he knows that Albertine invariably lies to him.[86] He has learned to decipher her 'hieroglyphics', but this does not prevent him from being the victim of a deception which, as he will discover later, surpasses even his most distrustful speculations. Nor is he willing to admit to Albertine herself that he is jealous. He tortures himself, but, 'in any case', whatever his doubts, he refuses to speak to her directly, 'for fear of making her think [him] jealous and so offending her'.[87] He dare not reveal his suffering. He would prefer her to believe that he no longer loves her. Now these two conditions go together: the unfaithful are even more inclined to lie when they see that their lovers are jealous. 'Besides, if jealousy helps us discover a certain tendency to falsehood in the women we love, it multiplies this tendency a hundredfold when the woman discovers that we are jealous.'[88] Hiding one's jealousy in the hope that this will avoid yet more lies, while knowing all along that it is too late. Listening, watching, inferring – all in silence.

Jealous intelligence is of a discontinuous, halting character. There are accesses of jealousy, intermittent jealousy; but there is also interminable jealousy and even 'delayed-action jealousy' (*une jalousie de l'escalier*).[89] 'What had abruptly drawn me closer to her – far more, fused indissolubly with her – was not the expectation of pleasure – even pleasure is too strong a word, mildly agreeable interest – but the grip of agonizing pain.'[90] This adverb – 'abruptly' – captures precisely the syncopated pace of erotic time. For there is a *tempo* to love as there is to music. Jealousy shatters that. It grips your heart. 'Abruptly', the narrator's hands, which clutch at his heart, begin to sweat when, one fine morning, Françoise informs him that Miss Albertine has left.[91] We are unpredictable even to ourselves.

There is a tragic realism in the wisdom of the jealous, a realism that recognizes the vagaries of the social landscape – Paris, the salons, the shops, the park of the Buttes-Chaumont, the beach at Balbec, the valley of Chevreuse, in short, the 'modern Gomorrah'. The same realism also admits to the destruction of trust. Never does Proust's text suggest that there might exist a reassuring and anodyne truth which the jealous man would have been condemned to ignore, precisely because of his misleading jealousy. Never does the search for things past end with a backward look, which might reveal that Swann, or Bloch or the narrator had been mistaken, or that Odette, or Rachel or Albertine might, in fact, have been innocent. These men are not Othello, nor are the women Desdemona. Quite the opposite. In the narrative construction of the novel, these mistresses are not devoted, faithful, reliable and unjustly accused companions. They are 'kept women', women of a certain 'type', as their lovers know very well. They are women who, above all, cultivate the 'habit of pleasure' (*l'habitude du plaisir*). Objectively, they are fugitives.[92] To imagine their dates, their affairs, their subterfuges, one does not need to fantasize about incredible, improbable escapades that never took place. All it requires is to remember, in detail, and with searing pain, situations, attitudes and inclinations one thinks one can guess at, or that one knows, more or less. The language of scientific experiment allows the narrator to explain how, from each barely perceived event, we may deduce others which, taken together, will create an image, pointillist, but coherent.[93] The language of medicine means not that jealousy is absurd and endogenous, but that it is painful and chronic. Chronic because a shattered trust will ensure that the jealous anxiety remains alive.

Some pleasure

One evening, Albertine announces that she wishes to attend a soirée to be given by Mme Verdurin (a soirée whose comings and goings occupy the whole of the volume called *The Captive* [*La Prisonnière*]). The reaction is immediate. The narrator understands at once. 'On that particular evening...[h]er object was to meet someone there to prepare some future pleasure.'[94] Is this paranoia? Certainly not! The narrator explains the reason for his 'certainty'. He has learned to interpret what people say, he admits, after, 'by their fault', he had lost his ability to trust. He now knows how to detect desires that are expressed unconsciously when someone blushes, or by moments of 'sudden silence'. This leads straight to the truth.[95] For there is a truth. Infidelity, sensuality and indefinite desire do exist. 'It is in fact one of the most terrible things for the lover that, whereas particular details – which only experiment or espionage among so many possible realizations would ever make known to him – are so difficult to discover, the truth on the other hand is so easy to detect or merely to sense.'[96]

Albertine's subsequent insistence that she is really not the least bit interested in Mme Verdurin's soirée sounds, to the narrator's disillusioned ears, like all too eloquent a denial. And it is a highly successful one. The truth is that she very much wants to go (or, at least, she wants to go out), but she hides it, just as she pretends that she is not looking at the beautiful women she passes in the street. Frequently in the past the narrator 'had seen her fasten on girls who came past...a sudden lingering stare, like a physical contact', which she invariably followed up with bold and allusive remarks. 'For some time past', however, probably since she became aware of her friend's jealousy, she had ceased making comments and now pretends not to notice anyone. This apparent distraction, as fixed at it was affected, was quite 'as revealing' as the 'magnetic swerve' had been before. Never had Albertine looked at erotically insignificant beings with 'so much fixity, or on the other hand with such reserve, as though she saw nothing'.[97]

It is by understanding this dance of lies and suffering, of suspicion and relief, of hope and disappointment that we can enter into the rhythm of the Proustian novel. If we wish to grasp the phenomenology of jealous love, we will have to follow the narrative scansion until the very end.

From doubts to inquiries, from denial to confirmation, the story culminates with the discovery that Albertine's infidelity had, after all, exceeded, in magnitude, intensity and regularity, even her lover's imagination. After her death, and when at last he has acquired a measure of indifference, the narrator completes his research into her past with a mission to Touraine and Balbec, which he entrusts to his valet, Aimé, and by interrogating their common friend Andrée, who, at his request, had accompanied Albertine on all her outings. In Balbec, Aimé sleeps with a charming laundry girl, who tells him how Albertine liked having sex with young women, including herself.[98] On the beach and in the showers at Balbec, Albertine had indulged in all kinds of erotic games with a 'tall woman older than herself', but most often with very young girls.[99] In Paris, Andrée, with whom the narrator himself is now having an affair, reveals to him, at last and unabashedly, the unimaginable: that Albertine had a taste for youngsters whom Morel (Charlus' lover) procured for him. She was able to carry on this voluptuous complicity with Andrée precisely because the daily intimacy which the narrator himself had created between them had placed her safely above suspicion. Andrée tells him how the duplicity of the two young women reached its height one afternoon when he returned home earlier than expected, bringing with him some highly scented lilacs. Andrée rushed out to meet him, claiming that he must leave at once and get rid of the flowers, because Albertine was allergic to them. It was all a hastily improvised ruse to distract him from what had been going on.[100]

The narrator was not, therefore, imagining things. On the contrary, what he had not realized was that the very person he had asked to chaperone his friend was taking advantage of the situation to make love with her under his very roof. He knew the truth, but he did not know the details. He was suspicious, but never enough, nor at the right time. He doubted, but never the right people. After the episode with the lilacs, Albertine had been unable to sleep for three nights, so afraid was she that he would find out about her goings-on. But he, despite his fertile imagination, never succeeded in working out what had actually happened. Like so many others at Balbec, Touraine and Paris, this particular 'little fact' had escaped him. Albertine's passion had a reality much closer in space and time than anything he could have envisaged.

And, for Proust, reality has the last word. 'The truth is the most cunning of enemies. It delivers its attacks at the point in one's heart where one was least expecting them, and where one has prepared no defence.'[101] Sometimes, when the truth dawns on us, it is an unexpected event that reveals the existence of past events – at a time when, fortunately, we have become indifferent enough to bear it. Now it is merely an 'unnecessary truth'. But, although it might have transpired too late to make us suffer, it can still remind us of just how much we have suffered when we were still in love.[102]

Problematic narcissism?

Scholarly readers of *Remembrance of Things Past* have for so long accustomed us to seeing Proustian jealousy as a kind of delirium that the language of reality, truth, event, may come as a surprise. Yet it is precisely in those terms that Proust describes the experience of jealousy. Only at the end, the very end, when we look back, do the pieces of our life, and of those whom we have loved and tried to know, finally emerge. Only then does the truth, in spite of everything, come to light.[103]

Of all the great sufferers from jealousy, Proust and his characters have been the most reviled. Nicolas Grimaldi, as we have seen, talks of the 'Proustian Hell'. Psychoanalysis revels in its condemnation. This 'little Marcel', although he may have been a genius, 'never got past or even reached the Oedipal stage of his development.' Since the novel handles the truth of experience with such a profusion of details, it means that its author must have remained trapped at this 'primary', infantile stage for his entire life. 'The jealous Proustian par excellence,' writes Éloisa Castellano-Maury, 'he who stamps and struggles with an oral and devastating violence, is first and foremost *His Majesty the Baby*.'[104] Even Julia Kristeva offers a clinical approach, speaking of 'the problematic frontiers of narcissism', 'the incursion of hatred into desire', the 'symbiosis of lover/loved' and 'over-interpretation'.

THE DESPAIR OF NOT BEING LOVED

'The jealous lover', she writes, 'devotes himself to *dissecting the sense of hatred* and/or his wound, rather than admitting the *independence of the beloved* or the incommunicability of lovers.'[105]

Proust's jealous lovers, however, do indeed have their eyes wide open to the independence of their loved ones. It is precisely because of such keen perception that they recognize in all fugitives their potential for flight. The jealous are fully aware of the abundant, transient, unknowable life of the other. They are curious about them because such people are more interesting than others. But the one thing which troubles them is sex. The habit of pleasure, the taste for passion, the need to enjoy and seduce – in short, the erotic availability of their mistresses – is the source of pain. And such pain is made even more disturbing by falsehood. It is eros which makes them suffer. The narrator is very clear on this point. Had he not detected, 'from that first day at Balbec', that Albertine was one of those girls 'beneath whose envelope of flesh more hidden persons stir, I will not say than in a pack of cards still in its box, a closed cathedral or a theatre before we enter it, in the whole vast ever-changing crowd?' So many beings in that one woman! But also, and above all: 'the desire, the voluptuous memory, the relentless search for all these persons'.[106] The loved one is filled with the past and the future, with memories and possibilities, with pleasures known and variable, and so on until infinity. This erotic infinity is made still more vertiginous by our own inclination to seduce, to seek for pleasure, to imagine new beginnings, to leaf through our cluttered memories. We, too, are full of images and desires.[107] We understand the other the better because we are also, in our turn, fugitives.

We are aware of the full extension of the seemingly 'boundless field of possibilities', and even of the fact that, despite our thirst for knowledge, we shall always be surprised by the 'real'. If what actually happened were to appear all of a sudden before us, we would still 'fall over backwards in a daze'.[108] The 'blindness of our credulity' always bears witness to a shred of confidence.[109] However realistic we may be about others, and ourselves, we are nevertheless constantly surprised by how vulnerable and naive we can be.

The jealous are narcissists, as are we all, and they, like us, live in a precarious balance between an 'excess' and a 'deficit' of self-love. Yes, but whatever our level of narcissism, losing the privilege of an erotic preference will always hurt. Yes, we wish to be loved in the singular, despite all our imperfections, in the hope that something will hang on to the other's desire. And, yes, if we are unfortunate enough to be in a relationship with someone who loves to seduce, and who lies to us about it all constantly, it takes time to break through the lies, to overcome the wish that the infidelities are not real, and finally to reach such a degree of certainty and pain that one decides either to break up or – if the slaughter ceases – to forgive.

Normally neurotic, we are all, like Swann and Proust's narrator, also normally jealous.

My indelicacy was hateful

We have to lay aside a legacy of preachy anaesthesia in order to read so much great literature. I will end this brief excursus with a contemporary autobiographical meditation: Catherine Millet's *Jealousy*.[110] It offers an unusually candid self-examination of jealousy. It is honestly right on target. It slices through the defensive envelope of shame to recount the immense effort required in putting a forbidden emotion into words. Millet is a self-confessed libertine. She has written a bestselling book, *The Sexual Life of Catherine M.*, describing in minute detail the complex, libidinous, unrestrained sex life she has led, with and apart from her husband. She fully believes, therefore, that she is in control of her desires and can anticipate all her emotions, when, suddenly by chance, she discovers that her husband has another sexual life, quite apart from hers.[111] Now she finds herself struggling with a sudden agony that is as astonishing as it was unforeseeable for her. The feeling comes from a sense of disintegration, dislocation, despair. 'The result', she writes, 'was an appalling physical sensation; a dry glacial wave came over my body.'[112] Now she finds herself overwhelmed by the need to ask more questions, to know more, and to reveal what she already knows, yet she is paralysed by fear of the other's anger and misunderstanding, and especially by the pure and simple mortification of having to confess to what she feels.[113] 'I invented countless strategies for letting him know, without actually telling him...'[114] Detours, allusions, the hope that the other might himself say something before one has to beg, capitulation and, finally, confession.[115] Truly a paradoxical passion, jealousy! It compels you *not to confess* to the passion itself, when one should have every reason and every right to demand a confession from the other. 'My indelicacy [*indélicatesse*] was hateful,' Millet says of the curiosity that had driven her to search through her husband's papers, in those private spaces, where she had come upon photographs of a girl, and then upon his notebooks, which she 'lost herself in deciphering until the forest of signs closed over her head'.[116]

How many women, in the history of Western love, have been made to feel 'indelicate', paralysed by the fear of contempt, daunted by the risk of ridicule, shamed by the demands of privacy. Ancient women did not have this problem. Between Medea and Catherine Millet, we have lost our way in a maze of numbing niceties. We no longer throw scenes. We blame ourselves for what we suffer. We act as if nothing has happened. We entomb our feelings. We bow down to cruelty.

I wish to plead for a rediscovery of the noble jealousy of the ancients (without the killings).

5

ART OF LOVE, ART OF JEALOUSY

The treatment of a person as if s/he were a thing, possessed and ready for use, is commonly believed to be the basis of jealousy. Since a human being (especially a man) is inclined to appropriate all sorts of things for himself and to grow attached to them, he allegedly shows himself to be 'a poor and wretched creature with a sense of deprivation' in all spheres of life, including love. As a consequence of our false morals and of the undue extension of property rights over a 'being that feels, thinks, wills and is free', jealousy cannot fail to be an 'unjust feeling'.[1] Any good is treated as if it were a material good. This is why the Enlightenment, followed by Kant and Marx, attempted to discredit jealous love. We must now return for the last time to this misapprehension, whose history I have reconstructed, and reconsider a discourse that, for centuries, has theorized the proper use of eros: the arts of love.

The project to be loved

In neo-Kantian feminist thought, to take the place of the object is self-objectification. This place is therefore forbidden to any self-respecting person. Male desire supposedly makes a woman into a thing. Heterosexuality is, therefore, reifying. Ann Cahill, a judicious critic of the same arguments, speaks instead of 'derivatization'.[2] Women are always thought of in relation to men. Their erotic presence is 'derived' from male desire. We must not categorically refuse to accept the position of object, therefore, for we are living beings, embodied and 'enfleshed'. But we have to challenge the systematic subordination of our desire and, more generally, the failure to recognize feminine autonomy. Although attentive to the traps of all ancillary perspectives, this reflection is more respectful of the body.

This is good, but it is not enough.

We need to rediscover, beyond Simone de Beauvoir, the themes dear to French phenomenology. 'I never become quite a thing in the world,' Maurice Merleau-Ponty wrote in 1945, 'the density of existence as a thing always evades me, my own substance slips away from me internally, and some intention is always foreshadowed.'[3] Beyond their apparent abstraction, these words convey a simple truth: it is simply not possible to be there, like a thing, even if that is what you want. And no one has enough power to compel you to become a thing. Someone may well try to make you into a mere instrument, but s/he will never succeed. You, too, might long for a state of peaceful, self-satisfied, inert being in the world, but you will never attain such a state. *Some intention* of yours – be it a regret, a dream, a protest, an aspiration, you name it – will always disrupt that 'facticity' and disturb you. Both objectification and self-objectification are pre-empted by the very fact that human beings always wish, desire, want, hope, prefer. Compliance, submission, resistance or revolt: 'some intention', whatever it is, has always already overtaken the human subject.

Jean-Paul Sartre had written some memorable pages about love and desire a few years before Merleau-Ponty. A successful, versatile, avid womanizer in his personal life, Sartre situated himself in the perspective that was entirely his own and from the standpoint of his own experience. 'Thus it seems that to love is in essence the project of making oneself be loved,' he wrote.[4] The vantage point of desire is the receiving side of another person's erotic intent; it is the place of a hopeful, confident, impatient *object of* a welcome, sought-after, longed-for interest. '[The lover] is and consents to be an object.'[5] This is the aim of love. Sartre was thinking, of course, – and he was emphatic on this point – of an intentional object, not of an object/thing. I approach love in order to become, precisely and foremost, an *object of* desire. 'Thus the lover does not desire to possess the beloved as one possesses a thing; he demands a special type of appropriation. He wants to possess a freedom as freedom.'[6] 'Freedom' here is synonymous with 'desire'. A lover wants to 'possess' desire as desire, which means that 'possessing' is paradoxical. A lover yearns for the most aleatory delight in the world: the spontaneous, capricious, unpredictable, renewed, always versatile, often improbable and ultimately unenforceable penchant of another person for him/her.

For Sartre, therefore, to conflate the *object of* love with private property was completely absurd, and he did not hesitate to say so.[7] To speak about reification was a total misunderstanding. And it was wrong not on account of the mere impossibility – except in Kantian legalistic terms – of reducing persons to things, or even on account of the irrepressible transcendence of human intentions (as Merleau-Ponty had claimed), but because such a reduction was at odds with the purpose of erotic desire. A man in love, or under the ephemeral spell of a charming woman, had no wish to make her into a 'fungible' thing. The point was to make *himself* interesting, attractive, impressive, admirable and, with any luck, irresistible *for* her. She had to like him. Hence Sartre's indomitable endurance and inexhaustible efforts to conjure the fanciful, whimsical, and ever uncertain inclinations of Olga, Tania, Bianca...A lover had to be a brilliant suitor, not a rapist.

A lover does not, therefore, want the enslavement of the other. On the contrary, all s/he wants is to be the recipient, the addressee, the beneficiary of an erotic attention that is not mechanical, perfunctory, obligatory, but free.[8] I crave to be loved. And if I want to be loved I want the other to make me feel that I exist (for her/him) freely, unreservedly, at every moment. If this happens, then I will not be used and bypassed in view of some other ends, but I will, myself, be the goal of the other person's intentions. I will be an 'unsurpassable end' (*une fin indépassable*). I will be saved from any utilitarian usage (*ustensilité*). The beloved makes me rather into a peculiar kind of 'object-limit of transcendence'.[9] To seduce a person is 'to risk assuming my object-state completely for the Other'.[10] I situate myself as a tentative, hypothetical 'object'; as a self-exposed, potentially fascinating 'object'; as a speaking, signifying 'object'. I wish to conquer that precious place in the eyes of that woman or that man, and I throw myself into an endeavour that might end in failure, disappointment and embarrassment – not to mention the unknown of the relationship that might ensue. I endanger myself to that effect. I venture into uncharted territory. And I do so whatever my gender. Once again, a man who pursues a woman *à la* Sartre is not a sexual predator but someone who has to know how to please by becoming pleasant. He has to strategize; he has to be persistent; he has to be humble enough to adjust to the wishes and tastes of his beloved; he does not shirk generosity; he tries to make scintillating conversation and, being Sartre, he writes long, beautiful, coruscating letters. Language is, above all, the way in which I propose myself to the other.[11] Sartre had learned how to speak to women.

Masochism and sadism

In tune with his conception of desire, Sartre sees eroticism realized in what he calls 'the caress'. It is the experience of my becoming a feeling flesh, in the unsettling experience (*trouble*) of my own desire, while I awaken the flesh of the other to the same sensations. To become flesh does not mean to treat myself and the other as a thing or, worse, to morph into a barbarous cannibal, hungry for a chuck of veal, but to become, in the time of love, a body entirely naked, abandoned to sensations, present here and now in its pure facticity. 'The same "enfleshment" (*incarnation*) affects both lovers'.[12] Sensuality is a communion of desires. 'Thus desire is an invitation to desire.'[13] If we read Sartre against the background of a Kantian harmony – intercourse is the mutual use of the sexual organs, an ignominious abdication of humanity, for a person who becomes a thing – we can hear, once again, the first strains of the same moral music. But here the tone is quite different. For Sartre, sensuality is a longed-for adherence to the sentient body, decontextualized from ordinary life – to the body made flesh. In heterosexual intimacy, a defenceless man lets go. A naked woman does the same. Both perceive each other in their pure presence. 'Immanence' is the name of the game, but immanence is shared. There are fleshy masses right there, but they touch each other. Skins press each other lightly. The lovers are '*indépassables*' for each other, which means, in less academic words, that they forget about tomorrow, 'for tomorrow never comes'. They do not worry, *in this particular moment*, whether their erotic abandonment to each other fits a proper relationship, equality or mutual recognition.

This is the moment when, in the Kantian kitchen, the flesh would turn to meat – the thigh to a chunk of round steak, the buttocks to boneless rump, the belly to tripe (or a pillow). But, in Sartre's bed, the flesh is neither a matter of butchery nor of home decor. The flesh is sensibility. The simultaneous 'enfleshment' of two lovers is not depersonalizing, dehumanizing, and therefore a degrading, bestial or shameful 'thingification' (*chosification*). It is, rather, a magical moment, sensuous and, unfortunately, ephemeral.[14]

The Kantian indictment of eros, however, looms large. Although the caress is saved from objectification, there are circumstances in which the object of desire may become something useful and serviceable: an object/thing. This occurs in masochism and sadism. In one case, I like to be treated 'as one object among others, as an instrument to be used'.[15] In the other, I do the opposite: I grab, I seize, I bind, I dominate and I treat my lover as a handy utensil (*objet ustensile*). My partner is a tool of my own pleasure, a functional device that I operate for my own sake and that I want to own immediately.[16] This kind of desire leads to sexual usage. Shame, Kant's leitmotiv, is reserved for masochism, in which one of the partners strives to be treated like an item of hardware. The quest for humiliation and physical pain is a desire to become nothing but a self-contemplating anatomical piece, at the mercy of the other. *That* is self-objectification. As a masochist, therefore, I blush. 'I am guilty due to the very fact that I am an object, I am guilty toward myself since I consent to my absolute alienation.'[17] It is Sartre, the reader of Kant, who speaks here. I sacrifice my humanity by making myself a thing.[18] Active 'thingification' is, symmetrically, peculiar to sadism: I take, and I see myself taking. I use, and I see myself using. I'm not troubled. I do not relinquish control. Instead I devote myself to the lucid, studied and orchestrated manipulation of chosen parts of other people's bodies. The elaborate, refined equipment the sadist requires in order to feel pleasure reveals his mastery of the erotic game. There is no shared abandonment, no spell. There are only machines to be operated, utensils to be manoeuvred. The body is exploited.

What is lacking in these ways of having sex is the double 'enfleshment' (*incarnation*) that makes the eroticism of the 'caress'. Somehow, like a professor of desire or a master of love, Sartre argues that there are good and bad ways of having sex.

The caress

Sartre relegates to perversion the capital sin of eros: the enjoyment of, with and by a partial object/cause of desire. This is where, yet again, the roast veal and the marrowbones lie in wait. Kant with Sade, then, and with Sacher-Masoch.[19] The conjugal contract, does not, of course, serve to legalize sexuality, as Kant claims. On the contrary: freedom must constantly regenerate love. Only the caress, through a communion of desires, spares the flesh from meaty decay. 'A contact with them [objects] is caress,' Sartre writes. 'My perception is not the *utilization* of the object and the surpassing of the present in view of an end...'[20] But, if a contact is a caress, it means that Kant was wrong: the sexual act is not 'use' (*Gebrauch*). I do not use the other as a means in view of my own pleasure. Sensuality is an 'unsurpassable' goal, as we have seen, sufficient unto itself.

The phenomenological writing on these gestures and sensations enters into such a profusion of details that one can read between the lines the sheer enjoyment of a man who loved to make love. Furthermore, it reveals an effort to think the value of sex as an end in itself. In response to the Kantian discourse, Sartre asserts that there is in the caress only the present, isolated from any context, detached from any surrounding situation, weaned away from any secondary purpose. No one possesses or uses the other. There are no people reduced to things. There are only objects of reciprocal desire, bodies that become flesh together. The dual incarnation of the lovers thus acquires a sort of innocence, an ethical legitimacy. And yet, although Sartrean eroticism happens out of a socially encoded situation and off duty, so to speak, it conforms to a norm. For Sartre, sadomasochistic playfulness leads into objectification and, for this reason, should be avoided. In order to open up the space–time of eros to the creativity of perversion, the theatrics of fantasy and the defining weirdness of an individual's erotic tastes, we need psychoanalysis (or personal experience). We need a morality that welcomes pleasure in the first place, to liquidate the premise that sex is immoral unless we sanitize it through marriage (Kant), freedom (Beauvoir), the caress (Sartre) or some other sanctimonious permission. But, although Sartre's love is constrained by the imperative to treat the other as an end, not as a means, what liberty there is in this erotic scenario! And what complexity!

Simone de Beauvoir, on the contrary, appears to theorize the intrinsic splendour of lovemaking but then ends up extending objectification to all erotic situations. She depicts heterosexual intimacy in enthusiastic terms. It is the instant that defies time, it is mutual generosity, it is a wondrous communion. But it can be so only hypothetically, if and only if Woman ceases to be treated as an object, which means almost never: not in any form of marriage, for the matrimonial bond is the complete negation of free desire, and rarely in adultery. Whenever and wherever men establish Woman as the Other, frigidity is the response. The female body resists the very situation in which Woman, as a person, finds herself constrained and from which she proves unable to escape. The body, therefore, can only feel if there is genuine reciprocity in a relationship. The *moral* and *political* quality of a couple is responsible for female physical pleasure.

Sartre sees the beauty of the flesh in touch. Desire targets the whole body, he writes, but 'attains it especially through masses of flesh which are very little differentiated, grossly nerveless, hardly capable of spontaneous movement, through breasts, buttocks, thighs, stomach: these form a sort of image of pure facticity.'[21] The encounter of these plump, yielding, inert curves lends charm to a way of loving which avoids grip and penetration. Beauvoir, however, makes these same 'masses of flesh' into an anatomical destiny. It is Woman who, as we have seen, is immersed in immanence, and who stays there, weighted down by her magmatic heaviness, her slabs of fat and folds of soft tissue. Woman is body-flesh-thing. Man transcends all this.

This foundational feminism casts suspicion not only onto gender inequality and social domination but also onto heterosexuality and the sexual act between women and men. In this way, Beauvoir endorses the Kantian reproach of objectification but redirects it in one direction only: man objectifies and instrumentalizes Woman. This happens in society and has repercussions in the bedroom. Not only because a man might act in an exceedingly impetuous, proprietary, predatory fashion, but also because, if he does so, a woman cannot but fail to respond with the sensations of her own body. The body utters a moral judgement. No reciprocity, no sensuality. We know the consequences of this train of thought. In order to redeem the sexual act, to wrest it from objectification, it is absolutely necessary to ascertain the type of relationship that serves as a framework for the erotic encounter – forgetting that the pure and simple presence of the naked flesh is precisely disjointed from its 'surroundings'. If only it were true that a nice, sentimental, egalitarian romance guarantees great sex! Respect is a duty, of course, but it is no aphrodisiac.

Art of love

There is, for Sartre, an art of love. There is none for Beauvoir.[22] Beauvoir inscribed the reduction of Woman to a thing in heterosexuality and could approve of such intercourse only on condition of a rapturous, instantaneous communion of body and soul, for a woman who had ceased to be an object. Sartrian sensuality, on the contrary, initiates an erotic didactic. You have to know how to make love.

Courtship is not just a sparkle of irrepressible lust. One has to work on it. The caress is not, like the ceremonial protocols of the sadist and the masochist, merely a question of pure and simple technique; it requires a concern for pleasure – for the other and for oneself. 'Enfleshment' is a languid and concentrated abandon which excludes the aggressive and, above all, the hasty manners typical of uncouth virility. Potency, effectiveness and performance give way to a different kind of capability, that of being overwhelmed by desire and pleasure. The caress is slow, ample, attentive to the arousal and enjoyment of the other. This kind of contact creates tactile exchanges between two bodies that meet in the *same* experience, personal and intimate.

Now all this is relevant to jealousy. Freedom excludes contractual fidelity, as we have seen, but love requires an object that is not, for all that, any old body or an interchangeable individual. I am looking for a personalized object that is as unique as I am and who loves my uniqueness. 'Actually what the lover demands is that the beloved should make of him an absolute choice.'[23] This highly ambitious demand, that the beloved should choose me absolutely, derives from the primordial perspective of desire. For the lover posits him-/herself, from the start, as a loveable object. He, she, wants to be preferred freely and spontaneously, but also specifically and exclusively. '…each of the lovers is entirely the captive of the Other inasmuch as each wishes to make himself loved by the Other to the exclusion of anyone else.'[24] This, paradoxically, is the active role in love: to achieve a totally exclusive passivity. I expect love in return, and in the singular.

As soon as you embrace this perspective, you are in the right sensuality. For, in any erotic moment, my incarnation will solicit the incarnation of the other. Desire invites desire. What makes the difference between perversion and caress is, in fact, the quality of the loveable object. In one case, it is one object among others. In the other, it is a singular object – even during a brief encounter. 'When you are here, with me, this room has no walls, but trees,' sings Gino Paoli. The sky in a room.

Pleasure, displeasure and jealousy

The couple Beauvoir–Sartre, however, demands the abolition of jealousy. The fulfilment of this commitment was much more complicated than expected, as we have seen. Neither Beauvoir nor Sartre was an ordinary person, and Beauvoir's bisexuality was to play an essential part in their agreements. But it is not their success or their failure that interests us. What is important for our purpose is the way in which Sartre could think, together, both the wandering liberty of desire and the creation of situations of amorous complicity. Love is free, and yet it requires singularity. Even in a passing situation, or in parallel, multiple affairs, there is an instant of uniqueness. I know that here and now the other person desires me – me, unquestionably me, to the exclusion of everyone else – and I know so because s/he is free to desire whomever s/he wishes. If s/he fancies me, it must be an 'absolute choice'. This shared freedom, lived in shared sensuality, is what protects the sexual act from Kantian objectification. But precisely because the other person's desire is so elusive, the capture of such desire calls for an art of love.

Who speaks of pleasure thinks already of displeasure. Defined negatively, from Homer to Freud, pleasure is the cessation of pain. As the children of Cura – that is, of Care, as Heidegger put it – we are all thrown into the world mortal, anxious and vulnerable. We extricate ourselves from this condition by creating punctual situations of enjoyment. This is the hedonistic project. Radical hedonism, however, cannot be sunny, overexposed and oblivious of the negative. It cannot be selfish either. We all aspire to the pleasant. But the pleasure of one may sometimes cause the pain of the other.

Jealousy is the experience of this imbrication of pleasure and pain. Whenever it surprises us, whenever we, or someone else, suffers from it, it is a passion that tears apart the dream of a fusional delight to be enjoyed in common among all at the same time. It shows us that infantile omnipotence is over, that no one can now count on unconditional love, that the intoxicating ecstasy, or the passing recreation, of one person may bring about the annihilation of another. There is no general will, no collective, egalitarian, contagious pleasure: there are only singular interactions made up of preferences that call for reciprocity. If one wants to assert one's own pleasure at all costs, one must forbid another to suffer for it; one must dare to be cruel, one must preach anaesthesia, one must impose silence. Here come the adjectives: shabby, petty, cruel, small, shady, sad, bourgeois, ridiculous, shameful, hateful, paranoid, pathological. Here come the scholarly reprimands, in their Stoic and libertine, political or medical versions.

Jealousy unnerves us. It reminds us that pleasure is not inexhaustible and innocuous. It exposes the fragility of our longings, both given and wished for, mutually and 'singularly'. Jealousy recognizes gallantry, coquetry, while drawing limits. It has been forbidden and made so painful to admit because we do not want to know that pleasure can displease and that our desire can suddenly become undesirable. It has been repressed because it is normal.

We must rethink, with Aristotle and the tragic poets, recognition as gratitude and jealousy as a form of erotic anger, as excruciating as it is justified. We must rediscover, with Epicurus, Hobbes and Freud, the anchoring of our life in pleasure and pain. We must rethink, with Stendhal, Proust and Freud, always, the realism of jealous love, the disappointment of not being loved, and the temptation to disavow whatever may be the cause. We must question, from our personal experience, the reasons for an ethic of love. To be loveable and to be loved, to be faithful while thinking about the potential suffering of the other, in a probabilistic perspective: it does not look like anything, but it is a good thing. Art is the only real antidote to cruelty. Praise of hedonism. Praise of an art of love. Praise of sensuality. All this is good *and* pleasant.

We need an erotic ethic. Sartre can help us because he invites us to subtract sensuality from the great Kantian reproach. At the same time, however, his condemnation of jealousy is implacable. 'A cuckold, of course, makes us die laughing.'[25] Cruelty triumphs. Moreover, that is what the theatre is made for. Above all, Sartre is the champion of a transparency which provokes jealousy while also forbidding it.

The great master of an art of love, who recognizes the jealous 'lesion' while offering advice about how we can play with it, is an ancient poet-philosopher: Publius Ovidius Naso. It is by returning with him to a distant and yet culturally fascinating past that we will finish our journey.

The Art of Love

At the very beginning of the Christian era, Ovid composed a poem of unbelievable insolence: *The Art of Love*. It consists of three books that offer us a palinody of love and a vindication of poetry. For Ovid, this rewriting was a matter of some urgency, because, on the one hand, the elegiac poets Propertius, Tibullus and Catullus never ceased speaking of erotic misery while, on the other, the philosopher poet Lucretius theorized only the inevitability of just such despair.

Here is but a small sample of the plaintive, whimpering, but also recriminatory tone of elegy.

Miser Catulle! O poor Catullus, stop your nonsense and, what you see lost, consider that it is well and truly lost. The sunny days of joyful love, kisses, sweet bites and voluptuous frolics are gone. The young woman does not come to you any more. May she regret it! But you, Catullus, resist: do not live like a wretch, do not live![26] Lesbia, his precious Lesbia, the only woman he has loved more than himself, now devotes herself to the most vulgar sex at the crossroads.[27] He hates her for that, but he still loves her.[28]

Propertius has a beautiful, sad nymph, Arethusa, write a letter to her dear Lycotas. Some characters will doubtless be effaced because of her tears! And if uncertain words were to escape his sight, she writes, it is because they were traced with an already dying hand. The absence of her beloved utterly consumes Arethusa. She worries for him and fears that calamity may strike. It would be better for him to be wounded on the battlefield rather than for another woman to engrave deplorable marks on his neck with her teeth![29] Unreadable and wet with tears, the poetic letter is all imbued with sadness, nostalgia and concern, but jealousy is the decisive emotion. Better dead than unfaithful! The thought of that beautiful skin covered in avid kisses is worse than the prospect of a heroic death.

As for Lucretius, in the poem *On the Nature of Things*, he offers us a philosophical explanation for all this, conducted in the name of reason. Love makes us blind. Words transform this blindness into foolish praise. The effect of this criticism is immense and terrifying. Lucretius reduces love to a gangrene of sex; desire, to an optical illusion; eroticism, to a category error; pleasure, to nothingness in motion. Bereft of any edifying intention, love poetry is nothing but idle talk laced with exotic words. Yet Lucretius is the only poet whom Ovid calls 'sublime'. His poems will perish, he writes, only when the same day brings the earth itself to an end.[30] Lucretian thought, therefore, presents Ovid with a unique challenge.

Lucretius' poem displays its own didactic programme: to prove that love must be unmasked, in its causes and in its nature. The reasons for its unpleasant effects – suffering, dependence and disappointment – must be understood in view of a radical purpose: to avoid love. This is what the poet teaches his recipient, young Memmius. *The Art of Love* will reverse this lesson: the poem will restore the rights of love, that is, its true nature, which is pleasure (not suffering), strategy (not dependence) and truth (not lies). Love is an injury, but not an illness, on condition that we learn the art rather than the reason – in other words, if we are not mistaken about a certain number of things: the movements of voluptuousness, the tempo of desire and the particular regime of erotic truth.

The high point of this theory of love is jealousy. We must discover the aesthetic knowledge that allows us to experience the volatility of Love – a winged God – without being his tragic victims, as Lucretius would have us be, and as the elegiac poets complain unceasingly that we are. There is a discord between anti-erotic reason and the art of love.[31] Reason makes us fear jealousy. Art teaches us, if not how to master it, at least how to use it properly.

The art of jealousy

In love, which Ovid knows from having experienced it in his own flesh, at his own risk and peril, we touch upon the true nature of things. Love is lived in pleasure and pain. It is a physical and passionate feeling on which one must rely to understand how the world works. Love, in other words, is at the origin of Ovid's representation of the cosmos.

First, love is metamorphosis. 'For human beings, indeed, love is a transforming experience, whether one is lover or beloved.'[32] We can go still further. It is by starting with an intimate and intelligent knowledge of love that, for Ovid, we can discover beforehand the law which governs the world around us: the fact that, as he has Pythagoras put it in Book 15 of the *Metamorphoses*, everything is in flux (*cuncta fluunt*). A liquid ontology supports the poet's thought. This liquid ontology is erotic. Then, since love flies and travels, it is, necessarily, jealous. The wings of the god Amor reveal its fickle character. Love moves from one body to another, from one detail to another. Jealousy always accompanies amorous feelings. 'I confess [*confiteor*]: I love only if I am hurt,' says the poet.[33] The explicit, emphatic and audacious confession of his jealousy gives us the key to the art of loving. The master (*magister*) himself knows no other love than that which produces a 'lesion'. This is what he needs to crystallize.

I understand Ovid's narrative meditations as 'thoughts'.[34] I would also add that, without announcing it programmatically, the poet takes part in debates over ideas dear to the Sceptics (on the reliability of perceptions) and the Epicureans (on the nature of pleasure). He also argues for the most radical denial of Stoic morality. On the nature of pleasure, *The Art of Love* theorizes a more truly Epicurean Epicureanism than Lucretius' authoritarian and tortured philosophy. Jealousy is at stake. On the truth of love, *The Art of Love* engages in a truly epistemological conversation. Jealousy is, once again, at stake. Against the Stoics, *The Art of Love* prescribes the intelligent and sensual enjoyment of affect. Jealousy is, as always, at stake.

To know how to love is to know how to be jealous.

Only you!

The universe of Lucretius is governed by chance. Sexual contact conforms to the following rule: to experience desire means to be struck by a simulacrum which excites the body and wounds the soul. It is a sudden shock, which occurs because infinitely subtle skins (whose appearance reproduces the silhouette of the bodies, from which they are detached) travel through the air and collide with other bodies, including those impalpable physical substances that are animal souls. The effect of this collision is a mechanical reaction: the blow causes the ejection of seed from the body that has been touched towards the body whose image, both aerial and material, has struck the soul, in the same way that blood will spring from a wound, directly into the face of the aggressor. This is Venus![35] That is desire! Nothing more. Then, if desire persists, the wound becomes envenomed, and we fall in love. Inflammation leads to swelling, attachment to obsession. To be healed, we now need a distraction. We must flee the *simulacra*, repel the cause of love, turn our attention towards other bodies, therein to redirect the seed. In short, love must be avoided.[36]

The Art of Love, by contrast, begins with an invitation to go out and look for someone to love. You must take the initiative and try to find her who will become the object of your desire. It is useless to hope for a sudden encounter. This is the artificial and artistic approach, as opposed to mere chance. The poet shakes up his male audience. To work! Get out! More precisely: do not rely on the automatic movement of bodies and images. It's up to you to make a move. You're the atom, so to speak. So: walk around, try to find yourself in the right place at the right time. If you so choose, go hunting, go fishing, discover, surprise the young woman to whom you will be finally able to say: 'You are the only one I like! You and you alone!'[37] The young woman, the Ovidian text adds, will not come to you, literally 'sliding through thin air'.[38] Sliding through thin air, coming out of the blue, so to speak, is precisely the way in which Lucretius' *simulacra* work. If a young woman were a *simulacrum*, she would fall into your lap. A woman, however, is not a *simulacrum*. This is the meaning of this sentence. From this revelation, a wise lover will be able to draw reasonable conclusions about the body, space, time, language and desire. And, of course, about jealousy.

First of all, if a girl is not a fluctuating film, then she is a dense, heavy and tangible body. Lucretius' decisive argument against love was that, in the most intimate and physical contact, we remain dissatisfied, like an unfortunate man who, although immersed in a river, is nevertheless tormented by an inexhaustible thirst. What we covet so intensely is, after all, only a rarefied texture which has struck us, but which the wind carries away.[39] Ovid refutes this. To him, to desire is not to take an impalpable and fleeting image for a body. A body is simply a body: it is, in turn, that face, that hair, those fingers, those feet, those lips – all those little bits that you stroke and embrace, name and flatter. By entering into the detail of the body through praise, erotic poetry opens up the perspective of another materialism: spontaneous movements, tangible bodies, voluptuous sensations. Desire is tactile and deictic: it touches this flesh that it indicates. It sticks to this tiny partial object, here and now. We can see here an ancient version of Sartre's caress.

Then, if you want to meet this body, it is up to you to locate it, through your own strenuous efforts.[40] You must not fear (or hope for) the inexorable, and perhaps disastrous, impact of a floating *simulacrum* at random. You have control over your movements and intentions. Like a hunter, a fisherman or a soldier, and, less metaphorically, like a dynamic Roman man, go and dine in town, go to the theatre, the circus, the Forum, the Field of Mars and the gardens.

We are in the city of Venus, after all, where all the beautiful women of the world reside. Rome is a labyrinth that one must come to know in all its corners suitable for felicitous encounters. Rome is yours, lucky young man: take the time to explore it! Instead of prescribing, as Lucretius had, that one should flee from or repress a loveable object which would be first unexpected, and thereafter haunting, Ovid recommends the exact opposite: go after her!

Finally, by projecting yourself into the world in search of a young woman, you will discover an individual whom you will choose, single out and make unique. You will say to her: 'You are the only one I like!' This is a speech-act which places its recipient in a category apart: a declaration of love crowns the effort of the Ovidian lover.

Preference marks the transition from indefinite desire to love, by separating one particular object of desire from all others. This predilection, whose importance for the philosophers of the eighteenth century we have seen, reverses the Lucretian perspective. Venus is not the shock of any *simulacrum* onto a physically receptive body and soul. It is a deep and focused attention. Attachment is not a hazardous and morbid fixation but the promise of happiness that emanates from this person, and from her alone. From one end to the other of this discourse, desire is a matter of time. Seduction operates differently at different hours of the day and night. Mastering luck requires a search for moments that lend themselves to encounters. One must know how to choose the appropriate ones. But it is the art of waiting which tests the competence of a suitor. While the Lucretian *simulacrum* takes you by surprise, urban love requires endurance, because what interests you is that precise person whose expectation you expect in return. Whereas, for Lucretius, time causes either the degeneration of the erotic wound or the cannibalistic impatience of the lover who despairs of ever being able to possess even the most flimsy of *simulacra*, in *The Art of Love*, time is a suitor's best friend.[41] Let women learn how to keep men waiting. Let men learn how to wait. To delay and to temporize (*morari*) is not passive patience but active attention. Stay put, but available; be discreet, but ready, until the desire of this woman ripens and comes to gratify your own desire, 'singularly', as Hobbes would say. Wait until the miracle comes. The activity of waiting is, as we have seen, a discursive activity. That is the most fundamental lesson. Rape is violence because it goes against the other's desire, and it does so swiftly, brutishly; seduction is a proper use of time – a time for words.

One approaches love by posing as an object of desire, Sartre would say. More precisely, one projects oneself as a fascinating object, hopeful of captivating the desire of others, as a signifying object, earnestly eager to enchant the other by endlessly speaking and writing.

Ovid, the Epicurean

Lucretius' poem takes the form of a sublime popularization of Epicurus' thought.[42] At the heart of this thought is pleasure, *voluptas*. Now, in *On The Nature of Things*, sex, sensuality and love seem to have very little to do with pleasure. The sexual act is reduced to natural insemination, to be concluded quickly, without unnecessary voluptuous contortions, and with the fertilization of the woman.[43] Admittedly, there are very short intervals of voluptuousness. The seminal discharge brings physical pleasure and the intermittent relief from the pressure of desire.[44] But all the rest merely hurts, starting from the wound that the *simulacrum* inflicts on the soul until the onset of inflammation, insatiability, disappointment, regret, anguish and deceit. Love leaves a bad taste in the mouth: even the most voluptuous moments are tainted with bitterness.[45]

Lucretius' *maître à penser*, Epicurus, had dissociated passion and pleasure, but only by recommending that one think twice before yielding to eros, for it was necessary to calculate what impact it might have on one's own life and that of others. You tell me, he warns a young man, that you are filled with amorous intent. All well and good: follow your inclinations as you please, so long as you do not violate the laws, or undermine local customs, or cause harm to any of your relatives. Be certain, too, not to exhaust your flesh or to sacrifice your life. Since, however, the 'things of love' will hardly be profitable to you, you should just be glad that they do not harm you.[46] Like all pleasures, erotic pleasure must not be allowed to cause pain – or only the least possible. This evaluation of the possible consequences of our pursuit of pleasure is the hedonic calculus, or 'compensation' (*compensatio*). The Epicureans we encounter in Roman philosophical literature theorize it. As Cicero explains,

> Epicurus teaches all this about pleasure, one considers that one must always wish and seek pleasure itself, because it is pleasure, while, for the same reason, one must always flee pain, because it is pain. And the wise man will practice the 'compensation', so as to avoid pleasure, if this pleasure will cause greater pain; and he will endure a pain that causes a greater pleasure.[47]

Lucretius, however, goes much further. He separates physical sex from love of preference – a passion which for him is completely pathological.[48] The initial excitement is an ulcer (*ulcus*) that will become more and more painful (*vivescit et inveterascit*) unless we pass quickly to other desirable bodies, to whom we must transfer the motion of our soul (*animi traducere motus*). It is precisely the fixation on a particular person that is sick. It is a sure pain (*certus dolor*), a form of madness (*furor*), an increasingly aggravating trouble (*aerumna gravescit*). We need an anonymous plural.[49]

To turn away from the body whose semblance has struck us, for the benefit of other bodies, is the only possible cure. It is a radical approach. There are no other remedies, such as travelling, taking a trip to the country or a change of air. The elegiac poets had tried this kind of self-medication on themselves to no avail. Epicurus had argued that the only way to eliminate passion was to put an end to all encounters, conversations, and any life together.[50] It was simple and easy. For Lucretius, however, there is no sweet medicine. We must tear ourselves away from the *simulacrum* altogether, so as to reject all that nourishes love and, above all, threatens to change the trajectory of the seed. In a language that, by its intransigence, recalls the Stoics rather than Epicurus, Lucretius emphasizes the rapidity of the disease that love is, and the urgency to act immediately before anguish and pain take over. Soon, it will be too late. Unlike his predecessors, however, Lucretius advocates the use of sex to achieve this. We must look for other outlets for all that accumulated seminal fluid.

And then, at the core of it all, there is jealousy. For Lucretius, a man in love will necessarily always be jealous, because the possession of the beloved can never be complete. First of all, the desire to pierce/absorb the body of another (a *simulacrum*) by embraces, kisses and even biting is always in vain. Secondly, deception proliferates. Furtive smiles, secretive glances, complicitous gestures are, in fact, an integral part of the amorous experience.[51] When one is caught up in love, one is exposed to dissimulation, mendaciousness, disillusionment. Because we expect a complete fusion in the erotic contact, we can only ever be dissatisfied. Because *simulacra* float everywhere and may strike anyone, desire is always on the move. Vulnerability to jealousy is therefore fundamental. Love, as we have seen, turns to pathology as soon as the emission of the seed singles out one particular body and persists in aiming only at that one target. There is no question of reciprocity or even of satisfaction. It hurts, that's all. To wander around (*vagus*) with the 'wandering Venus' (*vulgivaga Venere*) is the obvious mechanical antidote to this blockage – the only one that works.

Ovid redefines all this. Sex is a pleasure. Love is also a pleasure. Art enhances and maximizes it in all sorts of ways: from the playful variation on the 'service of love' (that is, wooing devotedly), to the pleasant lifestyle that one endeavours to offer to the beloved (conversing, singing, dancing, playing, walking together, etc.) so as to entertain in every possible way, without ever complaining, to the analgesic and cunning handling of infidelity (sparing humiliation, without ever explaining), to the well-orchestrated joys of the bed (where enjoyment must be shared).[52] Above all, jealousy is rethought in a completely new way. Men and women are inevitably unfaithful.[53] Love is winged, and it is practically impossible to stop the little god in flight. Women are slightly less unfaithful than men. No doubt about it. And yet, the 'preceptor of love' explains, couples can build lasting relationships – if only all resist the will to know and the vanity of bragging.[54] Love is not frivolous: there is an injury, there is a 'lesion'. But, out of this wound, the poet has learned how to create voluptuousness. His art is analgesic.

The Art of Love rediscovers the original hedonism of Epicureanism. No less than Horace or Cicero's Epicurean characters, Ovid embraces and supports the reasons for pleasure. But he does so without warning. Epicurus is not named, nor is his authority acknowledged. But the essence of his philosophy is present nonetheless. The poem is filled with physical pleasure but also joy, enjoyment and gratitude for enjoyment. The words of pleasure are omnipresent; the descriptions of sexual acts are detailed. Ovid even recommends erotic manners that are comparable to Sartre's 'caress'.[55]

How about displeasure? We calculate it, we control it, we even feign it. We are not afraid to suffer a bit. And we are not afraid of jealousy either. Accept physiological sex, but avoid at all costs the pain of love! This was Lucretius' lesson. Look for pleasure! Enjoy everything, including the troubles you will have been able to convert into pleasure! This is Ovid's lesson. For the former, pleasure turns into displeasure at once. For the latter, pleasure can be found at every step in the amorous experience. It is as if Ovid had wanted to challenge his sublime model, Lucretius, only in order to out-master him. He is the true heir of Epicurus. He knows about *Voluptas*. He has understood the nature of things. Read in this perspective, *The Art of Love* acquires a cultural significance that goes far beyond its literary or ideological import. If love can be taught, mastered and shaped, then you need new ideas about language, time, movement, truth, fiction, pain and pleasure. You need a new ethic. You are a philosopher.

Pain, anger and love

Thus far, we have been able to read Ovid with Sartre, for they both share a rare and interesting vision of sensuality. Now, however, it is time to separate them radically. As soon as he begins to speak of jealousy, the Roman poet takes a step forward. Indispensable, justified, exciting and natural, jealousy is an integral part of the amorous experience. Love has wings. But one must abstain from making infidelity known. That is only cruel and may be disastrous. Farewell, transparency!

Jealousy presents an extreme challenge to Ovidian hedonism. We want to enjoy ourselves. We want to build lasting relationships, but we also like furtive flings and 'contingent' affairs. We want to have it all. Our pleasure, however, must not be acquired at the price of our partner's displeasure. The art of love is a balancing act. The premise of this demanding imperative is the seemingly selfish (but actually generous) lucidity typical of intelligent pleasure-seeking: to suffer is normal, frequent and highly predictable. In love, we have to expect erotic anger. And we have to respect it.

'My heart suffers, and love overflows with anger,' admits Hypsipyle, Jason's first wife, when Medea attracts and seduces him.[56] The fury of a woman who surprises a rival in her lover's bed is as natural as that of wild boars attacked by dogs, lionesses whose cubs are threatened, and vipers when they are disturbed.[57] The injured woman burns, rushes like a bacchante, while her body exhibits her despair.[58] Such a commotion may be fatal for the culprit. Ovid understands the reactive dynamics of anger very well. This is precisely what he intends to teach to the sentimentally uneducated. The only way to reconcile the various demands of a complicated erotic life – to take pleasure and to give pleasure, without feeling and without causing pain – is the *art* of love. Neither ridiculous nor necessarily murderous, Ovidian jealousy can only be pervasive in love. In order to revive the flame of a well-established (but, perhaps, lukewarm) love, one must know how deliberately to awaken suspicion.[59] Desire is indeed mimetic. But one must be as discreet as possible in polyamorous experiments and, should an actual infidelity be discovered, be prepared to deny the facts and then make love. With all their theatrics – paleness, scratches, dark looks, torn hair and flowing tears – scenes of jealousy should flatter an enlightened lover. How happy the one who can arouse such dramatic anger! The poet dreams of finding himself in exactly this enviable situation – that of the object of an 'absolute choice'. Let your mistress vent her ire, therefore, but cover her tears with kisses and, above all, make love, at once, at length and passionately. The bed is the place of Concord and Grace. Never mechanical and always erotic, sex has a superlative power, that of binding and pacifying all living beings, especially humans. This is how civilization began: through the works of Venus. Let lovemaking transform erotic anger into eroticism. The poem makes us follow this metamorphosis in real time.

Give kisses to the one who is crying! Give the pleasures of Venus to the one who is in tears! And there will be peace. This is the only way that anger dissolves. Let the fierce grief of the wrathful woman be appeased by pleasure. This is the only remedy worth taking.[60]

It sounds simple, but the whole of literature is full of ill-mannered, short-sighted, incompetent lovers and, consequently, of blood and fury. Why? Why are there so many tearful stories of sad, disenchanted, betrayed women who commit murder in revenge or kill themselves? Because, in the past, the art of love had not yet been discovered.[61] With his new and novel poem, Ovid makes obsolete two traditional genres of erotic discourse: elegy, that unquenchable whining, and tragedy, with its vindictive monsters. When she saw Cassandra with her own eyes, Clytemnestra stabbed Agamemnon to death. When she learned that her husband, Tereus, had slept with Philomela, her own sister, Procne carefully stewed her children and presented this unsavoury casserole to the boys' unsuspecting father. Of course, as one might expect, Ovid evokes Medea. 'The barbarous Phasian woman', the preceptor of love reminds us, 'avenged on her own children the crime of Jason and the violation of the conjugal faith.'[62] And, as we might have guessed, Ovid understands her. This is the portrait of anger. And there is justice in this anger. Venus injured takes up just arms (*iusta arma*), strikes in return, and causes the aggressor to lament.[63] The fault is with him who deceives without showing any regard for the other. Cautious lovers must fear these crimes. Transgressions must be concealed, and, once again, one must be wary of boasting.

As much as women have to learn how to behave in order not to suffer so much, men must acquire the skills required to treat them well and the ability to spare them the ache of anger. To understand the price of ignorance in these matters, we must read the *Heroides*.

Ovid composed this collection of epistolary monologues to be read as miniature tragedies. In these poems, a few 'heroines', namely the great protagonists of literary mythology – Dido, Ariadne, Helen, Sappho, Oenone, Deianira, Hypsipyle, Medea – write long letters to their lovers. These women in love have been abandoned, most often for other women. Each of them addresses the man who has hurt her so much by confessing and describing her feelings in detail. We are witnessing the rise of an excruciating, furious and utterly solitary agony – and the phenomenological account of such agony is presented to the very man who has caused the damage. He is not there to console. Instead he is being asked to recognize what he has done. The letters are provocative speech-acts: declarations of love, expressions of pain, confessions of jealousy. 'I saw, with a trembling heart, a woman's face,' Oenone writes to Paris. It was Helen, standing proud, euphoric, triumphant on the deck of the ship that brought the adulterous couple back to Troy. She stood there in full light, resplendent. She pressed herself eagerly against her lover. At this spectacle, Oenone's ire declares itself: she rips her dress into pieces, she strikes her chest with great blows, her nails plough into her cheeks, while she runs here and there bellowing and pouring torrents of tears.[64]

Always exemplary, Medea, in turn tells her story. At first, when she heard the songs in honour of Jason and his young bride, her blood ran cold. But when one of her children, innocent and jubilant, called out to her and urged her to come and watch the beautiful feast – Look, mummy! There is dad, covered in gold, leading the procession in his carriage – she explodes. Once again, the script is one of anger: torn clothes, beaten chest, scratched face.[65] Prayers, supplications – let her recover her bed! Why does he not come home, this man who is everything for her? But nothing happens. Absorbed in his new marriage, Jason fails to answer. Certainly, Medea does not know exactly what the great agitation of her soul is. 'I do not know what... [*nescio quid*],' she says. But we the readers, we know full well what is going on.[66] We know the sequel, especially in Seneca's version of the plot, since the philosophical correctness of these words did not escape his attention.

These heroines' poignant letters prove the worth of Ovid's own lessons to Roman youths. Do the very opposite of what I recommend – and you will see! In fact, it has all been seen already. Tragic intrigues contain no surprises. Inflict on a woman who loves you the ostentatious sight of your conquests, neglect to surround her with tenderness and sexual attention, ignore the detonating mixture of pain, ire and love that will follow your insults – and you will find yourself in the midst of a tragedy. Abandon this woman while she is in pain; remain blind to her sorrow; although she is not ashamed to show you how she feels, be deaf to her touching appeals and indifferent to her reminders that her life is intertwined with yours – and you will see! Sometimes it is you, young man, who will have cause to regret. Hercules treated Deianira without the slightest consideration. He brought home a war captive, Iole, and allowed her to march across the city, in broad daylight, radiant with happiness and covered with gold. Everyone admired her. The triumph of the rival! Deianira had always put up with the rumours of her husband's sexual exploits, but now she found herself the unwilling spectator of a public epiphany. Hercules' infidelity was there, flagrant and irrefutable – in her face, and for all to see.[67] In a desperate attempt to get her man back, Deianira resorted to what she imagined was a love potion, but the remedy proved instead to be a poison. Instead of recovering him, she killed him. If Hercules and Deianira had read *The Art of Love*, the former would have learned that the unfaithful have to be considerate, and the latter that there is only one magic: the pleasures of Venus.

The art of pleasure

We can appreciate *The Art of Love* even better by exploring what lies behind this didactic *mise en scène*. In his youth, the poet himself had tried his hand at the plaintive amorous poetry which is the elegy. How did he behave then, we may ask, and had he already learned his own lesson?

Ovid's first work, *Loves* (*Amores*), is made up of brief poems in the first person. The poetic Ego experiences passion, albeit in his own way. He puts into practice the kind of creativity the preceptor recommends in *The Art of Love*. In the manifesto of the collection (*Loves*, 2, 4) he not only admits that in every woman there is a little something that will touch him, but he deploys his linguistic creativity by changing the idiosyncrasies of particular individuals (that others might consider defects) into causes of desire. This is an exercise in imagination, attribution and translation. The poet's 'personal' experience is already a theory of love.

His desire does not simply move from woman to woman, he says, but from detail to detail. His love is *ambitiosus*, eager, all-embracing.[68] Anything is a sufficient cause for him to be touched (*causa tangor ab omni*).[69] 'There is no certain beauty that invites my loves. There are always a hundred causes which make me love.'[70] Variety is consistent with continuity. What acts on the poet is not the objective and undeniable (*certa*) shape/beauty (*forma*) of a whole body but a cause of desire – literally: a *causa* – which is as uncertain and subjective as it is powerful. Any detail may become erotically significant in his eyes, although for another man it might either not be worth mentioning or even off-putting. For such details are not necessarily 'beautiful'. One crucial reason for this to happen is that a woman is trying to please by applying herself to *cultus*, namely dance, songs, poetry – or simply by walking in a certain way. 'Something in way she moves', as the song goes. At these moments, some intentionality flows from her embodied presence, as Merleau-Ponty would have put it. The poet tries to find a place in the trajectory of her desire, as Sartre would claim. The poet himself may also embellish one trivial aspect of hers by anticipating its erotic impact upon his hopeful imagination. He hyper-personifies her, as I would prefer to say.

If a woman turns her modest eyes to the ground, the poet is set on fire and finds temptations precisely in that very modesty. If a woman is shameless, he is taken, because she is not rough, which gives him hope that, once in a soft bed, she will keep moving for him. If she appears to be severe and to imitate the stern Sabine women, he still wants her but believes that she is only pretending, out of pride.[71] Desire is optative. She is not refined? Let her come to him, so that she will have the chance to become so.[72] Does she walk languidly? She captivates him because of her motion. Is another one unyielding? Oh, how soft she might become once she touches a man![73] Sometimes, the perception of an attractive novelty can become a direct compliment. *You*, because you are so tall, you match the ancient heroines and, in your abundance, you will spread out over the entire surface of the bed![74] If *you* are educated, you please by being gifted in the rare arts; if *you* are rough, you are appreciated because of your simplicity.[75]

All these bits and pieces – hair, fingers, eyes, hands, arms, sides – might be seen as a mere assortment of body parts, food for a priapic desire ever ready to assault an objectified woman, not a person in her entirety. This non-person would then become a dismembered thing. But what are we to make of the gestures, the voice, the gaze, the attitudes, the manners of moving? What to make of the intellectual qualities? What of the characters, outlined here in a few brushstrokes? And what of the prism of literature and art, through which Ovid, like so many other writers, sees a lover's features? Think of Proust on Odette de Crécy as a Botticelli figure in Swann's eyes. So much more than the 'body' is eroticized! *Amor* brings everything to life and, far from turning a human being into a lifeless contraption, projects desire and motion onto a potentially loving partner who, although unpromisingly stiff or uncompromisingly austere, is still imagined optimistically and confidently as mobile and desiring – in bed. The partial perspective one has on a body creates a vivacious and interacting person – in bed. Certainly, it is the bed that is responsible for the situation of erotic, consenting, playful complicity. One has to accept that.

Already in the *Loves*, we can see a longing, charming, virtuoso conversationalist in action. Here, already, love is sceptical, relativist, libertine, eloquent, artistic and enjoyable. Love is also jealous. One evening, at a festive dinner, Ovid pretends to doze off, although in fact he is wide awake. He spies on the flirtatious connivance of his mistress, Corinna, with another guest. Believing that the narrator is sound asleep, they exchange glances, they talk to each other, they write words on the table with fingers dipped in wine, and finally they embrace and kiss passionately. A kiss is just a kiss, perhaps, but it upsets the viewer. The perspective of jealousy is exactly the same as that of love. The same detail that causes desire also causes pain. Those furious, darting eyes, those wet fingers tracing letters on the table, those tongues that touch each other: all of this is a torture. The poet had done all he could to see nothing, he says, but this scene unfolds in slow motion and in real time before his half-closed eyes. He feels hurt.[76] He will take revenge. In another poem his unfaithful mistress suspects that he has deceived her with her own servant. He denies this with all his strength before revealing to us, in yet another poem, that Corinna was quite right.[77]

Ovid's elegy is therefore ironic. Love is all about fractional peculiarities and trifling mannerisms. So, too, is jealousy. Infidelity is a continual, real temptation in an urban erotic culture. So, too, is jealousy. The two go together. The only defence against displeasure is discretion. Better to close your eyes for good and never confess to a misdemeanour. The master of love had learned his own lesson.

Here Ovid meets Jacques Lacan. Woman does not exist. Woman is not all. They are innumerable, those partial, minimal and virtually insignificant but actually distinctive attributes to which desire adheres. Objects of desire become significant for each of us only *because of* those distinctive details. Objects are fashioned and set apart in their silly uniqueness by language. And desire is metonymic: the part stands for the whole. As we will see in a moment in *The Art of Love*, one is allowed to mollify the flaws of the object of one's desire with words (*nominibus licet mollire mala*).

When love hurts

Ovid wrote a 'medical' work intended to help cure the pains of love. The *Remedies for Love* teaches us to unlearn the teachings of *The Art of Love*.[78] At first glance we might believe that this poem aims at disavowing pleasure and recovering a sinister, pathological, fatal vision of love. Love might be a disease to be healed or, better still, to be prevented, as it is for Lucretius; or it might be an intermittent affliction, as it is for the elegiac poets. We might even speculate that Ovid is merely amusing himself with a blame of love after having sung its praises, as if the *Remedies*, coupled with *The Art of Love*, were meant only to demonstrate his rhetorical prowess. It is not so. Ovid does not denigrate the amorous experience. He simply adds a sequel to the same narrative theory.[79] Love is a pleasure, but, under very precise circumstances, it can turn to displeasure. These circumstances amount to the infidelity of the beloved. If someone loves, and this love is good for him (*iuvat*), then let him burn happily (*feliciter ardens*) and enjoy himself (*gaudeat*)! But if one bears badly (*male fert*) the dominion of an unworthy woman, let him try the preceptor's cure lest he perish! The poet addresses precisely young men who might have been deceived (*decepti*) and who have been cheated (*fefellit*) by love.[80] In this case, we have to break up immediately.

As soon as a relationship begins to make us suffer, and in order to put an end to our misery, we must stop loving that particular person who is the cause of the pain. The poet, therefore, advocates a therapy not against love itself but against a particular love that you have to 'bear badly' (*male ferre*), because this individual woman is now unworthy and deceives you. One can imagine a situation, for instance, in which your mistress has not absorbed the message of *The Art of Love* and has taken a lover without the slightest consideration for your feelings. Or it could be, as in *Loves*, an awkward accident: she might try to be tactful by waiting for you to be fast asleep before she kisses her paramour, but unfortunately you are not, and therefore see all that is going on. It hurts. Jealousy is no less natural than infidelity. When one is forced to witness what happens, one cannot help feeling its pangs.

One has to make a truly hedonistic calculation. In order to escape from an abusive relationship, it is good to withstand temporary, inevitable, but controllable sorrow. In order to be well, the poet warns, one will have to stomach a lot of painful moments. 'And with this end in mind, will you refuse to endure anything?'[81] By applying the art of healing, you will manage to replace a sensual voluptuousness that might well be more attractive, but which now entails too much pain, by a new lesser, less demanding pleasure – for instance, gardening, hunting or travelling.[82] This is the literal application of what the Epicureans call 'compensation'. The wise man must 'shun a pleasure, if this pleasure will cause a greater pain; and he will bear a pain, which causes a greater pleasure.'[83] The strategy of the *Remedies* is based on the same Epicurean logic to which the precepts of *The Art of Love* conformed. On behalf of pleasure, Ovid appeals to our power first to make, and then to unmake, love. We do everything we can to create a situation which will be agreeable for both members of an amorous couple. Then it is quite possible that our partner (a young woman, in the *Remedies*) might become unworthy of us. Now, we have to do everything we can to reverse the situation so as to get back to the beginning. No one is immune to suffering, but everyone can be healed. The poet has tested his cure on himself. He knows how effective it is. As love is built by habit and time, it is by time and habit that love can be dismantled. Just as faked devotion becomes true, so 'he who can pretend to be healthy will be well.'[84] The art of love is always an art of time.[85] Nothing changes in the poet's theory that fiction can be converted into truth over time, or in his confidence that love undergoes perpetual change.

Jealousy, then, is not the hidden face of love, of which you must always be wary and which will constantly taunt you. That was the scenario of Lucretius' tragic Epicureanism. Ovid, as we have seen, rethinks all this. He instructs us not to focus our attention on those smiles and looks which are the 'little excursions' of gallantry. One must know how to play with indefinite desire and pretend that nothing is happening. He invites us to spare the other the spectacle of our infidelities, while at the same time suggesting that we intimate vague possibilities of seduction to refresh our erotic interest. While infidelity must never become cruel, jealousy can spice up the movements of desire. But, once again, jealousy and infidelity fall upon us as sudden events. If deceit and inconstancy strike us hard, we must put an end to the attachment so carefully cultivated.

Love and truth

Lucretius had denounced not only the ontological misconception of love but also, and above all, its vocation to deceive. Love and truth are incompatible. Love causes a cognitive confusion between the image and the body but also a constant misperception: true blindness. In turn, this optical dysfunction turns us into liars. A lover starts by taking an image for a body. Then, despite the objective reality of the body in question, he continues to see – and to put into words – this unrealistic image. Thus, a woman with a dark skin will have the colour of 'honey'; the one that is dirty and smelly will be 'natural'; a fat colossus will be a creature with charming curves; a woman of small stature 'one of the Graces', a 'grain of pure salt'.[86] The terms of praise Lucretius uses to mock love's rhetoric are often rare and refined Greek words. They corroborate visual distortions. Love makes you blind, but not mute. On the contrary, it fills you with eloquence. You contemplate, adore, magnify – and then speak. You attribute to women qualities they do not really possess.[87] Love lies in the details, especially in the adjectives.

From Lucretius' point of view, the compliments, amplifications and flatteries of which elegiac poetry represents a written crystallization can only be justified on this basis. His poem sheds a pitiless light on the hyperbolic panegyrics that Catullus, Propertius and Tibullus address to their beloveds. 'In the eyes of many, Quintia is beautiful,' Catullus says. 'For me, she has white skin, a tall body and a straight look. I recognize these qualities one by one, but do not say that she is "beautiful". There is no grace and no grain of salt in this great body. It is Lesbia who is beautiful, with all that is most beautiful, for she, and she alone, has stolen all the charms.'[88] Women can be described either as a collection of banal features that do not add up to any stirring attractiveness or as an outstanding, superlative and unique synthesis. This aesthetically unrivalled creature is the addressee of erotic poetry. Catullus writes of Lesbia's beauty. His poetry makes her *pulcherrima*. And this is precisely the elusive object of desire that for Lucretius is to be found nowhere on earth except in the pompous, unsighted and self-deceptive jargon of love.

As a result, everything sounds false – as in an opera. 'And the large woman shall be majestic; the petite one, adorably cute (*e la grande maestosa; la piccina ancor vezzosa*),' sings Mozart's and Da Ponte's Leporello, in a tone no less sarcastic than that of Lucretius. The women of Don Giovanni are all optical illusions. 'Provided she's wearing the little skirt, you know what he does!' (*Purché porti la gonnella, voi sapete quel che fà*). It is the female genus that interests Don Giovanni. For Lucretius, it is just a flimsy image that has touched a boy full of sap. This is Venus! A woman's peculiarities are only pretexts. Nothing but pathetic camouflage for an unnecessary fiction. This devaluation of the distinctive attribute that embellishes an entire body leads to a righteous condemnation of love. For it is precisely the seeming splendour of arbitrarily singled-out fragments – the size, the colour of the skin, the allure – that this kind of thought tries to neutralize. The model remains Plato, who teaches us to discover the neutral – *the* beautiful, *to kalon* – beyond its particular and rhetorically malleable incarnations. Once one holds the idea of eros, small bits of body, mannerisms and attributes become insignificant – you know what he does![89]

Ovid upsets all this. The art of love requires that a woman be treated with constant and absolute admiration. This is how you can persuade a *puella* to meet your desire in reciprocity. The miracle occurs because, in the long run, the verbal expression of your project to be loved solicits, inspires, conjures the desire of the other. By trying to be pleasant, we end up both pleasing and being pleased. This is reciprocity. The lover must know, above all, that all women desire to be desired. You must have confidence: sooner or later, you will succeed in your conquest. At worst, if one resists, then another will agree.[90] The Ovidian theory of love entails this certainty about female desire, a *cupido* that is less talkative than that of men but endowed with a livelier libido, and more disposed to fury.[91] Women care about comfort, flattery and voluptuousness. Lucretius paid very little attention to feminine pleasure. His erotic physiology was tailor-made to the male body. Ovid makes the narcissism of women, and their enjoyment of sex, the source of seduction. The desire to be desired places a woman always one step ahead.[92] The third book of *The Art of Love* reveals that the hunter, the soldier, the fisherman, for all their confident virility, will eventually take the bait, which, as if by chance, is always hanging in the right places. They are the prey. It's just a matter of time.

In order to achieve your ends, in short, it is not enough to be patient: you must cultivate this desire for desire; you must play with this inexhaustible feminine vanity. It's a language game. The women you meet will be many, different and, therefore, inevitably imperfect. *A fortiori*, do not spare praise! Do not be afraid to overstate non-existent charms or even to transform flaws into assets. It is permissible to attenuate, to alleviate, to soften (*molliri*) the defects with words.[93] While echoing Lucretius over the biases of gallant homage, Ovid nevertheless recommends the use of such stylistic embroideries instead of forbidding them. 'That which is blacker than an Illyrian, with a blood of pitch', let her be called 'dusk' (*fusca*). If she squints, let her be 'like Venus'. Does she look greenish? Then she resembles Minerva. Should her thinness give the impression that she is hardly alive, then portray her as 'delicately frail' (*gracilis*). The term 'skilful' (*habilis*) is appropriate to someone who is short, whereas a fat (*turgida*) woman is 'full figured' (*plena*). Make sure that each defect disappears by being overshadowed by a corresponding quality.[94]

Ovid advocates euphemism as an invaluable resource. It is not reprehensible, as Lucretius would have it, to enhance all these objectively imperfect bodies – bodies that happen to be tall or short, thin or large, blonde or brown, sophisticated or rustic, graceful or ill-built. Not only is it permissible (*licet*) to diminish, soften, mollify those imperfections; it is indispensable. Without verbal alterations, with only naked, raw anatomical descriptions, there would be no seduction at all. But seduce we must if we want to love. Since women will not fall into your lap, it is advisable to blandish those whose attention you hope to captivate. For Lucretius, the primary function of language is denotation. For Ovid, it is persuasion. There is a recipient: she will be delighted. This use of language is ultimately legitimate because these 'bespoken' adjustments are promising redescriptions of the body as it is. Charitable adjectives help orient the eyes towards a pleasant quality that is very close to a defect that is better left unspoken. In other words, 'full figure' still means that a woman is overweight, but to say so is simply nicer than blurting out: 'fat'! What is wrong with being nice? This is what erotic poems are all about. Consistently, Ovid responds to the hyper-realistic rationalization of love in the name of his art. By working through gradation and contiguity, speech creates a reality which is not counterfeit. Artful language shapes a new, more beautiful and more loveable body. Poetry works its magic: a true metamorphosis.

For those readers who might balk at this way of playing fast and loose with truthfulness, Ovid has a reassuring and interesting reply. Thanks to the flattering rewording of the beloved's appearance, and thanks to the repetition of strategically plausible compliments, what was not true at the beginning becomes true at the end. Women might see through the oratorical skills of their suitors, but they should accept being part of the game. 'Often the person who feigned really believes. O young women, be indulgent towards those who pretend: it will become true the love which in the beginning was false.'[95]

Love is made in time. Duration, patience and the ability to wait create the regime of truth that befits the erotic experience. There is no static antithesis between true and false statements, between sincerity and the intention of lying. What happens is rather the transformation of a lie into a truth. The same compliment that at first conveyed mere adulation will eventually signify the genuine admiration that is ultimately bestowed upon the beloved. This is love! Love becomes. It becomes true because it is spoken, and the fact of speaking changes the feelings not only of the interlocutor but also of the speaker. A fat woman becomes a full figure in the eyes of the beholder who keeps calling her '*plena*'. A poet is, therefore, the best of lovers. At the right time, all sorts of gentle blandishments must be allowed to flow over the face and hair, the tapered fingers and the delicate foot of the beloved: as water seeps into the sand, so smooth talk imbibes an imperfect body, polishes its surface, dissolves its asperities and embellishes its aspect.[96] Whereas Lucretius' aquatic metaphors speak either to the impossibility of pleasure or to the sad resignation to a dull, unexciting reasonableness, Ovid invents other fluids for other linguistic purposes.[97] In the art of love, streams of felicitous lines produce what is indubitably a rhetorical effect, but one that is aesthetic, plastic and, ultimately, metamorphic.

Jealousy and truth

We make love over time. We create a singularity by the ornamental enlargement of a detail: this is the Venus of Ovid. This is the true goddess of love! I have sketched out this larger picture so as to come finally to jealousy, for amorous displeasure has everything to do with how we handle the truth of love.

Lucretius had vehemently refuted the views of the Sceptics. More precisely, he had demolished their arguments about the senses. Remember that scepticism, in its neo-academic version as exemplified by Cicero's philosophical dialogues, was an important presence in Roman culture in the first century BCE. The importance of this radical criticism of our cognitive abilities could not be overstated. The Sceptics theorized the imperative to suspend judgement and withhold assent in the presence of any sensory experience. Firstly, they argued that the correctness of a perception is not self-evident, for there is no criterion of truth. No distinctive character will distinguish a truthful sensation from a false one.[98] In other words, we cannot trust our sense organs. Secondly, they insisted that whatever we perceive will appear to be there for us only from a certain point of view, at a certain distance, and from a given perspective. All these circumstances, therefore, give to our knowledge a situational peculiarity which can never be objective. Lucretius rejected this theory. We cannot doubt our perceptions, because the testimony of the senses is irrefutable. Only

ART OF LOVE, ART OF JEALOUSY

our interpretations of the evidence they provide may be faulty. Let us not be so audacious as to admit that the eyes can deceive! Abstain from attributing to the eyes a vice that in reality belongs to the soul![99] Once we are committed to the will to know the truth, reason helps us dissipate illusions and ambiguities. With Platonic contempt, Lucretius dismissed the sceptical challenge in its entirety.

Ovid, by contrast, recognizes the fallibility of the senses, advocates the cultivation of vagueness, and recommends the benefits of doubt.

The art of jealousy relies precisely on this cognitive stance: it is better not to put everything we do on display and not to know with certitude what the beloved is doing. In shady situations, one must cultivate the suspension of judgement and, by being thoughtful, tactful, considerate, allow the other person to enjoy the same protective haziness. On the one hand, Ovid recommends a young man not to flaunt his own infidelity right under the eyes of his mistress.[100] This would be a tragic mistake, as we have seen. On the other, he goes so far as to give practical advice to a lover who may have caught a glimpse of his lady friend hiding inside her house when he has been told that she has gone out. 'Do believe that she has gone out, and that what you see is false,' the poet advises.[101] Trust the maid, not your eyes! *They* must have made a mistake. Uncertainty is precious. The best thing is to know nothing at all.[102] Above all, we must not try to shed full light onto all that happens. Finally, Ovid insists that a man should refrain from bragging about the object of his love. For other men might be tempted. A friend, even the dearest one, if he believes what you are saying, may immediately become your rival. Men care for their pleasures, especially if they can be found at the expense of others.[103] The words that glorify the beloved must therefore remain discreet and secret. It is preferable not to trust your mates overmuch and always to be on your guard about your lover's fidelity. This is because love has wings and desire is mimetic, but also because praise has such power that it awakens desire. While lavishing homage on the beloved woman you must fear potential competitors, for the world is full of them.

Love is sceptical. Lucretius had made light and clarity the metaphors of reason. The study of nature must reveal the source of our mistakes in order to combat their causes and to make things clear.[104] In love, the unveiling of the true woman who lies beyond the embellishing veil of *simulacra* – a mediocre female carcass that might be ill-built, unwashed, disproportionate or stuttering, an unworthy individual who is probably unfaithful and always malodorous – was the purpose of the caustic rant on love's pathetic blindness. Ovid, on the contrary, theorizes the virtues of chiaroscuro. Art requires that one refrain from exposing everything to the full light of day, both metaphorically and physically.[105] One must respect the vagueness of certain situations, especially when the discovery of infidelity is at stake. Do not insist with the servant! Do not touch those tablets![106]

Consistently, when the time comes to break up, one must endeavour to remember as distinctly and clearly as possible the ugliness of the woman to be unloved. To this end, the poet recommends a language that is the exact opposite of seductive flattery: say that her legs are disgraceful, although it is not true; attribute to her the spiteful, uncharitable, disparaging version of any quality. The 'full figure' (*plena*) now becomes 'bloated' (*turgida*). You made her beautiful through euphemism; use dysphemism to make her repellent. Ask her to wear unsightly fashions; surprise her when she is not made up; have sex with someone else, no matter who that might be, then go on a date with her, which will enfeeble your desire; once in bed, examine carefully her physique, lest any of her shortcomings escape you. Open the windows! Keep your eyes fixed on her flaws![107] This therapy of offensive redescription as well as forced realism concerns, in particular, the woman's unfaithfulness. She took oaths she failed to respect; she obliged you to sleep on the ground outside. She prefers someone else, and she now finds your love merely tiresome! The nights she refuses to you, some common salesman is now enjoying! Try to thrust all these memories right there before your very eyes: *pone ante oculos*![108] Now it is time to be properly jealous and to stare at the beloved – at her imperfections and her perfidiousness – without rose-tinted spectacles. But be careful! Whereas normal jealousy for actual infidelity is liberating, the thought that you might have a genuine rival could rekindle your desire for the woman you want to leave. Beware of the imagination! Force yourself to look at the potential competitor with equanimity. The day you are able to kiss him as a friend will be the day that you will be completely healed.[109]

Love is a credulous thing

The story that best illustrates the art of jealousy is that of Procris and Cephalus.

Imagine that we are in a pastoral landscape of dense forests and hunting grounds on the outskirts of Athens. Glorious weather, blue sky, a cool breeze. Procris, one of the daughters of Erechtheus, the mythical king of the city, is married to a charming hunter, Cephalus. They make a loving couple. 'They said I was happy, and I was,' Cephalus remembers, in the *Metamorphoses*, while he tells the story of his misfortunes.[110] But then tragedy strikes. He often goes hunting in the woods. One day, the divine personification of Dawn, Aurora, sees him, falls for him and tries to seduce him. Cephalus tries to remain faithful to Procris. Despite the beauty of the goddess, he is devoted to his wife. Procris is in his heart. Procris is on his lips. He can speak about nothing but his passion for her and their beautiful lovemaking in the conjugal bed. Aurora grows impatient: let him keep Procris, then, although he will come to regret it! Suddenly, suspicion is sown in the lover's anxious mind. Why should he ever feel sorry for his loyalty? Is it because Procris might be unfaithful? He has been away from home, after all, and she is so attractive. And, above all, he knows himself: 'We, lovers, are afraid of everything.'[111] Cephalus meditates on his fears, on what he now believes and does not want to believe. He then makes the fatal, unfortunate decision to investigate (*quaerere*) and to test (*sollicitare*) the fidelity of his wife.

Aurora transforms him into a different young man. He is still Cephalus, but he is now unrecognizable. Like a character in Mozart's *Così fan tutte*, he calls at his own house as if he were a traveller visiting the land. His wife plays host. He woos her, he solicits her. Procris behaves irreproachably. Mourning her husband whose mysterious disappearance is devastating for her, she rejects the handsome stranger. Her pleasures, she says, are for one man only. Now, would this experiment not have been sufficient for any reasonable man? Cephalus asks himself the same question before admitting to his folly. But, in the throes of uncertainty, he is not satisfied with the results. He pushes his luck and presses Procris still more by promising her sumptuous gifts. Finally, he raises his bid so high that Procris begins to vacillate and wonder, in view of such generosity, what course of action she should take. She doubts (*dubitare*). At that point, Cephalus bursts into anger, reveals his identity, and overwhelms his wretched wife with harsh reproaches. Procris runs away.

The couple is destroyed, but later it is remade. The two spouses love each other again, are now more united than ever. They share an erotic flame, but also friendship and tenderness. Life begins all over again. But so does the narrative. Once again, Cephalus goes hunting in the woods. It is hot, very hot. The young man is enchanted by the breezes that refresh him. In the loneliness of the forest, he amuses himself by speaking aloud, appealing to this light wind, this pleasant air (*aura*) whose caresses are so delightful. He sings. 'Please, come here! O, fresh air [*aura*], how great a voluptuousness you are to me!' Someone (we do not know who) hears his silly song and is quick to tell Procris that her beloved Cephalus must be having an affair with a certain Aura. Might this, perhaps, be Aurora? Now the roles are reversed. It is Procris' turn to be suspicious. She faints in pain, believing herself to be the victim of an unfair destiny, complaining of being betrayed, fearing a crime that does not exist. She dreads a name without a body, and she suffers, the unhappy woman, as if from a true rival. She often doubts (*dubitat*), while at the same time hoping that she might be deluding herself. She refuses to give credit to the suggestion (*indicio fidem negat*), for she refuses to condemn her husband for his alleged crimes unless she sees them for herself (*nisi viderit ipsa*).[112]

Here Cephalus, who is still the narrator, pauses to reflect. 'Love', he cries, 'is a credulous thing!'[113] And yet, like Othello, like Marcel Proust, like Cephalus himself, Procris is not dreaming, not inventing, not looking for imaginary pretexts to be mistrustful. She is, as Shakespeare's Othello might have said of her, as he did of himself, 'one not easily jealous, but, being wrought / Perplex'd in the extreme.' And Shakespeare knew Procris' story very well.[114] Procris had complete confidence in her husband until an unexpected insinuation unsettled her. As always, in these cases, the problem was not her faith in her beloved – for she did trust him – but the plausibility of an intentionally and objectively disturbing revelation. Although she did not believe in it immediately, precisely in the hope that it might prove untrue, Procris decided to check with her own eyes. *Miserrima*! This is exactly what she should not have done. The investigations of signs, the experimental verifications of evidence, the testing of hypothesis, trust in the naked eyes and a reliance on autopsy are all forms of epistemic anxiety that utterly ruin love. For although Procris doubts, struggles and suspends her belief in hearsay, she also counts on the revelatory power of eyesight. Like other unfortunate characters, such as Narcissus, captivated by an odd *simulacrum* – the reflection of his own image in water, which he contemplates until he dies of self-love – Procris seems to follow the precepts of Lucretius rather than those of Ovid.[115] She is the dupe of her own eyes. She goes into the woods to check on Cephalus and hides in a bush to spy on him unobserved. But then she makes a noise and ends up pierced by one of her husband's arrows, as if she were his prey. Cephalus' jealousy had hurt her. Her own literally kills her.

The narrative thinking of the *Metamorphoses* conveys an erotic epistemology: one must learn not only to avoid hastiness and to withhold one's belief but also to tolerate uncertainty, suspicion and doubt and valiantly to endure this uncomfortable state of mind. This is not because of any axiomatic value that might be found in perplexity, but because the will to knowledge is counterproductive. First-hand empirical observation is promising, tempting, potentially reassuring, but it may also be deceitful. The rumour about Aura was false. But this does not make it absurd. After all, in the groves of pastoral poetry, hunters, shepherds and nymphs do just that: they fall in love. It would not have been the first time, as any reader of the poem knows only too well. It is in a context of high probability, therefore, that Procris, like Othello, demands 'ocular proof'. Sceptical, but not enough to leave it there; prudent, but not enough to put up with a nagging suspicion, Procris wants to go all the way – and have it all made clear. The tragedy of scepticism is set in motion. Trying to test a doubtful speech by seeing, the young woman makes herself invisible in the thick vegetation, but she accidentally produces indistinct sounds that Cephalus will not be able to understand. He will mistake her for an animal and kill her.

This story demonstrates just how the senses can produce catastrophic illusions, precisely when we go out of our way to bring everything to light. Thus, in *The Art of Love*, the preceptor warns Roman women: do not believe hastily! Impulsive credence may be pernicious: Procris will provide you with a convincing example.[116] As soon as she hears the malicious rumour about Cephalus' pleas to Aura, Procris loses her voice. Muzzled with pain, furious, she tears her dress, strikes her breast, claws her cheeks and, with her hair dishevelled, throws herself into the unbridled impetuosity of a bacchante. Once again, this is the portrait of erotic anger. All this suffering is precisely what the art of love helps you to pre-empt. Without reproaching your passions as such, the poem puts before you the effects of precipitation and the false testimony of the senses. Procris is unable to wait. She is too eager to know. She suspends her judgement, therefore, but not for long enough. Or, more precisely, as Cephalus says in the *Metamorphoses*: 'Love is a credulous thing... we lovers are afraid of everything.'

In his didactic mode, the poet offers to correct all of this: belief (do not believe what you perceive!), fear (keep trusting!) and haste (learn to wait!). It is a theory of the passions. Let us speculate! If Seneca were the creator of this Procris, who is so similar to Medea, he would advise her to refuse to consent to her erotic anger from the very moment she felt it stirring within her. Look how this monster allows herself to be carried away! Stop, before it is too late! This would be the Stoic lesson. Ovid, the Epicurean with his sceptic proclivity, invites his readers, instead, to bear uncertainty, to keep their judgement indefinitely suspended and to consider as true whatever protects love. The invitation to women not to fall into the trap of rash assent resonates with the recommendation addressed to men: perhaps you see your mistress inside the house when you are told that she has gone out. Perhaps? Then tell yourself that she is out! Do not believe your eyes, which also means that you should not run into trouble by attempting to double-check in person. Scepticism is part of a common and reciprocal strategy: do not seek to see all; do not allow others to see all. Discretion is the better part of love. In this way, both women and men may collaborate in upholding the enjoyment of Venus.

This is a beautiful programme: realistic, astute and ironic. It is also, of course, very difficult to follow. With the art of love, Jason would have been a gentleman and Medea would never have existed. But the world is full of cads like Jason, and Medea does not cease to exist. Icon of a jealousy without shame, she asks us to respect love.

CONCLUSION

Confessing the Unconfessable

Jealousy is normal. Not because we are stupidly wicked, but because another person's love and desire set us apart, enhance us, exalt us. Love individualizes us. And we want to protect this always fragile, and perhaps ephemeral, uniqueness. Our desire, as I have said so often, is directed precisely at the desire of the other. Love demands reciprocity. But love is free. The balancing act of reciprocity and freedom can only generate anxiety. This means that the erotic experience is the very opposite of an arrogant, guaranteed and definitive appropriation. Jealousy is, therefore, the very opposite of what a tradition of systematic blame has taken it to be.

Jealousy is realistic. Before dismissing it as an imaginary, even hallucinatory, disorder, we would do well to recognize it as the expression of an affect which is intense, frequently justified, and sometimes traumatic. Confining jealousy to a pathology of the imagination is an excuse for ignoring the wanderings of indefinite desire, for cutting off the wings of eros or, more prosaically, for underestimating the challenges of monogamy. It will also lead us to misread the fictional works that depict chance encounters, the fascination with beginnings, the thrill of desire, the appeal of pleasure, and the sometimes heartbreaking consequences of other people's amusements.

Jealousy is healthy. It is repression or denial which transforms it into a symptom. Once we admit the frail singularity of love, we can finally say: I am jealous. I am jealous because this person is something unique to me, even if I do not quite know why. If we speak out instead of remaining silent, if we come clean instead of disowning what we feel, we will be able to exchange the intimidation created by shame for a cathartic clarity. It is a way of not disavowing our desire and of making others understand just what it is to experience an event that makes us suffer so much.

Jealousy is useful. One of the most banal arguments against jealousy is that it is not a productive, helpful, practical passion. It is true: like love, jealousy trumps measurements, calculations and down-to-earth expediency. We would be better off without unnecessary sentimentality. To recognize what we happen to feel, however, is beneficial for ourselves and for others. By refusing to conceal our pain from our beloved, we let them know what the consequences of their actions are. Sometimes, as we very well know, infidelity is a frivolous, thoughtless, superfluous diversion. To take the measure of what it does to others may change one's sense of how worthwhile it really is. By opening up to our close friends, furthermore, we may find a welcome and constructive sympathy. What is really useless are silence, solitude and self-deception.

Jealousy is honest. To own up to our suffering requires an act of courage and humility. You cannot pretend to be so indifferent that the love of your beloved does not count, or so impassive that its loss could not touch you, or so invulnerable that desertion would leave you cold. You need a paradoxical strength to resist the temptation of denial and to refuse the shallow rhetoric of 'insecurity' or 'narcissism'. And you have to defy the most callous defence against jealousy: ridicule. You need the humble dignity to recognize that, for all your decency, irony and self-respect, life is putting you through a really bad time. For, if the love of this person is truly important to you, its eclipse can only wound you terribly.

Jealousy is worthy. If we define jealousy as a sub-species of envy, we frame our feelings within a demeaning prejudice. Envy is shallow, cowardly, destructive. If we try to redeem jealousy in general, as a reasonable claim to a favour we deserve, we might still disapprove of jealousy in love. We might believe that this particular claim is irrational (and, therefore, immoral), for love is not about merit. Yet, if we acknowledge that erotic desire is caused by idealized partial traits and aims at reciprocity, intimacy and singularity, then we can return amorous jealousy to where it belongs: in the very experience of love. Love does not merely qualify a pre-defined emotion. Love is a situation which generates this specific passion. If we are prepared to value eros, then we admit to the worth of the erotic anger we call jealousy. If, however, we despise love on account of its blindness and irrationality, then of course we want only to laugh.

CONCLUSION

Jealousy is pain. Rather than vanity, narcissism or lack of security and self-esteem, the realistic, salutary and honest perspective offered by normal jealousy enables us to see, first of all, the real pain it causes. As a result, reprimands and sarcasm ring false. The condemnation of jealousy is, above all, a form of cruelty. We may also ask ourselves why we try so hard to repress and deny this particular emotion. The answer must surely be that repression and denial form an infantile tactic of protection, always convenient and handy. And when this becomes a cultural norm – when we are told that we must heal, eliminate, eradicate this execrable passion – we are doubly encouraged to misrecognize what affects us. But, again: why the cultural norm? Why should love demand that we anaesthetize ourselves in this way? It would be easy to say that, in a world obsessed with personal development, security, and the trite promotion of an inflated Self, we have grown afraid of our own vulnerability to others. In this book, however, I have preferred to take a historical approach.

This narrative has led us from the tragedy of Medea to Ovid's *The Art of Love*, via a few modern turning points. I began and finished in the ancient world because it is there that I found two manners of thinking that are lucid, thought-provoking and profound. Firstly, in Greek tragedy, jealousy took the form of a spectacular and heroic, but immensely painful, erotic anger. This insight should be inspiring. Secondly, jealousy found a learned and luminous expression in the philosophical poetry of a preceptor of love, who insisted upon two complementary truths: that infidelity is a pleasure and that jealousy is a 'wound'. Like Proust, Stendhal and Freud, Ovid *knew*. He didn't insist, like the Stoics, Rousseau or Diderot's fictional characters, that jealousy was the most indelicate of feelings. He made no attempt to sugar over the double face of love.

We share in pleasure and pain. There is a cruel irony, therefore, in reciprocal infidelity. The more I come to know the sensations and the feelings of erotic freedom, the more easily I can judge just what the other, my adored other, might also be experiencing. The more I learn how to lie and take advantage of ambiguous situations, the more I know that my lover might do the same. Above all, the more entertained I am by a proliferation of pleasures and desires, the more I enjoy novelty, nonchalance, excitement, complicity, compliments – in short, my own delightful success – the more I am inclined to detect a similar taste in the person whom I love and for whom, by contrast, I would like to be the sole object of love. The more I know myself, therefore, the more perceptive I am about the other. To paraphrase

Stendhal, we could say that love is always imbued with 'vanity' (*amour de vanité*). But this is not a matter of social validation. Because I seek the other's desire, I know that s/he does so too, and not necessarily with me. My 'vanity' is their 'vanity'. Furthermore, the very 'passion of love' (*amour passion*) is a quest for a mirroring response. This is the most demanding of all: the gaze of the other and its exclusive appreciation of me are all the more precious and indispensable when I am profoundly in love. Then I am really 'alienated' in their desire, as Lacanian psychoanalysts would say, or, as I prefer to say, I confidently and gratefully accept to be the object of that desire. At my own risk and peril.

We need to be candid enough to recognize jealousy. With the same degree of sincerity, we have to admit the most obvious, the cruellest truth of all: adultery does you good (when you are the adulterer). Whether it is an amusing infatuation that offers a leisurely counterpoint to a stable relationship or a new love that may come ultimately to replace an existing commitment, erotic distraction can provide a sense of renewed youthfulness. It offers all the energy of a new beginning; it proves that one can still be attractive; it holds out the promise of new happiness. Those eyes of another colour which admire you differently; those different jokes, sometimes in another language or with another accent; those little habits that are the opposite of those of your spouse – sleeping with the window open, or waking up early in the morning, or eating Thai rather than French food... what a pleasure all that can be! And then, of course, there are all the novel erotic mannerisms. Everything is more interesting, even those things you don't particularly like.

More real than anything else, there is the body. A body that, for the many men (or women) who take younger mistresses, may be objectively more attractive because it is firmer, more toned, better proportioned, or may simply have some strangely captivating details. A body that is *maestoso* (majestic) might offer a refreshing variation after one that is *piccino* (cute petite), for instance. And, for the women (or men) who make love with a younger man, there is a body whose skin is tense across his muscles, whose penis is stiffer and swifter to arouse. Or, once again, there is just a distinguishing feature that gives, who knows why, the illusion of beauty. Infidelity creates intimacy with a foreign body which carries none of the marks of occasional accidents or signs of illness, or scars of surgery, or the traces of former pregnancies. It reveals an instant body which you have never seen growing fatter or losing weight, never seen being depilated, or massaged, or covered with creams and masks. A body without a history. Isn't that what we all seek by being sexually adventurous? No past. As long as the young person, brand new and incomparable, doesn't surprise you on the phone with your wife (for you cannot leave her for good), everything is unexpected. As long as you don't discover that, after all, all you are doing is carrying over into the present the luggage of the past, you win on every score.

Infidelity is the cause of the normal jealousy with which I have been concerned. This is the kind of jealousy that so often occurs in our monogamous, and yet polyamorous, societies. Because of an actual situation, infidelity is objectively damaging. Because the shock shatters our trust, it may create a new, apprehensive sensitivity. Infidelity is consequential. This is the uncomfortable truth we try to avoid whenever we focus on suspicion, imagination and paranoia, as if jealousy were the infamous self-feeding 'green-eyed monster' we encounter in Shakespeare's *Othello*. Jealousy is not a monster.

What then is the value of fidelity? Freely chosen, sometimes by self-compulsion, erotic loyalty is a gift made to someone we love. One can give many reasons for renouncing the temptations of eros' wings, but the least pretentious is to consider what effect an irreversible break-up, a light-hearted affair, or even a passing adventure would have on the person we love were s/he to learn about it. Leaving aside the demands of the categorical imperative or religious observance, the simple thought of pleasure and pain alone can provide us with a hypothetical compass. Simply ask yourself: if s/he knew, how would that make her/him suffer? Firstly, if we really love, the mere conjecture of this suffering might put us off. Secondly, the probability that s/he will know is often higher than expected. As Ovid suggests, many tragedies could be avoided if lovers were to practise this simple art of love.

This art says a resounding 'no' to the cult of 'transparency' and to the vision of love which is meant to justify such mercilessness. It is for this reason that I have discussed Simone de Beauvoir at such length, for she is responsible for a well-known redefinition of the couple, one grounded on the abolition of jealousy. In turn, her reduction of monogamy to property rights on women and her language of 'objectification' belong to a strand of feminist theory which is still highly influential, especially in the United States. This, as we have seen, is based on the opposition of person and thing and casts the heterosexual act as the treatment of a person as an object/thing. Immanuel Kant provided the philosophical and legal groundwork for this claim, and Beauvoir, in contrast to Sartre, followed in his footsteps. On this account, the thing/flesh/body that is Woman is also a piece of real estate or a commodity. I have attempted to reconstruct the genealogy and the subsequent vicissitudes of this idea, precisely because the harshest condemnation of jealousy presupposes the ignominy of ownership and the indictment of possessiveness.

Today, to embrace the role not of an 'object/thing' but, rather, of an 'object *of*' – desire, attention or admiration – has an intrinsic and paradigmatic value. We know that to solicit, to awaken, to maintain the desire of another person is to live our own desire as a form of complicity. We know, then, in a fundamental way, that we are engaged not in conquest, much less in appropriation, but rather in seduction. And what do I do when I want to seduce? I am not aggressive. I do not attack, rape or violate. Instead I make myself agreeable. If the other person does not welcome my erotic attention, it is up to her, or him, to say so. If someone says that they do not desire me, what they are saying, in effect, is that they do not want my desire, whose aim, in turn, is nothing other than to let me be desired. I give myself to the desire of another who is playing the same game. Making myself an object *of* desire means going to meet him or her with no pretence that I am making some disinterested, mystical, charitable altruistic gesture, but in the knowledge that two narcissistic creatures, two desires to please, two sexual and speaking beings may – perhaps – enjoy being the objects *of* each other's fancy. If I were to play with this language, I might say that what I am entering into is a relationship of intersubjectivity, but I can do so only by being a good sport at the game of inter*objectivity*. When two human beings try to make themselves erotically welcome, they utter more or less straightforward verbal messages, emit culturally coded signals, and invent all sorts of creative allusions. They perform a variously gendered and a sexually significant role. I take a shower, get dressed up and made up; I try to draw attention, to please and to make myself loveable – this is how I enact my own desire. I place myself in the path of another's desire, to be sure, but I do so in the hope of capturing it. I become even more of a subject of desire.

In an erotic culture where it is usual to despise charm, chastise gallantry and hound coquetry, what I have just written might seem frivolous, if not scandalous. My arguments might be misunderstood. It might be thought that I am not taking seriously the depersonalization of an 'object-thing', which is, in this logic, either a passive, innocent victim of sexual objectification or the unenlightened dupe of stereotypes, advertisements and other ruses of social conditioning. My response is that it is now high time to shed this tired language because it is based on a confusion between the notion of 'intentional object' (object *of*) and object-thing. This slippage has a Kantian provenance and still betrays the premise that sex is fundamentally dehumanizing; it needs to be redeemed, condoned or permitted. Such a premise generates a constant reproach. It also blinds us to the intentional and expressive situation of the body in the world. This is seduction.

We should not be afraid of seduction. We should, rather, learn how to handle it both honestly and artistically. In a culture of seduction, I am not ashamed to recognize my wishes, my strategies and even my cheating. Since I recognize that this also happens to others, I know that I might have to be jealous. If there exists an indefinite desire, then I will play with it. If there is love, I will fall for it. Am I, by doing this, in fact playing the hysteric, whose desire sustains the fantasy of the other? Yes, of course! Do I get lost, as a person? Of course not! I contribute to an aesthetic atmosphere while taking full responsibility for my own desire. In a heterosexual exchange, I expect from men that they should master the art of love, and that they should aim at me not as a cut of meat but as an embodied, enfleshed erotic presence, whose intentions always transcend the fact of anatomy. Exactly in the same logic – since I do desire the other's desire for me – I also expect reciprocity. I put on my lipstick and I am an adult.

A sexual morality which is lived in these terms is truly respectful of others' desire, daringly truthful about pleasure and pain (including jealousy), and infinitely less hypocritical, less invidious and less self-righteous than any ethical stance based upon neo-Kantian injunctions. The rhetoric of subjectivity results only in arrogance. Me, I, You, You. On the other hand, to recognize the desire of the other and to become its object – and to do this by means of a gesture, a way of walking, a perfume or a funny story – is something humbler, more ironic and infinitely more authentic. And that is, indeed, how it happens. Literature, the cinema and psychoanalysis have demonstrated ad nauseam the truth of this for quite a long time. It is by offering my desire to the other that I desire. In other words, my very desire is the gift I offer. It is also another struggle for recognition, because I begin by giving instead of demanding. But what I give is my desire – fragile, and yet mine. This is an erotic ethic. And, in the terms of this ethic, it is not up to women to learn how to become subjects, because they already know how to do that exceedingly well, and have always done so. It is, rather, heterosexual men (or, quite simply, men who find themselves in love with a woman) who have to learn how to be objects – objects *of* desire, able to cause desire. It is for the males who believe so strongly in the phallus to learn that what they possess are, in fact, penises. They have to learn how to come to terms with the transformations of their bodies, to accept the realities of ageing – as women have always done.

It is up to men to look at themselves through the eyes of women. It is they who must go to us, they who must please us. It is they who must imitate us, even in our jealousy. For our erotic anger has always eluded any metaphor of property. On the contrary: it is the expression of the intelligence of love. Women are the paradigm. Of course, such an ethic presupposes that pleasure is not an evil, that pleasure is, in fact, pleasant. Kant, who admired Lucretius, would be outraged. But the women who today, in the West, live in an unprecedented compatibility between human and civil rights, their own chosen habits, and their lived bodies know that multiple forms of enjoyment – the enjoyment of rights, of lifestyles, of physical sensations – belong to them as their most precious possession. Pleasure is on their side. It is a feminist point of view which is far more real today than any which dwells constantly upon 'objectification'. It is in this spirit that a revaluation of amorous jealousy acquires meaning.

Women are now ready to confess the unconfessable.

As Antoine de Courtin, a contemporary of La Rochefoucauld and the author of a *Treatise on Jealousy*, knew so well, when women rebelled against the infidelity of their husbands, it was because they imagined themselves to be their equals. They demanded mutual respect. For Courtin, this was an absurd piece of sophistry. Women are clearly inferior to their spouses and must therefore submit to them. If they see them 'given over to disorder', they have the right to offer sound advice, but always with gentleness, never with reproach or 'sour words'.[1] 'Who could describe', he wrote, 'the displeasure, the disgust and importunity, and the horror which a talkative woman arouses: screaming, imperious, quarrelsome, outrageous, carried away, cunning, obstinate, sad, and difficult – all of which are so many of the monsters to which jealousy gives birth?'[2] Those whom jealousy torments, Courtin insists, 'are ashamed to admit it'.[3] Jealousy is a forbidden passion.

Today, indifferent to mockery and proud of her sensuality, the 'talkative woman' couldn't care less.[4]

NOTES

INTRODUCTION

1 François de La Rochefoucauld, Maxim 472, in *The Maxims of François Duc de La Rochefoucauld*, etc., trans. F. G. Stevens, London: Humphrey Milford, 1940, p. 147.
2 Charles Louis de Secondat, Baron de Montesquieu, 'On Jealousy', in *My Thoughts (Mes Pensées)*, ed. and trans. Henry C. Clark, Indianapolis: Liberty Fund, 2012, paras. 483–509; http://oll.libertyfund.org/titles/2534. 'I had written a work entitled *History of Jealousy*; I have changed it into another: *Reflections on Jealousy*' (para. 483). On the relationship between jealousy and the famous seraglio in Montesquieu's *Persian Letters*, see C. Martin, 'Une "histoire de la jalousie"? Différence des sexes et différence des mœurs dans les *Lettres persanes*', in Christophe Martin (ed.), *Les Lettres persanes de Montesquieu*, Paris: Presses de l'Université Paris-Sorbonne, 2013, pp. 185–209.
3 La Rochefoucauld, Maxim 446, in *The Maxims of François Duc de La Rochefoucauld*, p. 139.
4 Stendhal, *Love*, trans. Gilbert Sale and Suzanne Sale, London: Penguin, 1975, pp. 127–8.
5 This is the prevailing approach to jealousy in contemporary analytic philosophy. See Kristján Kristjánsson,'Jealousy revisited: recent philosophical work on a maligned emotion', *Ethical Theory and Moral Practice* 19 (2016): 741–54. See also Daniel M. Farrell, 'Jealousy', *Philosophical Review* 89 (1980): 527–59; Michael J. Wreen, 'Jealousy', *Noûs* 23 (1989): 635–52; Aaron Ben-Ze'ev, 'Envy and jealousy', *Canadian Journal of Philosophy* 20 (1990): 487–516; Luke Purshouse, 'Jealousy in relation to envy', *Erkenntnis* 60 (2004): 179–204. For a good example of a historical understanding of the semantic, psychological and legal definition of jealousy in connection with, and as a redescription of, anger, see Dawn Keetley, 'From anger to jealousy: explaining domestic homicide in antebellum America', *Journal of Social History* 42 (2008): 269–97.

6 Jacques Lacan, *Transference: The Seminar of Jacques Lacan, Book VIII*, ed. Jacques-Alain Miller, trans. Bruce Fink, Cambridge: Polity, 2015, p. 32.
7 Jacques-Alain Miller, 'Des semblants dans la relation entre les sexes', *La Cause freudienne* no. 36 (1997): 7–15.
8 Denis Diderot, *Supplément au voyage de Bougainville*, in Diderot, *Political Writings*, trans. and ed. John Hope Mason, Cambridge: Cambridge University Press, 1992, p. 50.
9 Denis Diderot, 'Jalousie', in *Encyclopédie ou Dictionnaire raisonné des sciences, des arts et des métiers*, 1751–80, vol. VIII, p. 439.
10 Jean-Paul Sartre, *Being and Nothingness: An Essay on Phenomenological Ontology*, trans. Hazel E. Barnes, London: Routledge, 2005, pp. 366–7: 'The notion of "ownership", by which love is so often explained, is not actually primary. Why should I want to appropriate the Other if it were not precisely that the Other makes me be?'
11 Charles Pinot Duclos, *Mémoires pour servir à l'histoire des mœurs au XVIIIe siècle*, London, 1752, p. 38. In a lively conversation, this charming person discusses the nature of love with an inexperienced young man. 'We find the bourgeoisie reasonable enough,' she tells him, 'polite enough, or foolish enough not to be jealous.' The *Considerations* end with the triumph of constant love. Madame de Rétel's diagnosis of jealousy – a prejudice induced by education and fortified by habit, a foolish pride, a sentiment brought on by a lack of merit, a bad heart, an insupportable tyranny and a cruel folly (pp. 37–9) – echoes those of Denis Diderot and Jean-Jacques Rousseau.
12 Pierre Choderlos de Laclos, *Les Liaisons dangereuses*, trans. Richard Aldington, London: Routledge, 2011, p. 14.
13 Laclos, *Des femmes et de leur éducation*, in *Œuvres completes*, ed. Laurent Versini, Paris: Gallimard, 1979, p. 422.
14 Montesquieu, 'On Jealousy', para. 509.
15 I borrow the expression 'hatred of the bourgeois' (*haine du bourgeois*) from François Furet, *Le Passé d'une illusion: essai sur l'idée communiste au XXe siècle*, Paris: Robert Laffont/Calman-Lévy, 1995. For an example of the interpretation of jealousy as property, see Masha Belensky, *The Anxiety of Dispossession: Jealousy in Nineteenth-Century French Culture*, Lewisburg, PA: Bucknell University Press, 2008, pp. 3–5, and *passim*.
16 Jean-Luc Marion, *The Erotic Phenomenon*, trans. Stephen E. Lewis, Chicago: University of Chicago Press, 2008; Christophe Perrin, 'La Jalousie à l'honneur: J.-L. Marion après Proust', *Revue d'éthique et de théologie morale*, 278 (2014): 9–34.
17 Christine R. Harris and Ryan S. Darby, 'Jealousy in Adulthood', in Sybil Hart and Maria Legerstee, *Handbook of Jealousy: Theory, Research, and Multidisciplinary Approaches*, Chichester: Wiley-Blackwell, 2010, pp. 547–71.
18 Andreas Capellanus, On Love, ed. 2nd trans. Patrick Gerard Walsh, London: Duckworth, 1982, p. 282.

CHAPTER 1 BEING MEDEA

1 On the importance of focusing on the situation, not merely the word, and for a fruitful reading of a wide corpus of texts, see Massimo Pizzocaro, *Il triangolo amoroso: la nozione di 'gelosia' nella cultura e nella lingua greca arcaica*, Levante, 1994. The most significant recent contribution is Ed Sanders, *Envy and Jealousy in Classical Athens: A Socio-Psychological Approach*, Oxford: Oxford University Press, 2014. Sanders recognizes the jealousy of Medea as an erotic and social passion composed of multiple emotions. My own interpretation has developed independently over the years, but it converges, in large part, with Sanders's arguments. I take a more radical position, however, for anger does not figure as one emotion among others in the 'complex of jealousy'. It is, rather, the passion that structures Medea – the play as well as the character. By refuting recent readings, Sanders helps us to take a decisive turning point, for which I have been arguing for some time (Giulia Sissa, *Sex and Sensuality in the Ancient World*, New Haven, CT, and London: Yale University Press, 2008). In the history of sexuality and amorous passions, we must recognize the place of the protagonist: *eros*. This turning point also brings us closer to the work of Nicole Loraux, which was always attentive to the interweaving of the sexual and the social. See, for instance, *Tragic Ways of Killing a Woman*, Cambridge, MA: Harvard University Press, 1992. On the broken agreement between Jason and Medea, see Deborah Boedecker, 'Euripides' Medea and the vanity of *logoi*', *Classical Philology* 86 (1991): 95–112.
2 Aristotle, *Rhetoric*, 2, 2.
3 Aristotle, *Nicomachean Ethics*, 4, 5, 5–6. An insightful discussion of jealousy in connection with merit, pride and self-respect (therefore with anger and indignation), based on a serious engagement with Aristotle, can be found in Kristján Kristjánsson, *Justifying Emotions: Pride and Jealousy*, Abingdon: Routledge, 2003. 'What Aristotle says about anger can arguably be related, *mutatis mutandis*, to jealousy in a perfectly straightforward way' (p. 285). I share Kristjánsson's main argument, but I argue that, for a historical understanding of the emotions, we should start from definitions given in their context, then come to contemporary redefinitions, also taken in their own context. What 'we' (and controversially so, across cultures, moral theories, philosophical allegiances and individual scholarship) happen to think as 'jealousy', by emphasizing *competition*, was indeed anger in ancient Greece. It was a response to undeserved slights. In amorous situations, anger was 'erotic', as we shall see in a moment, because its cause was eros. Eros creates an expectation of reciprocity and singularity. He makes us inevitably irascible. The profound intelligence of Aristotle, which Kristjánsson rightly brings to the fore, is to focus on the dual dialectic of recognition. This is what matters. And it still matters – more than ever – when sex and love are at stake. Euripides' *Medea* and *Andromache* will show precisely the intrinsic irascibility of love. I agree with Kristjánsson, therefore, that jealousy is a form of morally justified

self-respect. I disagree, however, that jealousy is fundamentally akin to envy. On this account, I would be jealous whenever I feel that I deserve to be valued as much as (or even more than) an undeservedly favoured third party. If we start from there, we may be able to reassess jealousy in general, but we are also compelled to downplay the reasons for erotic attachment *as such*. If jealousy responds to a sense of unfairness, and love is not something one can ever deserve, then jealousy in love is irrational. It is only in a proper relationship, with its reasonable expectations, Kristjánsson argues, that we are entitled to claim faithfulness (pp. 240–95). But erotic love, I will argue in this book, is desire for the beloved's desire. Even before the establishment of such covenants, amorous jealousy is built into the art of love.

4   Aristotle, *Nicomachean Ethics*, 4, 5, 3–4.
5   Ibid., 4, 5, 5–6. On Aristotle's theory of anger, see Pierre Aubenque, 'Sur la définition aristotélicienne de la colère', *Revue philosophique de la France et de l'étranger* 147 (1957): 300–17. I do not agree on the interpretation of the slight as necessarily 'public'. The affront is 'manifest' (*phainomenê*) to the person who grows angry.
6   Ibid., 4, 5, 13–14.
7   Ibid., 3, 8, 11.
8   Ibid., 3, 8, 10–12.
9   René Girard, *Violence and the Sacred*, trans. Patrick Gregory, Baltimore: Johns Hopkins University Press, 1977.
10 Homer, *The Iliad*, trans. A. T. Murray, 1924, https://en.wikisource.org/wiki/The_Iliad_(Murray), 1, 113–15.
11 Ibid., 9, 335–42:

> Some he gave as prizes to chieftains and kings, and for them they abide untouched; but from me alone of the Achaeans hath he taken and keepeth my wife, the darling of my heart [ἄλοχον θυμαρέα]. Let him lie by her side and take his joy. But why must the Argives wage war against the Trojans? Why hath he gathered and led hither his host, this son of Atreus? Was it not for fair-haired Helen's sake? Do they then alone of mortal men love their wives, these sons of Atreus? Nay, for whoso is a true man and sound of mind, loveth his own and cherisheth her, even as I too loved her with all my heart [ἐκ θυμοῦ φίλεον], though she was but the captive of my spear.

See ibid., 19, 295–300, on the prospect of a marriage between Briseis and Achilles.

12 On the ambiguities of the relations between a powerful man and a war captive, see Ruth Scodel, 'The captive's dilemma: sexual acquiescence in Euripides' *Hecuba* and *Troades*', *Harvard Studies in Classical Philology* 98 (1998): 137–54, at pp. 138–9.
13 Julian Pitt-Rivers, *The Fate of Shechem or the Politics of Sex: Essays in the Anthropology of the Mediterranean*, Cambridge: Cambridge University Press, 1997, p. 1.

14 Euripides, *Medea*, 334. Out of the vast scholarship on Medea, see Donald J. Mastronarde, ed., *Euripides: Medea*, Cambridge: Cambridge University Press, 2002; Euripide, *Médée*, trans. Myrto Gondicas and Pierre Judet de la Combe, Paris: Les Belles Lettres, 2012; Seneca, *Medea*, ed. and trans. Anthony Boyle, Oxford: Oxford University Press, 2014; Deborah Boedeker, 'Euripides' *Medea* and the vanity of *logoi*'; Jenny Clay Strauss and S. I. Johnston, eds, *Medea: Essays on Medea in Myth, Literature, Philosophy and Art*, Princeton, NJ: Princeton University Press, 1997 (in particular, the essays by John Dillon and Martha Nussbaum, on tragedy and philosophy respectively); Remo Bodei, *Ira: la passione furente*, Bologna: Il Mulino, 2011; David Stuttard, ed., *Looking at Medea: Essays and a Translation of Euripides' Tragedy*, London: Bloomsbury, 2014.
15 Euripides, *Medea*, 96–7.
16 Aristotle, *Rhetoric*, 2, 6.
17 Especially in the antagonistic dialogue, at the core of the play: Euripides, *Medea*, 465ff. On the broken agreement between Jason and Medea, see Boedeker, 'Euripides' *Medea* and the vanity of *logoi*'.
18 Euripides, *Medea*, 20, dishonour (*atimazein*).
19 Ibid., 26, 165, 265, injustice (*adikein*).
20 Ibid., 44, 92–4.
21 Ibid., 121, 176, 447, 615, 870, 909 (*orgê*); 94, 98, 172, 520, 590, 898 (*cholos*); 108, 27, 1056, 1079 (*thumos*).
22 Ibid., 698, on Jason's 'great love' (*megas eros*) for his new bride; see also 491.
23 Ibid., 8, 152, 228, on Medea's love for Jason.
24 Ibid., 154–9.
25 To take the measure of the attitude of scholars confronted with Medea's tragic *eros*, see the articles in Stuttard's *Looking at Medea*, which mix the language of 'sexual jealousy' with the assumption that Medea should be considered a generic female hero. Ian Ruffel argues that Medea fights on behalf of justice, honour, betrayal. She 'implicitly rejects Jason's accusations of jealousy and sexually motivated affront' ('The Nurse's Tale', p. 79). This is wrong. Sex is indeed a motivation. Firstly, as we will see in a moment, Medea insists on her *eros*. Secondly, Jason speaks as a self-serving liar. He fails to recognize his wife's loving agency, which he attributes to divine influence. This allows him to minimize the help Medea has given to him in his quest for the Golden Fleece. He accuses his wife of reducing everything to the logic of the bed. And this allows him to claim that he is not marrying another woman for the sake of love. He cares only and exclusively for his very dear children! But the text exposes his lies: at the outset, he is ready to get married while accepting that Medea will go into exile along with the children. Jason even offers to help his miserable little family with a bit of money (*Medea*, 459–62). He does not object at all to the banishment of the children. Medea even uses her own concern for the boys, since their father couldn't care less, when she tries to persuade King Creon to give her one extra day in Corinth (ibid., 340–44). Jason accuses Medea of bringing everything down to sex, while making ridicu-

lous excuses about his own *eros*. Medea never disavows her love: the bed is no small thing for a woman!

26 Among the many allusions to the 'bed' – ibid.: *lechos*: 489, 555, 568, 571, 697, 1291; *lektra*: 140; the injustice that involves the bed (*eunê*): 265. Ed Sanders, one of the rare Hellenists who does justice to the evidence of Medea's sexual suffering, has enumerated the occurrences of terms in Homeric and tragic poetry which designate the bed. The highest frequency is found in *Medea*. See *Envy and Jealousy in Classical Athens*, pp. 130–68, especially p. 132. On the matrimonial bed, a centre-piece in the decoration of the houses where tragic women live and kill themselves, see Loraux, *Tragic Ways of Killing a Woman*.

27 David Konstan, 'Before Jealousy', in David Konstan and Keith Rutter, eds, *Envy, Spite and Jealousy: The Rivalrous Emotions in Ancient Greece*, Edinburgh: Edinburgh University Press, 2003, pp. 7–27, at p. 22: 'Aegeus' concern, like Medea's own, is focused throughout on the threat to her welfare, not her amorous sensibilities.'

28 Euripides, *Medea*, 696–7.
29 Ibid., 1367–8.
30 Tristan Alonge, 'Lo spettro di Medea in Tessaglia: l'*Andromaca* di Euripide come riscrittura della *Medea*', *MAIA: Rivista di letterature classiche* 60 (2008): 369–86, at p. 386.
31 Euripides, *Andromache*, 213–14. This is particularly striking, after a tirade in which Andromache addresses Hermione as an incompetent girl and boasts about 'not betraying herself' (ibid., 191). She sports 'her unsubdued spirit', as it has been misleadingly claimed by Katarina Synoudinou (*On the Concept of Slavery in Euripides*, Ioannina: University of Ioannina, 1977, p. 56), when she feels strong enough to chastise a younger woman from the standpoint of older age, but she recommends total acquiescence to the man to whom she has been given. Andromache also mentions a wife's duty to downplay the prestige of her own parents, should they overshadow her husband's family. Social superiority is associated with the claim to erotic attention, therefore to jealousy.
32 Euripides, *Andromache*, 222–5.
33 Ibid., 227–8.
34 Ibid., 240.
35 Ibid., 229–30.
36 Ibid., 207–25.
37 Ibid., 32–8 (translated by David Kovacs). Scodel, 'The captive's dilemma'.
38 Euripides, *Andromache*, 938–42.
39 Plutarch, *Advice to Bride and Groom*, 276d.
40 Demosthenes, *Against Neaera*, 122.
41 Ibid., 87.
42 Aeschines, *Against Timarchus*, 183.
43 In 'Greek tragedy: a rape-culture?' (*EuGeStA: Journal on Gender Studies in Antiquity*, no. 1, 2011), Nancy Rabinowitz argues that Euripides focuses on Andromache's origin but then makes her the mouthpiece of Greek values:

...she emphasizes her Asianness (the first word of the play is Ἀσιάτιδος) which would mark her as the ethnic other, an appropriate slave in fifth-century Athens. The play opens with her summary of her past life – the child-bearing wife of Hector, having seen her child Astyanax killed, and, in contrast, now bearing a son to her *master* (24–25)....

But actually Andromache has become a spokesperson for Greek patriarchal values, basically instructing Hermione on how to make herself attractive to her husband. When Andromache gives Hermione advice about how to keep a man, she does so not only on the basis of her marriage to Hector, but also on the basis of her 'successful' relationship with Neoptolemus. (pp. 15–16)

I disagree on this point. Andromache, I would argue, speaks on behalf of an Asian and even of a Thracian vision of submissiveness. She has been 'successful' with a Greek husband, precisely because she imported her docility into his household, which Hermione refuses to do. I agree with Rabinowitz, however, on Andromache's ambivalence about her sexual complicity with her master:

The wife mocks the concubine as a slave and war prize (155), but at the same time implies that Andromache likes sharing a bed with the son of her husband's killer (171–73). The ambiguity of the word ξυνεύδειν comes from the fact that a bedmate can be a wife or a concubine, and of course, either can be won in war....

Andromache has, as I say, accommodated herself remarkably well. The play reveals the thinly veiled hostility in the sanctioned marriage of Neoptolemus and Hermione, but it also suggests the possibility that what starts as rape may not continue to be rape throughout a relationship (p. 16).

44   Euripides, *Andromache*, 215–21: 'If you had had as husband a king in snowy Thrace, where one husband divides his bed in turn among many women, would you have killed them? If so you would have clearly branded all women with the charge of sexual insatiability. This is a shameful thing. And yet though we women suffer worse from this disease than men do, at least let us veil it decently from sight' (translation by David Kovacs).
45   Ibid., 220.
46   Ibid., 215–17.
47   On the Thracian provenance of slaves in Athens, see Margaret Miller, *Athens and Persia in the Fifth century BC: A Study in Cultural Receptivity*, Cambridge: Cambridge University Press, 1997, pp. 80–3.
48   We know of the existence of a few Colchidian slaves in Athens. See William Linn Westermann, *The Slave Systems of Greek and Roman Antiquity*, Philadelphia: American Philosophical Society, 1955, p. 14. See also Edith

NOTES TO PP. 26–32

Hall, *The Theatrical Cast of Athens: Interactions between Ancient Greek Drama and Society*, Oxford: Oxford University Press, 2006, p. 201.
49   Euripides, *Andromache*, 213–14.
50   Aeschylus, in *The Persians*, had vividly depicted this contrast in Atossa's dream.
51   We should also notice how Andromache and Medea speak about women in the plural: the former is concerned about their reputation of lustfulness, the latter about their miserable condition, at the mercy of the masters they have to 'buy' for themselves.
52   Sigmund Freud, 'Some Neurotic Mechanisms in Jealousy, Paranoia and Homosexuality' (1922), in *The Standard Edition of the Complete Psychological Works of Sigmund Freud*, vol. 18, London: Hogarth Press, 1955, pp. 223–32, at p. 223. In my quotations from this text, I have occasionally modified the translation by Joan Riviere.
53   Sigmund Freud, *Civilization and its Discontents*, trans. Joan Riviere, 3rd edn, London: Hogarth Press, 1955, pp. 37–8 (translation modified).
54   Freud, 'Some Neurotic Mechanisms in Jealousy, Paranoia and Homosexuality', p. 223.
55   Ibid.: 'There is not much to be said from the psychoanalytical point of view about normal jealousy. If anyone appears to be without it, the inference is justified that it has undergone severe repression and consequently plays all the greater part in his unconscious mental life.'
56   Jerome Neu, 'Jealous Thoughts' and 'Jealous Afterthoughts', in *A Tear Is an Intellectual Thing*, Oxford: Oxford University Press, 2000, pp. 41–67 and pp. 68–80. See also Madeleine Chapsal, *La Jalousie*, Paris: Gallimard, 1985.
57   Freud, 'Some Neurotic Mechanisms in Jealousy, Paranoia and Homosexuality', p. 223.
58   Euripides, *Medea*, 704 (*olola*). See 146–7, 277, on Medea's wish to be utterly destroyed and dead.
59   Ibid., 225–6.
60   Euripides, *Médée*, 'Introduction', pp. xxiv–xxv.
61   Euripides, *Medea*, 695–6.
62   Ibid., 692.
63   Ibid., 578. See also 17; 268–71; 489; 778.
64   Ibid., 695–707.
65   Ibid., 811–13, on the chorus changing their mind, when Medea announces her plan to kill the children.
66   Ibid., 1049–50. See also 381–3; 404–6; 797.
67   Ibid., 695. See also 461.
68   Florence Dupont, *'Médée' de Sénèque, ou Comment sortir de l'humanité*, Paris: Belin, 2000, p. 5.
69   Elaine Fantham, 'ΖΗΛΟΤΥΠΙΑ: A brief excursion into sex, violence, and literary history', *Phoenix* 40 (1986): 45–57.
70   Aristophanes, *Wealth*, 1014–15.
71   Plato, *Symposium*, 213d.
72   Juvenal, 6, 278.

NOTES TO PP. 32–33

73 Petronius, *Satyricon*, 45, 7; 69, 3.
74 Luc Brisson, 'La notion de *phthonos* chez Platon', in Frederic Monneyron, ed., *La Jalousie*, Paris: L'Harmattan, 1996, pp. 13–34.
75 Konstan, 'Before Jealousy'. For a critique of this approach, see Robert Kaster's review of David Konstan's *The Emotions of the Ancient Greeks: Studies in Aristotle and Classical Literature* (Toronto: University of Toronto Press, 2006) in *Notre Dame Philosophical Reviews*, 5 September 2006. Kaster criticizes Konstan for putting Greek literature in perspective from the standpoint of a 'modern' definition, which is simplistic. Konstan uses the definition of 'jealousy' in general, to be found in the *Oxford English Dictionary* as a feeling 'arising from the suspicion, apprehension, or knowledge of a rivalry'. He also mentions the definition of amorous jealousy as 'fear of being supplanted in the affection, or distrust of the fidelity, of a beloved one, especially a wife, husband, or lover'. Kaster finds these definitions inadequate because they do not attribute respect, loyalty and, above all, total devotion to the 'modern and romantic' couple. He then poses a fundamental question: are we sure that the ancients have never formulated a complex reflection on the 'good' that we fear to lose in jealousy? If we were to enrich the modern definition of jealousy, the distance from the ancients might dwindle. My own guiding question is rather: why do we want to deny that even the definition of the *OED* might apply to Hermione or Medea?
76 I fully agree with the arguments of Ed Sanders on this point (*Envy and Jealousy in Classical Athens*, p. vii). The lexical approach has a certain value, he writes, but also has its limits. Firstly, since envy (*phthonos*) is a vulgar emotion, it is usually attributed not to oneself but to others with connotations that modify the meaning. Secondly, 'there is no classic labelling for sexual jealousy.' It is precisely for this reason that 'a different, complementary approach is required, which reads the expressed values and actions of entire situations.' A multidisciplinary approach, attentive to psychoanalysis and anthropology, allows us to explore explicit theories, but also the 'more oblique paths' that these emotions take, in different genres. For a study of passions that does justice to their cultural context, without reducing them to purely social constructions, see Jon Elster's classic work, *Alchemies of the Mind: Rationality and the Emotions*, Cambridge: Cambridge University Press, 1999. In the ancient world, Elster claims, love was a 'proto-emotion', composed of an intense interest for a person, the desire to be with that person, the pain that their loss may cause, and a sentiment of jealousy towards a third party. Modern love 'frames' these phenomena in a more complex and conscious way, to the point that we expect to experience all these symptoms at once. I will argue that ancient fiction and philosophy already represent love in a fully conscious and highly complex way. It is remarkable, however, that Elster did not hesitate to include jealousy among the components of love.
77 Barbara Cassin, ed., *Vocabulaire européen des philosophies*, Paris: Seuil, 2004.

NOTES TO PP. 34–43

78 On the major argument, see Janine Fillion-Lahille, *Le De ira de Sénèque et la philosophie stoïcienne des passions*, Paris: Klincksieck, 1984; Richard Sorabji, *Emotion and Peace of Mind*, Oxford: Oxford University Press, 2000; Peter Stacey, 'The sovereign person in Senecan political theory', *Republics of Letters: A Journal for the Study of Knowledge, Politics, and the Arts* 2 (2011): 15–73.
79 Seneca, *De ira*, 2, 4.
80 Ibid., 2, 1, 3–6. See 2, 3.
81 Ibid., 3, 5, 7–8.
82 Ibid.
83 Sigmund Freud, 'The Question of Lay Analysis' (1926), in *The Standard Edition of the Complete Psychological Works of Sigmund Freud*, Vol. 20, New York and London: W. W. Norton, 1989, p. 75, and *passim*.
84 On the philosophical ground of Seneca's *Medea*, see Jörn Müller, 'Did Seneca Understand Medea? A Contribution to the Stoic Account of *Akrasia*', in Jula Wildberger and Marcia Colish, eds, *Seneca Philosophus*, Boston: Walter De Gruyter, 2014, pp. 65–94. See also Gregory Staley, *Seneca and the Idea of Tragedy*, Oxford: Oxford University Press, 2010.
85 Seneca, *Medea*, 49–52.
86 Ibid., 155.
87 Ibid., 907–10.
88 Ibid., 914–17.
89 Ibid., 943–4.
90 Ibid., 953.
91 Ibid., 991–2.
92 Ibid., 1016–17.
93 Ibid., 1019–20. On the focus on pain in Seneca's take on Stoic anger, see Katja Maria Vogt, 'Anger, Present Injustice and Future Revenge in Seneca's *De ira*', in K. Volk and G. D. Williams, eds, *Seeing Seneca Whole: Perspectives on Philosophy, Poetry and Politics*, Leiden: Brill, 2006, pp. 57–74.
94 Seneca, *De ira*, 3, 10, 2 (translation Aubrey Stewart).
95 Ibid., 3, 13, 1–2.
96 Ibid.
97 Ibid., 3, 3, 2. It is necessary to corroborate through argument (*coarguere*) how ugly anger can be, and to place this ugliness before the eyes (*ante oculos ponere*).
98 Ibid., 2, 36, 2–3.
99 Ibid., 2, 35, 5.
100 Ibid., 2, 35, 6.
101 Ibid., 2, 36, 5.
102 Ibid., 2, 35, 6.
103 Seneca, *Medea*, 849–69.
104 Seneca, *De ira*, 3, 3, 2: it is necessary *ante oculos ponere*...
105 Ibid., 3, 5, 3.
106 Ibid., 3, 4, 4.

NOTES TO PP. 43–47

107 Antonin Artaud, 'Compte rendu de la *Médée* de Sénèque (en version d'Unamuno) représentée par la compagnie de M. Xirgu au Palais des Beaux-Arts de Mexico, dans *El Nacional*, 7 juin 1936', in Juan Carlos Sánchez León, *L'Antiquité grecque dans l'œuvre d'Antonin Artaud*, Besançon: Presses universitaires de Franche-Comté, 2007, pp. 101–3.
108 Seneca, *De ira*, 2, 19, 4.
109 Ibid., 3, 5, 8.
110 Ibid., 3, 13, 1–2. See note 95 above.
111 Seneca, *Medea*, 917–19: For a similar phenomenology of suffering, see also Seneca, *Phaedra*, 101–3. Phaedra begins to feel erotically attracted to Hippolytus, her stepson. It is a pain, *dolor*, which crushes her. It is a nascent evil. An evil is nourished and grows and burns within, like the vapour that overflows from the cave of Etna (*alitur and crescit malum / et ardet intus qualis Aetneo vapor / exundat antro*). In his commentary of Seneca's *Medea*, Anthony Boyle interpreted *nescio quid ferox* as a simple conflict between different emotions, which is at odds with the Stoic theory of the unity of the soul (Seneca, *Medea*, ed. and trans. Anthony Boyle, Oxford: Oxford University Press, 2014, pp. civ–cv). For a comparison with pantomime, see Alessandra Zanobi, *Seneca's Tragedies and the Aesthetics of Pantomime*, London: Bloomsbury, 2014, pp. 136–7. Victoria Rimell has highlighted the spatial/dramatic/corporeal dimension of the oscillation between inside and outside: 'The labour of empire: womb and world in Seneca's *Medea*', *Studi italiani di filologia classica* 105 (2012): 211–37.
112 I have already discussed this argument at length, but see, in particular, Seneca, *De ira*, 3, 10, 2, on the imperative to stop the passions as soon as they are born, *cum primum oriuntur*.
113 Ibid., 2, 13, 3: 'Anger should be removed. This is partly admitted by those who say that it should be moderated [*hoc ex parte fatentur etiam qui dicunt minuendam*]. Let us proscribe it altogether: nothing useful could come of it [*tota dimittatur: nihil profutura est*].' Ibid., 3, 42, 1: 'Let us preserve ourselves from such a disease, let us purge our soul [*purgare*], let us uproot it [*careamus hoc malo purgemusque mentem et extirpemus radicitus*]....Let us not moderate anger, but let us remove it completely [*iram non temperemus, sed ex toto removeamus*].' It is possible, if only we try. The temperament of anger, on the contrary, is impossible.

On the Stoics versus Aristotle, see Fillion-Lahille, *Le De ira de Sénèque et la philosophie stoïcienne des passions*, pp. 203–20. Gregory Staley (*Seneca and the Idea of Tragedy*) underestimates the intransigence of Seneca's criticism of Aristotle.
114 Giulia Sissa, 'Pathos', in Cassin, *Vocabulaire européen des philosophies*.
115 Seneca, *De ira*, 3, 42, 1.
116 Ibid., 3, 3, 2; 3, 5, 3. For an interpretation of Aristotle and Seneca on tragedy and on the effects of the theatre, see Staley, *Seneca and the Idea of Tragedy*. Staley underestimates the intransigence of the Stoic theory of passions and the resulting anti-Aristotelian critique.

NOTES TO PP. 48–51

117 Aristotle, *Poetics*, 14.
118 Seneca, *Medea*, 910.
119 Pierre Corneille, *Médée*, in *Œuvres complètes*, ed. Georges Couton, Paris, Gallimard, 1980, vol. I, p. 253.
120 Ibid., 199, 1120 (Cléone), 749 (Nérine), 575 (Jason), 1497 (Créuse), 980 (Médée elle-même), 587 (Créuse de Jason), 1014 (Nérine évoque la jalousie d'Égée).
121 Pierre Corneille, 'Médée, Épître', in *Œuvres complètes*, vol. I, pp. 535–6.
122 Pierre Corneille, 'Examen', ibid., p. 540.
123 Corneille, *Médée*, 267, 1028, 947.
124 Ibid., 455.
125 Ibid., 345.
126 Ibid., 1385.
127 Ibid., 29–30.
128 Ibid., 9–17.
129 Ibid., 150–151.
130 Paul Bénichou, *Man and Ethics: Studies in French Classicism*, Garden City, NY: Anchor Books, 1971.
131 Pierre Corneille, *Œuvres complètes*, vol. III, p. 122.
132 Ibid., pp. 121–2.
133 On this, see Alessandro Schiesaro, *The Passions in Play: Thyestes and the Dynamics of Senecan Drama*, Cambridge: Cambridge University Press, 2003.
134 On the Christian context of Corneille's dramaturgy, see Marc Fumaroli, *Héros et orateurs: rhétorique et dramaturgie cornéliennes*, Geneva: Droz, 1996, pp. 40–3, 400–1.

> Would Medea be inculcated into the principles of canon law? For her, as for the canonists, the essence of marriage is not in the public blessing, in the presence of the priest, but in the commitment of reciprocal fidelity contracted formally by the two spouses. The *sacramentum* is consubstantial with the *jusjurandum*. The public blessing merely enshrines this word given and sworn freely. Hence the sympathy which Corneille obviously wishes to attract towards Medea is the consequence of the 'legal' force of the cause Medea herself so passionately advocates. (p. 401)

> The legal and religious background of marriage (which, in turn, is part of the Thomist tradition) reinforces the attenuating circumstances that Corneille could find to excuse Medea. It is not merely a way of charitably tolerating a passion but of putting forward the obligations of a sacrament.

135 Ibid., p. 504. In an otherwise flowery language, Amy Wygant writes:

> In a logic of jubilation and mirroring, the audience and the author take her side. Her crimes great and small, those prosecutable under the law and those worthy only of human pity, are taken by the audience onto itself in a complex of reactions that I call glammatology,

a neologism meant to reference not only glamour's old meaning as grammar, but also the loving reading whose object she was. On the one hand, the social body is glamorized, and several respects with the theory that lead to witchcraft accusations beyond the theatrical stage. (*Medea, Magic and Modernity in France: Stages and Histories*, Farnham: Ashgate, 2007, p. 23)

Wygant goes on to examine Corneille's Medea as a sorceress (pp. 80–139).

136 Corneille does not limit his clemency to Medea. In *Clitandre*, another jealous character, Dorise, survives the denouement of the play: the 'worm of jealousy', which throws our soul into 'frenzy', into 'blindness' and into 'disorder', causes a behavior that ought to be condoned, 'when all that it produces deserves to be excused' (Act. V, scene 6, 1797–1801). On the notion of 'interest', favour, example and, more generally, the relationship between personages and the public, see Déborah Blocker, *Instituer un 'art': politiques du théâtre dans la France du premier XVIIe siècle*, Paris: Honoré Champion, 2009; Joseph Harris, 'Corneille and audience identification', *Modern Languages Review* 104 (2009): 659–75.

137 In *La Jalousie dans la littérature au temps de Louis XIII: analyse littéraire et histoire des mentalités*, Geneva: Droz, 1981, Madeleine Bertaud affirms that, in her exaltation, 'Medea, in truth, is right, she knows herself and her confidence in herself arises from a Stoic attitude. Jealousy as a passion, a disease of the soul, could not produce generous actions in this tragedy. It nevertheless leaves intact the "great courage" (I-5, 313) of the heroine' (p. 467). We have seen how the Stoic theory of the passions, examined in detail, leads us in a completely different direction. A Stoic Medea would be inconceivable: this hyper-passionate woman is the opposite of the wise man. A Medea depicted *by* a Stoic, as a consequence, would be inexcusable: she would be Seneca's *monstrum*. Beyond this misunderstanding, this book is filled with analyses of philosophical and literary texts which shed light on the many debates about the value of jealousy.

138 On the alleged neo-Stoicism of Corneille and, more generally, on the reception of Seneca in the seventeenth century, see Staley, *Seneca and the Idea of Tragedy*; Jacques Maurens, *La Tragédie sans tragique: le néostoïcisme dans l'œuvre de Pierre Corneille*, Paris: Armand Colin, 1966; André Stegman, *L'Héroïsme cornélien*, Paris: Armand Colin, 1968; André Gabriel, 'Pierre Corneille, vierge et martyr', *Baroque* 12 (1987), http://baroque.revues.org/600; Mariette Cuenin-Lieber, *Corneille et le monologue: une interrogation sur le héros*, Tübingen: Narr, 2002, pp. 160–2; Jacqueline Lagrée, *Le Néostoïcisme: une philosophie par gros temps*, Paris: Vrin, 2010.

139 Pierre Corneille, 'Discours de la tragédie, et des moyens de la traiter, selon le vraisemblable ou le nécessaire', in *Œuvres complètes*, vol. III, pp. 142–3.

140 Corneille, 'Examen de *Nicomède*', in *Œuvres complètes*, vol. II, p. 643: 'In the admiration we feel for the virtue of Nicomedes, I find a way of purging the passions, of which Aristotle has not spoken, and which is perhaps more certain than that which he prescribed for the tragedy by

means of pity and fear. The love the play gives us for the virtue we admire fills us with hatred for the contrary vice.' Corneille corrects Aristotle by adding two passions even more passionate than pity and fear: love, and its opposite, visceral hatred.

141 A small sample of scholarship on Aristotelian *catharsis*: Donald Keesey, 'On some recent interpretations of catharsis', *Classical World* 72 (1978–9): 193–205; Stephen Halliwell, 'La Psychologie morale de la catharsis: un essai de reconstruction', *Études Philosophiques* 4 (2003): 499–517; William Marx, *Le Tombeau d'Œdipe: pour une tragédie sans tragique*, Paris, Minuit, 2012; Pierre Destrée, 'Aristotle on the Paradox of Tragic Pleasure', in J. Levinson, ed., *Suffering Art Gladly: The Paradox of Negative Emotions in Art*, London: Palgrave Macmillan, 2013, pp. 3–27; Giulia Sissa, 'Comédies potentielles', in Philippe Rousseau and Rossella Saetta-Cottone, eds, *Diego Lanza, lecteur des œuvres de l'Antiquité: poésie, philosophie, histoire de la philologie*, Lille: Presses Universitaires du Septentrion, 2013, pp. 123–52.

142 Pierre Corneille, 'Discours de la tragédie, et des moyens de la traiter, selon le vraisemblable ou le nécessaire', in *Œuvres complètes*, vol. III, pp. 142–3.

143 Augustine, *The City of God*, IX, 4–5; XIV, 8–9. See Terence H. Irwin, 'Augustine's criticisms of the stoic theory of passions', *Faith and Philosophy* 20 (2003): 430–47.

144 Thomas Aquinas, *Summa Theologiae*, Supplement to the Third Part, 65 ('On the Plurality of wives'), especially 'Objections' 8 and 9, and the respective 'Replies'.

145 Dante Alighieri, *Purgatorio*, XIII, 38.

146 On self-love in the *Maxims*, see Vivien Thweatt, *La Rochefoucauld and the Seventeenth-Century Concept of the Self*, Geneva: Droz, 1980. More generally, on jealousy in the seventeenth century, see Bertaud, *La Jalousie dans la littérature au temps de Louis XIII*. See especially the illuminating pages on the neo-Stoics and their critics inspired by Aristotle, namely Jean-Pierre Camus, bishop of Belley, who described the baneful consequences of jealousy in many of his narratives. See also Anna Karolina Dubois, 'La Conception du tragique dans les récits brefs de Jean-Pierre Camus', *Réforme, humanisme, renaissance* 73 (2011): 163–77.

CHAPTER 2 A FORBIDDEN PASSION

1 Kristján Kristjánsson, 'Jealousy revisited: recent philosophical work on a maligned emotion', *Ethical Theory and Moral Practice* 19 (2016): 741–54; See also Daniel M. Farrell, 'Jealousy', *Philosophical Review* 89 (1980): 527–59.

2 Kristjánsson, 'Jealousy revisited', p. 744.

3 Denis Diderot, 'Hobbisme', in *Encyclopédie ou Dictionnaire raisonné des sciences, des arts et des métiers*, 1751–80, Vol. VIII, p. 232 (hereafter cited as *Encyclopédie*). On Hobbes's reception in France, see Noel Malcolm, *Aspects of Hobbes*, Oxford: Oxford University Press, 2002, pp. 493–510.

NOTES TO PP. 61–63

4 Thomas Hobbes, *Leviathan* (1651), I, vi. Cf. *Elements of Law*, VII, 1–2. On the importance of the passions in modern philosophy and their relationship with respect to the classical tradition, see Susan James, *Passion and Action: The Emotions in Seventeenth-Century Philosophy*, Oxford: Oxford University Press, 2000. *On Human Nature* constitutes the first part of Hobbes's *Elements of Law, Natural and Politic*, first published in 1640. An anonymous and incomplete French translation appeared in 1662.
5 Hobbes, *Leviathan*, XIII, x.
6 Hobbes, *Elements of Law*, IX, xxi.
7 Ibid., IX, v.
8 This formulation is in keeping with the version in *Leviathan* I, vi, 'Aversion with opinion of *Hurt* from the object FEARE. The same with Hope of avoyding that Hurt by resistance COURAGE. Sudden *courage* ANGER.' By 'hurt', Hobbes means 'harm'. This does not necessarily, however, imply an intention to 'wound' the self-respect of another, which would be 'contempt'.
9 Hobbes, *Leviathan*, II, xxvii.
10 Thomas Hobbes, *A Brief of the Art of Rhetorick Containing in Substance all that Aristotle Hath Written in His Three Books on That Subject*, 2, 2:

> ANGER is desire of Revenge, joyned with grief for that he, or some of his, is, or seems to be *neglected*.
>
> The object of *Anger* is always some particular, or individual thing. In *Anger* there is also pleasure proceeding from the imagination of revenge to come.
>
> To *Neglect*, is to esteem little or nothing: and of three kinds.
>
> 1 *Contempt*.
> 2 *Crossing*.
> 3 *Contumely*.
>
> *Contempt*, is when a man thinks another of little worth in comparison to himself.
>
> *Crossing*, is the hinderance of another man's will without design to profit himself.
>
> *Contumely*, is the disgracing of another for his own pastime.

11 In the *Elements of Law*, IX, v, Hobbes says of anger that 'It hath been commonly defined to be grief proceeding from an opinion of contempt', and in *A Brief of the Art of Rhetorick* 2, 2, that one of the 'common opinions' of anger is a belief that one has been 'neglected'.
12 Thomas Aquinas, *Summa theologiae*, Ia., IIae., q. 46. art. 1.
13 Ibid., q. 46, art 7.
14 Ibid., q. 46, art. 2.

15 Ibid., q. 46, art. 3.
16 This is, of course, in direct contrast with the Stoic view of anger, which offers no justification for what it holds to be a bestial and destructive passion. See, for instance, the *De ira* of Seneca (discussed above, pp. 34–6), for whom there is nothing great or noble in anger (*magnum, nhil nobile est*).
17 Cf. Hobbes, *A Brief of the Art of Rhetorick*, 2, 2: 'And such as think they deserve well.
    And such as grieve to be hindered, opposed, or not assisted. And therefore sick men, poor men, lovers, and generally all that desire and attain not, are *angry* with those that standing by, are not moved with their wants.'
18 Hobbes, *Leviathan*, I, vi.
19 Hobbes, *Elements of Law*, IX, xvi.
20 Hobbes, *Leviathan*, I, vi.
21 Ibid., I, viii.
22 Hobbes, *Elements of Law*, XXVIII, 28, iii. See Paul Hoffmann, *La Femme dans la pensée des Lumières*, Paris: Ophrys, 1977, pp. 254–67. This remarkably broad work allows us to follow the debates on gender difference, on sexuality and on love, in the eighteenth and nineteenth centuries. My approach is different, since I am concerned with the guiding question of the 'unconfessable' and the subjective costs of the condemnation of jealousy. Hence my concern for the connection of the law and the emotions. Hobbes's account of the natural law, for instance, is incomplete unless we read it together with his account of the passions, both of which are the subject of the first book of the *Elements of Law*.
23 Hobbes, *De cive*, VI, 16: '*Theft, Murther, Adultery* and all the *injuries* are forbid by the Lawes of nature.'
24 Aquinas, *Summa theologica*, Ia., IIae., q. 28, art. 2.
25 Ibid., q. 28, art 2.
26 See Diderot's comments in the article 'Hobbisme' in the *Encyclopédie*, Vol. VIII, p. 232: 'He had translated Euripides' *Medea* into Latin verse at an age when most children did not even know its author's name.' And see Gianluigi Goggi, 'Diderot et Médée dépeçant le vieil Éson', in A.-M. Chouillet, ed., *Colloque international Diderot*, Paris: Aux Amateurs de livres, 1985, pp. 173–83.
27 See Robert Derathé, *Jean-Jacques Rousseau et la science politique de son temps*, Paris: Vrin, 1995.
28 Diderot, *Encyclopédie*, Vol. VIII, p. 232. See Leland Thielemann, 'Hobbes dans l'*Encyclopédie*', *Revue d'histoire littéraire de la France* 51 (1951): 333–46, and 'Diderot and Hobbes', *Diderot Studies* 2 (1952): 221–78; and Madeleine Morris, 'Le huitième volume de l'*Encyclopédie* et *Le Neveu de Rameau*', *Recherches sur Diderot et sur l'Encyclopédie* 5 (1988): 33–44.
29 Jean Starobinski, *Jean-Jacques Rousseau: Transparency and Obstacle*, trans. Arthur Goldhammer, Chicago and London: University of Chicago Press, 1988, p. 293.

NOTES TO PP. 69–75

30 Jean-Jacques Rousseau, 'Discourse on the Origin and the Foundations of Inequality among Men', in *The First and Second Discourses, together with the Replies to Critics and Essay on the Origin of Languages*, ed. and trans. Victor Gourevitch, New York: Harper & Row, 1986, pp. 159–62.
31 Ibid., p. 160.
32 Ibid., p. 163.
33 Ibid., pp. 164–5.
34 Ibid.
35 Ibid., p. 164 (translation modified).
36 Ibid., p. 170.
37 Ibid., p. 175.
38 Ibid.
39 Jean-Jacques Rousseau, *Emile or On Education*, trans. Barbara Foxley, London: J. M. Dent, 1921, p. 392 (translation modified).
40 Ibid., p. 393.
41 Ibid.
42 Ibid., p. 175 (translation modified).
43 Ibid., p. 392.
44 Ibid., p. 394 (translation modified).
45 Ibid., pp. 369–70.
46 Ibid., p. 372.
47 Ibid., p. 175 (translation modified). This opposition, described in a language which is almost identical, is also to be found in Charles Pinot Duclos, *Considérations sur les mœurs de ce siècle*, Amsterdam, 1752. Duclos was very close to Rousseau. His influence on the latter's political ideas has been analysed by Maurizio Viroli, *Jean-Jacques Rousseau and the 'Well-Ordered Society'*, Cambridge: Cambridge University Press, 1988. Duclos opposes two types of love: 'that ardent, but indeterminate desire, for which anything is fodder, which never settles on any one object and whose violence makes any choice impossible', on the one hand, and that which 'attaches the will to an object to the exclusion of all others', on the other (p. 330). The same dichotomy appears in the *Mémoires pour servir à l'histoire des mœurs au XVIIIe siècle*, London, 1752: 'The taste which I felt very early for women became, after a short while, so strong that I was in no position to choose one in particular. They all made the same impression on my heart, or rather on my senses' (p. 9; see also p. 36). On the place of libertine love in the moral education of young men, see May Sansregret, 'L'évolution du corps moral, ou comment la fatuité mène à la vertu dans les *Mémoires pour servir à l'histoire des mœurs au XVIIIe siècle* (1752) de Charles Pinot Duclos', in Isabelle Billaud and Marie-Catherine Laperrière, eds, *Représentations du corps sous l'Ancien Régime*, Laval: Presses Universitaires de Laval, 2007, pp. 147–62.
48 Rousseau, *Emile*, pp. 175–6.
49 Diderot, *Encyclopédie*, Vol. VIII, p. 232:

> The relationship of a body with that of another consists in their equality or inequality, in their similarity or difference. The

NOTES TO PP. 75–80

> relationship is not a new accident but a quality of both bodies before a comparison between them has taken place. The causes of the accidents of the two correlatives are the causes of their correlation. The idea of quantity is born from the idea of limit. There is no big or small except by comparison. The rapport between them is an evaluation of quantity by comparison, and that comparison is either arithmetic or geometric.

50 Rousseau, *Emile*, p. 175.
51 Ibid., pp. 174–5.
52 Ibid., p.175.
53 Ibid.
54 Ibid., p. 176.
55 Hobbes, *Elements of Law*, IX, xvi.
56 Rousseau, *Emile*, p. 174 (translation modified).
57 Ibid., pp. 175–6.
58 Ibid., p. 175 (translation modified).
59 Ibid., p. 392.
60 Jean-Jacques Rousseau, *Lettre à M. D'Alembert* (1758), in *Œuvres complètes*, Vol. V, pp. 1–125.
61 Jean D'Alembert, *Lettre à M. Rousseau, citoyen de Genève, sur l'article Genève, tiré du septième volume de l'Encyclopédie, avec quelques autres pièces qui y sont relatives*, Amsterdam: Zacharie Chatelain, 1759.
62 Jean-François Marmontel, *Apologie du théâtre, où Analyse de la lettre de Rousseau, citoyen de Genève, à M. D'Alembert au sujet des spectacles* (1758–9), in Raymond Trousson, ed., *Jean-Jacques Rousseau*, Paris: PUF, 2000, p. 165:

> But when the gradations are well executed, when one is allowed to see the souls of Phaedra or Medea convulsed by the same feelings which arise in us too, prey to the same reflections, divided by the same remorse, proceeding little by little, and finally precipitating to commit crimes hideous to nature, we suffer as they do. And it is this return to ourselves which generates the principle of pity, and also of fear.

63 Denis Diderot, *Supplément au voyage de Bougainville*, in *Diderot: Political Writings*, ed. and trans. John Hope Mason, Cambridge: Cambridge University Press, 1992. On the complexities of the text, see R. Niklaus, 'Diderot et Rousseau: pour et contre le théâtre', *Diderot Studies* 4 (1963): 153–89; Susan Pinette, 'Diderot's dialogic difference', *French Review* 81 (2007): 339–50; Andrew Cowell, 'Diderot's Tahiti and Enlightenment sexual economics', *Studies on Voltaire and the Eighteenth Century* 332 (1995): 349–64; Colin Davis, 'Backward, forward, homeward: encounters in Ithaca with Kant and Diderot', *Eighteenth Century: Theory and Interpretation* 40 (1999): 219–33; Suellen Diaconoff, 'Diderot's mas-

carades: the jeux of je', *Diderot Studies* 27 (1998): 68–81; Andrzej Dziedzic, 'Liberté, propriété et sexualité dans le *Supplément au voyage de Bougainville*', *Chimères* 25 (2001): 45–55; Yves Giraud, 'De L'exploration à l'utopie: notes sur la formation du mythe de Tahiti', *French Studies* 31 (1977): 26–41; Claudia Moscovici, 'An ethics of cultural exchange: Diderot's *Supplément au voyage de Bougainville*', *Clio* 30 (2001): 289–309; Rita Goldberg, *Sex and Enlightenment: Women in Richardson and Diderot*, Cambridge: Cambridge University Press, 1984; Alice Parker, 'Did/erotica: Diderot's contribution to the history of sexuality', *Diderot Studies* 22 (1986): 89–106.

64 Diderot, *Supplément au voyage de Bougainville*, p. 50.
65 Diderot, *Encyclopédie*, Vol. VIII, p. 449.
66 Georges-Louis Leclerc, count of Buffon, *Histoire naturelle générale et particulière: avec la description du Cabinet du Roy*, Paris: l'Imprimerie royale, 1752, Vol. IV, p. 81.
67 Ibid., p. 82:

> All that is good in love, therefore, belongs as much to animals as it does to us; and even if it would seem that in animals this feeling can never be pure, they appear to have a smaller portion of what is less good – by which I mean jealousy. With us this passion always supposes some distrust of ourselves, some dull knowledge of our own weakness. Animals, on the contrary, appear to be all the more jealous because they have more strength, more ardour, and are more used to pleasure. This is because our jealousy depends on our ideas, and theirs on feeling. They have enjoyed pleasure, and wish to do so again. They feel their own strength, and they therefore reject any who attempts to take their place. Their jealousy is not reflective. They do not turn it against the object of their love. They are jealous only of their pleasures.

68 Rousseau, *Emile*, p. 392. On the birth of females in hot climates, and the fear that the risk of disequilibrium might also extend to the males, see ibid., pp. 332–4. Rousseau makes no mention of what the women themselves think or feel. A correlation between polygyny and an absence of jealousy among the husband's compliant wives may be found in Montaigne's account of 'savages' in his essay 'On the Cannibals' (in *The Complete Essays*, trans. M. A. Screech, London: Penguin, 1987, p. 239 [translation modified]):

> The men take several wives; the higher their reputation for valour, the more of them they have. One of the beautiful features of their marriages is that the jealousy which our wives employ in order to impede our friendship and tenderness towards other women, theirs have to the same degree in order to procure them for them. Being more concerned for their husbands' reputations than for anything

NOTES TO PP. 83–85

else, they take care and trouble to have as many companions as they can, as that is a testimony to their husbands' valour. Our wives will scream that this is marvel. But it is not. It is a virtue proper to matrimony, but from an earlier age. In the Bible, Leah, Rachel, Sarah and the wives of Jacob all made their fair handmaidens available to their husbands, and Livia connived at the lusts of Augustus against her own interests. Stratonice, the consort of King Deiotarus, not only provided her husband with a very beautiful chambermaid who served her but carefully brought up their children and lent a hand in enabling them to succeed to her husband's rank.

69 Rousseau, *Emile*, p. 177.
70 Rousseau, 'Discourse on the Origin and the Foundations of Inequality among Men', pp. 164–5.
71 The 'dystopic' aspects of the Tahitian paradise have not, of course, been overlooked by scholars, but it is still necessary to emphasize the ironical nature of the dialogue. See, for instance, Tzvetan Todorov, *Nous et les autres*, Paris: Seuil, 1989; Sharon A. Stanley, 'Unraveling natural utopia: Diderot's *Supplement to the voyage of Bougainville*', *Political Theory* 37 (2009): 266–89; Kate Tunstall, 'Sexe, mensonges et colonies: le discours de l'amour dans le *Supplément au voyage de Bougainville*', *Littératures classiques* 69 (2009): 15–34. See Pamela Cheeks, *Sexual Antipodes: Enlightenment, Globalization and the Placing of Sex*, Stanford, CA: Stanford University Press, 2003, pp. 152–8, for a postcolonial reading where the main consideration is the ambivalence of the 'blood' of the French as a bearer of both contagion and the possibility of a genetic improvement of the Tahitians. No mention is made either of the lesson in universalism Orou delivers to the chaplain or of the highly nuanced exchanges between 'A' and 'B'. A thorough analysis of the text may be found in Wilda Anderson, *Diderot's Dream*, Baltimore: Johns Hopkins University Press, 1990, and in Sankar Muthu, *Enlightenment against Empire*, Princeton, NJ: Princeton University Press, 2003, pp. 48–59. Muthu claims that, in Diderot, 'the conceptualization of the New World's societies ultimately subverted the noble savage tradition.' He compares and contrasts Rousseau and Diderot on the subjects of women, love and jealousy (pp. 64–5).
72 Diderot, *Supplément au voyage de Bougainville*, pp. 63–4.
73 Ibid., p. 48. On the juridical and classical underpinnings of this distinction, which, as we shall see in the following chapter, is both philosophically and politically crucial, see Roberto Esposito, *Le persone e le cose*, Turin: Einaudi, 2014. For Diderot and women, see, above all, Dominique Lecourt, *Passions, sexe, raison*, Paris: PUF, 2013.
74 Diderot, *Supplément au voyage de Bougainville*, p. 65.
75 Ibid., p. 68.
76 Ibid., p. 65.
77 Ibid., p. 74.

78 Denis Diderot, *Lettres à Sophie Volland*, Paris: Gallimard, 1984, p. 16. See also J. Geffriaud Rosso, 'Les demi-silences de Mademoiselle Volland: sur la jalousie', *Diderot Studies* 2 (1995): 109–24.

> A number of the dialogues with Madame d'Holbach or Madame Le Gendre, although they claim to be mere badinage, are in fact veiled declarations, made all the more piquant and exalting by the fact that Diderot practises the art of the unspoken, of the innuendo, of a speech which is hidden but no less expressive. And the repeated declarations to Sophie that follow the (accurate?) account of those fiery dialogues are perhaps the fruit of a bad conscience, a liberating confession made with – who knows? – the satisfaction of a man of letters at having written a beautiful page by showing off his noble feelings. (p. 120)

79 Diderot, *Lettres à Sophie Volland*, p. 107.
80 Ibid., p. 37. Diderot makes numerous allusions to Medea, above all to her skills as a magician, and in particular in connection with the rejuvenation of Aeson. On this, see Amy Wygant, *Medea, Magic and Modernity in France: Stages and Histories*, Farnham: Ashgate, 2007, pp. 187–206.
81 Denis Diderot, *Réfutation d'Helvétius*, 2, 3.

> Man has created society to be able to struggle with the greatest advantage against his constant enemy, nature. But, not satisfied with conquering it, he wished to triumph over it. As he found the hut more comfortable than the cavern, he began to dwell in huts. But what an immense distance there is from there to a palace! Is life better in a palace than in a hut? I doubt it. How much pains has mankind taken in order to add to his lot only superfluities and to complicate to infinity the accomplishment of his happiness!

82 Ibid., 2, 8.
83 Ibid., 2, 3:

> I do not think, like Rousseau, that we should destroy them whenever we can, but I am convinced that human industry has gone far too far and that, had it been stopped much earlier, had it been possible to simplify its work, we would be none the worse.... I believe that there is also a moment in civilization, a moment which is more propitious to the happiness of man in general and far less removed from the wild condition than one imagines. But how can we return to it when we have gone astray, and how can we stay there when we have got there? Alas, I have no idea!

84 Ibid., 2, 6.

85 Stendhal, *Love*, trans. Gilbert Sale and Suzanne Sale, London: Penguin, 1975, p. 45 (translation modified).
86 Ibid., p. 47.
87 Ibid., p. 45.
88 Ibid., p. 47.
89 Ibid., p. 112.
90 Ibid.
91 Ibid.
92 Ibid., p. 46.
93 Ibid.
94 Ibid., p. 45.
95 This episode is described in the section entitled *The Salzburg Bough*, ibid., pp. 284–92.
96 Ibid., p. 118.
97 Ibid., p.112. See La Rochefoucauld, Maxim 446, in *The Maxims of François Duc de La Rochefoucauld*, etc., trans. F. G. Stevens, London: Humphrey Milford, 1940, p. 139.
98 Stendhal, *Love*, p.112.
99 Ibid., p. 118.
100 Ibid., p. 112.
101 Ibid., pp. 111–24.
102 Ibid., pp. 116–19.
103 Ibid., pp. 112–17.
104 Stendhal, *The Red and the Black*, trans. Robert M. Adams, New York and London: W. W. Norton, 2008, p. 291.
105 Ibid., p. 292.
106 Ibid., p. 294 (translation modified).
107 Ibid., p. 291 (translation modified).
108 Ibid., p. 229.
109 Ibid., p. 326.
110 Ibid., p. 347 (translation modified).
111 Ibid., p. 352.
112 Ibid., pp. 324, 291.
113 For a discussion of this text see pp. 50–66 above.
114 Victor Del Litto, *La Vie intellectuelle de Stendhal: genèse et développement de ses idées (1802–1821)*, Paris: Slatkine, 1962, pp. 146–9.
115 Hobbes, *Elements of Law*, IX, xxi.
116 Yves Ansel, 'Amour de l'idéologie et idéologie de l'amour', in Daniel Sangsue, ed., *Persuasions d'amour: nouvelles lectures de De l'amour de Stendhal*, Geneva: Droz, 1999, pp. 21–39 and 35–7.
117 Del Litto, *La Vie intellectuelle de Stendhal*, p. 86; Stendhal, *Pensées*, 1, 124. See Raymond Trousson, *Stendhal et Rousseau: continuité et ruptures*, Geneva: Slatkine, 1986, p. 43.
118 On the Rousseauist sensibility of the young Henri Beyle, see Del Litto, *La Vie intellectuelle de Stendhal*, pp. 33, 271.
119 The varieties of crystallization are numerous. Here are two key passages from *Love* which show the dissonance between the frequently mediocre

NOTES TO PP. 98–104

qualities of the actual person and the lover's perception of his or her worth.

> 'Ah, I understand', said Ghita, 'at the moment you begin to be interested in some woman, you do not see her *as she really is*, but only as it suits you to see her. You compare the flattering illusions which this wakening arouses, with the pretty diamonds which cover this leafless branch of hornbeam in winter – and which are apparent, mark you, only in the eyes of this young man who is falling in love.'
>
> 'And that', I continued, 'is why the conversations of lovers sound so absurd to sensible people who are unaware of the phenomenon called crystallization.'
>
> 'Oh you call it *crystallization*,' laughed Ghita. 'Well, then will you crystallize for me?' (Ibid., p. 287)
>
> 'No matter whether it be in the forest of Arden or at a Coulon Ball, you can only enjoy idealizing your beloved if she *appears* perfect in the first place. Absolute perfection is not essential, but every perceived quality must be perfect. Only after several days of the second crystallization will the beloved appear perfect in all respects. It's quite simple; you only need to think of perfection to perceive it at once in your beloved. (Ibid. pp. 57–8)'

120 Ibid., p. 80.
121 Rousseau, *Emile*, p. 393 (translation modified).
122 Stendhal, *Histoire de la peinture en Italie*, ed. Victor de Litto, Paris: Gallimard, 1996, cap. 117. See also cap. 111 on Othello. Stendhal had intended to write a Medea, which he claimed to be 'a superb subject which has not yet been done'. See Georges Kliebenstein, 'Stendhal face au grec', in M.-R. Corredor, *Stendhal à Cosmopolis: Stendhal et ses langues*, Grenoble: ELLUG, 2007, pp. 25–59, at p. 31.

CHAPTER 3 SEXUAL OBJECTS AND OPEN COUPLES

1 Marcel Hénaff, *Le Don des philosophes: repenser la réciprocité*, Paris: Éditions du Seuil, 2012.
2 Jacques Lacan, *Transference: The Seminar of Jacques Lacan, Book VIII*, ed. Jacques-Alain Miller, trans. Bruce Fink, Cambridge: Polity, 2015, pp. 3, 11–12 and *passim* (*Le Séminaire* VIII. *Le Transfer*. Paris: Éditions du Seuil, 1991 & 2001, p. 11; 21 and *passim*).
3 Ibid., p. 145.
4 Martha Nussbaum, 'Objectification', *Philosophy and Public Affairs* 24 (1995): 249–91, at p. 257.
5 Rae Langton, *Sexual Solipsism: Philosophical Essays on Pornography and Objectification*, Oxford: Oxford University Press, 2009, pp. 228–9. For this very brief overview of objectification, I am indebted to the

thoughtful synthesis by Evangelia Papadaki, 'Feminist Perspectives on Objectification', *Stanford Encyclopedia of Philosophy* (summer 2014 edn), ed. Edward N. Zalta, http://plato.stanford.edu/archives/sum2014/entries/feminism-objectification/.

For a critical discussion and an interesting move from the language of 'objectification' to that of 'derivatization', see Ann Cahill, *Overcoming Objectification: A Carnal Ethics*, Abingdon: Routledge, 2010. I share Cahill's arguments on objectification as a way of speaking and thinking that obliterates the corporeal incarnation of a gendered human being. But I will argue that the imaginary experience of the erotic works not only through the logic of gender (placing the female in a position that is always relative to the male, as was the case for Luce Irigaray and Simone de Beauvoir) but also via an anxious *projection of desire* upon a subject whose special attention we expect. And this projection of desire is a hypothetical, uncertain, apprehensive, hopeful, wishful thinking, not merely the insensitive attribution of a self-serving will on behalf of the desiring subject. I will come back to these arguments in chapter 5.

6   Kant's position is upheld and defended by a number of moral philosophers, such as Barbara Herman, 'Could it Be Worth Thinking about Kant on Sex and Marriage?', in *A Mind of One's Own: Feminist Essays on Reason and Objectivity*, ed. Louise Antony and Charlotte Witt, Oxford: Westview Press, 1993, pp. 53–72.

7   Immanuel Kant, AK 4:429, *Groundwork of the Metaphysics of Morals* (1785), in *Practical Philosophy*, ed. and trans. Mary J. Gregor, Cambridge: Cambridge University Press, 1996, p. 79:

> Beings the existence of which rests not on our will but on nature, if they are beings without reason, still have only a relative worth, as means, and are therefore called *things*, whereas rational beings are called *persons* because their nature already marks them out as an end in itself, that is, as something that may not be used merely as a means, and hence so far limits all choice (and is an object of respect).

8   Ibid., p. 80 (AK 4:429); see also: p. 79 (AK 4:428).
9   Ibid.
10 Ibid., pp. 79–80 (AK 4:429). See Leslie Green, 'Pornographies', *Journal of Political Philosophy* 8 (2000), pp. 27–52.
11 Immanuel Kant, *The Metaphysics of Morals*, Part 1: *The Doctrine of Right*, §22 (AK 6:276).

For a thorough discussion of these arguments, see John Ladd's introduction to *Metaphysical Elements of Justice: Part I of The Metaphysics of Morals*, trans. John Ladd, Indianapolis: Hackett, 1999, pp. xv–lviii; Reinhardt Brandt, 'Kants Eherecht', in Maximilian Bergengruen, Johannes Friedrich Lehmann and Hubert Thüring, eds, *Sexualität, Recht, Leben: die Entstehung eines Dispositivs um 1800*, Munich: Wilhelm Fink, 2005, pp. 113–32; Friederike Kuster, 'Verdinglichung und Menschenwürde: Kants

Eherecht und das Recht der häuslichen Gemeinschaft', *Kant-Studien* 102 (2011): 335–49.
12 Kant, *The Metaphysics of Morals*, Part 1: *The Doctrine of Right*, §11 (AK 6:260).
13 Ibid., §24 (AK 6:276).
14 Ibid., §24 (AK 6:277).
15 Ibid., §26 (AK 6:278).
16 Ibid., §24 (AK 6:277).
17 Ibid., §25 (AK 6:278).
18 Ibid., §25 (AK 6:278).
19 Ibid., §25 (AK 6:278).
20 Ibid., *Appendix*, 3 (AK 6:359). In this supplemental section, Kant clarifies his argument.
21 Ibid.
22 Ibid., AK:6:358, footnote.
23 Fanny Karaman and Stanley C. Ruchelman, '*Usufruct*, bare ownership, and U.S. estate tax: an unlucky trio', http://publications.ruchelaw.com/news/2016-09/Usufruct-Code-2036.pdf.
24 Kant, *The Metaphysics of Morals*, Part I: *The Doctrine of Right*, *Appendix*, 3 (AK 6:359) (italics in the original; emphasis added).
25 Ibid., §25 (AK 6:278), p. 427. On the logic of this argument, see Carole Pateman, *The Sexual Contract*, Stanford, CA: Stanford University Press, 1988, pp. 168–73; Evangelia Papadaki, 'Sexual objectification: from Kant to contemporary feminism', *Contemporary Political Theory* 6 (2007): 330–48, and 'Feminist Perspectives on Objectification'. The language of acquisition and reciprocal possession through the usage of the sexual parts is pervasive in *The Doctrine of Right*, §24 and §27.
26 Ibid., *Appendix*, 3 (AK 6:359).
27 Ibid., §26 (AK 6:278).
28 Immanuel Kant, *Lectures on Ethics*, AK 27:385, in Kant, *Lectures on Ethics*, ed. Peter Heath and J. B. Schneewind, trans. Peter Heath, Cambridge: Cambridge University Press, 1997, p. 156.
29 Immanuel Kant, *The Metaphysics of Morals*, Part II: *Metaphysical First Principles of the Doctrine of Virtue* (Doctrine of the elements of ethics), §7 (AK 6:424–5), in *Practical Philosophy*, pp. 548–50.
30 Kant, *Lectures on Ethics*, AK 27:632 in *Lectures on Ethics*, p. 373 (Vigilantius §95); see also ibid., pp. 380–1 (AK 27:641–2):

> A contravention against the end of nature is not only demeaning of humanity in our person – we also make ourselves the object of the greatest abhorrence, whether our lust be vented upon ourselves, or upon an object of the same sex.... All these *crimina contra naturam* involve a bestial element, i.e., they demean man below the beasts, among whom there is indeed no commonality, but nevertheless a mating of opposite sexes, and likewise among the same animals. If these crimes are compared with suicide, feeling already tells us that the suicide is not contemptible in the same degree.

NOTES TO PP. 113–122

31 Immanuel Kant, *Religion within the Boundaries of Mere Reason*, ed. Allen Wood and George di Giovanni, Cambridge: Cambridge University Press, 1998, p. 95n (AK 6:80).
32 Ibid.
33 Kant, *Lectures on Ethics*, p. 156 (AK 27:386). To be an object of sexual desire is a debasement of one's humanity, as opposed to being an object of respect. See *The Metaphysics of Morals*, Part II: *Metaphysical First Principles of the Doctrine of Virtue*, §11 (AK 6:435): *Die Menschheit in seiner Person ist das Objekt der Achtung*.
34 Immanuel Kant, *Anthropology from a Pragmatic Point of View*, ed. Robert B. Louden, Cambridge: Cambridge University Press, 2006, Preface, p. 4 (AK 7:120). Michel Foucault, 'Introduction à l'*Anthropologie*' [1964], in Kant, *Anthropologie du point de vue pragmatique*, Paris: Vrin, 2008.
35 Kant, *Anthropology from a Pragmatic Point of View*, p. 205 (AK 7:304).
36 Ibid., p. 206 (AK 7:305).
37 Ibid.
38 Ibid., p. 206 (AK 7:304–5).
39 For a more extended discussion of this text (*Some Neurotic Mechanisms in Jealousy, Paranoia and Homosexuality*) see pp. 162–4.
40 Ibid., pp. 205–6 (AK 7:304), note a; p. 212 (AK 7:310).
41 Foucault, 'Introduction à l'*Anthropologie*'.
42 Immanuel Kant, 'Appendix' to *The Metaphysics of Morals*, Part I: *The Doctrine of Right* (AK 6:358–9). Kant insists on the novelty of his contribution also in his letter to Christian Gottfried Schütz, which I will discuss in a moment.
43 Ibid., p. 127–8 (AK 6:359–60).
44 Immanuel Kant, *Correspondence*, ed. and trans. Arnulf Zweig, Cambridge: Cambridge University Press, 1999, #195, pp. 520–2 (AK 12:181–3).
45 Ibid., p. 521 (AK 12:182).
46 Ibid.
47 Ibid.
48 Ibid., p. 522 (AK 12:183).
49 Michel Foucault, 'Introduction à l'*Anthropologie*', p. 25.
50 G. W. F. Hegel, *Elements of the Philosophy of Right*, ed. Allen Wood, trans. H. B. Nisbet, Cambridge: Cambridge University Press, 1991, §75, p. 105 (translation modified).
51 Ibid. (emphasis added).
52 Ibid., §167, p. 207:

> Marriage is essentially *monogamy*, because it is personality or immediate exclusive *individuality* [*Einzelheit*] which enters into and surrenders itself to this relationship, whose truth and *inwardness* (*the subjective form of substantiality*) consequently arise only out of the mutual and *undivided* surrender of this personality. The latter attains its right of being conscious of itself in the *other* only in so far as the other is present in this identity as a person, i.e. as atomic individual-

ity [*nur insofern das andere als Person, d. i. als atome Einzelheit in dieser Identität ist*].

53 Ibid., §163, p. 203.
54 Lucretius, *On the Nature of Things*, IV, 1070–4. I have developed this argument in *Amor Mora Metamorphisis Roma*, in Matteo De Poli, ed., *Maschile e femminile: genere ed eros nel mondo Greco: Atti del Convegno Padova 22–23 Ottobre 2009*. Padua: Acta Sileni, 2010, pp. 7–38 [in English].
55 Kant, *The Metaphysics of Morals*, ed. and trans. Mary Gregor, Cambridge: Cambridge University Press, 1996, §24 (AK 6:277). Cf. AK 6:325, where *venus volgivaga* is a euphemism for prostitution, to be regulated by the state.
56 Hegel, *Elements of the Philosophy of Right*, §161, p. 201, Addition.
57 *Hegels handschrifliche Zusätze zu seiner Rechtsphilosophie*, ed. G. Lasson, Leipzig: Meiner, 1916, part 3, p. 85.
58 Rae Langton, *Sexual Solipsism: Philosophical Essays on Pornography and Objectification*, Oxford: Oxford University Press, 2009.
59 Luce Irigaray, *J'aime à toi*, Paris, Grasset, 1992, p. 60.
60 Lacan, *Transference*, p. 146.

> And we need to know – how can we ever forget this question? – what function is served by the fact that (in this elective, privileged relationship which is the love relationship) the subject with whom, among all others, we have a bond of love is also the object of our desire. If one brings out the love relationship while holding in abeyance its anchor, pivotal point, centre of gravity, or hook, it is impossible to say anything that is not simply a crock.
>
> In the other perspective, and analytic work demonstrates this, everything revolves around the privileged or unique point constituted somewhere by something we find in a being only when we truly love. But what is it? *Agalma* – the object we have learned to discern in analytic practice. (p. 148)
>
> The psychoanalytical object is the something that is the aim of desire as such, the something that emphasizes one object among all the others as incommensurate with the others. The introduction in analysis of the function of the partial object corresponds to this emphasis on the object (*C'est ce quelque chose qui est la visée du désir comme telle, qui accentue un objet entre tous d'être sans balance avec les autres. C'est à cette accentuation de l'objet que répond l'introduction en analyse de la fonction de l'objet partiel.*)...But if this object 'impassions' you, it is because hidden inside it is *agalma*, the object of desire. This is what makes it weighty (*ce qui fait le poids*); this is why it is important to know where this fabulous

object is, what its function is, and where it operates in inter- and intra-subjectivity. (p. 146)

61 On the literal origins of these terms, see Frédéric Vandenberghe, *A Philosophical History of German Sociology*, trans. Carolyn Shread, Abingdon: Routledge, 2009, pp. 8–9.
62 Karl Marx, *Capital*, I, IV, 14.1.
63 Vandenberghe, *A Philosophical History of German sociology*, pp. 8–9.
64 Louis Althusser, *For Marx*, trans. Ben Brewster, London: Verso, 2010, p. 195.
65 Ibid., p. 197, n. 7.
66 Ibid., p. 190.
67 On the genesis and complexity of Simone de Beauvoir's thought, revisited in recent (especially Anglo-American) philosophy and political theory, see the synthetic and very enlightening overview by Éliane Lecarme-Tabone, 'Le couple Beauvoir–Sartre devant la critique féministe', *Les Temps Modernes*, no. 3 (2002): 19–42. See also Debra Bergoffen, *The Philosophy of Simone de Beauvoir: Gendered Phenomenologies, Erotic Generosities*, Albany: State University of New York Press, 1997; and 'Simone de Beauvoir', *Stanford Encyclopedia of Philosophy* (fall 2015 edn), ed. Edward N. Zalta, https://plato.stanford.edu/archives/fall2015/entries/beauvoir/.
68 Simone de Beauvoir, *The Second Sex*, trans. Constance Borde and Sheila Malovany-Chevallier, New York: Vintage Books/Random House, 2009, p. 211: 'But when woman is delivered to the male as his property, he claims that her flesh be presented in its pure facticity. Her body is grasped not as the emanation of a subjectivity [*le rayonnement d'une subjectivité*] but as a thing weighted in its immanence [*une chose empâtée dans son immanence*]; this body must not radiate to the rest of the world, it must not promise anything but itself: its desire has to be stopped.'
69 Ibid., p. 193:

> Each one tries to accomplish itself by reducing the other to slavery. But in work and fear the slave experiences himself as essential, and by a dialectical reversal the master appears the inessential one. The conflict can be overcome by the free recognition of each individual in the other, each one positing both itself and the other as object and as subject in a reciprocal movement.

70 Ibid.:

> History has shown that men have always held all the concrete powers; from patriarchy's earliest times they have deemed it useful to keep woman in a state of dependence; their codes were set up against her; she was thus concretely established as the Other. This condition served males' economic interests; but it also suited their ontological and moral ambitions. Once the subject attempts to assert

himself, the Other, who limits and denies him, is nonetheless necessary for him: he attains himself only through the reality that he is not. That is why man's life is never plenitude and rest, it is lack and movement, it is combat.

71 Ibid., p. 26. See also p. 35:

But what singularly defines the situation of woman is that being, like all humans, an autonomous freedom, she discovers and chooses herself in a world where men force her to assume herself as Other: an attempt is made to freeze her as an object and doom her to immanence, since her transcendence will be forever transcended by another essential and sovereign consciousness.

72 Ibid., p. 195.
73 Ibid., p. 198.
74 Ibid., p. 114. The whole argument is developed on pp. 103–14. See, in particular, pp. 111–12: 'Venerated and revered for her fertility, being *other* than man, and sharing the disquieting character of the *other*, woman, in a certain way, kept man dependent on her even while she was dependent on him; the reciprocity of the master–slave relationship existed *in the present* for her, and it was how she escaped slavery.' On the difference between woman and slave, see pp. 99–100.
75 Ibid., pp. 118–19.
76 Ibid., pp. 206–13, namely p. 211:

The ideal of feminine beauty is variable; but some requirements remain constant; one of them is that since woman is destined to be possessed, her body has to provide the inert and passive qualities of an object. Virile beauty is the body's adaptation to active functions such as strength, agility, flexibility, and the manifestation of a transcendence animating a flesh that must never collapse into itself.... But when woman is delivered to the male as his property, he claims that her flesh be presented in its pure facticity.

77 Ibid., p. 211: from the most 'primitive' societies to more refined cultures, men appreciate a full womanly figure.

The buttocks are the part of the body with the fewest nerve endings, where the flesh appears as a given without purpose. The taste of people from the East for fleshy women is similar; they love the absurd luxury of this fatty proliferation that is not enlivened by any project, that has no other meaning than to be there. Even in civilizations of a more subtle sensibility, where notions of form and harmony come into play, breasts and buttocks were prized objects because of the gratuitousness and contingency of their development.

78 Ibid., p. 212: 'Makeup and jewels were also used for this petrification of the body and face.'
79 *The Second Sex* is consistent in its transhistorical reconstruction of this perspective. Men objectify women, and women comply. Scholars writing on Beauvoir, however, disagree on her views on the body. From a vast scholarly literature: Judith Butler, 'Sex and gender in Simone de Beauvoir's Second Sex', *Yale French Studies* 72 (1986): 35–49; and 'Gendering the Body: Beauvoir's Philosophical Contribution', in Ann Garry and Marilyn Pearsall, eds, *Women, Knowledge, and Reality: Explorations in Feminist Philosophy*, Boston: Unwin Hyman, 1989; Penelope Deutscher, 'Bodies, lost and found: Simone de Beauvoir from *The Second Sex* to Old Age', *Radical Philosophy* 96 (1999): 6–16; Sarah Fishwick, *The Body in the Work of Simone de Beauvoir*, Oxford and New York: Peter Lang, 2002. For a discussion of different interpretations, see Patricia Moynagh, 'Beauvoir on Lived Reality, Exemplary Validity, and a Method for Political Thought', in Lori Jo Marso and Patricia Moynagh, eds, *Simone de Beauvoir's Political Thinking*, Urbana: University of Illinois Press, 2006, pp. 11–30. See also the comments on Beauvoir's and Sartre's disagreement about the harem as a paradigmatic situation in which the former sees transcendence as being especially difficult for the women involved; the latter claims that freedom, however limited, is always still possible.
80 Beauvoir, *The Second Sex*, p. 242:

> So as to tear woman from nature, so as to subjugate her to man through ceremonies and contracts, *she was elevated to the dignity of a human person; she was granted freedom*. But freedom is precisely what escapes all servitude; and if it is bestowed on a being originally possessed by malevolent forces, it becomes dangerous. And all the more so as man stopped at half measures; he accepted woman into the masculine world only by making her a servant, in thwarting her transcendence; the freedom she was granted could only have a negative use; it only manifests itself in refusal. *Woman became free only in becoming captive*; she renounces this human privilege to recover her power as natural object. By day she treacherously plays her role of docile servant, but by night she changes into a kitten, a doe; she slips back into a siren's skin, or riding on her broomstick, she makes her satanic rounds. Sometimes she exercises her nocturnal magic on her own husband; but it is wiser to conceal her metamorphoses from her master; she chooses strangers as her prey; they have no rights over her, and she remains for them a plant, wellspring, star, or sorceress. So there she is fated to infidelity. (Emphasis added)

81 As we will see in a moment, Allen Wood (*Kant's Ethical Thought*, Cambridge: Cambridge University Press, 1999, pp. 256–60, 396–7) argues that Sartre derived his views on sex, to a large extent, from Kant. See Jean-Paul Sartre, *Being and Nothingness: An Essay on Phenomenological Ontology*, trans. Hazel E. Barnes, London: Routledge, 2005, pp. 339–79.

NOTES TO PP. 137–138

Wood also acknowledges the presence of the Kantian heritage in Beauvoir's thought and American feminism, in particular in the works of Andrea Dworkin. See also Allen Wood, *Kantian Ethics*, Cambridge: Cambridge University Press, 2008, pp. 224–39. I will discuss later (in chapter 5) the difference between Simone de Beauvoir's and Jean-Paul Sartre's endorsement of the Kantian language of sexual objectification.

82 On Beauvoir and Kant, see Sara Cohen Shabot, 'On the question of woman: illuminating De Beauvoir through Kantian epistemology', *Philosophy Today* 51 (2007): 369–82; William Wilkerson, 'A Different Kind of Universality: Beauvoir and Kant on Universal Ethics', in Shannon M. Mussett and William S. Wilkerson, eds, *Beauvoir and Western Thought from Plato to Butler*, New York: SUNY Press, 2012, pp. 55–74.

83 Simone de Beauvoir, *The Ethics of Ambiguity*, trans. Bernard Frechtman, New York: Citadel Press, p. 18. 'We also meet it [humanism] in Marxism which, from one point of view, can be considered as an apotheosis of subjectivity. *Like all radical humanism, Marxism rejects the idea of an inhuman objectivity and locates itself in the tradition of Kant and Hegel*' (emphasis added).

84 Beauvoir, *The Second Sex*, p. 194:

> This embodied dream is, precisely, woman; she is the perfect intermediary between nature that is foreign to man and the peer who is too identical to him. She pits neither the hostile silence of nature nor the hard demand of a reciprocal recognition against him; by a unique privilege she is a consciousness and yet it seems possible to possess her in the flesh. Thanks to her, there is a way to escape the inexorable dialectic of the master and the slave that springs from the reciprocity of freedoms.

85 Ibid., p. 530:

> Physical love draws its strength and dignity from the joy lovers give each other and take in the reciprocal consciousness of their freedom; thus there are no degrading practices since, for both of them, their practices are not submitted to but generously desired. But the principle of marriage is obscene because it transforms an exchange that should be founded on a spontaneous impulse into rights and duties; it gives bodies an instrumental, thus degrading, side by dooming them to grasp themselves in their generality.

86 Ibid., p. 476.
87 Ibid.
88 Ibid., p. 456:

> In any case, she feels passive: she is caressed, penetrated; she undergoes intercourse, whereas the man spends himself actively. It is true that the male sex organ is not a striated muscle commanded by

will; it is neither plowshare nor sword but merely flesh; but it is a voluntary movement that man imprints on her; he goes, he comes, stops, resumes, while the woman receives him submissively; it is the man – especially when the woman is a novice – who chooses the amorous positions, who decides the length and frequency of intercourse. *She feels herself to be an instrument: all the freedom is in the other.* (Emphasis added)

See also pp. 465–6 on women refusing to be caressed.

89 Ibid., p. 476. See also pp. 475, 859:

Many modern women who claim their dignity as human beings still grasp their sexual lives by referring back to a tradition of slavery: *so it seems humiliating to them to lie under the man and be penetrated by him, and they tense up into frigidity*; but if reality were different, the meaning sexual gestures and postures symbolically express would be different as well.... If, however, both assumed it with lucid modesty, as the correlate of authentic pride, they would recognize each other as peers and live the erotic drama in harmony. (Emphasis added)

See also pp. 756–7 on women being educated to be objects, thus to alienate themselves in their body, and on puberty as the revelation of the body as passive and desirable. Eroticism and narcissism are mutually exclusive: 'Making herself carnal object and prey contradicts her self-adoration: it seems to her that lovemaking disfigures and defiles her body or degrades her soul. Some women, therefore, choose frigidity, thinking they can thus preserve the integrity of their ego' (p. 779).

Man's attitude is thus of extreme importance. If his desire is violent and brutal, his partner *feels changed into a mere thing in his arms*; but if he is too self-controlled, too detached, he does not constitute himself as flesh; *he asks woman to make herself object without her being able to have a hold on him in return.* In both cases, her pride rebels; *to reconcile her metamorphosis into a carnal object with the demands of her subjectivity, she must make him her prey as she makes herself his. This is often why the woman obstinately remains frigid.* (p. 466: emphasis added)

90 Ibid., p. 787: in the emotional experience of love, something similar occurs: 'Since she has being alienated herself in another, she also wants to recover herself: she has to annex this other who holds her being.' (*S'étant aliénée en un autre, elle veut aussi se récupérer*).

91 Ibid., p. 475:

The asymmetry of male and female eroticism creates insoluble problems as long as there is a battle of the sexes; they can easily be settled when a woman feels *both desire and respect in a man*; if he covets her in her flesh while recognizing her freedom, she recovers her essentialness at the moment she becomes object, she remains free in the submission to which she consents. (Emphasis added)

92 Ibid., p. 533: 'The truth is that physical love can be treated neither as an absolute end in itself nor as a simple means; it cannot justify an existence: but it can receive no outside justification [*aucune justification étrangère*]. It means it must play an episodic and autonomous role in all human life. This means it must above all be free.' Ibid., p. 780: 'in truly mutual love, sexual pleasure is justified [*le plaisir est justifié*]; the woman can gloriously assume her sexuality because she transcends it; arousal, pleasure, and desire are no longer a state but a gift; her body is no longer an object: it is a song, a flame.'

93 Wood, *Kant's Ethical Thought*, pp. 256–60, 396–7. According to Beauvoir, sexual instrumentalization culminates with marriage:

> Eroticism is a movement toward the Other, and this is its essential character; but within the couple, spouses become, for each other, the Same; no exchange is possible between them anymore, no giving, no conquest. If they remain lovers, it is often in embarrassment: they feel the sexual act is no longer an intersubjective experience where each one goes beyond himself, but rather a kind of mutual masturbation. That they consider each other a necessary tool for the satisfaction of their needs is a fact conjugal politeness disguises…(*The Second Sex*, pp. 531–2)

94 See chapter 5, pp. 193–200. On Sartre versus Beauvoir on these questions, see Christine Daigle, 'Sartre and Beauvoir on Embodiment and Sexuality', in Alfred Betschart, Manuela Hackel, Marie Minot and Vincent von Wroblewsky, eds, *Jean-Paul Sartre: eine permanente Provokation – une provocation permanente – a Permanent Provocation*. Frankfurt am Mein: Peter Lang, 2014, pp. 227–40.

95 On the complexity of the philosophical relation between Beauvoir and Merleau-Ponty, see Sara Heinämaa, *Toward a Phenomenology of Sexual Difference*, Lanham, MD: Rowman & Littlefield, 2003 (the author focuses on the phenomenological genealogy of Beauvoir's views of the body, from Husserl and Merleau-Ponty); Ulrike Björk, 'Simone de Beauvoir and Life', in Lester Embree and Thomas Nenon, eds, *Husserl's Ideen*, Berlin: Springer, 2013, pp. 351–64 (Björk revisits the same reconstruction and argues for Beauvoir's mostly indirect knowledge of phenomenology via *Phenomenology of Perception*, of which she wrote a review); and Suzanne Laba Cataldi, 'The Body as a Basis for Being: Simone de Beauvoir and Maurice Merleau-Ponty', in Lester Embree and Wendy O'Brien, eds, *The Existential Phenomenology of Simone de Beauvoir*, London: Springer, 2001, pp. 85–106. Laba Cataldi rightly rejects the simplistic reading of *The Second Sex* as misogynistic (on account of its depiction of Woman), but

NOTES TO P. 140

she downplays the difference with Merleau-Ponty. According to Beauvoir, women across history are really stuck in immanence. They can live their entire lives in situations where transcendence is so difficult that they 'sink' into immanence. Merleau-Ponty claims that a body is *never* a mere object, as we will see in chapter 5. Interestingly, Judith Butler, notwithstanding her admiration for Beauvoir and her criticism of Merleau-Ponty, engages with him rather than with Beauvoir in her appeal to phenomenology to think the performativity of gender. See 'Performative Acts and Gender Constitution: An Essay on Phenomenology and Feminist Theory', in Katie Conboy, Nadia Medina and Sarah Stanbury, eds, *Writing on the Body: Female Embodiment and Feminist Theory*, New York: Columbia University Press, 1997, pp. 401–18. Phenomenology has gained traction among feminist theorists. See Kathleen Lennon, 'Feminist Perspectives on the Body', *Stanford Encyclopedia of Philosophy* (fall 2014 edn), ed. Edward N. Zalta, https://plato.stanford.edu/archives/fall2014/entries/feminist-body/.

96 On embodiment, and more generally on the phenomenology of the 'feminine experience', I am in agreement with Camille Froideveaux-Metterie, whose theoretical voice is emerging in French polyphonic feminism. I discovered her work only after the publication of the French edition of the present book (*La Jalousie: une passion inavouable*, Paris: Odile Jacob, 2015). See *La Révolution du féminin*, Paris: Gallimard, 2015, and 'Le sujet féminin entre incarnation et relation', in Camille Froideveaux-Metterie and Marc Chevrier, eds, *Des femmes et des hommes singuliers: perspectives croisées sur le devenir sexué des individus en démocratie*, Paris: Armand Colin, 2014, especially pp. 64–77, where Froideveaux-Metterie argues:

> The feminine obsession with the marks left by age on their faces is not a simple narcissistic anxiety for the disappearance of a beautiful self-image. It is also a sign of a particular sensitivity to the inexorable progress of an existence placed under the sign of deprivation and decrepitude. The care that women take of their appearance should not be understood as a simple reaction to the social and masculine injunctions to beauty and youth; it is a quasi-metaphysical concern by which the link of consubstantiality between the female subject and her body is expressed.

97 Beauvoir, *The Second Sex* p. 193:

> Once the subject attempts to assert himself, the Other, who limits and denies him, is nonetheless necessary for him: he attains himself only through the reality that he is not. That is why man's life is never plenitude and rest, it is lack and movement, it is combat. Facing himself, man encounters Nature; he has a hold on it, he tries to appropriate it for himself. But it cannot satisfy him. Either it realizes itself as a purely abstract opposition – it is an obstacle and

NOTES TO PP. 140–141

remains foreign – or it passively submits to man's desire and allows itself to be assimilated by him; he possesses it only in consuming it, that is, in destroying it. In both cases, he remains alone; he is alone when touching a stone, alone when digesting a piece of fruit. The other is present only if the other is himself present to himself: that is, true alterity is a consciousness separated from my own and identical to it.

98 Ibid., p. 193.
99 Ibid., p. 194.
100 Ibid., p. 212:

> The role of dress is both to link the body more closely to and to wrest it away from nature, to give a necessarily set artifice to palpitating life. Woman was turned into plant, panther, diamond, or mother-of-pearl by mingling flowers, furs, precious stones, shells, and feathers on her body; she perfumed herself so as to smell of roses and lilies: but feathers, silk, pearls and perfumes also worked to hide the animal rawness from its flesh and odor. She painted her mouth and her cheeks to acquire a mask's immobile solidity; her gaze was imprisoned in the thickness of kohl and mascara, it was no longer anything but her eyes' shimmering ornamentation; braided, curled or sculpted, her hair lost its troublesome vegetal mystery. In the embellished woman, Nature was present but captive, shaped by a human will in accordance with man's desire. Woman was even more desirable when nature was shown off to full advantage and more rigorously subjugated: the sophisticated woman has always been the ideal erotic object.
>
> On modern, bourgeois obsession for fashion: ibid., p. 657: 'The coquettish woman is not only alienated in things, she wants to be a thing, and without an intermediary she feels insecure in the world.... A successful dress creates in her the character of her dreams; but in a soiled, ruined outfit, she feels demeaned.' 'When women dress for the sake of other women, the reason must be to arouse their jealousy' (p. 659).

101 For a polyphonic, yet mostly non-moralistic, ironic and timely reflection on fashion and feminism, see Jessica Wolfendale and Jeanette Kennett, *Fashion – Philosophy for Everyone: Thinking with Style*, Oxford: Wiley-Blackwell, 2011. See in particular the contribution by Marguerite La Caze, 'A Taste for Fashion', on Kant, with a brief discussion of Simone de Beauvoir:

> Simone de Beauvoir, in *The Second Sex*, criticizes fashion from a feminist point of view, but could the problems she finds in fashion be overcome? She warns against women using clothes as a substitute

for genuine projects such as writing, art or a political project: 'The purpose of the fashions to which she is enslaved is not to reveal her as an independent individual, but rather to offer her as prey to male desires; thus society is not seeking to further her projects but to thwart them.' The limiting of independence Beauvoir describes is not an inevitable characterization of fashion; it is fashion as lived through an oppressive world where women have no projects of their own. (p. 202)

I thoroughly agree.

102 On the critique of Engels, see Beauvoir, *The Second Sex*, pp. 88–93, especially p. 91:

True, the division of labour by sex and the oppression resulting from it bring to mind class division in some ways: but they should not be confused; there is no biological basis for division by class; in work the slave becomes conscious of himself against the master; the proletariat has always experienced its condition in revolt, thus returning to the essential, constituting a threat to its exploiters; and *the goal of the proletariat is to cease to exist as a class*. We have said in the introduction how different woman's situation is, specifically because of the community of life and interests that create her solidarity with man and due to the complicity he encounters in her: she harbours no desire for revolution, *she would not think of eliminating herself as a sex: she simply asks that certain consequences of sexual differentiation be abolished*. (Emphasis added)

103 Ibid., p. 118.
104 Ibid.
105 Ibid., p. 241.
106 Ibid., p. 119.
107 Ibid., pp. 242–3.
108 Ibid., p. 122.
109 Ibid., p. 242.
110 Ibid., pp. 243–4: 'Just as in primitive society the male sex is secular and woman's is laden with religious and magic qualities, today's modern societies consider man's failings harmless peccadilloes; they are often lightly dismissed...'
111 Karl Marx and Frederick Engels, *Manifesto of the Communist Party* [1848], ed. Samuel Moore, trans. Frederick Engels [1888], in *Marx/Engels Selected Works*, Moscow: Progress, 1969, Vol. I, pp. 15–16.
112 Simone de Beauvoir, *The Prime of Life*, trans. Peter Green, Harmondsworth: Penguin, 1965, p. 22: 'Sartre was not inclined to be monogamous by nature: he took pleasure in the company of women, finding them less comic than men....He explained to me in his favourite terminology. "What we have", he said, "is an essential love; but it is a good idea for us also to experience *contingent* love affairs."'

113 Jean-Paul Sartre, *Lettres au Castor et à quelques autres*, Paris: Gallimard, 1983, Vol. I *(1926–1939)*, p. 208.
114 Ibid., p. 185.
115 Ibid., p. 223.
116 Ibid., p. 272. Sartre is drafted into the army, and the good little Beaver is 'courageous and perfect, as always'.
117 Ibid., p. 189. Martine Bourdin opens up with Sartre: '*I am jealous of Simone de Beauvoir.*' Sartre replies that this 'derives from a right feeling'. And he goes on to praise his addressee.
118 Simone de Beauvoir, *A Transatlantic Love Affair: Letters to Nelson Algren*, New York: New Press, 1998, p. 207.
119 On this question, see a number of biographies of Simone de Beauvoir: Deirdre Bair, *Simone de Beauvoir: A Biography*, New York: Simon & Schuster, 1990; Hazel Rowley, *Tête-à-Tête: Simone de Beauvoir and Jean-Paul Sartre*, New York: HarperCollins, 2004; Ingrid Galster, *Beauvoir dans tous ses états*, Paris: Tallandier, 2007.
120 Simone de Beauvoir, *Letters to Sartre*, trans. Quintin Hoare, London: Vintage, 1992.
121 Bianca Lamblin, *A disgraceful affair*, trans. Julie Plovnick, Boston: Northeastern University Press, 1996.
122 Gisèle Halimi, Interview, 'Beauvoir et moi', *L'Express*, 15 January 2009, www.lexpress.fr/culture/livre/ne-vous-resignez-jamais_823266.html.
123 Sartre, *Lettres au Castor et à quelques autres*, Vol. I, p. 17, letter to Simone Jolivet.
124 Herbert Goldhamer and Edward A. Shils, 'Types of power and status', *American Journal of Sociology* 45 (1939): 171–82.

CHAPTER 4 THE DESPAIR OF NOT BEING LOVED

1 Nicolas Grimaldi, *Essai sur la jalousie: l'enfer proustien*, Paris: PUF, 2010, pp. 8–9. 'The drama of jealousy would then be, as it is in the theatre, an imaginary drama. At the same time that he is the victim, he (the jealous lover) is in reality a victim of nothing but his own imagination. Or, rather, it is he himself who, in playing it out, affects himself with a feigned suffering, a theatrical suffering' (pp. 90–1). Grimaldi summarizes his argument thus:

   1) As it is unrelated to reality, jealousy is purely phantasmic.
   2) Since it is invented, developed, maintained and lived as a fiction, it has the structure and status of a game.
   3) Because it is a game, one is even more inclined to pretend that one believes that, in fact, one does not believe in it...Jealousy is a scenography of the imaginary. (p. 91)

   'Jealousy is not some defensive reaction against the possibility of a risk, a danger or a loss. Jealousy has no relation at all to reality' (p. 10).

2 Ibid., p. 52; and see p. 17.
3 Ibid., p. 91.
4 Ibid., p. 10.
5 Ibid., p. 17.
6 Christophe Perrin, 'La Jalousie à l'honneur: J.-L. Marion après Proust', *Revue d'éthique et de théologie morale* (2014), no. 1, p. 278, §13 and n. 76.
7 Ibid., n. 76:

> This is an account of an unpublished fragment of the seminar by the professor of metaphysics, which we attended, recorded and transcribed, held in the Sorbonne during the academic year 2001–2002 with the title 'The phenomenology of others: the question of love'. Jean-Luc Marion says what he does, and does what he says, unlike Piero Bargellini and Gaëlle Obiégly who – in their respective eulogies on jealousy ('Elogio della gelosia', *Chiodi solari*, Brescia: Morcelliana, 1952, pp. 81ff., and *Petit éloge de la jalousie*, Paris: Gallimard, 2007) – had provided less of a defence than an illustration of jealousy.

8 Ibid., §14.
9 François de La Rochefoucauld, Maxim 324, in *The Maxims of François Duc de La Rochefoucauld*, etc., trans. F. G. Stevens, London: Humphrey Milford, 1940, p. 105. This self-esteem is not only undermined but also very ill-placed: 'Infidelity ought to extinguish love, and no man should be jealous when he has reason to be. It is only those who give no cause for jealousy who are worthy to arose it' (ibid., p. 115). In other words, we should be jealous of a person who, thanks to her loyalty, *deserves* such profound attention. Those who are truly unfaithful are simply not worthy of our jealousy. This paradox resonates with the words of Descartes, who condemns amorous jealousy on the grounds that it reveals not only the perceived unworthiness of the one who feels jealous, but also the inferior quality of the object of love itself. 'And a man who is jealous of his wife is scorned…It is not even she that he loves, properly speaking; it is only the good he imagines to consist in having sole possession of her, and he would not be apprehensive about losing this good if he did not judge that he was unworthy of it or that his wife was unfaithful' ('Article 169: Wherein it is blameworthy', in *The Passions of the Soul*, trans. Stephen Voss, Indianapolis: Hackett, 1989, p. 112).
10 Max Rouquette, *Médée*, scene 5, 17–19: 'The other, that stupid virgin, who believes that she is entitled to the hero and that, sweet and trembling, Medea will simply go away.' Rouquette's Medea focuses on the sex of her rival, a reissue of the Golden Fleece and a cyclical conclusion of the history of the Argonauts: 'A girl, like the young Medea, comes to meet the man and catches him in the net of her golden fleece. So my time is coming to an end' (5: 8–10).

11 As happened with Valerie Trierweiler's account of her relationship with the French president, François Hollande, in 2014. After he abandoned her for Julie Gayet, Trierweiler wrote a searingly honest account of the affair: 'I was delighted to see I was not the only jealous partner. I will readily admit it: I am jealous. I have been jealous with every man I have loved. I do not know how not to be when I am in love' (*Thank You for This Moment: A Story of Love, Power and Betrayal*, trans. Clemence Sebag, London: Biteback, 2015, pp. 281–2).
12 Sigmund Freud, 'Some Neurotic Mechanisms in Jealousy, Paranoia and Homosexuality' (1922), in *The Standard Edition of the Complete Psychological Works of Sigmund Freud*, vol. 18, London: Hogarth Press, 1955, pp. 223–32, at p. 223.
13 Ibid.
14 Ibid. As we shall see in a moment, Freud adds here that there are two other levels of jealousy, caused by the projection of unconscious desires of infidelity and repressed homosexuality.
15 Ibid., p. 224.
16 Ibid., pp. 223–5.
17 On the subject of gallantry, see Claude Habib, *Galanterie française*, Paris: Gallimard, 2006.
18 Melanie Klein and Joan Riviere, *Love, Hate and Reparation*, London: Hogarth Press, 1937.
19 Joan Riviere, 'Jealousy as a Mechanism of Defence' (1932), in *The Inner World and Joan Riviere: Collected Papers, 1920–1958*, ed. A. Hughes, London: Karnac Books, 1991, pp. 104–15, at p. 114.
20 Betty Denzler, 'Miroir trompeur: la jalousie et le narcissisme', *Revue française de psychanalyse* 61 (1997): 39–44. See, in the same issue, Danielle Labrousse-Hilaire's 'La Jalousie en son absence: à propos d'un choix d'objet chez la femme' (pp. 83–100), which begins with apt observations about how jealousy has been discredited in the philosophical tradition as well as in feminist culture, before going on to present clinical cases of repressed jealousy in women alienated from their mothers, afflicted by a fragile narcissism caught between primary and secondary homosexuality, and systematically attracted by Don Juans. Once again, everything is explained by the choice of the love-object, considered as an unconscious preference for a situation that will inevitably lead to jealousy. There is no attention given to the hope that this might happen otherwise, to the lies of the other, or to the attraction of 'fugitives' (see pp. 186–7 above), often far more interesting than others.
21 Willy Pasini, *La Jalousie*, Paris: Odile Jacob, 2001. This book provides an overview of the clinical account of jealousy and the research on the subject in modern neurobiology.
22 Hildegard Baumgart, *Jealousy: Experiences and Solutions*, Chicago: University of Chicago Press, 1990, p. 44.
23 Ibid., pp. 4–9.
24 On the various strains of psychoanalysis and, above all, on the theories of the self that run counter to the tragic vision of subjectivity at its heart,

see Elizabeth Roudinesco, *Why Psychoanalysis?*, New York: Columbia University Press, 2003.

25 Jean-Paul Hiltenbrand, 'Présentation', *La Revue lacanienne* (2012), no. 2: 7–15. In his introduction to a series of very interesting articles, Hiltenbrand discusses the 'current clinical upsurge' of amorous jealousy. He also draws attention to the difficulty of positioning jealousy between 'a normal and a universal affect', on the one hand, and an explosive passion, on the other. He therefore does justice (in the language of possession, however, which Freud does not use and which, as we have seen, can be very misleading) to normal jealousy: 'Jealousy belongs more specifically to the experience of love and desire, for in some way to love is also to desire the exclusive possession of the object' (§2). But Hiltenbrand also identifies, in neurosis, an element of psychosis. Whatever 'the recent troubled actuality' (§5) may be, he claims, jealousy is constituted in the past. The jealous person allegedly commits a capital mistake, which is to replace the symbolic Other with an imaginary other. The symbolic is the Other as language and as the source of meaning (the 'Name of the Father'). 'The jealous person makes this Third Other *(ex)ist*; it is there that his intelligence is to be found, but he does so only by removing the ambiguity and casting suspicion on an imaginary third party' (§6). Whereas the healthy 'speaking being' *(parlêtre)* has properly established the Symbolic – with all its usual functions: loss, lack, hole *(perte, manque, trou)* – the jealous person identifies the Third Other with an actual, threatening third party. The judgement of a jealous person is, therefore, clouded (§5). Once again, the *event* that causes jealousy is being defused. See, however, Charles Melman's 'Baisse un peu la jalousie' (ibid., p. 17), which makes a different claim, namely that jealousy will always mean the foreclosure of the phallus (i.e., the inability to represent the symbolic) in the narcissistic face-to-face of a couple.

26 'When you are here with me in this room / There are no walls, but only trees...' From *Il cielo in una stanza*, a song by Gino Paoli, recorded by Mina in 1960. It is a text as moving as the erotic situation was apparently ephemeral. See *Il Corriere della Sera*, http://cinquantamila.corriere.it/storyTellerThread.php?threadId=PAOLI+Gino.

27 Marcianne Blévis, *Jealousy: True Stories of Love's Favorite Decoy*, New York: Other Press, 2009.

28 Anne Deburge-Donnars, 'Enfin jalouse?', *Revue française de psychanalyse* 81 (1997): 67–82, at p. 77.

29 Jerome Neu, 'Jealous Thoughts' and 'Jealous Afterthoughts', in *A Tear Is an Intellectual Thing*, Oxford: Oxford University Press, 2000, pp. 41–67 and pp. 68–80, at p. 73. The *Revue française de psychanalyse* dedicated vol. 75/3 (2011) to the subject *Jalousie, projection, paranoïa*. See, in particular, the article by Bernard Chervet, 'La jealousie', pp. 713–30, which develops the notion of desire for desire. Paul-Laurent Assoun too places jealousy where it should be, namely in the very experience of love and in the intelligence of what he calls the 'constitutive alienation of the subject to the desire of the other'. See *Leçons psychanalytiques sur la jalousie*,

Paris: Anthropos, 2000, and 'La jalousie ou le symptôme amoureux', *Pause santé* 15 (2011):

> This movement of jealousy across the scene of the unconscious recalls Freud's remark to Ludwig Binswanger in 1920 that 'jealousy...seems to be able to give us the deepest understanding of psychic life, both normal and pathological' – precisely because it reveals the constitutive alienation of the desire of the subject to the other's desire. This is what the subject seeks to unravel in the course of psychoanalysis. It is still necessary, however, to distinguish the current neurotic forms from their psychotic crystallizations. Jealousy, if it is omnipresent, reveals each time the unconscious position of the subject between desire, love and enjoyment [*jouissance*].

For a critical study of the meaning of 'narcissism', see Elisabeth Lunbeck, *The Americanization of Narcissism*, Cambridge, MA: Harvard University Press, 2014.

30 Jacques Lacan, *Family Complexes in the Formation of the Individual*, trans. Cormac Gallagher, www.lacaninireland.com/web/wp-content/uploads/2010/06/FAMILY-COMPLEXES-IN-THE-FORMATION-OF-THE-INDIVIDUAL2.pdf, pp. 27, 26.

31 This is the type of jealousy mentioned by Annie Ernaux in 'L'occupation' (2002), in *Écrire la vie*, Paris: Gallimard, 2011, pp. 877–909. A film was made of this book, with the title *L'Autre* ('The Other'), by Patrick Mario Bernard and Pierre Trividic. The fixation on the other woman, however, is not as monomaniacal as the beginning of the novel suggests. 'I wanted to get him back,' says the narrator.

> I remembered above all the early days of our story together, the use I made of the 'magnificence' of his sex, as I have written in my diary. It was not the other woman, in the end, that I saw in my place; it was above all me, such as I would never be again, loving and *sure of his own love for me*, and on the brink of what had not yet taken place between us. (p. 885)

Of course, in reading this poignant book, one might focus on the title, which alludes to the haunting, mysterious and omnipresent thought of the other woman. But the passage I have quoted provides the key to the true nature of the 'triangular' fantasy. What truly matters, what really hurts, is that the desire of the beloved is no longer there. 'No doubt the greatest suffering, as well as the greatest happiness, *comes from the Other*' (p. 898, emphasis added) – the other whose love we love.

32 Jacques Lacan, *Family Complexes in the Formation of the Individual*, p. 26.

> By demonstrating the structure of infantile jealousy, experimental observation of the child and psychoanalytic investigation have

NOTES TO PP. 171–177

brought to light its role in the origins of sociability and consequently of knowledge itself as human knowledge. The critical point revealed by these investigations is that jealousy at its most fundamental does not represent biological rivalry but rather a mental identification. See note 30 above.

33 Jacques Lacan, *Transference: The Seminar of Jacques Lacan, Book VIII*, ed. Jacques-Alain Miller, trans. Bruce Fink, Cambridge: Polity, 2015, pp. 51–2.
34 Ibid., p. 56.
35 Ibid., p. 52.
36 On the history of the place of jealousy in the psychoanalytic tradition, see Phil Mollon, *Shame and Jealousy: The Hidden Turmoils*, London: Karnac Books, 2002.
37 Lacan, *Transference*, p. 144, and see Marie-Magdeleine Chatel, 'Pour introduire à la frérocité', *Littoral 30: La Frérocité* (1990): 7–10, at p. 9.
38 Sappho, 31.
39 I share the conviction of René Girard, Martha Nussbaum and Stanley Cavell that the best reflections on love are to be found in narrative, whether dramatic or lyric. See René Girard, *Deceit, Desire and the Novel: Self and Other in Literary Structure*, Baltimore: Johns Hopkins University Press, 1965; Martha Nussbaum, *The Fragility of Goodness: Luck and Ethics in Greek Tragedy and Philosophy*, Cambridge: Cambridge University Press, 1986; and Stanley Cavell, *Disowning Knowledge in Seven Plays of Shakespeare*, Cambridge: Cambridge University Press, 2003. I am not, however, necessarily in agreement with all their readings and interpretations of their chosen texts.
40 William Shakespeare, *Othello*, Act I, scene i.
41 Ibid., Act I, scene ii; Act I, scene iii; Act IV, scene i.
42 Ibid., Act I, scene i.
43 The Greek word is *phthonos*, the Latin, *invidia*. Plato, *Laws*, 731a-e; Aristotle, *Rhetoric*, 2, 10.
44 *Othello*, Act I, scene iii.
45 Ibid., Act II, scene i.
46 Ibid., Act III, scene iii.
47 Ibid.
48 Ibid., Act IV, scene i.
49 Ibid., Act II, scene iii.
50 Ibid., Act IV, scene ii. The speaker here is Iago's wife Emilia:

> I will be hang'd, if some eternal villain,
> Some busy and insinuating rogue,
> Some cogging, cozening slave, to get some office,
> Have not devised this slander;
> I'll be hang'd else.

NOTES TO PP. 177–179

51 Othello, Act III, scene, i – Iago: 'If imputation and strong circumstances – / Which lead directly to the door of truth – / Will give you satisfaction, you may have't.'
52 Plutarch, *How to tell a Flatterer from a Friend*. Erasmus translated this little moral treatise into Latin and circulated it among his humanist friends. See Plutarch, *Moralia*, Vol. 1, trans. Frank Cole Babbitt, Cambridge, MA: Harvard University Press, 1927. See Yvonne Charlier, *Érasme et l'amitié, d'après sa correspondance*, Paris: Les Belles Lettres, 1977, pp. 57–60. An English translation by Philemon Holland was published in London in 1603.
53 On Shakespeare's knowledge of this tradition, see Robert Evans, 'Flattery in Shakespeare's *Othello*: the relevance of Plutarch and Sir Thomas Elyot', *Comparative Drama* 35 (2001): 1–41; Blair Worden, 'Shakespeare's Politics', in Catherine Alexander, ed., *Shakespeare and Politics*, Cambridge: Cambridge University Press, pp. 22–45, especially p. 35: 'Of all the sins of the court, none is more pervasive in Shakespeare's plays than flattery'; David Colclough, 'Talking to the Animals: Persuasion, Counsel and their Discontent in Julius Caesar', in David Armitage, Conal Condren and Andrew Fitzmaurice, eds, *Shakespeare and Early Modern Political Thought*, Cambridge: Cambridge University Press, 2009, pp. 230–45.
54 *Othello*, Act I, scene i. Iago flatters Cassio by praising his honesty and stressing the love he has for him. 'When devils will the blackest sins put on, / They do suggest at first with heavenly shows, / As I do now' (Act II, scene iii).
55 See, for instance, the exchanges between Othello and Iago in Act III, scene iii. See also Judith Weil, *Service and Dependency in Shakespeare's Plays*, Cambridge: Cambridge University Press, 2005, pp. 50–79, who provides an analysis of power and servitude in Shakespeare. This is very useful, since it reveals a number of sociological nuances in the texts. It does not, however, touch directly on the question of flattery and envy. Jealousy becomes a 'jealousy of service'. Traumatized by servitude and blinded by possessiveness, Othello allegedly reveals himself to be incapable of reciprocal love. Weil also demonstrates very well what Shakespeare was able to do in *Antony and Cleopatra* with Plutarch's *How to tell a Flatterer from a Friend* (pp. 91–104).
56 *Othello*, Act V, scene i: 'O brave Iago, honest and just, / That hast such noble sense of thy friend's wrong! / Thou teachest me.'
57 Ibid., Act III, scene iii.
58 Ibid., Act III, scene iv. The speaker is Emilia.
59 Ibid., Act I, scene iii.
60 Ibid.
61 Ibid., Act III, scene iii.
62 The allegorical representation of Envy, as it first appears in Ovid's *Metamorphoses* (2, 775–82), is a woman with an oblique stare, a green chest filled with bile (*pectora felle virent*), and a deathly pallor. Her tongue is impregnated with poison (*lingua est suffusa veneno*); she feeds on vipers

and never laughs, except at the suffering of others. She suffers, in turn, however, from the success of others, which makes her claw at herself (*carpitque and carpitur*).

63 *Othello*, Act III, scene iii.
64 Ibid., Act III, scene iv.
65 Ibid., Act I, scene iii.
66 Cf. Baumgart, *Jealousy*. See also the classic study by André Green, *The Tragic Effect: The Oedipus Complex in Tragedy*, Cambridge: Cambridge University Press, 2011. Here the emphasis is on homosexuality. See also, along the same lines, Louis Lo, *Male Jealousy: Literature and Film*, New York and London: Continuum, 2008, pp. 84–107, at 17 (love is a *folie à deux*); Melman, 'Baisse un peu la jalousie', p. 17; and Cléopâtre Athanassiou-Popesco, 'L'intolérance à la jalousie dans l'*Othello* de Shakespeare', *Revue française de psychanalyse* 61 (1997): 140–52:

> He [Iago] takes possession of Othello's passion in order to degrade it into a destructive fire and transform the 'natural' jealousy that accompanies any revivification of Oedipal emotions into a poison, which dissolves the ego into its primal elements and makes it incapable of re-creating its relationships. In this way, jealousy then becomes a delirium of jealousy. (p. 142)

67 Stanley Cavell, 'Epistemology and tragedy: a reading of Othello (together with a cover letter)', *Daedalus* 108 (1979): 43.
68 Shakespeare, *Othello*, trans. Yves Bonnefoy, Paris: Gallimard, 2001, p. 36. For other examples of interpretations which blame Othello, see the critical overview by Harry Berger Jr., 'Acts of silence, acts of speech: how to do things with Othello and Desdemona', *Renaissance Drama* 33 (2004): 3–36.
69 *Othello*, Act V, scene ii.
70 Ibid.
71 William Shakespeare, *Julius Caesar*, Act I, scene ii. Cf. *Macbeth*, Act I, scene iii. On the representation of the social and psychological interdependence of Shakespeare's characters, see Stephen Greenblatt, 'Shakespeare and the Ethics of Authority', in David Armitage, Conal Condren and Andrew Fitzmaurice, eds, *Shakespeare and Early Modern Political Thought*, Cambridge: Cambridge University Press, 2009, pp. 64–79.
72 *Othello*, Act I, scene iii; and see Act I, scene ii; Act I, scene iii; Act IV, scene i.
73 Ibid., Act V, scene ii; Act I, scene iii.
74 The first reaction of Desdemona's father, Brabantio, to the news of her marriage to Othello is, however, similarly contemptuous of 'the Moor' and his 'sooty bosom', and claims that he could only have seduced Desdemona 'with foul charms; / Abused her delicate youth with drugs or minerals / That weaken motion' (Act I, scene ii).
75 On the flatterer as poisoner, see David Colclough, 'Talking to the Animals: Persuasion, Counsel and their Discontents in *Julius Caesar*', in David

NOTES TO PP. 182–186

Armitage, Conal Condren and Andrew Fitzmaurice, eds, *Shakespeare and Early Modern Political Thought*, Cambridge: Cambridge University Press, 2009, pp. 217–33.
76 René Girard, *Shakespeare: les feux de l'envie*, Paris: Grasset, 1990.
77 The attribution of social insecurity to Othello, on the basis that he is not Venetian, is all the more inappropriate given that, on this point, Shakespeare modified significantly his original source, Giovanni Battista Giraldi Cinzio's novella *Gli Hecatommithi* (3.7.), which duly emphasizes Othello's cultural and moral strangeness. When she sees her husband become sullen and suspicious, Disdemona (*sic*) reproaches him for his irascible character and his warm blood: 'You Moors are so warm by nature that the smallest thing provokes you to anger and vengeance.' Faced with his growing jealousy, she begins to regret her choice of an exotic husband: 'Let Italian women learn from me not to get together with a man whom nature, Heaven, and way of life separates from us!' Shakespeare's Desdemona never talks like this. Shakespeare emphasizes, deliberately and systematically, the love that Othello inspires and the esteem in which he is held. On the issue of race and colour, see Phyllis Natalie Braxton, 'Othello: the Moor and the metaphor', *South Atlantic Review* 55 (1990): 1–17.
78 *Othello*, Act III, scene iv; Act IV, scene i.
79 'O curse of marriage, / That we can call these delicate creatures ours, / And not their appetites!' Ibid., Act III, scene iii.
80 Marcel Proust, *Remembrance of Things Past*, vol. III: *The Captive*, trans. C. K. Scott Moncrieff and Terence Kilmartin, New York: Vintage Books, 1982, pp. 86–7. 'Even if you hold them in your hand such persons are fugitives. To understand the emotions which they arouse, and which others, even better-looking, do not, we must realize that they are not immobile but in motion, and add to their person a sign corresponding to that which in physics denotes speed.'
81 Ibid., p. 88.
82 René Descartes, *Les Passions de l'âme*, Paris: Gallimard, 1988, p. 256.
83 La Rochefoucauld, Maxim 28, in *The Maxims of François Duc de La Rochefoucauld*, p. 13: 'Jealousy is, in a certain sense, a right and reasonable feeling, since it conduces to the preservation of something we possess, or think we possess: envy, on the other hand, is a kind of fury, which cannot tolerate the good fortune of others.' Jealousy is inevitable and obstinate: 'Jealousy and love are born twins; but the former often outlives the latter' (Maxim 361, ibid., p. 115). Another maxim, however, states that 'Jealousy feeds on doubt; and either develops into rage, or disappears, as soon as doubt gives place to certainty' (Maxim 32, ibid., p. 13). This brings La Rochefoucauld closer to Descartes.
84 Proust, *The Captive*, p. 88.
85 Ibid., p. 81.
86 Ibid., p. 86.
87 Ibid., p. 81.
88 Ibid., p. 85.

NOTES TO PP. 186–188

89 Ibid., p. 81.
90 Ibid., p. 342.
91 Ibid., p. 422.
92 Ibid., p. 88.
93 Proust, *Remembrance of Things Past*, Vol. III: *The Fugitive*, trans. C. K. Scott Moncrieff and Terence Kilmartin, New York: Vintage Books, 1982, p. 524:

> Besides, is not a single small fact, if well chosen, sufficient to enable the experimenter to deduce a general law which will reveal the truth about thousands of analogous facts? Although Albertine might exist in my memory, as she had successively appeared to me in the course of her life, only as a series of fractions of time, my mind re-establishing unity in her, made her a single person, and it was on this person that I wished to arrive at a general judgment, to know whether she had lied to me, whether she loved women, whether it was in order to associate with them freely that she left me.

94 Proust, *The Captive*, p. 83.
95 Ibid.
96 Ibid., pp. 83–5.
97 Ibid., p. 85.
98 Proust, *The Fugitive*, p. 535:

> The young laundry girl confessed to me that she enjoyed playing around with her girl friends and, seeing that Mlle Albertine was always rubbing up against her in her bathing wrap, she made her take it off and used to caress her with her tongue along the throat and arms, even on the soles of her feet which Mlle Albertine held out to her. The laundress undressed too and they played at pushing each other into the water. After that she told me nothing more, but being always at your service and ready to do anything to oblige you, I took the young laundry-girl to bed with me. She asked me if I would like her to do to me what she used to do to Mlle Albertine when she took off her bathing dress. And she said to me: (If you could have seen how she used to wriggle, that young lady, she said to me (oh, it's too heavenly) and she got so excited that she could not keep from biting me.) I could still see the marks on the laundry-girl's arms. And I can understand Mlle Albertine's pleasure, for that young wench is really a very good performer.

99 Ibid., pp. 525–6:

> According to her the thing that Monsieur supposed is absolutely certain. For one thing, it was she who looked after Mlle Albertine whenever she came to the baths. (Mlle A) came very often to take her shower with a tall woman older than herself, always dressed in

NOTES TO PP. 188–189

> grey, whom the shower attendant without knowing her name recognized from having seen her often going after girls.... But (Mlle A) came most often with girls younger than herself, especially one with very red hair.

100 Ibid., pp. 612–14:

> Ah! We spent many happy hours together; she was so caressing, so passionate. But it wasn't only with me that she liked to enjoy herself. She had met a handsome young man at Mme Verdurin's called Morel. They came to an understanding at once. He undertook – having her permission to enjoy them himself, for he liked little novices, and as soon as had set them on the path of evil would abandon them – he undertook to entice young fisher-girls in remote villages, or young laundry-girls, who would fall for a boy but might not have responded to a girl's advances...I must confess that in the early days of her stay with you she hadn't entirely given up her games with me...You were bringing a big bunch of it [lilac] home with you which enabled me to turn my head away and hide my confusion.

The story of the lilacs is told in detail in *The Captive*, pp. 48–9.

101 Ibid., p. 396.
102 *The Fugitive*, p. 615:

> What, so that truth which I have sought for so long, which I've so dreaded, is nothing more than these few words uttered in the course of conversation, words to which one cannot even give one's whole attention, because one isn't alone!...The habit of thinking prevents us at times from experiencing reality, immunizes us against it, makes it seem no more than another thought. There is no idea that does not carry in itself its possible refutation, no word that does not imply its opposite. In any case, if it was true, it was by this time the sort of useless truth about the life of a dead mistress that rises up from the depths and reveals itself when we can no longer have any use for it.

103 Proust, *The Captive*, p. 517:

> And yet how often we had expressed them, those painful, those ineluctable truths which dominated us and to which we were blind, the truth of our feelings, the truth of our destiny, how often we had expressed them without knowing it, without meaning it, in words which doubtless we ourselves thought mendacious but the prophetic force of which had been established by subsequent events...Lies and errors falling short of the profound reality which neither of us perceived, truth extending beyond it, the truth of our natures, the

NOTES TO PP. 189–190

essential laws of which escape us and require time before they reveal themselves, the truth of our destinies also.

104 Éloisa Castellano-Maury, '*Sua cuique persona*: la jalousie dans l'œuvre de Proust', *Revue française de psychanalyse* 61 (1997), pp. 153–61, at pp. 156 and 158.
105 Julia Kristeva, 'Le Temps, la femme, la jalousie selon Albertine', Lecture presented during a study day organized by Francis Marmande and Sylvie Patron, 27 January 2007, for students and teachers of the modern *khâgne* (the two-year preparation for entry into the '*grandes écoles*'):

> Whenever I have encountered it, either personally or in my patients, jealousy appeared to me as a 'hijacking' [*détournement*] of hatred. The lover idealizes his/her loved one, but it is his/her own self, grounded on the problematic boundaries of narcissism, that he/she carries to its heights in the challenging experience of passion.... As an incursion of hatred into desire, jealousy conveys aggression in an inverted form, as a love which reaches out towards an imaginary other who turns that aggression away from oneself. Rather than hating his/her *self*, the lover becomes jealous of a beloved other. This pseudo-object never appears to be specific or different – it is only inferior to the lover's idealizing desire, and it is necessarily treacherous. Should this be the case, the intermittent lucidity of the lover could only lead him/her to the ruin of the self-construction which is his/her love. But the jealous person is neither depressed nor sick. He/she has no time to fall back on him-/herself or on a time of his/her own. In the fire of his/her jealous obsession, he/she painfully deciphers his/her executioner's time and takes a painful pleasure [*jouit douleureusement*] in the signs of his/her vacuousness or treachery. Thus his/her agressivity towards the loved/beloved symbiosis, from which he/she is unable to detach him-/herself, is metamorphosed into an excess of interpretation. The jealous person, therefore, gives him-/herself over *to dissecting the sense* of hatred and/or of the wound, rather than admitting to the *independence of the beloved* or to the incommunicability of lovers. (www.kristeva.fr/albertine.html)

106 Proust, *The Captive*, p. 89.
107 Ibid., pp. 22–3. The narrator opens his window to gaze on some laundress, baker, dairymaid or other passer-by – all of them women more desirable than Albertine, because they are unknown – so long, that is, as Albertine, by her own desire or by the desire she excites in others, becomes more desirable once again. See also p. 762:

> And yet perhaps, had I myself been entirely faithful, I should have suffered because of infidelities which I would have been incapable of conceiving, whereas what it tortured me to imagine in Albertine was my own perpetual desire to find favour with fresh ladies, to plan

fresh romances, was to suppose her guilty of the glance which I had been unable to resist casting, the other day, even when I was by her side, at the young bicyclists seated at tables in the Bois de Boulogne. As we have no personal knowledge, one might almost say that we can feel no jealousy save of ourselves. Observation counts for little. It is only from the pleasure that we ourselves have felt that we can derive knowledge and grief. Cf., pp. 79–80.

108   Ibid., p. 87.
109   Ibid., p. 91.
110   Catherine Millet, *Jealousy*, trans. Helen Stevenson, New York: Grove Press, 2009. The original French title was *Jour de souffrance* (Day of suffering).
111   Catherine Millet, *The Sexual Life of Catherine M.*, trans. Adriana Hunter, New York: Grove Press, 2003.
112   Millet, *Jealousy*, p. 85.
113   Ibid., p. 133.
114   Ibid., p. 108.
115   Ibid., p. 109.
116   Ibid., pp. 84–5.

CHAPTER 5 ART OF LOVE, ART OF JEALOUSY

1   Denis Diderot, *Supplément au voyage de Bougainville* [1772], in *Diderot: Political Writings*, ed. and trans. John Hope Mason, Cambridge: Cambridge University Press, 1992, p. 68.
2   Ann Cahill, *Overcoming Objectification: A Carnal Ethics*, Abingdon: Routledge, 2010. For an example of the language of objectification (petrification, risk of losing mental health, etc.), see Tanjare McKay, 'Female self-objectification: causes, consequences and prevention', *McNair Scholars Research Journal* 6/1 (2013), http://commons.emich.edu/mcnair/vol6/iss1/7. See also Claudia Moscovici, *From Sex Objects to Sexual Subjects*, Abingdon: Routledge, 1996.
3   Maurice Merleau Ponty, *Phenomomenology of Perception*, trans. Colin Smith, London: Routledge, 2002, p. 191.
4   Jean-Paul Sartre, *Being and Nothingness: An Essay on Phenomenological Ontology*, trans. Hazel E. Barnes, London: Routledge, 2005, p. 375.
5   Ibid., p. 367.
6   Ibid., p. 364.
7   Ibid., pp. 366–7: 'The notion of "ownership", by which love is so often explained, is not actually primary. Why should I want to appropriate the Other if it were not precisely that the Other makes me be?'
8   Ibid., p. 367.
9   Ibid., p. 368.
10 Ibid., p. 371.
11 Ibid., p. 372.

12 Ibid., p. 395:

> But if the desire flows back from the situation upon the being who is in situation and to corrode the Other's relations to the world. The movement of desire which goes from the surrounding "environment" to the desired person is an isolating movement which destroys the environment and cuts off the person in question in order to effect the emergence of his pure facticity... As soon as I throw myself toward the Other's facticity, as soon as I wish to push aside his acts and his functions so as to touch him in his flesh, I incarnate myself, for I can neither wish nor even conceive of the incarnation of the Other except in and by means of my own incarnation.... for I desire only with my trouble, and I disrobe the Other by disrobing myself; I foreshadow and outline the Other's flesh only by outlining my own flesh.

13 Ibid., p. 396.
14 Ibid., p. 376: 'At the start, each of the consciousnesses can at any moment free itself from its chains and suddenly contemplate the other as an object. Then the spell is broken; the Other becomes one mean among means.'
15 Ibid., p. 378.
16 Ibid., p. 399.
17 Ibid., p. 378.
18 Ibid.
19 On Sartre and Lacan, see Clotilde Leguil, *Sartre avec Lacan: corrélation antinomique, liaison dangereuse*, Paris: Navarin, 2012.
20 Sartre, *Being and Nothingness*, p. 392.
21 Ibid., p. 396.
22 Simone de Beauvoir, *The Second Sex*, trans. Constance Borde and Sheila Malovany-Chevallier, New York: Vintage Books/Random House, 2009, p. 475: 'What is necessary for such harmony are not technical refinements but rather, on the basis of an immediate erotic attraction, a reciprocal generosity of body and soul.'
23 Sartre, *Being and Nothingness*, p. 370. Merleau-Ponty criticizes this conception of love. See E. de Saint-Aubert, *Du lien des êtres aux éléments de l'être: Merleau-Ponty au tournant des années 1945–1951*, Paris: Vrin, 2004, p. 181: 'Love is jealousy, and, like any form of jealousy, it wants the impossible.' This is how Merleau-Ponty understood Sartre, especially on Proust.
24 Sartre, *Being and Nothingness*, p. 375. I am talking here about Sartre's thought, not his amorous life, of his erotic style as it emerges from the writings of Beauvoir or Sartre's mistresses, namely Bianca Lamblin, who, in her own autobiography, *Mémoires d'une jeune fille dérangée* (which we discussed in chapter 3), called him a 'cad' (*mufle*). For the biographies that reconstruct the liaisons of Sartre and Beauvoir, see Hazel Rowley, *Tête-à-tête: The Tumultuous Lives and Loves of Jean-Paul Sartre and Simone de Beauvoir*, New York: HarperCollins, 2009; C. Seymour-Jones, *A*

Dangerous Liaison: A Revelatory New Biography of Simone de Beauvoir and Jean-Paul Sartre, New York: Overlook Press, 2009.
25 Jean-Paul Sartre, *The Family Idiot: Gustave Flaubert 1821–1857*, trans. Carol Cosman, Chicago: University of Chicago Press, 1987, p. 168.
26 Catullus, *Poems*, 8.
27 Ibid., 58.
28 Ibid., 85.
29 Propertius, *Elegies*, 4, 3, 1–6; 26.
30 Ovid, *Loves*, 1, 15, 23.
31 I have discussed this contrast elsewhere. See Giulia Sissa, *Sex and Sensuality in the Ancient World*, New Haven, CT: Yale University Press, 2008; 'Amor mora metamorphosis Roma', in Mattia De Poli, ed., *Maschile e femminile: genere ed eros nel mondo greco*, Padua: SARGON, 2010, pp. 7–38. The argument in this chapter draws on this article (written and published in English), but I have not repeated the detailed textual demonstrations or the complete bibliographical references.
32 W. S. Anderson, 'Multiple change in the *Metamorphoses*', *Transactions and Proceedings of the American Philological Association* 94 (1963): 1–27, at p. 8.
33 Ovid, *The Art of Love*, 3, 598: '*En ego confiteor: non nisi laesus amo.*'
34 I therefore find myself in agreement with Carlos Lévy's claim that *The Art of Love* is a 'non-philosophical response to philosophy'. This response follows the same absolute coherence as the systems it rejects. Love is an 'irremediably dual reality'. Ovid articulates pleasure and pain in a theory in verse. This is innovative. See Carlos Lévy, 'Aimer et souffrir: quelques réflexions sur la "Philosophie dans le boudoir" de l'*Ars amatoria*', in Laurence Boulègue et Carlos Lévy, eds, *Hédonismes: penser et dire le plaisir dans l'Antiquité et à la Renaissance*, Lille: Presses Universitaires du Septentrion, 2007, pp. 161–72, at pp. 162 and 169.
35 Lucretius, *On the Nature of Things*, IV, 1058 (*Haec Venus est nobis!*).
36 Ibid., 1063–74. See also 1146.
37 Ovid, *The Art of Love*, 1, 42.
38 Ibid., 1, 43: '*Haec tibi non tenues veniet delapsa per auras.*' Each of the words in this line – *tenues, tibi veniet, delapsa, per auras* – belongs in Lucretius' language when he speaks of *simulacra*. I have developed this intertextual argument in 'Amor mora metamorphosis Roma'. On air in Latin poetry, see Armelle Deschard, *Recherches sur aura: variations sur le thème de l'air en mouvement chez les Latins*, Louvain: Peeters, 2002, pp. 134–5, on the expression '*delapsa per auras*'. Deschard does not mention the allusion to Lucretius.
39 Lucretius, *On the Nature of Things*, IV, 1094–6.
40 Ovid, *The Art of Love*, 1, 35: *quod amare velis reperire labora.*
41 Ibid., 3, 447–73: *mora semper amantes incitat*; 3, 752 (*maxima lena mora est*). Sensuality demands that lovemaking should not be hasty (2, 717–18).
42 And for a sublime reader, as Gian Biagio Conte argues in *Genres and Readers: Lucretius, Love Elegy, Pliny's Encyclopedia*. Baltimore: Johns Hopkins University Press, 1994.

NOTES TO PP. 208–210

43 Lucretius, *On the Nature of Things*, IV, 1263–77. On the body in Lucretius' thought, see Mayotte Bollack, *La Raison de Lucrèce: constitution d'une poétique philosophique avec un essai d'interprétation de la critique*, Paris: Minuit, 1978.
44 Lucretius, *On the Nature of Things*, IV, 1117.
45 Ibid., 1134: *surgit amari aliquid*.
46 Epicurus, *Vatican Sentences*, 51.
47 Cicero, *Tusculan Disputations*, 5, 95. See also Epicurus, *Letter to Menoeceus*, 129.
48 Pierre Vesperini, *La 'philosophia' et ses pratiques de Ennius to Ciceron*, Rome: École française de Rome, 2012, pp. 354–5:

> These three maxims (pleasure as sovereign good, political abstentionism, the indifference of the gods) would not have been suitable in an epic destined for a senator of the Roman people. Thus, in the eulogy of Epicurus in Book III, pleasure (*voluptas, gaudium*) is replaced by the *commoda* – which makes Epicurus' doctrine seem less threatening. What Cicero called *genus orationis lubricum* (in *Against Piso*) is more acceptable (*decus*). In the same way, erotic pleasures are denounced, whereas Epicurus, whose bust may have been placed during his lifetime in the temple of Aphrodite in Paphos, does not conceive of good outside (among others) the 'pleasures of Aphrodite'. His Garden included at least six hetaerae, one of whom was Leontion, whom he and Metrodorus loved (*erasthenai*). In fact, the greater part of the *epicurea* selected by Lucretius is constituted by Epicurean physics. So that, if we had only Lucretius to give us an idea of the doctrine of Epicurus, we would see in it a variant of pre-Socratic physics and not what it was above all else, namely a theological doctrine from which an ethic was derived.

49 Lucretius, *On the Nature of Things*, IV, 1063–73. See William Fitzgerald, 'Lucretius' cure for love in the *De rerum natura*', *Classical World* 78/2 (1984): 73–86, on the consistency of Lucretius' anti-erotic cure and the kinds of movements he theorizes in the universe: fixation/attachment versus mobility and wandering desire.
50 Epicurus, *Vatican Sentences*, 18.
51 Lucretius, *On the Nature of Things*, IV, 1137–40.
52 Ovid, *The Art of Love*, 2, 107–372. Much of Book 2 is devoted to good manners once the couple is formed. Essential is a mixture of softness, gentleness, compliance, devotion and admiration. On discretion and falsehood: 2, 389–424. On erotic pleasure: 2, 703–44; 3, 769–808. On pleasure in Ovid: Thomas Habinek, 'The Invention of Sexuality in the World of Rome', in Thomas Habinek and Alessandro Schiesaro, eds, *The Roman Cultural Revolution*, Cambridge: Cambridge University Press, 1997, pp. 23–43, especially pp. 30–6; 'Aimer et souffrir: quelques réflexions sur la 'Philosophie dans le boudoir' de l'*Ars amatoria*'.
53 Ovid, *The Art of Love*, 2, 17–20.

NOTES TO PP. 210–217

54 Sissa, *Sex and Sensuality in the Ancient World*.
55 Victoria Rimell, *Ovid's Lovers: Desire, Difference and the Poetic Imagination*, Cambridge: Cambridge University Press, 2006, pp. 89–94, has seen very clearly the importance of caressing in erotic situations.
56 Ovid, *Heroides*, 76: 'Hypsipyle to Jason'.
57 Ovid, *The Art of love*, 2, 373–7.
58 Ibid., 378–80.
59 Ibid., 435–6.
60 Ibid., 435–90.
61 Ibid., 3, 41–2: 'Do you want me to tell you what caused your loss? You did not know how to love. You lacked the art. It is art that perpetuates love [*Quid vos perdiderit, dicam? Nescistis amare; defuit ars vobis; arte perennat amor*].'
62 Ibid., 381–2.
63 Ibid., 399.
64 Ovid, *Heroides*, 65–74: 'Œnone to Paris'.
65 Ibid., 141–54: 'Medea to Jason'.
66 Ibid., 212.
67 Ibid., 119–36: 'Deianira to Hercules'.
68 Ovid, *Loves*, 2, 4, 49.
69 Ibid., 31.
70 Ibid., 9–10: *Non est certa meos quae forma invitet amores. Centum sunt causae*.
71 Ibid., 11–15.
72 Ibid., 37.
73 Ibid., 23–4.
74 Ibid., 33–4.
75 Ibid., 16–17.
76 Ibid., 2, 5.
77 Ibid., 2, 7 and 8.
78 Giampiero Rosati, 'The Art of *Remedia amoris*: Unlearning to Love?', in Roy K. Gibson, Steven Green and Allison Sharrock, eds, *The Art of Love: Bimillennial Essays on Ovid's Ars amatoria and Remedia amoris*, Oxford: Oxford University Press, 2006, pp. 143–65. On the *Remedies* as a form of connivance within the genre of the diatribe (primarily Horace and Lucretius) and, therefore, as 'a remedy against a form of literature' (elegy), see Ovid, *Rimedi contro l'amore*, ed. Caterina Lazzarini, with an introduction by Gian Biagio Conte, Venice: Marsilio, 1986, pp. 42–8. Conte rightly emphasizes the anti-elegiac strategy while acknowledging that Ovid prescribes a cure not for love as such, but for a botched affair to be terminated. I agree, but I argue that the poet/doctor of the *Remedies* completes the mission of the poet/preceptor of *The Art of Love* by helping those who, notwithstanding the lessons of the Art, happen to suffer, mostly through jealousy. I would also add that the poem offers a remedy not only against elegy but also against tragedy.
79 On the *Remedies* as the fourth book of *The Art of Love*, and on the strategic deferrals of the poem(s) as the narrative enactment of a theory

of desire, see Francesca Martelli, 'The End of the Affair', in *Ovidian Revisions: The Editor as Author*, Cambridge: Cambridge University Press, 2013.

80 Ovid, *Remedies for Love*, 13–16; 41–2; 15–44. Ruth Rothaus Caston analyses the theme of the cure of love, confronting the elegiac poets (Tibullus, Propertius and Ovid), on the one hand, and the philosophers (Lucretius and the Stoics in Cicero's dialogues), on the other. She insists on analogies between the two discourses but also on a final divergence: philosophers recommend philosophical arguments, while poets enjoy their inability to heal themselves and rely, instead, on their poems (*The Elegiaic Passion: Jealousy in Roman Love Elegy*, Oxford: Oxford University Press, 2012, pp. 29–47). This is a very useful work, but it dilutes Ovid's thinking. Ovid is not merely one elegiac poet among others. The remedies he prescribes are supposed to act effectively, but they are advocated only, and specifically, in cases where a woman begins to make the poet suffer. Ovid's love is not 'elegiac' – that is, plaintive and doomed to failure. It is a mischievous, smart pleasure that *sometimes* turns into displeasure. It is in these precise circumstances that a cure must be applied. Caston also states that the *Remedies* echo the philosophy of Cicero and Lucretius when they teach the unhappy lover how to rid himself of his passion. Ovid allegedly 'incorporates' the opinions of these philosophers (distancing oneself, changing air, seeking other partners) by also adding his own. 'Fundamentally, though, Ovid does not stand apart from the philosophers' approach, except, of course, in so far as he offers advice to the other side, too' (pp. 34–5). But, again, Ovid is not merely a philosopher among others. He shares neither Stoic ethics nor the anguished Epicureanism of Lucretius.

81 Ovid, *Remedies for Love*, 226: '*Ut valeas, multa dolenda feres*'; 231: '*Ut valeas animo, quicquam tolerare negabis?*'
82 Ibid., 103, 138, 197.
83 Cicero, *Tusculan Disputations*, 5, 95.
84 Ovid, *Remedies for Love*, 497–504: '*Qui poterit sanum fingere, sanus erit.*'
85 On the art of time (*ars temporis*), see Martelli, *Ovidian Revisions*, pp. 74–5.
86 Lucretius, *On the Nature of Things*, IV, 1153–70.
87 Ibid., 1154: '*et tribuunt ea quae non sunt his commoda vere*'.
88 Catullus, *Poems*, 86.
89 Plato, *Republic*, V, 274.
90 Ovid, *The Art of Love*, 1, 269–70: '*prima tuae menti veniat fiducia, cunctas posse capi*'; cf. 1, 343.
91 Ibid., 342: '*acrior libido*'.
92 Ibid., 710: '*cupit illa rogari*'.
93 Ibid., 2, 657: '*Nominibus mollire licet mala.*'
94 Ibid., 641–62.
95 Ibid., 1, 613–16: '*Verus amor fiet, qui modum falsus erat.*'
96 Ibid., 618–20.

NOTES TO PP. 222–226

97 Lucretius, *On the Nature of Things*, IV, 1284–5.
98 Cicero, *Academica (Lucullus)* 2, 18 and *passim*.
99 Lucretius, *On the Nature of Things*, IV, 379 ('let us not admit at all that the eyes deceive!' *nec tamen hic oculos falli concedimus hilum*); 386 ('abstain from attributing to the eyes this flaw of the soul!' *animi vitium hoc oculis adfingere noli*); 479 ('the senses cannot be proven wrong!' *neque sensus posse refelli*); 462–72. See Myles Burnyeat, 'Protagoras and self-refutation in later Greek philosophy', *Philosophical Review* 75 (1976): 44–69, at p. 57 n. 22, and 'The up-side-down back-to-front sceptic of Lucretius IV 472', *Philologus* 122 (1978): 197–206; Tobias Reinhardt, 'To See and to Be Seen: On Vision and Perception in Lucretius and Cicero', in Katherina Volk and G. Williams, eds, *Roman Reflections: Essays on Latin Philosophy*, Oxford: Oxford University Press, 2017.
100 Ovid, *The Art of Love*, 2, 373–410.
101 Ibid., 521–2: '*Dicta erit isse foras, quom tu fortasse videre; isse foras, et te falsa videre puta.*'
102 Ibid., 555: '*melius nescisse fuit.*'
103 Ibid., 1, 737–52.
104 Lucretius, *On the Nature of Things*, IV, 1188–9: '*protrahere in lucem.*'
105 See Sissa, *Sex and Sensuality in the Ancient World*.
106 Ovid, *The Art of Love*, 2, 543: '*Ne tange tabellas!*'
107 Ovid, *Remedies for Love*, 317–418. These are tactics of self-deception, but they are 'deceptive' only as long as one is unlearning to love (211–12). The end is to come to think exactly like that.
108 Ibid., 299–306.
109 Ibid., 543–8, 767–98.
110 Ovid, *Metamorphoses*, VII, 698–9: '*hanc mihi iunxit amo; felix dicebar eramque.*'
111 Ibid., 719: '*cuncta timemus amantes.*'
112 Ibid., 798–865, for the long vicissitudes of Procris, the jealous bacchante, and Cephalus, the outdoor singer. Numerous studies on this episode are generally concerned with literary and intertextual resonances or with the sexual mores of the characters in other versions of the myth. For a synthesis, see Frederick E. Brenk, *Clothed in Purple Light: Studies in Vergil and in Latin Literature, including Aspects of Philosophy, Religion, Magic, Judaism, and the New Testament Background*, Stuttgart: Franz Steiner, 1999, pp. 166–75. For a study that pays attention to the interpretation of signs and raises the question of Procris' feminine subjectivity as a hermeneutical exercise, see Lowell Bowditch, 'Hermeneutic Uncertainty and the Feminine in Ovid's *Ars amatoria*', in Ronnie Ancona and Ellen Greene, eds, *Gendered Dynamics in Latin Love Poetry*, Baltimore: Johns Hopkins University Press, 2005, pp. 271–95. For a study that thematizes vision, see Gregory Hutchinson, 'Telling Tales: Ovid's *Metamorphoses* and Callimachus', in Dirk Obbink and Richard Rutherford, eds, *Culture in Pieces: Essays on Ancient Texts in Honour of Peter Parsons*, Oxford: Oxford University Press, 2011, pp. 239–61. See also Ralph Johnson, 'Confabulating Cephalus: Self-Narration in Ovid's *Metamorphoses*', in

Todd Breyfogle and David Greene, eds, *Literary Imagination, Ancient and Modern: Essays in Honour of David Greene*, Oxford: Oxford University Press, 1999, pp. 127–38. Johnson translates '*credula res amor est*' (love is a credulous thing) by 'love is not sceptical', but he does not mention the true scepticism that Ovid puts to work in the text. For a theoretical and philological approach to Ovid which does justice to the structuring themes of deception and error, see Phillip Hardie, *Ovid's Poetics of Illusion*, Cambridge: Cambridge University Press, 2002. In this context, Hardie discusses the significance of Aura/Aurora and the Ovidian reception by Petrarch, whose beloved is called Laura, a name that generates infinite puns about Laura/*l'aura* (the air) within a theory of desire based on absence, elusiveness and lack (pp. 74–9). For a diffident reading of Cephalus' sentiments towards Aurora/Aura, see Rimell, *Ovid's Lovers*, pp. 97–103.

113 Ovid, *Metamorphoses*, VII, 826. See also *Heroides*, VI, 21.
114 Lisa Starks-Estes, *Violence, Trauma, and Virtus in Shakespeare's Roman Poems and Plays: Transforming Ovid*. London: Palgrave Macmillan, 2014, pp. 173–83.
115 Phillip Hardie, 'Lucretius and the Delusions of Narcissus', in Peter Knox, ed., *Oxford Readings in Ovid*, Oxford: Oxford University Press, 2006, pp. 123–42.
116 Ovid, *The Art of Love*, 3, 685–: '*Nec cito credideris; quantum cito credere laedat exemplum vobis non leve Procris dabit.*' The narrative runs: 3, 683–746. Roy Gibson, *Ovid, Ars amatoria, Book 3*, Cambridge: Cambridge University Press, 2003.

CONCLUSION

1 *Traité de la jalousie ou Des moyens d'entretenir la paix dans le marriage* [1682], Amsterdam: Pierre Mortier, 1696, pp. 123–4.
2 Ibid., p. 128.
3 Ibid., p. v.
4 Ibid., p. 55.

INDEX

adultery 232
  adulterous women in classical Athens 24–5
  Beauvoir on 143–4
  Hobbes on 66
  see also infidelity
Aeschines 24
Alonge, Tristan 22
Althusser, Louis 137, 150–1
  Pour Marx 131–2
analytic philosophy 58
ancient Greece 4, 8
  comic jealousy in 29–30, 31–2
  and Freudian psychoanalysis 28–9, 173
  the jealousy of the ancients 54, 59, 102, 192
  language of jealousy in 30–3
  and polygyny 143
  see also anger; erotic anger; Euripides; Stoicism
Andromache (Euripides) 21–3, 25–7, 55, 112, 144, 147
anger
  Aquinas on 55, 62–3
  Aristotle on 4, 9–10, 10–12, 18, 45–6, 60, 66
  cholos 16, 17, 18
  in Corneille's *Medea* 49–50
  disappearance of rightful anger 58–9
  Hobbes on 64–5, 66
  and Hobbes's theory of the passions 61–2
  and jealousy as suffering 160
  and the jealousy of the ancients 54, 59, 102
  and the jealousy of the moderns 5, 59, 102
  orgê 16, 17, 18
  in Ovid's *The Art of Love* 210–14
  Rousseau on 76–7
  Seneca on 34–5, 39–43, 47
  Stendhal on 96
  and Stoicism 45, 55
  thumos 11, 13–14, 16, 17
  see also erotic anger
Aquinas, Thomas 55–6, 62–3, 66, 99
aristocratic view of jealousy 5–6
Aristophanes 29, 31
Aristotle 169, 202
  on anger 4, 9–10, 10–12, 18, 45, 66
  heroic passion of 60
  on infanticide 47–8
  on the passions 54
  Rhetoric 31, 62, 64, 176
The Art of Love (Ovid) 202–12, 214, 216, 217, 218, 231
  the art of jealousy in 204–5
  and credulity 227

293

The Art of Love (Ovid) (cont.)
  and Epicureanism 204, 205, 207–10
  and Lucretius 203, 205–6, 208–9
  pain, anger and love in 210–14
  simulacra in 205–6, 207, 208, 209
Artaud, Antonin 43
Athenian tragedy *see* ancient Greece
Augustine, St 66
  The City of God 55

Baumgart, Hildegard
  Jealousy: Experiences and Solutions 166–7
Beauvoir, Simone de 5, 133–50, 169, 194, 233–4
  The Ethics of Ambiguity 137
  La Femme rompue 149
  and the Hegelian dialectic 136–7, 140, 143
  L'Invitée 149
  and Kantian ethics 135–7, 138, 139, 140–1, 143, 144, 146
  on the objectification of women 132–9, 151–2, 199
  open relationship with Sartre 145–50, 157–8, 200–1
  The Second Sex 132, 134–5, 137, 140, 142–5, 146, 147
  on sexual pleasure 198–9
Beauvoir, Sylvie Le Bon de 148
bestiality 113
Bienenfeld, Bianca 145, 147, 148, 149
blogs 7
bodies
  and infidelity 232–3
  objectification of 134–5, 139–40
  and second-wave feminism 152–3
  see also women's bodies
Bonnefoy, Yves 180, 181
Bougainville, Louis-Antoine de 79–80
Bourdin, Martine 146
bourgeoisie
  and jealousy 5, 6, 28–9, 101
  Kant and bourgeois love 137

Buffon, Georges-Louis Leclerc, count of
  Natural History 82–3

Cahill, Ann 193
cannibalism metaphor
  Schütz on Kant's conception of marriage 118–20
Capellanus, Andreas 8, 93, 99
  On Love 56
capitalism
  Marxism and reification 131
Caribbean peoples, Rousseau on 69–70
Castellano-Maury, Éloisa 189
categorical imperative 104–5
Catullus 219
Cavell, Stanley 180–1
celibacy, monastic 114
cholos 16, 18
Christianity
  Aquinas on the passions 55–6
  Kant on sexuality and 113–14
  and *Medea* 54
  and Stoicism 55
Cicero 208, 210, 222
comic jealousy
  in ancient Greece 29–30, 31–2
communism
  of early mankind 100
  Communist Manifesto (Marx and Engels) 145
compensation
  and healing 217–18
Corneille, Pierre 50–4, 60
  Discours de l'utilité et des parties du poème dramatique 50
  The Examination 49
  and Hobbes's theory of the passions 60
  Medea 5, 48–52, 56
  and Seneca 52
Così fan tutte (Mozart) 225
Courtin, Antoine de
  Treatise on Jealousy 236
Crécy, Odette de 215
credulity and love 224–8

INDEX

cruelty
  and open couples 150–1
  theatre of 43
crystallization of love
  in Stendhal 88–96, 97, 98, 125, 166, 184
cultural repression 3

D'Alembert, Jean 78–9, 81, 98
Dangerous Liaisons (Laclos) 6
Dante Alighieri
  Divine Comedy 56
Deburge-Donnars, Anne 168–9
Deianira and Hercules 213–14
Del Litto, Victor 97
delayed-action jealousy
  in Proust 186
Demosthenes 24
denial
  and repression 171–3, 229–30
derivatization of women 193–4
Descartes, René 125, 184, 185
desire
  and jealousy 6–7
Diderot, Denis 5, 59, 67, 78, 82, 155, 231
  Encyclopédie 85
    Buffon's article on virginity 82
    entry on jealousy 81–2
    'Hobbisme' 67–8, 75
  The Indiscreet Jewels 6
  letters to Sophie Volland 85–7
  Refutation of Helvétius 86, 87
  Supplément au voyage de Bougainville 79–80, 83–5, 87
Discourse (Rousseau) 68, 69–72, 74, 76, 98–9, 101
Don Giovanni (Mozart) 119, 161, 219
Duclos, Charles 5–6, 158

Elements of the Philosophy of Right (Hegel) 121–3, 124
Émile (Rousseau) 68, 71–7, 78, 98–9
Engels, Friedrich 142
  The Origin of Family and Private Property 100

envy 3, 58, 230
  in *Othello* 176
Epicureanism
  and compensation 217–18
  and Ovid's *The Art of Love* 204, 205, 207–10
Epicurus 202
Erasmus 179
Ernaux, Annie
  L'Occupation 149
erotic anger 4, 57, 236
  in ancient Greece 4, 9–10, 10–12, 15–19, 47, 62, 231
    epic poetry 12–14, 15
  and Freudian psychoanalysis 28–9
  and the aristocracy 5–6, 10–12
  and jealous speech-acts 175
  and jealousy as suffering 161
  in Ovid's *The Art of Love* 211–12
  and reciprocity 15, 16, 24
  Rousseau on 76–7
  in Seneca's *Medea* 44–5
  and Stoicism 45–8
  see also anger
erotic ethic 235–6
eroticism
  and objectification 127–9
Euripides 6, 101
  Andromache 21–3, 25–7, 55, 112, 144, 147
  Medea 17–21, 22, 26, 28–30, 34, 67, 160
  tragic erotic anger in 17–19, 47–8
evolutionary biology 7
existentialism, post-Kantian 142

families
  formation of the monogamous family 100–1
Family Complexes in the Formation of the Individual (Lacan) 170–1
fear, Hobbes on jealousy and 65

INDEX

female sexuality 82
  and honour cultures 14
  in Tahiti 84
feminism
  and intersubjectivity 102
  and Marxism 101
  and objectification 127, 129–30
  second-wave 121, 152–3
  and self-objectification 151–3, 193–4
  Woman as a sexual object 132–42, 233–4
  see also Beauvoir, Simone de
La Femme rompue (Beauvoir) 149
Fichte, J. G. 131
flattery and friendship
  in *Othello* 177–8
Foucault, Michel
  on Kantian jealousy 115, 117
Frankfurt School 132
Freud, Sigmund 202, 231
  Civilization and its Discontents 162
  on normal jealousy 27–8, 162–4
Freudian psychoanalysis 7, 162–73
  and the end of the tragic 164–6
  and jealousy as suffering 161
  and the medicalization of jealousy 167, 173
  repression 36–7, 40, 169, 171–3
  see also Lacan, Jacques; normal jealousy
friendship and flattery
  in *Othello* 177–8
Fumaroli, Marc 51

gender
  and the Hegelian dialect 133
  and self-objectification 152–3
  see also men; women
gender roles
  and jealousy in classical Athens 23–5
  and marriage 55–6
Gherardi, Mme (la Ghita) 90, 91, 97, 98, 164

Giotto
  allegory of Wrath (fresco) 43–4
Girard, René 182
Greece *see* ancient Greece
Gregory of Nyssa 63
Grimaldi, Nicolas 155, 189

habits
  and second-wave feminism 152–3
Halimi, Gisèle 148–9
healing
  and compensation 217–18
Hegel, Georg Wilhelm Friedrich 75, 131
  Elements of the Philosophy of Right 121–3, 124
  gender and the Hegelian dialectic 133, 135, 136–7, 140, 143
  on marriage 144
Heidegger, Martin 201
Helen of Troy 212–13
Hénaff, Marcel
  Le Don des philosophes 102
Hercules and Deianira 213–14
heroic anger
  Aristotle on 45–6, 60, 67
Heroides (Ovid) 212–14
Hiltenbrand, Jean-Paul 167
Hobbes, Thomas 60–2, 63, 64–7, 202, 207
  Diderot on 67–8
  and Euripides' *Medea* 67
  on jealousy 65–6
  Leviathan 60, 65
  and normal jealousy 163
  On Human Nature 60, 65, 96
  Rousseau and 67, 68, 74, 76, 77
  on the singularity of love 64–5, 66–7, 76, 77–8
  and Stendhal 96–7, 99
  theory of the passions 60–2
Holbach, Paul-Henri Dietrich, baron d' 60
homosexuality 113
  repressed 163
honour cultures, anger in 14, 62
Horace 210

INDEX

humanism
  in Marx 131–2

The Iliad 12–14, 15
  Achilles and heroic anger in 45–6
immanence
  and the art of love 196
  of women 132, 135, 141, 142, 143, 199
incest, Hobbes on 66
infanticide
  in *Medea* 47–8, 49, 51–2, 79
infidelity
  Beauvoir on 135–6, 143, 144–5
  Courtin on 236
  and jealousy 7, 8, 101, 230, 231, 232–3
  Kant on 115–16, 135–6
  open couples 145–53
  Ovid on 216, 217
  projection and normal jealousy 163, 164–6
  truth and jealousy 223
  see also adultery
injustice and jealousy 2, 4
  in Euripides' *Medea* 29
intention
  and the project to be loved 194
interobjectivity 234
intersubjectivity 102–3, 234
Irigaray, Luce 126

Jaucourt, Louis de 81, 82
Jealousy (Millet) 149, 191–2
Jealousy: Descriptive Psychology and Psychoanalysis (Lagache) 167
Jealousy: Experiences and Solutions (Baumgart) 166–7
Jolivet, Simone 145, 149
Julie, or the New Heloise (Rousseau) 98
Julius Caesar (Shakespeare) 181
justice of the bed 172
  in Athenian tragedy 16, 18
Juvenal 32

Kant, Immanuel 80–1, 104–24, 128, 198, 236
  Anthropology from a Pragmatic Point of View 115, 116–17, 119–20, 135
  categorical imperative 104–5
  Hegel's criticism of 121–3
  on jealousy 115–17
  and Lucretius 123–4
  and Medea 123
  Metaphysics of Morals 105–8, 116, 117–18, 119, 135
  neo-Kantian self-objectification 151–3, 193
  and objectification 124–5, 126, 129–31, 132, 135–7, 138, 139, 144, 146, 151, 153, 199, 201, 233–4
  post-Kantian existentialism 142
  and Sartre on the art of love 196–7, 198
kinship
  and the formation of the monogamous family 100–1
Klein, Melanie 164–5
Konstan, David 20
Kosakiewicz, Wanda 146
Kristeva, Julia 189–90
Kristjánsson, Kristján 58
Kundera, Milan 157

La Rochefoucauld, François de 16, 17, 59, 156, 173, 236
  Maxims 1, 3, 56, 57
  and normal jealousy 184
  and *Othello* 181
  and Stendhal 91, 92
Lacan, Jacques 4, 90, 125, 167, 172
  Family Complexes in the Formation of the Individual 170–1
  and intersubjectivity 102–3
  and Ovid 216
Lacanian psychoanalysis 232
Laclos, Pierre Choderlos de 99
  Dangerous Liaisons 6

INDEX

Lagache, Daniel
  Jealousy: Descriptive Psychology and Psychoanalysis 167
Langton, Rae 103–4, 125
Letter to D'Alembert (Rousseau) 78–9, 98
Leviathan (Hobbes) 60, 65
L'Invitée (Beauvoir) 149
love 2, 7
  Aquinas on 55
  the art of 199–200
  and credulity 224–8
  the project to be loved 193–6
  and *simulacra* 205–6, 207, 208, 209, 223–4, 226
  and truth 218–4
  in Euripides' *Medea* 19–21, 29
  freedom and reciprocity in 229
  in Freudian psychoanalysis 28
  Hobbes on the singularity of 64–5, 66–7, 76
  and normal jealousy 166
  and objectification 126–7
  Rousseau on love and jealousy in *Émile* 72–7
  Rousseau on the invention of 69–72
  Stendhal on 87–93, 97, 98, 99, 166, 184
  suffering in 159–61
  and truth 218–22
  see also self-love
Love, Hate and Reparation (Klein and Riviere) 164–5
Loves (Amores) (Ovid) 214–16, 217
Lucretius 236
  on jealousy and truth 222–3, 223–4
  on love and truth 218–19, 220–1, 222
  On the Nature of Things (De rerum natura) 123–4, 203–4, 205–6, 208–9, 217
Lukács, György 132

Machiavelli, Niccolò 179
Marion, Jean-Luc 7, 155–6

Marmontel, Jean-François 79
marriage
  Aquinas on 55–6
  Beauvoir on 137, 142–5
  in Euripides' *Andromache* 21–7
  Hegelian 144
  Hobbes on monogamous marriage 65–6
  Kant on reciprocal possession in 81, 105–12, 106, 115–17, 144, 153
    Hegel's objection to 121–3
  Marxist thought on 100–1
  and the persons/things distinction 85
  Rousseau on 68
  see also monogamy; polygamy
Marx, Karl 130, 131, 143, 193
Marxism 5, 100–1
  and Beauvoir's *The Second Sex* 142, 144–5
  and objectification 130, 131–2, 133, 137, 139
masochism 138, 197, 198, 200
masturbation 106, 113, 136
Medea 150–1, 231
  and jealousy as suffering 159, 161
  and normal jealousy 164
  and *Othello* 183
  and Ovid's *Metamorphosis* 228
  and Ovid's *The Art of Love* 211, 212, 213
  Rousseau on 78–9
  see also Corneille; Euripides; Seneca
medicalization of jealousy 167, 173
men
  and the erotic ethic 235–6
  and jealousy in classical Athens 23–5
Merleau-Ponty, Maurice 128, 132, 146
  and Ovid's *Loves (Amores)* 215
  and the project to be loved 194, 195
Merteuil, Isabelle de 6, 101

298

INDEX

Metamorphoses (Ovid) 204
   Procris and Cephalus story 224–8
Millet, Catherine 6, 101
   Jealousy 149, 191–2
   The Sexual Life of Catherine M. 191
monastic celibacy 114
monogamy
   Aquinas on 55
   Beauvoir on 144–5
   Kant on jealousy and 111, 116–17
   objectification 81
   see also marriage; sexual fidelity
Montaigne, Michel de 157
Montesquieu, Charles de Secondat, baron de 2, 6
moralism and jealousy 167
Morgan, Lewis 100
Mozart, Wolfgang
   Così fan tutte 225
   Don Giovanni 119, 161, 219

narcissism 230, 231
   and normal jealousy 168, 169–70
   Proust on jealousy and 189–91
natural law, Aquinas on 55
natural man
   Rousseau on 69–70, 70–1, 74
   Stendhal on 90
neo-Aristotelianism 62
Neu, Jerome 28, 35, 169
normal jealousy 8, 27–8, 162–70
   and the end of the tragic 166–70
   and infidelity 233
   as pathological 146–6, 164
   in Proust's *Remembrance of Things Past* 184–91
   see also Freudian psychoanalysis
Nussbaum, Martha 103, 104

objectification 5, 80–1, 103–4, 124–39, 233–5
   and the art of love 196–7, 198
   and eroticism 127–9
   interobjectivity 234

in Kant 124–5, 126, 129–31, 132, 135–7, 138, 139, 144, 146, 151, 153, 199, 201, 233–4
   and open couples 145–51, 146
   and the project to be loved 193, 194–5
   rights, habits and bodies 151–3
   Woman as a sexual object 132–42, 199, 233–4
   see also persons/objects distinction; reification; self-objectification
Oedipal triangle 163, 164, 168, 171
On Human Nature (Hobbes) 60, 65, 96
On the Nature of Things (Lucretius) 123–4, 203–4
open couples 145–51
   Althusser and cruelty 150–1
   Sartre and Beauvoir 145–50, 151
The Origin of Family and Private Property (Engels) 100
Orou (Tahitian man) 79–80, 81, 84–5, 87, 99, 100
Othello (Shakespeare) 167, 175–84, 186, 226
   flattery and friendship in 177–8
   jealousy in 178–80, 233
   and Ovid's *Metamorphoses* 226
the Other, Woman as 133–4, 198
Ovid 6, 8, 99, 101, 139, 169, 202–28
   Heroides 212–14
   and jealous speech-acts 174
   on jealousy and truth 223, 224
   on love and truth 220–1, 222
   Loves (Amores) 214–16, 217
   Metamorphoses 204
      Procris and Cephalus story 224–8
   The Remedies for Love 216–18
   see also The Art of Love (Ovid)

Padua
   Cappella degli Scrovegni 43–4
pain
   and the crystallization of love 94
   in Euripides' *Medea* 17–18

299

INDEX

pain (cont.)
  and jealousy as suffering 159, 161, 165
  and normal jealousy 168
  Ovid on the pains of love 210–14, 216–18
  and pleasure 12, 201–2, 231–2, 235
  Proust on jealousy and 185–7, 190
  in Seneca's *De Ira* 35–6, 38
  in Seneca's *Medea* 38, 44–5
  and Stoicism 46
Paoli, Gino 200
Paris 8
passions
  Aristotle on anger and 45
  Corneille on the passions 52–4
  Hobbes's theory of the passions 60–2
  jealousy as a forbidden passion 54–7
  Rousseau on 69–70
  Seneca on Stoicism and 46–7
performativity
  and women 140
Perrin, Christophe 156
persons/objects distinction 85
  in Kant
    protecting persons from dehumanization 104–5
    reciprocity and matrimonial possession 105–12
    and sexual desire 5, 112–15
  see also objectification
Petronius
  Satyricon 32
phenomenology 7, 142, 155–6
  and erotic anger 12
  and the project to be loved 194
  see also suffering, jealousy as
Pitt-Rivers, Julian 14
Plato 29, 220
  Laws 176
  Symposium 31–2
pleasure
  in Aristotelian ethics 21
  displeasure and jealousy 200–2

and objectification 104
  in Ovid's *Loves (Amores)* 214–16
  and pain 12, 201–2, 231–2, 235
  in Proust's *Remembrance of Things Past* 187–9
  in Seneca's *Medea* 38
  Stendhal on love and 90
  and Stoicism 46
  see also sexual pleasure
Plutarch 177
polyamorous relationships 7, 101–2
polyandry 56, 66
polygamy/polygyny
  Aquinas on 55
  Beauvoir on 143
  Hobbes on 66–7
  Kant on jealousy and 115–16, 153
  and possession 112
  Rousseau on 83
  wives of polygamous husbands 7, 26, 101, 157
possessiveness, Rousseau on 71–2
power
  and objectification 152
primitivism
  Diderot on 86–7
  and Stendhal 99
  see also natural man
private property
  Beauvoir on 142, 144–5
  Marxism and 101, 139
  and the project to be loved 195
  Rousseau on 68, 69, 70–1
  see also property rights
procreation, Kant on 106
Procris and Cephalus story 224–8
projection
  and normal jealousy 163, 164–5
Propertius 219
property rights 5, 6, 193
  Kant on
    matrimonial possession and 108–12
    sexual desire and 114–15
  see also private property

INDEX

prostitution 114
Proust, Marcel 6, 99, 143, 169, 202, 215, 226, 231
   and Beauvoir 149
   Remembrance of Things Past 155–6, 160, 184–91
punishment
   Aquinas on anger and 63
   in Corneille's *Medea* 50–2

rape 207
reciprocity 6, 58, 101–2, 230
   and anger 15, 16, 24, 54
   ethics of 156
   and freedom in love 229
   Hobbes on 64
   and jealousy as suffering 161
   Kant on reciprocal possession in marriage 81, 105–12, 106, 115–17, 144, 153
      Hegel's objection to 121–3
   in love and truth 220
   and open couples 146, 148
   Rousseau on 73–4, 77
   and seduction 235
   and Stendhal's crystallization of love 96
The Red and the Black (Stendhal) 93–6, 97, 164
Refutation of Helvétius (Diderot) 86, 87
reification 129–32, 135, 136
   and Kantian ethics 81, 117, 124, 129
   see also objectification
The Remedies for Love (Ovid) 216–18
Remembrance of Things Past (Proust) 155–6, 160, 184–91
   fugitives in 184–5, 186–7
   narcissism in 189–91
   the pain of jealousy in 185–7
   pleasure in 187–9
repression 229–30
   in Freudian psychoanalysis 36–7, 40, 165, 169, 171–3
   in Seneca's *De ira* 39–40

revenge
   in Seneca's *Medea* 44–5
Rhetoric (Aristotle) 31
rights
   and second-wave feminism 152
rivalry, jealousy of 82, 163
Riviere, Joan 164–5
Roman law
   person/things distinction 85
Roman poetry *see* Ovid
Roman tragedy
   Seneca's *Medea* 4–5, 32, 34, 37–8, 42–3, 48, 51, 178, 213
   and *zelotupia* 32
Rosso, Jeannette Geffriaud 86
Rouquette, Max 160
Rousseau, Jean-Jacques 59, 67–79, 100, 155, 231
   and Diderot on primitivism 86–7
   Discourse 68, 69–72, 74, 76, 98–9, 101
   Émile 68, 71–7, 78, 98–9
   and Freudian psychoanalysis 170
   Julie, or the New Heloise 98
   Letter to D'Alembert 78–9, 98
   on *Medea* 78–9

sadism 138, 197, 198, 200
Sappho 6, 175
Sartre, Jean-Paul 5, 145–50, 234
   Lettres au Castor et à quelques autres 145
   open relationship with Beauvoir 145–50, 151–2
   and Ovid on love 210, 215
   and reification 132
   on sex 138–9
   on sexual pleasure 194–8, 199
Satyricon (Petronius) 32
Sceptics
   on jealousy and truth 222–3
Scholastic philosophy 62, 63, 66
Schultz, Court Chaplain 118
Schütz, Christian Gottfried
   on Kant's conception of marriage 118–21
Scodel, Ruth 14

INDEX

seduction 234–5
self-criticism and jealousy 28
self-esteem
  and normal jealousy 162, 166, 169
self-love, jealousy as 57, 158–9
  Rousseau on (*amour-propre*) 68, 69, 71, 74, 75–6, 78, 158
self-objectification 151–3
  and the project to be loved 193–4
Seneca 157
  and Corneille 52
  De ira 34, 39–42, 44
  Medea 4–5, 32, 34, 37–8, 42–3, 48, 51, 178, 213
  On Anger 52
  and Stoicism 46–7, 48, 55
  Thyestes 51
sex and sexuality
  Beauvoir on heterosexual intercourse 137–9
  and the erotic ethic 235–6
  Hobbes on 65–6
  Kant on
    the degradation of humanity 112–15
    Hegel's objection to 121–3
    reciprocity and matrimonial possession 81, 105–12, 106, 115–17
  and objectification 135
  in Ovid's *The Art of Love* 205–10
  Rousseau on 68–9, 71
  see also female sexuality
sexual fidelity 85
  Kant on reciprocity and 108, 111–12, 117
  see also infidelity
The Sexual Life of Catherine M. (Millet) 191
sexual objects *see* objectification
sexual pleasure
  in ancient Greece 21
  Beauvoir on 198–9
  and objectification 127–9
  in Ovid's *The Art of Love* 207–10
  Sartre on 194–8, 199
sexual promiscuity
  and early mankind 100
  Lucretius on 124
Shakespeare, William
  Julius Caesar 181
  see also Othello
shame and jealousy 1–2, 3
  and Freudian psychoanalysis 165
siblings, competition between 170
Simmel, Georg 132
simulacra
  and the art of love 205–6, 207, 208, 209, 223–4, 226
speech-acts of jealousy 174–5
  in Ovid's *Heroides* 212–14
  see also Othello (Shakespeare)
Starobinski, Jean 68–9
Stendhal (Henri Beyle) 3, 6, 8, 50, 59, 65, 67, 87–99, 101, 128, 202, 231–2
  and Beauvoir 149
  and the crystallization of love 88–96, 97, 98, 125, 166, 184
  and Hobbes 96–7, 99
  and jealousy as suffering 154
  Love 87–93, 97, 98, 99
  and normal jealousy 163
  The Red and the Black 93–6, 97, 164
  and Rousseau 98–9
Stoicism 34–48, 56, 231
  and anger 45, 55
  and jealous speech-acts 174
  and jealousy as suffering 158, 159, 161
  and *Medea* 4–5, 34, 37–8, 40–3, 44–8, 52, 54
  and objectification 129
  and Ovid's *The Art of Love* 204, 205
  and the passions 46–7, 53
  and the pathologization of jealousy 173
  and repression 37, 39–40
  and Seneca 46–7, 48, 55
subjectivity 103–4, 235
  and women's bodies 141–2

INDEX

suffering, jealousy as 154–61
   denial and repression 171–3
   healing 217–18
   and jealous speech-acts 174–5
   normal jealousy 163
   and self-love 158–9
Supplément au voyage de Bougainville (Diderot) 79–80, 83–5, 87
Symposium (Plato) 31–2

Tahiti
   in Diderot's *Supplément* 79–80, 81, 83–5, 87
theatre of cruelty 43
thumos (passionate energy) 11, 13–14, 16, 17, 18
Thyestes (Seneca) 51
Tibullus 219
transcendence of women 142
transparency, cult of 233
Treatise on Jealousy (Courtin) 236
truth
   and jealousy 222–4
   and love 218–22

Vandenberghe, Frédéric 130
vanity and jealousy 3, 57, 158–9, 231–2
   Buffon on 82
   normal jealousy 162
   in *Othello* 181–2
   Rousseau on 72–3

virginity of women 82
virtue and erotic anger 11
Volland, Sophie
   Diderot's letters to 85–7

websites 6
the will
   and Hobbes's theory of the passions 61
women
   and erotic anger in Athenian tragedy 15–17
   frigidity in 138, 198
   Kant on 115–17, 120–1
   and the price of polygyny 157–8
   Stendhal on female jealousy 91–2, 96
   truth about appearances and character 218–22, 224
   Woman as a sexual object 132–42, 199, 233–4
women's bodies
   and honour cultures 14
   and infidelity 232–3
   objectification of 134–5, 139–40, 151–2, 153
   and subjectivity 141–2
Wood, Allen 138–9

zelos (zeal) 31
zelotypia/zelotupia 29, 31–2, 33